THE
LIGHT
OF
THE
PAST

Published by AMERICAN HERITAGE PUBLISHING CO., INC

THE
LIGHT
OF
THE
PAST

A Treasury of HORIZON
A Magazine of the Arts

ok *Trade Distribution by* SIMON AND SCHUSTER, INC.

HORIZON is published every three months
by American Heritage Publishing Co., Inc.,
551 Fifth Avenue, New York, N.Y. 10017.
Single copies: $5.00; Annual subscriptions:
$16.00 in U.S. & Canada, $17.00 elsewhere

PHOTO GRISH SHABANIAN

ABOVE: *King Xerxes of Persia among the ruins of ancient Persepolis.* TITLE PAGE: *A view of the Roman Forum*

Contents

Introduction   *By* GILBERT HIGHET

When we started HORIZON, we wanted it to be free to explore in any dimension. We thought of it, very broadly, as a magazine of ideas and the arts. It would be a mistake, we decided, to limit its readers and its authors to one single art or one single field of intellectual discourse. Ever since September, 1958 (Volume I, Number 1), we have used, in planning and selecting articles for HORIZON, one central principle: does it tell us something new about life? does it describe and explain some human achievement? does it, in fact, move toward a new horizon?

Now, six years later and looking back, we see not a plan but an intelligible pattern emerging. In those six years we read hundreds of articles and discussed thousands of ideas and printed a few score. One of the chief areas in which good ideas came up and good essays were offered to us was history. History in the broadest sense: not "the register of the crimes, follies, and misfortunes of mankind," as Gibbon called it; nor "bunk," as Henry Ford described it before setting out to create his historical museum; nor "the history of class struggles," as Marx misinterpreted it; nor "the biography of great men," as his contemporary Carlyle heroized it; but the entire record of the past—carved, painted, written, monumentalized, or concealed, buried like a Pharaoh's death chamber or reared in the eye of heaven like a cathedral, the whole of man's past both on and off the record.

Therefore we have collected, from the first six years of HORIZON, some of the best articles on history that we have been privileged to publish. They reflect a good deal of the life of the human race.

History is probably more alive for us than it has been for any preceding generation. First, because of the magnificent achievement of the archaeologists: what Columbus did for geography, what Einstein did for space time, that Schliemann did for history in 1870 when he struck the first spade into a Turkish hillock and turned up Troy. Until then scarcely anyone, however learned and imaginative, had conceived the notion that the dead past was everywhere around us, beneath our feet, waiting for resurrection. Since then the past has in large measure been reborn. Graves in Mycenae have given up the armor, the very face masks, of heroes who lived before Agamemnon; Egypt, Iraq, Cambodia, Turkestan, Peru—from all of them mighty monuments of human will and imagination have been unearthed. With infinite effort lost languages have been recovered, forgotten scripts have been read, sacred texts have been set free from cave prisons, vanished masterpieces of Greek poetry have emerged from the rubbish heaps of Egypt. More recently the archaeologists have gone up into the air. Flying over a centuries-old farm, they can detect and photograph the outlines of a Roman villa or a Celtic fortress which has been utterly un-

known to those who have lived above its ruins. Meanwhile underwater archaeology is only beginning. Cousteau's invention of the aqualung is barely twenty years old, and already divers using it have found masses of valuable things in the shallow coastal waters of the Mediterranean. Greek and Roman records tell us that many cargoes of priceless statuary were sunk near the shores of that treacherous sea. Hitherto only sponge divers have known of these sunken hulls. Now they are being searched out and mapped.

Archaeology was once a hobby. So was coin collecting. Now these and other scholarly diversions have become important disciplines in historical research. In fact, the concept of history has, in the past fifty years or so, been immensely extended. No longer is it drums and trumpets, no longer is it a tangle of political maneuvers, elections, revolutions, and annexations; it is more now than class warfare and trade routes, inventions and monopolies.

Furthermore, for many generations history was ordinarily limited to the exploits of a single nation or group of nations. It is not even yet the history of mankind. Nor can it ever be, until mankind exists as an intelligible unit. But history is now—on the broadest scale—the history of civilizations spread widely through space and time: modern Europe, modern America (North and South), Japan trying to bridge the centuries, the British Commonwealth trying to span the world, and Islam, and Byzantium, and Rome, and Israel. It is also, equally important, the story of their impacts upon one another. The history of a single nation is unreal, the history of one civilization is incomplete, unless it also includes the impacts of other nations and cultures upon it and describes their effects. No one can understand Russia who does not know that Norsemen started it, Byzantines civilized it, Tartars brutalized it, Frenchmen refined it, and German-trained officials and German thinkers dragged it reluctantly into modernity. The Capitol in Washington is a Roman building elaborated on a Greek model because the American republic was based on the ideals of Greek and Roman republican government; and the Washington Monument is simply an adaptation of the Egyptian obelisks that Roman conquerors brought back from Egypt. Half of history is the history of distinctive civilizations. The other half is the story of cross-culture conflicts and cross-culture fusions.

Straight history explains the life of ideas, the history of institutions, and the careers of great men. One of the deathless ideas is the dream of the earthly paradise, the perfect state: Henry Grunwald traces its career in "From Eden to the Nightmare." Another is male sexuality incarnate, ruthless, irresistible, immune to both impotence and boredom: Don Juan. Begotten in 1630 by Tirso de Molina, he was murdered in 1903 by George Bernard Shaw, who wrote *Man and Superman* in order to dominate his own libido. This is Mr. Grunwald's theme in "The Disappearance of Don Juan." Two institutions which distorted the life of humanity in the past, and are still potentially alive—slavery and witchcraft —are analyzed by M. I. Finley of Cambridge University and H. R. Trevor-Roper of Oxford; while Christopher Herold invades the symbolic fortress of conservatism in "The Pleasures of the Bastille," and shows that it was not at all like the "corrective" prisons of modern authoritarian states.

During that seminal century, the seventeenth, three great men changed Western culture: Bacon, Pascal, and Louis XIV. All three ended their lives in melancholy and bitter failure. They attempted too much. What they achieved is set down by Loren Eiseley, who sees Bacon as the head of a revolution in scientific method; Morris Bishop, who describes Pascal as a tormented hybrid of saint and scientist; and William Harlan Hale, who shows in "The Minister's Fatal Showplace" that young Louis, on his visit to a palace built by one of his own servants, determined that henceforth he and he alone would be the center of wealth, and power, and glory.

History deals also with conflict and co-operation between cultures. The great conflict which affects all modern life and will shape all future history is that between the white and the non-white peoples. To describe it completely would take many volumes, but in "The Image of the White Man" John Maass shows us the simplest and yet the strangest aspect of it: that different members of the human race do not *look* quite human to one another.

Reading the Bible with an open imagination, everyone is struck by the Song of Solomon: so sensual, so happy, so frank, it sounds very different indeed from the other books of the Old Testament. The correct thing is to explain it, not as a book of love lyrics, but as an allegory of mystical union between Christ and his Church or between God and his chosen Hebrew people. But in "O Ye Daughters of Sumer!" Samuel Noah Kramer produces a much earlier parallel for these Israelitish hymns: a group of songs expressing the delight of the Sumerian goddess Inanna in her mortal lover; and so, behind this mysterious and beautiful book, we recognize the age-old religious experience of the Holy Marriage.

East and West: it is not true that the twain shall never meet. They constantly meet, in conflict or conquest or exploitation or exchanges of goodwill. Alfred Duggan's short but elegant confrontation of Richard Lionheart and Saladin shows how conflict can be transformed into something like harmony; while C. A. Robinson's superb study of Alexander the Great, overrunning and then revivifying half the known world, is a masterpiece of clear, energetic writing by a scholar who truly loves and admires his subject.

Past and Present: these also are separate cultures. Yet they affect and alter one another. Present reinterprets Past. Past molds and strengthens Present. So a gentleman of the Renaissance was largely educated to follow ideals drawn from the high culture of Greece and Rome, as Iris Origo shows in her study of the Italian school in the sixteenth century. Professor Finley chose a more difficult subject when he selected the unreal "Year One" to show the connection between Roman power, over seven hundred years old, and the new-born faith which was to transform it.

All archaeological discovery is surprising to the layman. Little oases of human life existed here and there far earlier than we can imagine. We know they held civilized men and women, not hominoid animals, for in the debris we find evidence of orderly living, and works of art. Some of the hunters who both pursued and painted wild beasts are described by James Mellaart in "Man's First Murals"; and an underground settlement of Middle Eastern farmers who had enough leisure to make statues of fair women is evoked in Jean Perrot's "Cave-Dwelling Carvers of Five Thousand Years Ago."

After the breakthrough from stone to metal came the Age of Bronze. Its marvelously complex trade routes, which conveyed useless but precious things such as amber far afield through the Western world, are analyzed in Geoffrey Bibby's "Before the Argo." After the Argonauts came the Homeric heroes, whose world, in spite of our earnest explorations, still contains much that is beautiful and unexplained: in his "Homer's Age of Heroes" Sir Maurice Bowra delimits history, so far as it is possible to do so, from myth.

Michael Grant, surveying the Roman emperors as portrayed on their own coins, strikes a contrast between the idealized faces meant for propaganda and the realistic portraits created by true artists. Fernand Auberjonois sensitively describes the resurrection of a forgotten sculptor of medieval France, and Basil Davidson suggests that the culture of ancient Africa must, on the basis of its fine statuary and other evidences of civilization, be graded upward. Last in this group is an essay inspired by several discussions at the editorial table of HORIZON. My friends used to ask me as a classicist how much we really knew about the great books of Rome and Greece, and how we could possibly be sure that we had anything like their true texts. I tried to answer these questions in "The Survival of Records."

Outside the general field of historical knowledge lie three essays in this book. Loren Eiseley in "The Time of Man" surveys our whole evolutionary history and compares the flint knife to the Parthenon. Arthur Clarke's "In the Light of the Sun" moves outside this planet to the life of the solar system, a vast experience in which the collective existence of mankind is but a moment. Finally, a man who is both historian and philosopher, Herbert Muller, examining the "Misuses of the Past," shows that all attempts to crush the life of humanity into a single mold, to force "laws" upon historical change, or to extrapolate its movements into "inevitable progress" are radically wrong. The past, the present, and the future are either meaningless discontinuities, or they are the experience of mankind, with nothing omitted, distorted, degraded, or deified. The past is what makes us; and we are making both the past and the future.

HOMER'S AGE OF HEROES

The classical Greeks knew it only by legend.

But modern scholars have found at

Mycenae the capital city of the lost civilization

that inspired the *Iliad* and the *Odyssey*

By C. M. BOWRA

In the last hundred and fifty years, scholars have done an enormous amount of work on the Homeric poems in their desire to find out when and how they were composed and what truth, if any, lies behind their stories. At times the critically minded might well ask to what end all this work was leading. The bits of the puzzle did not seem to fit; there was fierce disagreement on most fundamental points. But slowly and quietly, despite many false starts, progress has been made. The bits are coming together, and we can see the general pattern. Archaeology has brought the

Trojan War back from legend to history; the comparative study of oral epics has shown how Homer must really have worked; the discovery and decipherment of documents from the Greek past of 1200 B.C. have thrown unexpected lights into what seemed to be a lost world. The inspiration of a few men of genius and the solid support of many hard-working inquirers have changed the whole character of Homeric studies, and we can now relate Homer to his historical background and see how he worked and what he worked on.

The classical Greeks believed that at a period in the past, which our system of chronology would place from about 1400 to about 1200 B.C., their ancestors had been a race of supermen, of heroes, who were endowed physically and mentally beyond the common lot and who lived for action and the glory which it brings, especially through prowess in battle. Such a belief in a heroic past is to be found in many peoples, and for parallels we need look no further than the great Germanic migrations from the fourth to the sixth century A.D. or to the cycles of high adventure which the French connect with Charlemagne in the ninth century, or the Russians with

With a shower of spears and arrows Homeric warriors meet the charging lion on this bronze dagger found in a tomb at Mycenae. To the ancient Greeks, proud of their bravery and physical perfection, lion hunting was a sport—as well as a defense of their homes and flocks. Homer compares the clash of Trojan and Greek on the battlefield to mountain lions who "depopulate the stalls and waste the fold." This dagger, finely inlaid with gold and silver, bears out Homer's description of the huge body shields, some in figure-eight shape, which warriors of both armies carried on the battlefield of Troy.

"Agamemnon's death mask" (opposite title page) was found during Schliemann's excavations at Mycenae.

Homer   *Schliemann*   *Ventris*

Vladimir Monomakh of Kiev in the twelfth century, or the Yugoslavs with the fall of the old Serbian kingdom to the Turks at the battle of Kosovo in 1389. With such beliefs the Greek tradition of a noble past has much in common, and like them, it found its expression in heroic, narrative song. From what must once have been a vast mass of songs, we have only the *Iliad* and the *Odyssey*, which the Greeks, without hesitation, ascribed to Homer. In all their pristine strength and splendor these epics stand at the dawn of European literature as its first and in some ways its most remarkable achievement.

The *Iliad* and the *Odyssey* survive in isolation. Of other poems resembling them we have only a few stray lines, and of Homer himself we know next to nothing. He says not a word about himself, offers no personal judgments, and hardly ever speaks, even in the first person. External traditions about him are late, contradictory, and untrustworthy. Where all is darkness it is not surprising that some scholars have decided that he did not exist or at least did not compose the two poems, and many alternatives have been sought to what is regarded as the uncritical gullibility of the Greeks about him. The case for some kind of multiple authorship has appealed to many whose standards of literary criticism come from books composed in conditions very unlike those of the Homeric poems and who are unable to understand that in the course of centuries literature has changed its habits. For some one hundred and fifty years the Homeric poems have been carved into pieces by minute analysis and explained variously as combinations of single short lays, or expansions of original, basic poems, or ingenious transformations of poems dealing with quite different subjects. Yet all this labor has led to no single point of agreement. Each analyst believes he has found the solution, but he has no disciples. Something seems to have gone wrong, and we can in fact see what it is.

The fundamental error of the analytical method is that it treats the Homeric poems as if, like modern books, they were written to be read. They belong to a different, much older art. They were not written but recited, not read but heard, and the difference accounts for the peculiarities which have troubled modern scholars but did not trouble the Greeks. Before the invention of writing, all poetry was recited or sung, and the practice still flourishes in many regions where not everyone is literate, or books are confined to limited, special fields like law and theology, or recitation is still enjoyed for its own sake as a dignified and agreeable pastime.

The oral poet works quite differently from the poet who writes. Recitation is his only means of making his work known, and his first duty is to keep his audience's attention at all costs. If he bores or confuses them, he loses their interest and, with it, his source of livelihood. His technique, which comes from generations of practiced bards, tells him what to do. Above all he must not allow his story to become too complicated; he must deal with one and only one thing at a time, with all the clarity and firmness of outline of which he is capable. This means that he sacrifices much that the writer of books thinks indispensable. In oral art the moment a theme has done its task it is dismissed without ado, and no attempt is made to tidy the loose threads. The need to stress the special character of each dramatic occasion may lead to inconsistencies with what is said elsewhere. A long poem, whose performance may last for several days, may be loose in construction just because each episode must be complete in itself. A passage which performs one task in one place may be repeated word for word in another place to perform a slightly different task. The audience does not know what it is to turn over pages to see if everything fits exactly, and it is content with the fleeting situation as the spoken word reveals it. Oral poetry has its own rules, which are well known to us from a large mass of poems collected from many parts of the world where the art is still vigorous and popular. It is by the standards of this art that Homer must be interpreted and judged.

Our knowledge of Mycenaean civilization springs in large measure from the work of the three men on the opposite page: the ancient poet and two amateur archaeologists. Homer's picture of an age of heroes, though accepted by the classical Greeks, had been generally dismissed as legend until Heinrich Schliemann, a German businessman, set out to prove its truth. In 1870 he uncovered the site of Troy and six years later began his excavation of the ruins of Mycenae. Schliemann's lead was followed up by Sir Arthur Evans on Crete and by Carl W. Blegen on the mainland. The next great breakthrough came in 1952, when Michael Ventris, a young English architect, deciphered the Linear B script found on tablets at Knossos, Pylos, and Mycenae. The tablets proved to be largely commercial records, but they show that the people spoke an archaic form of Greek and had a highly organized business and political life. The tablet shown at right is a record of a commercial transaction in wool.

Although the *Iliad* and the *Odyssey* were composed for recitation and show all its familiar marks, each has its own mastering design and its own kind of unity. In the *Iliad* the whole poem hangs upon the wrath of Achilles, and though other episodes are introduced on a generous scale to make it indeed a tale of Troy, it is the wrath which gives a unity to the whole. The last book picks up the themes of the first and tells the end of the wrath with which all the action began.

The *Odyssey* is composed in three movements: the first tells of the anarchic condition of Ithaca in the absence of Odysseus, the second of his many adventures between his departure from Troy and his final arrival on Ithaca, the third of his vengeance on Penelope's suitors after his arrival. In each movement the characters are admirably consistent, life-like, and even at times complex. The rich, elaborate, and traditional language shows no real variation between one section and another, and the poetical vision is sustained throughout. Devices, such as similes or the repetition of conventional themes for the arming of warriors or the conduct of sacrifices or putting boats to sea, are managed with admirable judgment and made to provide variety just when it is needed. Both the *Iliad* and the *Odyssey* are clearly artistic wholes, and such interpolations as they may contain do not disturb the main pattern.

It does not necessarily follow that both poems are the work of the same poet. There are certainly differences between them, in temper, in language, in pace, in construction, and in outlook, but these are less than between *Romeo and Juliet* and *The Tempest* or between *Comus* and *Samson Agonistes*. All considered, the *Odyssey* looks very like a later work by the author of the *Iliad* and may have been intended to be in some sense a sequel to it. The poems were probably composed between 750 and 700 B.C., since such a date fits the latest datable details in them. They belong to a period from which almost no other literature survives, and their origin was certainly in Ionia on the eastern coast of the Aegean Sea.

There is no reason to think that their author's name was not Homer.

Between the events of which Homer tells and the lifetime of the poet himself there is a gap of some five hundred years. Another three centuries separate Homer from the classical Greeks of the Golden Age. These later Greeks believed that the main events of his poems were historically true, but of the poet's lost world they knew almost nothing—far less than we do today. It remained for modern research, moving on three main lines of discovery, to unearth an advanced civilization which corresponds in many respects to that of which Homer sang.

The first move came from archaeology, when in 1870 a retired German businessman, Heinrich Schliemann, who was obsessed by a passionate love of Homer, drove a deep trench into the traditional site of Troy near the southeastern shore of the Dardanelles. Three years later, after digging through many levels, he found what he thought to be the city of Priam and its treasure. But what he identified as Homeric Troy was, in fact, a city which flourished at least a thousand years earlier than any possible city of Priam, and at the end of his life Schliemann knew that he had not discovered what he sought. It fell to his successors, and especially to the University of Cincinnati expedition led by Professor Carl W. Blegen, to identify, in a higher level at the same site, the ruins of the city which must indeed be the Homeric Troy. Schliemann also attacked sites on the Greek mainland, notably at Mycenae, where he uncovered a royal graveyard where the bodies lay intact in all their gold masks and ornaments. The work his inspired insight inaugurated has been continued ever since, and each year it has added to our knowledge of this rich and spectacular past.

The heroic age of which Homer sang has its historical counterpart in this Mycenaean civilization, which had its beginnings in Crete, notably at Knossos. About 1450 B.C. Knossos waned and Mycenae waxed, developing its own new

TEXT CONTINUED ON PAGE 18

P.-J. LAUNAY

The Lion Gate

Mycenae

The citadel of Mycenae, rising high above the Argive plain, was the stronghold, according to Homeric tradition, of Agamemnon, "king of men" and leader of the Greek armies against the Trojans. The walls are built of stones so huge that the Greeks of the classical age thought they must have been set in place by the Cyclopes. Actually the fortress palace was built between 1500 and 1300 B.C. and was destroyed by the "Dorian" invaders barely a century after Mycenaean power reached its apogee in the conquest of Troy. Mycenae had been a ruin for thirteen hundred years when the Greek traveler Pausanias saw it in the second century A.D. "There still remain," he wrote, "parts of the city wall, including the gate, upon which stand lions." The lions still stand guard, though headless, at the gate near the Grave Circle (right), which Pausanias thought to contain the tombs of Agamemnon and his family. Heinrich Schliemann, who excavated the tombs, likewise thought the skeletons he found were those of Homer's royal family, but modern archaeologists date them four centuries earlier. The golden treasure which the tombs yielded proves that even then Mycenae was a center of wealth, power, and artistic accomplishment unrivaled on the continent of Europe.

GEORGES VIOLLON, RAPHO

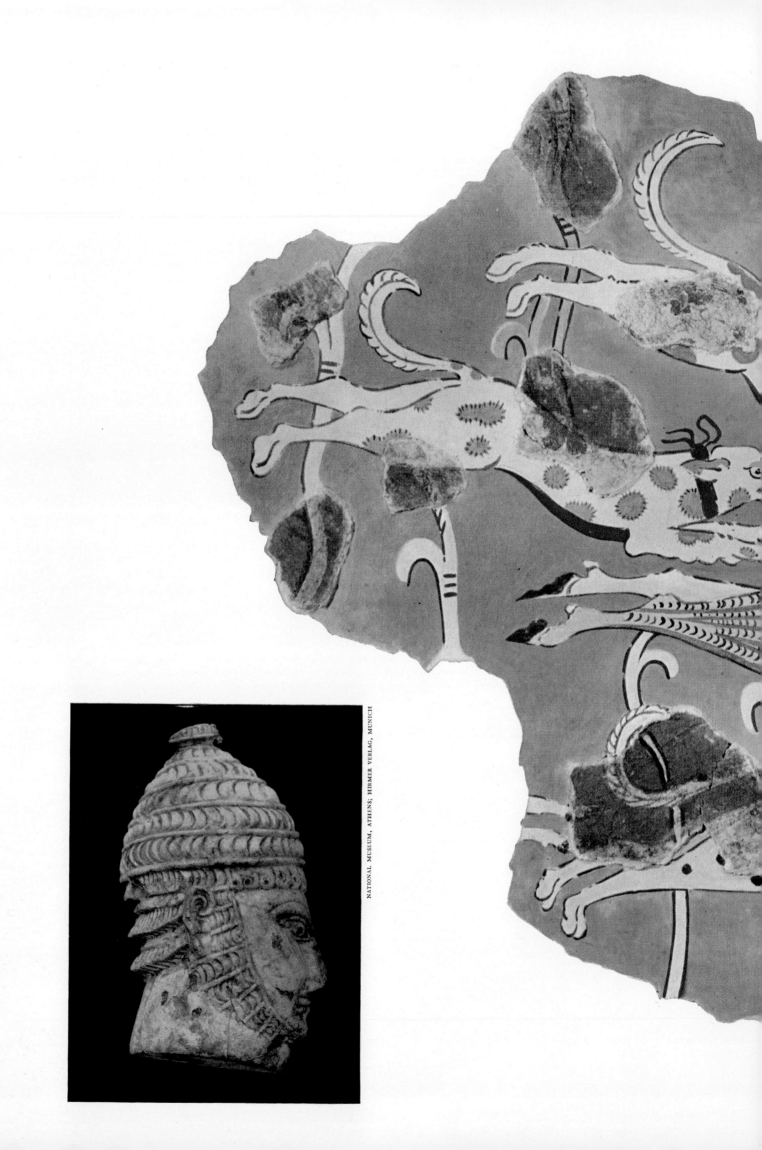

The Boar Hunt

Tracking the wild boar with hunting dogs was an exciting sport to the Mycenaean lord. The spectacle provided Homer with a simile for the Trojan attack on the Greeks:

> "So two wild boars spring furious from their den,
> Roused with the cries of dogs and voice of men . . ."

A painting of such a boar hunt adorned one wall of the palace of Tiryns, ten miles south of Mycenae. From the surviving fragments, which appear as dark spots in the picture, archaeologists made this reconstruction. Boars' teeth were prized for making helmets like that on the Mycenaean carved ivory figure (bottom left). Odysseus wore such a helmet in night operations against the Trojans. Homer reported, "A boar's white teeth grinn'd horrid o'er his head."

VATICAN MUSEUM, ALINARI

HARISSIADIS–NATIONAL MUSEUM, ATHENS

Homer's warriors were imagined by the Greeks of the classical age as handsome, noble figures like Achilles (above), shining in his famous armor adorned with the Medusa head. The ancient heroes' picture of themselves was far less flattering. On the Warrior Vase from Mycenae (right) the fighting men of 1200 B.C. are depicted as long-nosed, chinless types who seem more startled than eager to be marching to war.

TEXT CONTINUED FROM PAGE 13

movements in the fine arts and its own characteristic pattern of life. That it was fashioned for war is clear from the vast scale of its Cyclopean fortifications, from the rich variety of weapons found in its graves, from the many scenes of battle which its artists delighted to portray on gold or ivory or gems or pottery. Yet the Mycenaean world did not exist only for war. It made notable achievements in the fine arts, and its works and wares found markets in distant lands from the Adriatic to Syria. A power like this one was fully capable of maintaining a war such as that against Troy, and tradition may well be right in saying that the expedition was led by the king of Mycenae. But the Mycenaean civilization, which had many seats in the Peloponnesus and even northward as far as Thessaly, came to an abrupt and violent end about 1200 B.C., when its towns and citadels were destroyed and its material culture fell into rapid decay. The destroyers probably came from the northwest and, even if they were related racially to the Mycenaeans, were vastly inferior to them in culture. By 1200 the Dark Age of Greece begins.

A second, much less abundant source of information comes from Egyptian and Hittite records. The Egyptians were much troubled by the "Peoples of the Sea," and among these we may recognize two names which Homer uses for his Greeks—Achaeans and Danaans. The first took part in an attack against Egypt from the west about 1230 B.C. and were routed by Merneptah; the second peoples were among the confederates of a concerted invasion by land and sea about 1182 B.C. and were routed in the Nile Delta by Ramses III, who had reliefs of the battle carved on a pylon at his temple at Medinet Habu. The Hittite records, found in their ancient capital of Boghazköy, contain tantalizing references to the Ahhiyawans, who cannot be other than the Achaeans, and who played a considerable part in Hittite foreign affairs in the fourteenth and thirteenth centuries, first as allies and later as raiders by land and sea. They were classed as a great power; and in one document in particular the king of Ahhiyawa is mentioned as being the equal of the kings of the Hittites, the Egyptians, and the Babylonians, only to have his name

"The rushing chariot and the bounding steed" of 1400 B.C. are depicted on the Mycenaean vase at left. By 450 B.C., when the Attic volute krater below was made, classical artists had added two horses and romanticized the legend of heroic times. But the design of the chariot remains basically the same in art as it did in fact for more than a thousand years.

A MYCENAEAN CHARIOT

AS SEEN BY A MYCENAEAN ARTIST (ABOVE)

. . . AND BY THE CLASSICAL GREEKS (RIGHT)

erased, as if in the interval he had forfeited his title to honor.

From the Egyptian and Hittite documents we get a clear enough picture of Achaeans, living probably on the Greek mainland but with outposts in Asia Minor and Cyprus, who through their ships pursued a policy of expansion toward the east and the southeast, aiming eventually at seizing land in Egypt. In such conditions an attack on Troy would have had its place; for Troy, which stood near the narrowest point of the crossing from Europe to Asia and seemed to have been a tributary of the Hittites, would have had to be captured before Asia Minor could be invaded from the northwest. For the Achaeans such a policy would have been almost a necessity, and we can understand why the Trojan War took place. The Achaeans, who are known alike to Homer and to the Egyptians and Hittites, are evidently the same people as those known to archaeology as Mycenaeans.

Neither archaeology nor foreign records tells us much about the internal organization of Mycenaean society, or indeed whether its members were authentic Greeks. For this information we must rely on the clay documents found in Mycenaean sites, first at Knossos and later in great quantities at Pylos in the southwestern corner of the Peloponnesus. These were deciphered in 1952 by a young English architect, Michael Ventris, who proved beyond doubt that they contain an archaic form of Greek. In one of the great tragedies of historical scholarship, Ventris was killed in 1956 in a road accident, but his epoch-making discovery had been made, and he left a rich legacy for others to develop.

The Mycenaean script, which is adapted from an earlier script current in Crete, whose reported decipherment has raised much controversy, is a syllabary, and its eighty-seven signs stand either for vowels or for consonants followed by vowels. Such a syllabary is far less efficient than an alphabet and contains many ambiguities owing to its lack of sufficient signs. This probably did not matter to its original users, who must have been officials who kept records only for certain purposes and were well acquainted with what the signs meant by convention. The documents are for the most part

inventories of possessions, offerings to gods, documents on land tenure, military orders, and lists of men and women allotted to certain tasks. They contain not a trace of anything that can be called literature and have more than a touch of the précis in their manner. But their value is incalculable. They prove that the Mycenaeans were Greeks; that they had a highly organized system of government, were certainly quite as rich as Homer believed, worshiped some of the gods known to him, and had names very like those which he gives to Greeks and Trojans—including both Achilles and Hector, though neither of these has any claim to be Homer's original.

From these three sources we get, quite independently of Homer or other Greek source, a well-established notion of the Mycenaean world, of its wealth, its fine arts, its expanding and aggressive policies, and its ability to wage war. From it we may turn to the site of Troy and specifically to the level known as VIIa, a rebuilding of the city after the earthquake of circa 1280 B.C. This level keeps the old walls and gates, but has otherwise been refashioned for the needs of war. Empty spaces have been filled with houses; food supplies were kept in earthenware vessels dug into the floor; internal communications were improved by paved roads. About 1240 this city was destroyed by fire, and layers of ashes, calcined stones, burned bricks (to say nothing of corpses in the main

streets and under the walls) tell the same story. This was the Troy of which Homer knew, and its destruction was the work of invading Achaeans. It does not matter that it can have been no more than a fortress, covering some five acres. What matters is that it guarded the way into Asia, and the Achaeans captured and destroyed it. It was the last great event in their heroic legend. Story told that its capture cost the Achaeans dear, and that afterward disaster fell upon them. Within fifty years their great cities and fortresses of the mainland suffered the same fate as Troy, and the Mycenaean world came to an end. A few survivors escaped by sea to Ionia and brought with them the songs of their homeland and the memories of its heroic deeds.

It is of this heroic age that Homer tells, directly in the *Iliad* and less directly in the *Odyssey*. His information about it was extensive and surprising. He knew that Troy had been besieged and taken by an Achaean confederacy under the king of Mycenae, that among the Trojan allies were people who looked like Hittites, that Achaeans like Bellerophon had been active in an earlier generation in Asia Minor, that they did not hesitate to raid Egypt. He also knew more surprising details which meant nothing to his own age and can only be memories of the Mycenaean world. He consistently speaks of bronze weapons, and though he knows about iron, he does not mention that it was used for war. The helmets of his

King Nestor's Palace and Bathtub

In Pylos, the traditional realm of the wise King Nestor, excavations have uncovered the remains of a sixty-room palace. The throne room in the foreground of the picture at left may be the hall where, in the Odyssey, *Nestor counseled Telemachus, Odysseus's son, in his search for his father. Upon his arrival at Pylos, the weary Telemachus was bathed by Polycaste, Nestor's beautiful daughter. A terracotta bathtub, decorated with spiral patterns and containing a broken kylix (right), found in the palace area lends reality to Homer's account of this ancient hospitality. King Nestor's palace was destroyed by fire around 1200 B.C.*

warriors have plumes and horns like those on the Warrior Vase from Mycenae (see page 18). His Ajax carries a shield "like a tower" (pages 10–11), which was normal in the fourteenth century but went out of use soon afterward. He speaks of such characteristic Mycenaean things as sword hilts riveted with silver or gold studs, of silver work inlaid with gold, of palaces with upper floors and rooms opening on vestibules and courtyards, of open precincts for the gods instead of temples. His shield of Achilles is made in a technique like that used in the inlaid dagger blades from Mycenae; he gives to Nestor a cup with images of doves on the rim, and such a cup, made of gold, has been found (see page 23). When he tells of the slaughter of men and animals at a great man's funeral, he is confirmed by a tomb at Dendra. He knows about the towers and gates of Troy and, more surprisingly, about the structure of its walls. Because of their unusual batter below the perpendicular ramparts, Patroclus is able to climb them up to the point where Apollo casts him down.

Homer knows of the gold of Mycenae, of the *temenos*, or special piece of land, allotted to princes and mentioned in Mycenaean documents, of thrones inlaid with ivory ornaments such as have been found in more than one place, of bronze greaves like those found in Cyprus and the Peloponnesus. He has heard of even remoter objects and situations. When Odysseus goes out on night operations, he wears a felt cap covered with boars' teeth (page 16); though such caps were common before 1300 B.C., they went out of use afterward. He gives an account of Egyptian Thebes which seems to come from the fourteenth century, when Amenhotep III decorated temples with floors and doors of gold and silver and built pylons which survive for Homer as a hundred gates. Homer's knowledge of the Mycenaean age is extensive, and through it he sets his story in a heroic past when men were wealthier and more powerful than in his own day.

At the same time many of Homer's details come from ages later than the Mycenaean. His dead are not buried but burned, a practice which seems to have started soon after the Trojan War. Though he knows about Thebes, he believes Egypt is so far away that even birds take a year to cross the sea from it. His warriors do not fight from chariots, like the Mycenaeans, but use them simply as a means of transport to places on the battlefield where they dismount and fight on foot. Instead of two horses his chariots usually have four. From his own time or near it come descriptions of the wealth of Apollo's shrine at Delphi, the Gorgon on the shield of Agamemnon, the wheeled tripods of Hephaestus, the advance of infantry in close line in battle, the structure of the brooch of Odysseus with its two pins fitting into sheaths, the part played by Phoenicians in the seafaring life of the *Odyssey*. Above all in his similes, which bear no relation to the

Mycenaean world, he draws from his own observation and touches on many subjects which lay outside his heroic theme but touched him intimately by their simple and varied appeal.

Why does Homer draw on the material of different centuries? How does he know anything about the Mycenaean world? The answers would be easy if we could believe that he inherited written texts of Mycenaean poems and that he drew upon them for material before bringing it up to date to suit his contemporary audience at points where it might be unintelligible. However, though the Mycenaeans used writing, there is no evidence that they used it for poetry, and, more important, it is clear that when the Mycenaean civilization perished, its system of writing perished with it. This is indeed an extraordinary, almost unparalleled phenomenon, and it can be explained only by the hypothesis that the scribes were a small class whose work the new conquerors did not understand and did not use. At any rate, on all the thousands of potsherds which originated between circa 1200 and 750 B.C., when the new Phoenician alphabet was introduced into Greece, there is not a single inscribed letter, and we are forced to conclude that Homer cannot have learned about the past from any written records. He may conceivably have seen some Mycenaean objects preserved as heirlooms, and he almost certainly knew the site of Troy (though not Ithaca), but even this would not account for his knowledge of the Mycenaean world. How did he find it?

As so often with Homer, the answer comes from looking at other oral poets who tell of the past. They do not learn from books; their knowledge of the past, which is often impressive, comes from oral tradition. Such a tradition may last for centuries, and this is what happened in Greece. We cannot doubt that heroic songs existed in the Mycenaean age, and it is even possible that the magnificent meter of the hexameter had already been invented, since Mycenaean Greek, as we can see from the tablets, falls easily into it. Bards passed on to their successors not only names and stories, metrical devices and tricks of narrative but something much more substantial and useful—a large number of formulaic phrases covering most needs of the heroic story and ready for use when the poet needed them. Such formulas were indispensable to oral composition and were fashioned with much care through many centuries until, by Homer's time, they met almost every want in his story. Oral poets operate less with single words than with phrases, and these phrases have been polished and perfected by generations until they have a true distinction of their own. Some of these formulas in Homer are extremely ancient, and he himself may not quite have known their original meaning, but they belonged to the tradition in which he learned his craft, and for that reason he used them. He could and no doubt did supplement them with new phrases of his own making, but these old formulas were his link with the past, and it is through them that he knew so much about an age which was at least five hundred years before his own. Whenever we come across something indubitably ancient in the *Iliad* or the *Odyssey*, we may be sure that it came to Homer through a long succession of bards whose art can be traced back to Mycenaean times.

Homer seems to have supplemented this traditional knowledge with a knowledge of the actual site of Troy. His story in the *Iliad* makes hardly any mistake in geography; and though many of the points may seem unimportant, like the course of the Scamander, or the distance from the city to the Achaean camp, or the plants and bushes on the plain, they

"Mycenae, Rich in Gold"

Homer's admiration for the skill of Mycenaean goldsmiths is borne out by the treasure found in the tombs of the Grave Circle. The cup, which is reproduced a little larger than actual size on the facing page, is hammered from a single sheet of metal with handles bearing two golden birds. It is called "Nestor's Cup" because of its resemblance in miniature to the huge embossed goblet which the king of Pylos took with him to the Trojan battlefield.

> *"It was set with golden nails, the eared handles upon it were four,*
> *And on either side there were fashioned two doves of gold, feeding,*
> *And there were double bases beneath it.*
> *Another man with great effort could lift it full from the table,*
> *But Nestor, aged as he was, lifted it without strain."*   (Iliad, *XI*)

NATIONAL MUSEUM, ATHENS; HIRMER VERLAG, MUNICH

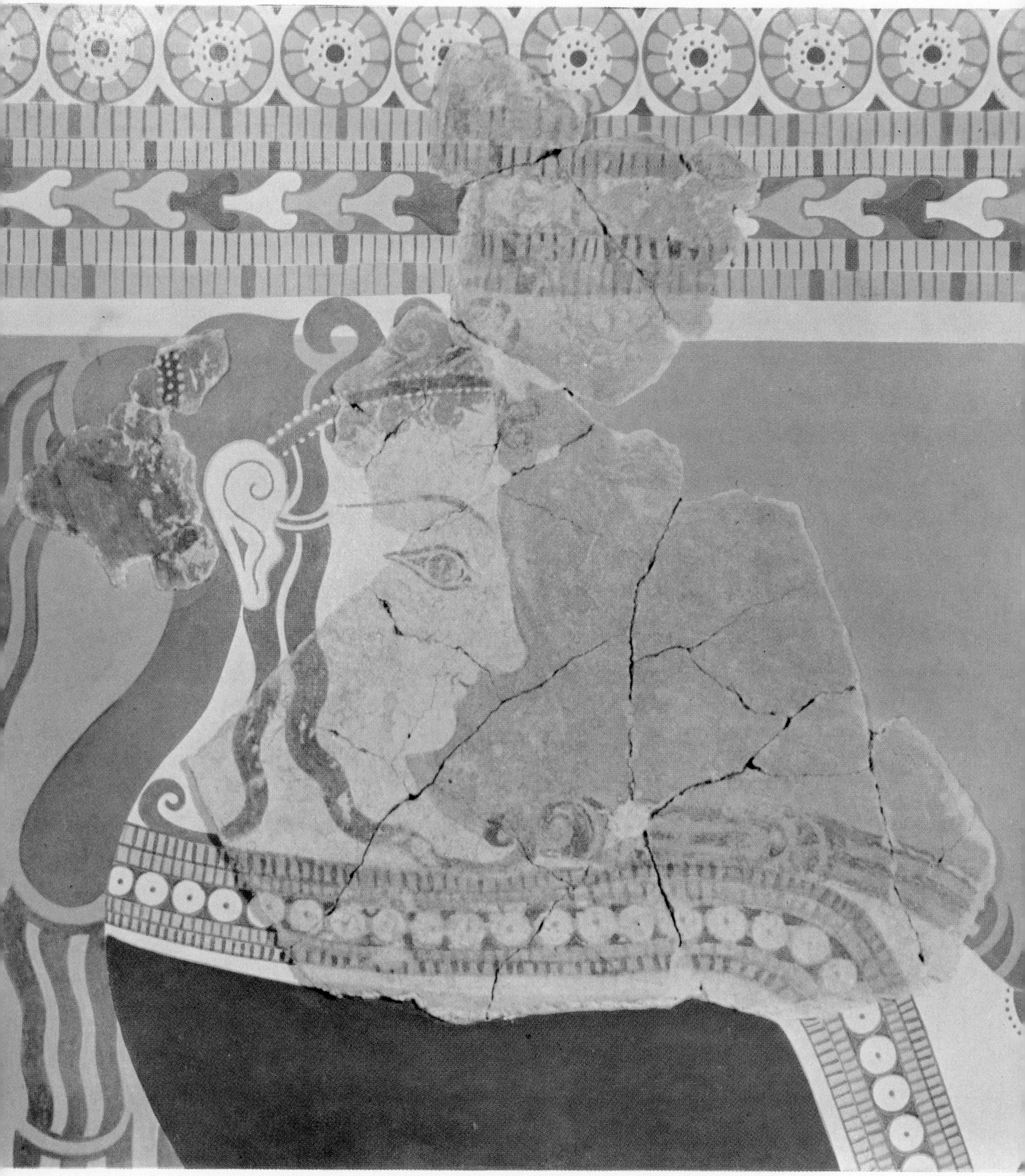

all indicate that he knew more about the battlefield than even his formulas can have given him. Indeed, even today, when we stand on the ruins of Troy and look over the plain, we feel that we can see why his masterpiece fits so well into the landscape. The Troy he saw was certainly in ruins, but he knew that it had been a great city, and he took advantage of his local knowledge to create such scenes as those of Andromache on the tower seeing the dead body of her husband dragged behind the chariot of Achilles or Priam going out at night across the plain to ransom the body of his dead son from the terrible man who has killed him. Among these ruins, which were old even in his time, Homer created again an ancient tale and gave to it a strength which it surely never had before.

Homer is not a historian, and he lived long before scientific history was invented. His re-creation of the past in poetry is not historical because it combines competing elements which come from some six centuries. No doubt, too, he made his own improvements on legends, and we have no right to presume that all he says is true. What he tells is what he himself believed because the Muse had told it to him. By the Muse he means the divine power of creative song which he knew in himself and rightly regarded as the daughter of Memory, because it was indeed a people's memory that had preserved so much for him. We do not know how he performed his songs. He himself makes bards sing to kings at their courts, and perhaps this is what he himself did, though it would not prevent him from singing also at religious festivals and public gatherings. Nor do we know how his poems were written down. It is most unlikely that his pupils memorized them and passed them by word of mouth to later generations, since for this there is no parallel in oral performance; indeed, it is alien to the methods of such composition. The easiest explanation is that since he himself was alive when the wonderful art of writing returned to the Greeks in the form of the Phoenician alphabet, he dictated his poems to someone who knew it and the written texts were guarded by professional bards who recited them to later generations. Yet he remains an oral poet who uses all the devices of this special craft and draws his art from a long tradition. His aim was more to delight than to instruct, but he believed that men delighted to hear of the glorious doings of men and that such doings, and the sufferings which they bring, find a reward and a consolation in song. To this task he gave his incomparable gifts. He learned the ancient formulas and used them as if they were fresh as the morning for his vision of the heroic generations who once belonged to his race and whose memory was treasured through all the changes and catastrophes of the intervening years.

Sir Maurice Bowra, a leading scholar of the ancient Greek world, is warden of Wadham College, Oxford. His books include Problems in Greek Poetry *and* Heroic Poetry. *Among his best-known works is* The Greek Experience, *an evaluation of the Greek spirit through its philosophy, as developed from the time of Homer to the fall of Athens in the year 404 B.C.*

She could be Helen

But all we know is that she adorned a wall of the palace of Tiryns in the thirteenth century B.C. Starting with fragments, which appear as darker areas, archaeologists used other paintings as a guide to reconstruct the figure of a stately, curly-haired woman. She wears the embroidered, open-bodiced dress that Mycenaean women adopted from Crete.

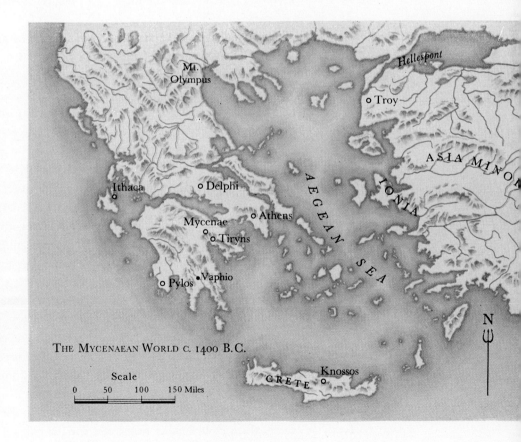

THE MYCENAEAN WORLD C. 1400 B.C.

Scale
0   50   100   150 Miles

FROM THE CLASSIC EARTH

In 1959 two laborers were repairing a sewer in Piraeus, the seaport of Athens, when they stumbled on a hoard of masterpieces of Greek sculpture lost since antiquity and lying barely a yard beneath the pavement. Of the eight works found, the marvels are four bronze statues, which HORIZON was enabled to photograph through the courtesy of Ionnis Papadimitriou, Director of Antiquities for the Greek government. They are presented here virtually as they came from the earth, with fissures, marks of corrosion, and particles of soil still on them.

First, opposite, is the upper portion of a figure of the goddess Artemis, standing five feet high. A Hellenistic work of the fourth century B.C., its warm grace and air of thoughtful quiet exemplify the finest qualities of that sculptural period. Unquestionably the greatest of the finds is the magnificent *kouros*, or youth, shown overleaf—probably a representation of the god Apollo. Made in the late sixth century B.C., this slightly more than life-size figure is the earliest statue in bronze that has yet come to light from the soil of Greece. While it still conveys the stylized simplicity of the archaic, its forms reveal the gentle swell of life and the naturalness that characterize the art of the classic period.

On the left-hand page thereafter appears the larger than life-size head of a girl, her eyes set with semi-precious stones and fixed in a serene gaze. Close to the school of Praxiteles, the whole statue sums up what was best in Greek art near the close of the fourth century B.C. The final page presents a figure of Athena in her splendor. More than seven feet high, it is a triumph of a sculptor active near the beginning of the fourth century. The goddess is heroic and magisterial in her great helmet, adorned with shapes of owls and griffons. Across her breast is fitted the *aegis*, in its center the head of Medusa with its hair of serpents.

Some evidence on the site has led scholars to theorize that the works may have been brought together at Piraeus as part of a shipment of artistic loot destined for Rome, and that the warehouse containing them may have burned during the pillaging of Athens and Piraeus by the troops of the dictator Sulla in 86 B.C. Whatever the circumstances, at some ancient moment they were buried and forgotten, and their cover of oblivion perfectly preserved them from further marauders for the gaze of our own time.

PHOTOGRAPHS BY D. A. HARISSIADIS, ATHENS

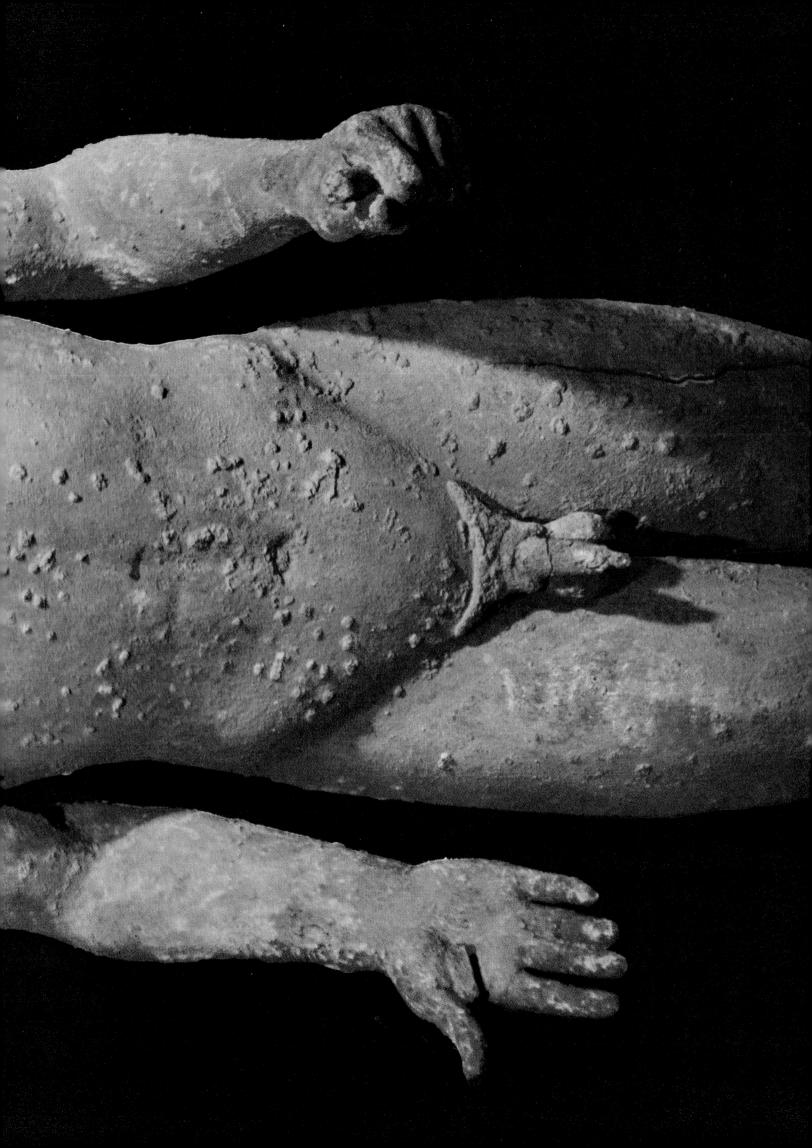

More than 8,000 years ago an artist painted on the wall of a village dwelling at Çatal Hüyük, in what is now Turkish Anatolia, a pioneer portrayal of the activities of his neolithic fellow men. The photograph below shows a detail of his work as recently discovered. At right is a sketched reconstruction of his mural as a whole: the inset square indicates the area of the original fragment below. The figures show men hunting, dancing, engaging in acrobatics, and beating a drum.

MAN'S FIRST MURALS

The scholar who recently discovered them presents startling works of
prehistoric art that were an indirect result of man's first revolution

Today we can no longer measure man's early cultural achievements only in terms of classical Greece or of the Bronze Age civilizations of Egypt, Mesopotamia, or Crete; new archaeological discoveries show that these eras had forerunners of no less importance. Among them is the highly sophisticated culture that flourished nine thousand years ago at Çatal Hüyük, a recently uncovered city on Turkey's Anatolian plateau. Dating from the Early Neolithic period, roughly 6600 to 5800 B.C., the Çatal Hüyük site has brought to light jewelry, hunting equipment, household utensils, statuettes and other religious objects, and—most significantly—the earliest murals ever found on man-made walls.

This center of art was found during an archaeological survey of the surrounding plain, which I led in 1958, and excavations there were begun in the summer of 1961. Although it will require another decade to uncover all of Çatal Hüyük, the largest neolithic site yet known in the Near East, the discoveries we have made thus far hint at the extraordinary achievement, at a very early date, that this site represents.

Çatal Hüyük covers thirty-two acres in the center of the fertile plain of Konya, in the foothills of the Taurus Mountains. Its people were among the first to live in village farming communities in which plant domestication and stock-breeding, primarily of cattle, provided a significant part of the food supply. Their houses are crowded around courtyards or on narrow lanes, presenting a most urban appearance, and they are characterized by a convenience of layout that is strikingly "modern": two or more rooms, a raised platform, or divan, a bench, sometimes a plaster cupboard with shelves, a grain bin, and an isolated, meticulously arranged cooking area with a built-in wall oven. The growth of a settled community apparently provided an opportunity for the Çatal Hüyük dwellers to decorate their houses; and the ornamentation varies from panels, recesses, and painted hearths to, in one large building, work in plaster relief.

The character of this culture betrays a neatness, attention to detail, and sophistication far beyond what even the most sanguine of archaeologists would have expected to find at so early a period. And its wall paintings, illustrated on these pages, constitute its greatest surprise.

The paintings were executed on the interior walls of houses or shrines, with a brush, in freehand application of flat wash against white or cream-colored plaster, with a relatively wide assortment of colors that include shades of red, pink, mauve, white, buff, black, and—in one instance—pale yellow. Perhaps the most significant aspect of the art is that several different styles are evident, indicating the work of a number of different artists.

The earliest of the work now being recovered is purely geometric, similar to the designs on the woven mats or textiles also found at the site. In later works at Çatal Hüyük the human figure emerges: a group of four males dressed in white loincloths and animal skins, a small figure of a plump woman dressed in leopard skin, and some other fragments of figures and "portraits."

The more recent, and better preserved, paintings (shown opposite and on the two following pages) are almost exclusively concerned with hunting or hunting ritual scenes. One of the main panels in a shrinelike building contains a mural of considerable scope, depicting a number of men hunting red deer; a huge aurochs bull, six feet long, dominates one entire wall. But of all the paintings at Çatal Hüyük the mural on the east wall of this same shrine (opposite) must have been, at the time it was fully intact, the most spectacular. Even in the four slight fragments that survive there is evidence of outstanding technical dexterity. The earliest of the scenes shows thirteen men in three rows, performing a ritual dance in which they are disguised as leopards. The sense of motion in the dancing and acrobatics, and the rendering of true and distorted perspective in this and the deer-hunting scene (page 35), is remarkably well projected.

What is the origin of this art? Until investigations of Çatal Hüyük's earlier, lower levels are completed, it would be premature to offer even hypotheses. Nothing yet is known of the beginnings of the neolithic culture that flourished there only to become extinguished; nor do we know, from other excavations in Anatolia so far, whether the culture was any more than local.

Similarities have been pointed out between the Çatal Hüyük murals, the upper paleolithic Lascaux cave paintings in southern France (about 20,000 B.C.), and the neolithic Tassili frescoes in the Sahara (8000 to 3000 B.C.); and there is certainly an analogous preoccupation with lively scenes in which the human element is dominant. However, with so little knowledge of these early periods it may be unjustifiable to speculate about resemblances between expressions of art that are separated by such vast regions of what is still artistically, if not archaeologically, *terra incognita*.

With or without such formidable comparisons, Çatal Hüyük stands as an instance of man's emergence, in a very early community, through agriculture into art.

By JAMES MELLAART

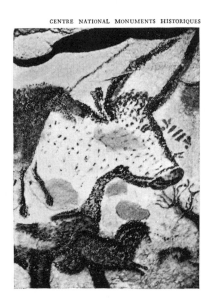

Though separated by thousands of years and thousands of miles from the new-found murals at Çatal Hüyük in Turkey, the cave painting of a bull at Lascaux in southern France (left) and the rendering of antelopes found at Tassili in North Africa (below) show a strong resemblance in style and spirit to such Çatal Hüyük figures as those shown here. Each culture apparently arrived at these similar themes and styles independently. The Lascaux cave painting dates from more than 20,000 years ago, the Tassili art from about 5,500 years ago, and the Çatal Hüyük murals from 8,000 to 9,000 years ago.

The enormous wall painting of an aurochs bull (opposite, in a sketched reconstruction) was recently found in a "shrine" room in neolithic Çatal Hüyük along with the portrayal of a deer hunt, below. The bull is surrounded by numerous fragmentary figures that apparently represent either hunters or worshipers, and other evidence found at the site suggests that this painting was connected with an early cult. The horns of bulls were preserved at Çatal Hüyük either in small plastered rooms or set in plaster near the hearth, which seems to indicate the beginnings of the bull cult so characteristic of the Near East and the Mediterranean at a later date. The awesomeness of the bull, six feet long in the original, and its great size relative to the figures around it, suggests a mood of veneration rather than a hunting scene.

The deer-hunt mural is especially noteworthy for its acute sense of perspective. Partly stylized and partly naturalistic, the painting achieves a three-dimensional effect through the turned heads of the stags and through a proper rendering of linear perspective in the treatment of the antlers. It also exemplifies a preoccupation with live action that is typical of the Çatal Hüyük murals. At bottom a wounded stag attempts to bolt free from its attackers; at upper right a doe shields its fawn from the pursuing hunters; and at left the leader of the hunt appears ready to cope with any, and all, of the animals missed by the other hunters.

The author of the article on p. 33, James Mellaart, directed the excavations that uncovered the Çatal Hüyük murals and is currently lecturer in prehistoric archaeology at the University of Istanbul.

THE TIME OF MAN

Once he was thought a fallen angel; then we found him to be a descended ape. Today, new finds are revolutionizing our ideas about his origins and the growth of that unique great brain which he may yet put to fatal use

It is a curious thought that as I sit down to write this essay on the history of our species, I do so in the heightened consciousness that it may never be published: a holocaust may overtake it. Tomorrow I may lie under tons of rubble, precipitated into the street along with the paper on which this history is scribbled. Over the whole earth—this infinitely small globe that possesses all we know of sunshine and bird song—an unfamiliar blight is creeping: man—man, who has become at last a planetary disease and who would, if his technology yet permitted, pass this infection to another star. If I write this history in brief compass it is because, on the scale of the universe, it is but an instant, shot with individual glory and unimaginable shame. Man is the only infinitely corruptible as well as infinitely perfectible animal.

The story I here record contains many gaps and few names. Most of what has gone into the making of man is as nameless as the nothing from which he sprang and into which, by his own hand, he threatens to subside. He has wandered unclothed through earth's long interglacial summers; he has huddled before fires in equally millennial winters. He has mated and fought for a bare existence like earth's other creatures. Unlike these others, however, he has clothed his dreams in magic that slowly became science— the science that was to bring him all things. And so, because of the dark twist in his mind, it has; it has brought him even unto death.

This story, then, is written in a kind of fatal haste—to be read by whom, I wonder? Or does it matter? Man is the talking animal. I shall talk to myself if necessary. I feel my own face before the mirror, touch the risen brain vault over the gray layer of cells that has brought us to this destiny. I lift up my hands under the light. There is no fur, black upon them, any longer.

For a moment I wish there were—for a moment of desperate terror I wish to hurtle backward like a scuttling crab into my evolutionary shell, to be swinging ape and leaping Tupaiid; yes, or sleeping reptile on a stream bank—anything but the thing I have become. He who enters history encounters burdens he cannot bear, and traps more subtle than his subtlest thought. No one quite knows how man became concerned with this torrent called history. He contrives it out of his own substance and then calls it an "act of God" when the tanks grind forward over his own body.

A strange animal, indeed: so very quiet when one turns over the mineral-hardened skull in a gravel bed, or peers into that little dark space which has housed so much cruelty and delight. One feels that something should be there still, some indefinable essence, some jinni to be evoked out of this little space which may contain at the same time the words of Jesus and the blasphemous megatons of modern physics. They are all in there together, inextricably intermixed, and this is how the mixture began.

There are innumerable detailed questions of dating and of detailed anatomical analysis and interpretation of those scant human remains which through gaps of hundreds of

By LOREN EISELEY

thousands, even of millions of years, enable us to secure brief glimpses of our nameless forerunners. For more than a hundred years—ever since the theory of evolution became biologically demonstrable—these facts have been accumulating. To catalogue them, to debate their several arguments, would require volumes. It is my intention in this article merely to select for discussion a few key items which continue to intrigue the educated layman, and which may help him to comprehend not alone a few of the mileposts of his long journey but which may give him as well a better comprehension of his own nature and the built-in dangers it contains. The moment is topical, for it is within the past few years that discoveries have been made which may drastically change our ideas about our earliest past.

We will begin with a warning: more than 90 per cent of the world's animal life of past periods is dead. Though it flourished in some instances longer than the whole period of human development, somewhere along its evolutionary path one of two things happened. It vanished without descendants or was transformed, through still mysterious biological processes, into something else; just as man is now something quite different from what he was ten million years ago. This leads to the inescapable conclusion that, contrary to popular impression, evolution is not something "behind" us—the impression we may get while staring into museum cases.

So long as life exists on the planet, it is still changing, adjusting, and vanishing as natural forces—and among them we must now count man—may dictate. Thus life is never really perfectly adjusted. It is malleable and imperfect because it is always slipping from one world into another. The perfectly adjusted perish with the environments that created them. It is not really surprising, when one thinks about it, that man, who evolved with comparative rapidity, should be among earth's most dangerous juvenile delinquents.

He is literally compounded of contradictions, mentally and physically. He is at one and the same time archaic and advanced. His body and his mind are as stuffed with evolutionary refuse as a New England attic. Once he comes to accept and recognize this fact, his chances for survival may improve. He has come halfway on a trembling bridge toward heaven, but the human brain in its loss of life-preserving instincts passes also along the brink of sanity. Here is a great poet, John Donne, speaking three centuries ago of the power of the human intellect:

Inlarge this Meditation upon this great world, Man, so farr, as to consider the immensitie of the creatures this world produces; our creatures are our thoughts, creatures that are borne Gyants; that reach from East to West, from Earth to Heaven, that doe not onely bestride all the Sea, and Land, but span the Sunn and Firmament at once; My thoughts reach all, comprehend all. Inexplicable mistery; I their Creator am in a close prison, in a sicke bed, any where, and any one of my Creatures, my thoughts, is with the Sunne, and beyond the Sunne, overtakes the Sunne, and overgoes the Sunne in one pace, one steppe, everywhere.

Man, in short, has, like no other beast, tumbled into the crevasse of his own being, fallen into the deep well of his own mind. Like modern divers in the sacrificial wells of the Maya, he has drawn from his own depths such vast edifices as the Pyramids, or inscribed on cave walls the animals of his primitive environment, fixed by a magic that inhabited his mind. He retreats within and he appears outward. Even the fallen temples of his dead endeavors affect, like strange symbols, the minds of later-comers. There is something immaterial that haunts the air, something other than the life force in squirrel and chipmunk. Here, even in ruin, something drawn from the depths of our being may speak a message across the waste of centuries.

A little while ago I handled a flint knife, from Stone Age Egypt, running my hand over its beautifully rippled surface. A human mind, an artist's mind, whispered to me from the stone. I held the knife a long time, just as in another way I might hold in my mind the sunlit Parthenon, feeling some emanation, some re-entering power deriving from minds long past but flooding my own thought with renewed powers and novelties. This is a part, a mystical part if you will, of man's emergence into time and history.

When he entered into himself, as no other animal on the globe is capable of doing, he also entered the strangest environmental corridor on the planet, one almost infinite in its possibilities, its terrors, and its hopes. It was the world of history, of symbolic thought, of culture. From the moment when the human brain, even in its dim red morning, crossed that threshold, it would never again be satisfied with the things of earth. It would heft a stone and make of it a tool grown from the mind; fire would become its instrument; sails on the invisible air would waft it far; eventually a little needle in a box would guide men to new continents and polar snows. In each case there would also be the aura of magic. The powers would not be what we of today call natural; around them would hover a penumbral mystery drawn from the abysses of the mind itself. Time and the foreknowledge of death would rise also in that spectral light. Of the fears that beset our dawning consciousness, the brown bone on the shores of a vanished lake bed will tell us nothing. It will tell us only how we changed.

From whence did we come? Over and over again the scholar is asked this question by those who forget the wounds and changes in the bone. Do they ask upon which continent we first stood dubiously erect? Do they ask from what limb in an ancient forest we first hung and by some idle quirk dropped down into the long grass that first received us? Do they want to know at what point we first asked a question of some wandering constellation in the night sky above our heads? Or from what marsh we first dragged our wet amphibian bodies up the shore? Or from what reptilian egg we sprang? Or from what cell in some far, steaming sea?

No, the question has to be contained and caught within the primate order to which we and all manner of ring-tailed, wide-eyed lemurs, blue-chinned monkeys, and enormous apes belong. With these we share certain facets of a common bodily structure that speaks of ancient relationships. In a strange, figurative way there was a time far back along the evolutionary road when all this weird array might be seen to shrink to a single tree shrew, a single ratty insectivore upon a branch. Man, at that moment, was one of many potentials. He was and was not, and likewise all his hairy and fantastic kin. They all quivered there upon that single branch in one frail body—Socrates, Confucius, and Gargantua, along with the organ-grinder's monkey.

The student asks you, as a child his mother, "Where did I come from?" "Son," you say floundering, "below the Cambrian there was a worm." Or you say, "There was an odd fish in a swamp and you have his lungs." Or you say, "Once there was a reptile whose jaw bones are in your ear." Or you try again. "There was an ape and his teeth are in your mouth. Your jaw has shrunk and your skull has risen. You are fish and reptile and a warm-blooded, affectionate thing that dies if it has nothing to cling to when it is young. You are all of these things. You are also a rag doll made of patches out of many ages and skins. You began nowhere in particular. You are really an illusion, one of innumerable shadows in the dying fires of a mysterious universe. Yesterday you were a lowbrowed skull in the river gravel; tomorrow you may be a fleck of carbon amid the shattered glass of Moscow or New York. Ninety per cent of the world's life has already gone. Perhaps brains will accomplish the work of extinction more rapidly. The pace is stepping up."

"Life," a cynical philosopher once shrewdly observed, "is a supremely illogical business. One can become dark from excess of light." This statement is so directly applicable to the study of human evolution that it ought to preface any survey of our past. At first glance everything is simple. We have a bone here, a skull there. Teeth grow smaller, brains grow larger. The upright posture undoubtedly preceded by perhaps a million years or more the appearance of a face and brain faintly comparable to our own.

Even after the brain began to grow, it was long shielded by a shell of bone as thick as a warrior's helmet. It was as if nature itself was dubious of the survival of this strange instrument, yet had taken steps to protect it. I like to think that with the invention of a brain capable of symbolic thought—and, as an unsought corollary, philosophy—something behind nature rejoiced to look out upon itself. That massively walled brain, even in its early beginnings, had taken life two billion years to produce. But the future of no invention can be guaranteed. As in the case of other forms of life in the past, extinction may come about some millennia hence from "natural" causes. Or—as we are constantly reminded by our experts—life's most dazzling invention may, through the employment of its own wizardry,

MAN'S FAMILY TREE: 1965 VERSION

Recent discoveries have thrown new light upon man's evolutionary history, but "only the dim light of morning," in Loren Eiseley's phrase, so far illumines our knowledge of human origins. The chart opposite reflects today's complex view of primate evolution, in contrast to the straight-line concept of a century ago (see insert). Various living primates—survivors of a process of some sixty million years during which most forms vanished—are shown at the top in typical postures. The heavy lines ascending to them are diagrammatic only, taking the place of myriad untraceable networks of intersecting, converging, and parallel lines (suggested by the lighter strokes). Glacial periods are indicated in gray; the deepening browns of remoter geological epochs are a reminder that these are not drawn to scale.

A hundred years ago, scientists—working with only living forms and a single fossil, the Neanderthal skull, as evidence—thought modern man had descended directly from the apes by way of Neanderthal man (as the traditional "family tree" at lower right indicates). But as more fossils have been found and studied, this conception has changed radically. It is now known that man clearly could not have evolved from any present-day species; rather, both he and the apes must have evolved independently from some rudimentary common ancestor, now extinct.

A primitive ape from the Miocene epoch, Proconsul, may have been such a forerunner. A later creature, Oreopithecus, found in the coal fields of Tuscany, may have been close to the early human line. The next fossil in ascending order on the chart, Zinjanthropus, was discovered only in 1959; he appears to be one of the slender, erect-walking man-apes called Australopithecines, whose skeletons and teeth show stronger resemblances to man than to apes. Their brain was apelike in size, but the fact that shaped stone implements were found alongside Zinjanthropus indicates he was a toolmaker—that is, a man. In 1961 he was dated by a new radioactive-decay process at the astonishing age of nearly two million years, three times the estimate for other Australopithecines. If this date proves correct, man will be known to have emerged much earlier than has been thought.

Java and Peking men are evolutionary brothers, similar to each other and, except for their massive skulls and small brains, to ourselves. The classic Neanderthals, or "cave men," however, now seem to have reached an evolutionary dead end in the late Pleistocene; some Neanderthals may have contributed genetically to Homo sapiens, but the type is no longer considered our direct forerunner. Indeed, before human evolution can be traced with any certainty, still unknown forms of man or pre-man, particularly from the long, dark Pliocene epoch, must be unearthed. Zinjanthropus may be a harbinger of just such discoveries.

ILLUSTRATIONS DAVID GREENSPAN

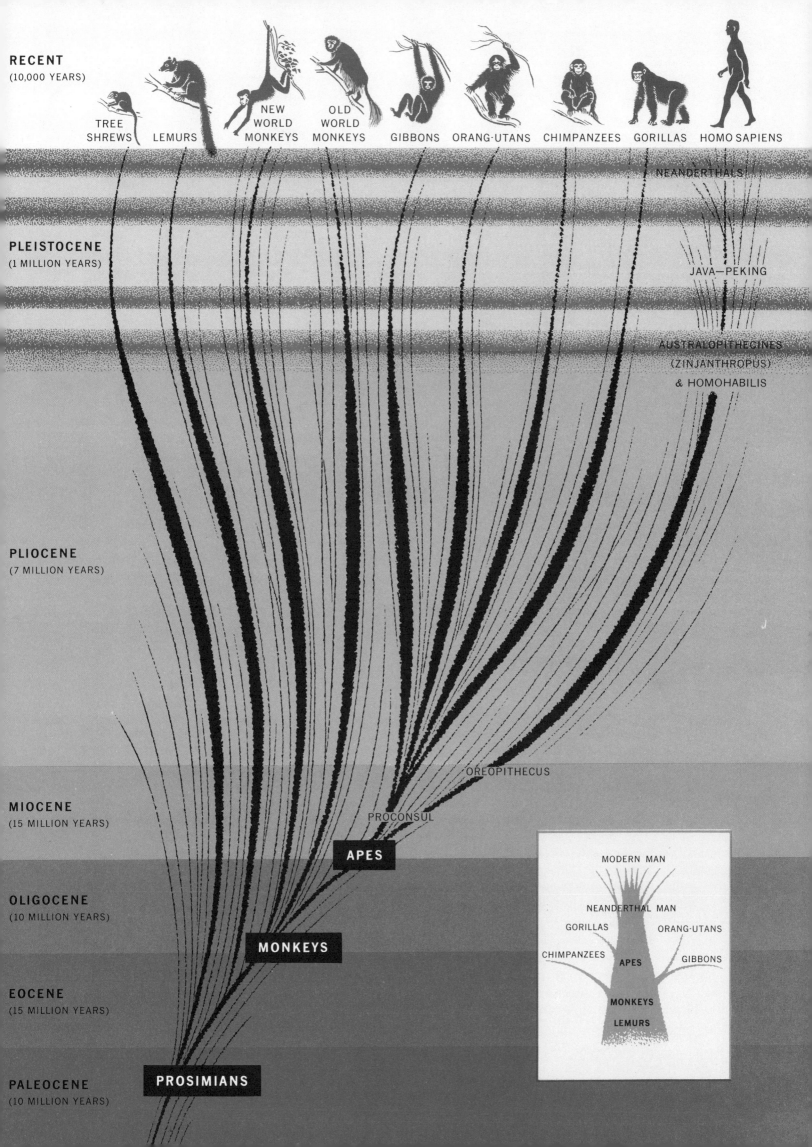

RECENT
(10,000 YEARS)

TREE SHREWS   LEMURS   NEW WORLD MONKEYS   OLD WORLD MONKEYS   GIBBONS   ORANG-UTANS   CHIMPANZEES   GORILLAS   HOMO SAPIENS

NEANDERTHALS

PLEISTOCENE
(1 MILLION YEARS)

JAVA–PEKING

AUSTRALOPITHECINES
(ZINJANTHROPUS)
& HOMOHABILIS

PLIOCENE
(7 MILLION YEARS)

OREOPITHECUS

MIOCENE
(15 MILLION YEARS)

PROCONSUL

APES

OLIGOCENE
(10 MILLION YEARS)

MONKEYS

EOCENE
(15 MILLION YEARS)

PALEOCENE
(10 MILLION YEARS)

PROSIMIANS

MODERN MAN

NEANDERTHAL MAN

GORILLAS   ORANG-UTANS

CHIMPANZEES   GIBBONS

APES

MONKEYS

LEMURS

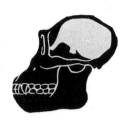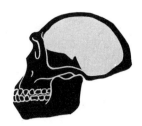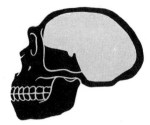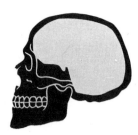

Man has become man through a phenomenal growth of the primate brain, chiefly in the frontal areas that control memory and speech. But while these diagrams compare the skulls of a present-day ape (left) and Homo sapiens *(right) with* *fossils in between (in sequence,* Australopithecus, *Peking, and Neanderthal man), mystery surrounds our direct lines of ancestry and the rise of what Dr. Eiseley calls this "strange instrument"—the gray matter that is our ultimate weapon.*

soon be able to erase itself completely from the earth, in a matter not of millennia, but of minutes.

For the human brain, magnificent though it be, is as yet imperfect and bears within itself an old and lower brain—a fossil remnant, one might say—geared to the existence of a creature struggling to become human, and dragged with him, unfortunately, out of the Ice Age. This ancient brain, capable of violent and dominant re-emergence under various conditions of stress, contains, figuratively speaking, claws—claws which by now can be fantastically extended.

Life *is* illogical, and if one looks long and steadily at evolution and at man in particular, the illumination provided by fossil skulls can produce, paradoxically, some profound shadows. In the early history of anthropological studies, when we possessed few human remains but much acquaintance with our living relatives in the trees, the story had seemed simpler: somewhere, not too far back in time, an ape had gotten down from his tree, driven to the ground, possibly, by a growing desiccation of the landscape. In time natural selection had altered an arboreal foot for bipedal progression, and the hands, once used by our ancestors for the manipulation of the branches among which they dwelt, were now employed in the exploration and eventual remaking of the world into which they had intruded. There is, indeed, a certain semblance of truth in this account, but with every discovery of the past few decades, the story has had to be modified if not rewritten. Even today, while no reasonable man doubts the reality of human evolution, its precise pathways are hazy, and far gaps in time and space make the exact succession of forms difficult if not impossible to determine.

It is easy when bones are few, to stick to a single line of ascent or to give a simple version of events (see insert chart, "Man's Family Tree, Old Style," page 39). But bones also have their limitations. We cannot trace the living races far into the past. We know little or nothing about why man lost his fur. Consider the mistakes to which our descendants, a million years forward in time, would be liable in trying to reconstruct, without a single written document, the events of

today. To tell the truth, though theories abound, we know little about why man became man at all.

We know as much—and as little—about our own ancestors as we do about some other missing creatures from the geological record. Why, for example, do bats hurl themselves so suddenly upon us, fully formed, out of the Paleocene era? They emerge with comparative rapidity in the dawn of mammalian history. In fact they bear a distant relationship to ourselves. How they became bats and not men is one of those evolutionary problems which involve the interplay of vast and ill-understood forces operating over enormous lengths of time.

The light being thrown upon our history is truly only the dim light of morning. I often think, on taking off my shoes at night, that they clothe an awkward and still imperfect evolutionary instrument. Our feet are easily sprained or injured, and somehow comical. If they had not been reshaped in some long venture on the early grasslands, we would not find it so satisfactory now to brace them artificially in shoes. The sight of them is chastening to pride. The little toe is attractive to the student of rudimentary and vanishing organs; the over-all perspective is a rude palimpsest, a scratched-out and rewritten autobiography whose first anatomical pages were contrived in some arboreal attic.

Among these living shards and remnants of the past, however, it is easy to linger and be lost. I remarked that we know little about why it was necessary to become man at all. There are many parallelisms in the other parts of nature. Complex social life has arisen several times in diverse insect orders. There are flying marsupials as well as flying placental mammals. But man, the thinker, has occurred but once in the two billion years that may be the length of life's endurance on this planet.

He is an inconceivably rare and strange beast who lives both within himself and in his outside environment. With his coming came history, the art of the mind imposing itself upon nature. There has been no previous evolutionary novelty comparable to this save the act of creation itself. Man, imperfect transitory man, carries within him some uncanny spark from the first lightning that split the void. He alone can dilate evil by drawing upon the innocent powers contained in nature; he alone can walk straight-footed to his own death and hold the world well lost for the sake of such intangible things as truth and love.

Yet let me suggest once more that we look long and clearly at ourselves, our strange and naked bodies, our evolutionary wounds, wracked as we have been through trees and lion-haunted grasslands and by the growing failure of instinct to guide us well. Let us take care, for beyond this point in time, brains and sympathy—the mark of our humanity—will alone have to guide us. The precedent of the forest will be wrong, the precedent of our dark and violent mid-brains will be wrong; everything, in short, will be wrong but compassion—and we are still the two-fold beast. Why did we have to be man, we ask ourselves, as the Christians of another day must have asked: "How can man be made whole? How can he be restored to the innocence he knew before the Fall?"

In one of those great insights that embellish the work of the stylist and philosopher George Santayana, he wrote sadly: "The Universe is the true Adam, the Creation the true Fall." He saw, that wise old man who has left us, that to come out of the blessed dark of nonbeing, to endure time and the disturbances of matter, is to be always subject to the unexpected even if it masquerades as "natural law." With the unexpected comes evil, the unforeseen, the moment's weakness. Life—even nonhuman life—becomes parasitic, devours its fellows, until a Darwin looking on may call it "devil's work." The creation falls and falls again. In mortal time, in Santayana's sense, it must ever fall. Yet the falling brings not only strange, dark, and unexpected ends to innocent creatures but also death to tyrannous monsters.

The very novelties of life offer renewed hope to the spirit that works upon intransigent matter and lends us our willingness to endure our time. For us, for this little day we inhabit so unthinkingly, much has been suffered. A gray and shadowy and bestial thing had to become a man. Gleams, strange lights, half-caught visions of both love and abominable terror, must have dogged our footsteps. Disease destroyed us in infancy. We were abruptly orphaned, and great teeth struck us down. We were fearful of the dead who haunted our dreams. We barked and gabbled until, at some unknown point in time, the first meaningful invented sounds in all the world were heard in some lost meadow. The creature had stumbled, with the growth of speech, into a vast interior world. Soon it would dominate his outer world.

A short time ago most of us who work in this graveyard of the past would have said that a brain which we could truly denominate as human was perhaps no older than the lower Ice Age, and that beyond the million years or so of Ice Age time, man, even lowbrowed, thick-skulled man, had vanished from our ken. If, that far back, he still walked, he was not a tool-user; if he still talked, his thoughts had found no

lasting expression upon the objects of his outer world. It appeared to us, not that he had vanished in the seven-million-year epoch of the Pliocene, but rather that he was a thinly distributed ground ape, a late descendant upon the upland grasses, still teetering upon a dubiously adapted foot from one sparse clump of trees to another.

In July, 1961, our ideas were destined to change drastically. They were to change not so much because of a newly described form of early man from Africa—we had grown used to that—but rather because of what a new method of dating was to tell us about humanity in general.

Over the previous thirty years a startling series of discoveries in South and East Africa had revealed that the simplified versions of single-line human evolution were very unlikely to be true. It was soon realized that African humanity has a very ancient history—more ancient than, at present, we can demonstrate for any other part of Asia or Europe. I am not now speaking of problematic early relatives of ours such as *Oreopithecus* from the Tuscan coal mines of Italy, but of tool-using creatures walking upon the ground.

Deep in the Olduvai Gorge in Kenya lay hand axes of enormous antiquity. Even more primitive pebble tools were found in various regions in South Africa. Man—some kind of heavy-browed man—had long roved the uplands of that game-filled continent. Darwin's guess that Africa might prove to be the original home of man was taking on renewed interest, even though very ancient remains such as Peking Man had been located in the caves of Choukoutien, and a series of early forms had also turned up in Java. It must be remembered also that the inhospitable desert break between Africa and southwestern Asia has not always existed. In early ages it is likely that freedom of movement between these two regions was far more simple for primitive man and beast than has been true in historic times. Hence, since so much of Asia remains archaeologically unknown, it would be premature to decide that Africa alone contains the full story of the human past. That it has provided us with more clues to early human development than any other region, however, it would now be idle to deny.

All through the past few decades the labors of such pioneer scientists as Robert Broom, Raymond Dart, L. S. B. Leakey, and J. T. Robinson have succeeded in turning up amid the breccia of ancient cave deposits a hitherto totally unsuspected and apparently cultureless group of ape-men, or perhaps one should say man-apes. Instead of gorilloid, long-fanged creatures lately descended from the trees, such as the early Darwinists would have envisaged, these creatures, of whom numerous remains and several species have been recovered, brought dramatically home to us a largely unsuspected aspect of the human story, anticipated on theoretical grounds only by Darwin's great contemporary Alfred Russel Wallace.

The idea of the gorilloid nature of early man as advanced

by many nineteenth-century scientists was not borne out by the new-found fossils. Instead, the bones proved to be those of rather slightly built, erect-walking "apes" with massive molar teeth unaccompanied by projecting canines. In short, the animals turned out to be a rather variable lot of short-faced, small-brained creatures already adapted for walking on their hind feet. Long arguments developed as to whether these creatures of some 500 cubic centimeters of cranial capacity—roughly akin to the brain size of a modern chimpanzee or gorilla—could have made crude tools, or at least utilized the long bones of slain animals as clubs or stabbing weapons. This was possible—but difficult to prove.

One thing, at least, had become evident. The man-apes represented not recently arboreal apes but, instead, an unsuspected variety of erect-walking anthropoids whose foot adaptation to a ground-dwelling existence was already greatly perfected. In Tertiary times large primates had not been confined to the trees. Instead, they had successfully brought their old-fashioned arboreal bodies down onto the grass and survived there—a feat of no mean magnitude. By some evolutionary neurological quirk they had acquired an upright posture which had freed the forelimbs from the demands of locomotion. Man bears in his body clear signs of an early apprenticeship in the trees. We now began to suspect, however, that man had served his arboreal apprenticeship much farther back in time than many scholars had anticipated. It also became evident that the number of forms and datings of what soon came to be called the Australopithecine man-apes could only suggest that not all of them were direct human ancestors. These African creatures hinted rather of a variety of early man-apes, not all of whom had necessarily taken the final step of becoming human.

A group of apes had entered upon a new way of life in open park land and grassland. Arboreal apes are not carnivorous; they are primarily vegetarians. But these man-apes, or perhaps I should say *some* of these man-apes, had become killers of game. Their massive jaws, however, are not evidence of this fact. Massive molar teeth may mean only the consumption of certain types of uncooked vegetation. It is the broken bones of animals in the caves they frequented which suggest that some species, at least, had become killers, using their unloosed forelimbs as weapon wielders. As for the brain, perhaps though still small, the upright posture had given this organ some qualitative advantage over the brains of our living relatives, the great apes.

Still, we had to look upon these creatures as essentially an odd, humanlike ape. Like any other animal, they had intruded into and adapted themselves to a grassland existence; it seemed unlikely that they could speak. It appears unlikely, also, that all these creatures survived to become men; some may have been living fossils in their own time. The last of them may have been exterminated by the spread of man himself. But they indicate that the bipedal apes were well adapted to survive upon the ground without entering extensively upon a second road of conquest.

It remained for the direct human ancestors, from whatever bipedal group they may have sprung, to precipitate the final stage in man's development: the rise of the great brain, still marked by its ferocious past. For man entered, with the development of speech and its ever-growing product, culture, into the strangest and most rapidly changing environment on the planet, an environment limited only by his own creativeness. He entered into himself; he created society and its institutions. The exterior, natural world would be modified and pushed farther and farther back by the magic circle in which he had immured himself. Some societies would dream on for millennia in a world still close to nature; other roads would lead to the Greek thinkers and the Roman aqueducts. The history of the world-changers had begun.

We can still ask of this varied group of fossils, why did man have to be? No answer comes back. He did not have to be any more than a butterfly or a caterpillar. He merely emerged from that infinite void for which we have no name.

In 1959 Dr. L. S. B. Leakey found at Olduvai the massive-jawed, small-brained creature who has come to be known as *Zinjanthropus*. The creature would appear to be not too distant in its anatomy from some of the known, and possibly much later, man-apes. It, however, is remarkable for two reasons. First, it was found in association with clearly shaped stone tools, long known but never found in direct contact with human remains. Thus this creature was not merely a user of chance things which he picked up; he was a thinker who shaped. Second, in 1961 Doctors J. F. Evenden and Garniss Curtiss of the University of California announced that *Zinjanthropus* was nearly *two* million years old. They had dated the creature by a new "clock" involving the use of potassium-argon radioactive decay. If this dating method is correct, the history of tool-using man will thus have been carried back almost a million years before the Ice Age—and recently Dr. Leakey has reported another find, *Homo habilis,* from the same vicinity. The latter he believes to be closer to the human line of ascent than *Zinjanthropus*.

Previously I have mentioned that man's mental development, so far as its later, bigger-brained phase is concerned, has seemed rapid. Dr. Leakey's finds can be interpreted in two ways: as suggesting that the incipient steps leading to the emergence of the large brain began earlier than we have anticipated, or that man drifted in a static fashion on this simple level for a long period before some new mutation or latent dynamism generated a new leap forward in brain size. Little in the way of advanced cultural remains is known before the later Pleistocene, so that the appearance of these tool-using creatures of such archaic countenance is an amazingly disturbing element to our thinking.

Have all our lower Ice Age discoveries been underestimated as to time? And what of the other, the seemingly later yet more primitive Australopithecines? Are they, then, true

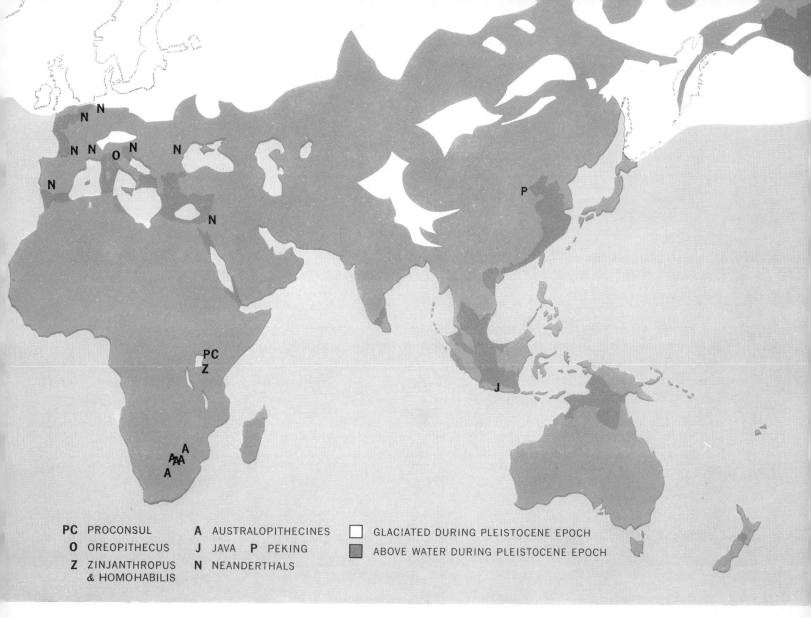

PC PROCONSUL   A AUSTRALOPITHECINES   □ GLACIATED DURING PLEISTOCENE EPOCH
O OREOPITHECUS   J JAVA   P PEKING   ▨ ABOVE WATER DURING PLEISTOCENE EPOCH
Z ZINJANTHROPUS   N NEANDERTHALS
    & HOMOHABILIS

Where did man begin? Anthropological science, starting in Europe, found its first fossils (the Neanderthals) near home. Then came the discoveries of Java and Peking men. In our generation, finds of great antiquity in Africa (the Australopi-thecines and Zinjanthropus) have lent new interest to Darwin's guess that Africa might be our ancestral home. Glacial periods, by lowering sea levels and linking Africa and Java to the Eurasian continent, may have aided man's spread.

cousins rather than ancestors—survivals of an even more remote past? We do not know. We know only that darkest Africa is not dark by reason of its present history alone. Contained in that vast continent may be the secret of our origin and the secret of the rise of that dread organ which has unlocked the wild powers of the universe and yet taught us all we know of compassion and of love.

Those ancient bestial stirrings which still claw at sanity are part, also, of that dark continent we long chose to forget. But we do not forget, because man in contemplation reveals something that is characteristic of no other form of life known to us: he suffers because of what he is, and wishes to become something else. The moment we cease to hunger to be otherwise, our soul is dead. Long ago we began that hunger; long ago we painted on the walls of caverns and buried the revered dead. More and more, because our brain lays hold upon and seeks to shape the future, we are con-

scious of what we are, and what we might be. "No man," wrote John Donne, "doth exalt Nature to the height it would beare." He saw the great discrepancy between the dream and the reality.

Great minds have always seen it. That is why man has survived his journey this long. When we fail to wish any longer to be otherwise than what we are, we will have ceased to evolve. Evolution has to be lived forward. I say this as one who has stood above the bones of much that has vanished, and at midnight has examined his own face.

A leading student and writer in his field of the science of man, Dr. Loren Eiseley is the author of Darwin's Century, The Firmament of Time, *and* The Mind As Nature. *Once Provost of the University of Pennsylvania, he is now University Professor of Anthropology and the History of Science.*

CAVE-DWELLING CARVERS
OF 5,000 YEARS AGO

A troglodyte culture in the Negev yields a trove of ivory figurines

By JEAN PERROT

An aerial view of the excavated area at Safadi shows the underground chambers of the troglodyte settlement of 3500 B.C. The tunnels (right) often reached a depth of 23 feet. From the workshop of a cave-dwelling carver comes the woman's head in ivory (opposite page), with appropriately big, staring eyes, and holes cut in the skull for the purpose of stringing the piece as a pendant.

Fifteen centuries before Abraham settled in Beersheba and five hundred years before the Pyramid Age in Egypt, a foreign population entered Palestine from the northeast. These pastoral people, who probably came from the steppes bordering the Syro-Arabian desert, became the first dwellers in the Negev, the southern, semiarid region of Israel. Their remarkable settlements, dating back more than 5,000 years, have been uncovered by recent excavations at Safadi and Abu Matar, near Beersheba.

The villages constructed by this people were entirely subterranean. They are composed of extensive caves dug straight down into the alluvial soil on the banks of the wadi, or dry river-bed. The discovery of this troglodyte way of life could finally explain the cave-dwelling Horites whom Biblical scholars were always surprised to find mentioned as living in this caveless part of the country.

Such a subterranean settlement offers protection from the searing heat of the day, the chill of the night, and the biting wind-borne sands of the desert. It seems less likely that security from enemy tribes was the reason for building underground, since the absence of weapons or fortifications reflects rather a life of peace centered around trade and agriculture.

Distributed around a central communal hall

PHOTOGRAPHS ARIEH VOLK

and admirably preserved to this day, the underground dwellings were found complete with their furnishings: decorated pottery, basalt basins and pedestaled bowls, ornaments, bracelets, necklaces, bone and ivory objects. Copper tools, the oldest yet found in Israel, were made on the spot by casting. Since copper ores are not found in the immediate vicinity, the evidence of a copper industry at Beersheba suggests commercial relations before 3000 B.C. with the Jordanian plateau, a source of copper ore, basalt, and other hard stones, or even with the metallurgical centers of the Caucasus.

The most remarkable finds are the ivory figurines. The local production of these objects was established by the discovery of an ivory carver's workshop, complete with tools, a workbench, and the raw material—an elephant tusk. Although elephants are known to have existed in Syria, it is also possible that an active ivory trade was carried on with Africa, down the channel of the Red Sea.

These statuettes, found in the dwellings, may represent worshipers standing in ritual nakedness before a divinity, or may be connected with some magical or other religious practices. They bear some resemblance to pre-Dynastic Egyptian figurines, but are superior in the delicacy of conception and vigor of execution. The simplicity of execution produces a certain stiffness in general attitude but vitality is not absent, and the sensitiveness of the artist to the grace of the female body is clearly evident in the figure of the pregnant woman. Unrelated to any previously known school in the Middle East, the Beersheba figurines provide the first glimpse of an amazingly early and original school of art.

Jean Perrot, head of the French Archaeological Mission in Israel, directed the Beersheba excavations which uncovered the Safadi caves.

Probably connected to a fertility cult was the statuette (far left) of a pregnant woman with an exaggerated navel. The male figure (above left) wearing an incised "Libyan sheath" over the genitals was found (below) in a cache with other objects. The holes in the head and cheeks of the male head (below left) were for inserting tufts of hair. Other pieces include an ivory pin in stylized bird shape and a woman's head with hair swirled in a bun supporting an animal headdress.

Sumer's Language of Love

INANNA

GU-DA-LA *(embrace)*

GIS-GU-ZA *(throne)*

MU-TI-IN *(bridegroom)*

HI-LI-ZU *(your allure)*

LAL-AM *(honey)*

KU-KU-DA *(sweet)*

SHA-ZU *(your heart)*

KI-AG *(love)*

SHU-TAG *(caress)*

SIR-SHA-HUL-LA
(songs that rejoice the heart)

AMAUSHUMGALANNA

NA *(bed)*

KULIANNA

AMA-MU *(my mother)*

SIPAD *(shepherd)*

DUMUZI

O Ye Daughters of

New light on the Biblical book commonly known as Solomon's Song of Songs has been cast by current archaeological discoveries in Sumer, the Mesopotamian kingdom that flourished in the third and second millenniums B.C. On the clay tablets excavated there love poems have been found remarkably similar in form to that most sensuous of Biblical texts. The Song of Songs is like no other book in the Old Testament. In fact, it seems to be nothing more than a loosely organized collection of love poems. No wonder there has been considerable debate about the propriety of including it in the Biblical canon at all; although once included, it came to be regarded as an allegory, with Jahweh in the role of the lover and the Hebrew people in the role of His bride.

Modern scholarship, however, cannot accept this fanciful interpretation. To judge from what we now know of the history and culture of the ancient Near East, there is good reason to believe that at least some portions of the Song of Songs were originally sung during the *hieros gamos,* or "sacred marriage," between a king and a votary of Astarte, the Canaanite goddess of love and procreation.

The Canaanite rite itself had roots deep in the history of Mesopotamia; it derived from the Tammuz-Ishtar cult, which was in turn a counterpart of the Dumuzi-Inanna cult of ancient Sumer. In the course of recent years a considerable amount of Sumerian literary material has been unearthed which emphasizes the importance of the Sumerian legacy to Biblical literature. For some time past a highly competent German expedition has been making significant discoveries at Erech, an important Sumerian city-state two hundred miles south of modern Baghdad; while an expedition of the University Museum of the University of Pennsylvania has found tablets of basic importance for the understanding of the Dumuzi-Inanna cult at Nippur, which was the cultural center of Sumer, located about sixty miles northwest of Erech.

Dumuzi was a prominent ruler of Erech in the third millennium B.C. The tutelary deity of the city-state was Inanna, a goddess who throughout Sumerian history was deemed to be primarily responsible for sexual love and fertility. As the Sumerians became more nationally minded, however, there arose the seemingly quite plausible and not unattractive idea that the king of Sumer, no matter who he was or from what city, must become the husband of the life-giving goddess Inanna of Erech. Eventually the dogma was actually put into ritual practice with the consummation of a marriage ceremony, probably repeated every New Year, between the king and a specially selected priestess from Inanna's temple.

To lend prestige and authority to the rite, it was desirable to attribute the symbolic marriage to an earlier time, and the honor of being the first mortal to wed the deity not unnaturally fell to Dumuzi, the Erech ruler who had become such a memorable figure in Sumerian legend. Moreover, the premarital courting and wooing of Inanna by Dumuzi became a favorite subject of Sumerian bards. We now possess numerous examples of their poems on this theme (two of them are reproduced on these pages) showing the extent to which the Biblical canticles were anticipated. To be sure, aesthetically speaking, the songs in Solomon's Song of Songs, with their concrete, rich, and impassioned imagery, are far superior to their stilted, repetitive, and relatively unemotional forerunners. But there is little doubt today that more than a few of the expressions, implications, situations, and allusions in the Biblical masterpiece have their origins in ancient Sumer.

Samuel Noah Kramer is Clark Research Professor of Assyriology at the University of Pennsylvania and the author of History Begins at Sumer.

Sumer!

One of the most charming of the Sumerian love songs is recorded on a two-column tablet (a portion of which appears at left) now in the Hilprecht collection of the Friedrich-Schiller University of Jena in East Germany. It might almost be entitled "Fooling Mother." In the poem, after an amorous tête-à-tête, Inanna, the Sumerian Venus, pleads with Dumuzi, her mortal sweetheart and future husband, who is also variously known as Kuliana, Amaushumgalanna, and Kulienlil:

> Come now, set me free, I must go home,
> Kulienlil, set me free, I must go home,
> What can I say to deceive my mother,
> What can I say to deceive my mother Ningal?

Dumuzi has a ready answer:

> I will tell you, I will tell you,
> Inanna, most deceitful of women, I will tell you.
> [Say] 'My girl friend took me with her to the public square,
> There a player entertained us with dances,
> His chant, the sweet, he sang for us.'
> Thus deceitfully stand up to your mother,
> While we by the moonlight take our fill of love;
> I will prepare for you a bed pure, sweet, and noble,
> The sweet day will bring you joyful fulfillment.

Another of the best preserved Sumerian love lyrics is inscribed on a tablet from Nippur now in the Istanbul Museum of the Ancient Orient. It would probably have been recited by a priestess of the goddess Inanna, as a part of the rites of holy marriage between the goddess and King Shu-Sin, who reigned in Sumer about 2000 B.C.

> Bridegroom, let me caress you,
> My precious caress is more savory than honey,
> In the bedchamber, honey filled,
> Let us enjoy your sweet allure,
> Lion, let me caress you,
> My precious caress is more savory than honey.
>
> Bridegroom, you have taken your pleasure of me,
> Tell my mother, she will give you delicacies,
> My father, he will give you gifts.
>
> Your spirit, I know where to cheer your spirit,
> Bridegroom, sleep in our house until dawn,
> Your heart, I know where to gladden your heart,
> Lion, sleep in our house until dawn.
>
> You, because you love me,
> Give me pray of your caresses,
> My lord god, my lord protector,
> My Shu-Sin who gladdens Enlil's heart,
> Give me pray of your caresses.
>
> Your place goodly as honey, pray lay [your] hand on it,
> Bring [your] hand over it like a gishban-garment,
> Cup [your] hand over it like a gishban-sikin garment.

By SAMUEL NOAH KRAMER

FROM *Histoire de la Marine*, L'ILLUSTRATION, PARIS 1942

An Egyptian ship of the Eighteenth Dynasty loads a cargo of rare flora and unchained baboons from Punt, in this relief from Queen Hatshepsut's temple at Deir el-Bahri.

Looking back through the centuries of the earth's exploration from the nineteenth to the thirteenth, we see the known world shrinking steadily as our eyes pass Livingstone, Cook, Magellan, Columbus, Vasco da Gama. Peering back beyond Marco Polo, we see the horizons closing in upon Europe and the southern shores of the Mediterranean. When we think of the world at the time of the Crusades, we see only this small area lighted up, known and traversed; beyond it lie the dark regions of *terra incognita*.

For the inhabitants of that area at that time, the picture was true; that was the way they looked upon their world. For us, of course, this view is parochial in the extreme. There were other lighted areas. The Arabs occupied one that stretched from Transoxiana and the region of Bombay to Morocco. The Chinese knew the world from Ceylon to Japan. The Polynesians were getting a fair grasp of the layout of the Pacific. But it is true of all these areas that they were patches of light in a world mainly dark, that the unknown was vastly greater than the known, and that the fringe regions were the abodes of mermaids, rocs, and sea serpents, of fabulous riches and fabulous dangers.

As we go further back in time, the darkness closes in even more. To the north there is a brief flash, Vinland the Good, found and then lost again. But otherwise there is a gradual and regular diminution in the area of the known world. Oddly enough, the fall of Rome did not affect this historic movement. A larger area was known and traversed in the depth of the Dark Ages than at the height of the Roman Empire. About A.D. 1100 a guidebook was published in Iceland giving the best routes for travelers to Constantinople and Jerusalem; about A.D. 500 the golden horns of Denmark bore pictures of the New Year festival in Constantinople. Yet only four centuries before, in A.D. 100, Scotland had been unknown territory to the Romans.

Four hundred years earlier, in 325 B.C., there was another flash of illumination when the Greeks, under Alexander, reached the Indian Ocean. But backwards from Alexander the darkness closes in rapidly. Herodotus, describing the known world, scarcely got beyond Egypt and the nearer frontiers of Bulgaria and Persia (although a Greek physician at the Persian court, writing about 500 B.C., had given an account of Persia and India for Greek readers). And Homer, singing in 900 B.C. or thereabouts of events then three hundred years in the past, clearly regarded his heroes as ventur-

Although it was long thought that Western man's explorations began with Jason's legendary voyage, archaeologists now find that in a still earlier millennium, Mediterranean traders journeyed as far as India and Sweden with such goods as ivory, amber, and bronze

BEFORE THE ARGO

By GEOFFREY BIBBY

ing into the fabulous fringe areas if they sailed outside a triangle bounded by the Dardanelles, Crete, and the western islands of Greece.

The bard cannot be accused of a parochial outlook. A few centuries after Homer, Ashurbanipal, ruler of Assyria, the greatest power of the time, wrote of an embassy from Gyges, the king of Lydia, as coming from "a district across the sea, a remote place, of which the kings, my fathers preceding me, had not heard the mention of the name." Yet Nineveh was no farther distant from Lydia than Chicago is from New York.

It would seem that in going back further we are nearing the beginning of things, that another century or so will take us to a time when the world that lay over the hill or around the headland from a man's own village was the Great Unknown, when the whole world showed nothing but feeble sparks of light, each invisible to the next.

Certainly the Greeks of Homer's time believed that the period before the Trojan War (by the archaeologist's reckoning, say 1300 B.C.) was just such an era of isolation. The legends of the time are full of stories of kings' sons—Jason, Oedipus, Theseus—banished or carried off as children to be brought up in the next parish, apparently without the news

ever crossing the hill. Tales of long voyages survive from that period, that of the Argonauts being the most detailed, but the Argonauts were clearly portrayed as having no idea where they were going. They sailed in the general direction in which the ram with the Golden Fleece had flown a generation before, and by the time they reached the Dardanelles, they were in the mythical lands of nymphs and magic wells.

So there, it would seem, we have the whole story: a continuous expansion of man's knowledge of his world, commencing about 1000 B.C. and progressing over a period of three millennia, from complete darkness to complete light— a satisfying background before the onward leap to the stars.

And yet—what came before? The Greeks were satisfied to begin the history of exploration—and indeed all history— with the Argonauts. There *was* no history before Jason and his generation, the warriors of the Age of Bronze, when, as Hesiod wrote, "armor was of bronze and tools were of bronze; for black iron was not yet." Go further back and you come to the Ages of Silver and of Gold, said Hesiod, the time of the Noble Savages, nameless and innocent and content.

But today we cannot be content with this. We who are preparing to explore space have already for a hundred years

and more been engaged in the exploration of time, and the simple answers no longer suffice. While Livingstone was following the Zambezi River, Rawlinson was deciphering the cuneiform script of the Babylonians, even as Champollion had learned to read the hieroglyphs of the ancient Egyptians. With the later unraveling of the Sumerian, the Hittite, and, most recently, the Urartean languages, and the "Linear B" * script of Crete and Mycenae, written history has become available to us from a period of slightly more than a thousand years before ever the *Argo* sailed. And written history has been checked, supplemented, confirmed or disproved, and illustrated by the work of the archaeologist, while his diggings, his potsherds and stratifications, his pollen analysis and radioactive carbon dating have brought within the definition of history the actions and movements of men and of peoples in regions and in eras that no ancient writing, deciphered or undeciphered, has ever described. Using this new evidence, what can we say of man's knowledge of his world during the centuries and millennia that preceded the three thousand years of ever-widening horizons which led from the *Argo* to the moon rocket?

Evidence of contacts between the Aegean and northen civilizations during the Bronze Age has been found at Stonehenge, England. Dagger carvings on one of the sarsen stones (below) resemble the bronze blade found in excavations at Mycenae (right).

If the apparent ignorance shown by the contemporaries of Homer and Ashurbanipal of the world beyond their horizon leads us to expect the people of the preceding thousand years or so to have been preoccupied with digging their own cabbage patch and happily ignorant of their neighbor's patch, we are due for a series of surprises.

In Mesopotamia, and in particular at Ur of the Chaldees, in graves which can be dated to about 2500 B.C., there have been found sixteen round soapstone seals such as were used to sign or mark cuneiform tablets. But these are of a peculiar character; they are not the usual cylinder-type seal used generally during that period in Mesopotamia. Forty seals of the same type have recently been found on a little island off the Kuwait coast, a little way down the Persian Gulf; 225 similar seals have been found on Bahrein Island, 250 miles farther south by east; and three more have been unearthed from the ruins of Mohenjo-daro, one of the two cities of the enigmatic Indus valley civilization in faraway Pakistan. Moreover, some of the Mesopotamian seals are inscribed in the still undeciphered script that was current on the banks of the Indus. The conclusion is inescapable that well over a thousand years before the *Argo* sailed for Colchis, Indus valley merchants were in the habit of sailing to Mesopotamia, or that Sumerian merchants voyaged to India, or both.

The seals are not the only evidence. In the temples of Ur, clay tablets from this period have been discovered that are, in effect, bills of lading, lists of cargo carried by ships chartered for trading voyages to the island of Bahrein, 350 miles away. The return cargo lists show that, at Bahrein, the ships took on freight coming from a land far off to the east known as Meluhha. And these cargoes included such characteristic Indian treasure as ivory, gold, and carnelian.

In Eridu, not far from Ur, were found two clay tablets in-

* See "Homer's Age of Heroes" by C. M. Bowra, page 13.

ALISON FRANTZ FOR THE MYCENAE EXCAVATIONS

scribed about 1400 B.C., which proved on decipherment to be file copies of letters sent by a trading house of that city to its agents on Bahrein. The letters confirm the booking of a passage for a lady passenger and complain of the delay in shipment of a cargo of dates. The one extraordinary thing about them is their date.

At Deir el-Bahri, in Upper Egypt, stands the magnificent temple-tomb of Queen Hatshepsut, who ruled Egypt from 1502 to 1480 B.C. Its walls are covered with hieroglyphs and paintings depicting the most important events of her reign. And to judge by the space given to it, not the least important of her exploits, in her own eyes, was the dispatch of a successful expedition to a land she calls Punt. There has been much speculation among the learned as to the precise location of Punt. Identification is made more difficult by the fact that the ancient Egyptians themselves were clearly in no doubt as to where Punt lay. Accordingly, they included no directions for reaching it. All we know of the route thither is that it was by sea, beyond the Bab el Mandeb, the southern gate of the Red Sea. There is every reason to believe that Punt lay in Africa; Somaliland, Kenya, and points south have all been suggested as locations. The vegetation and animal life of Punt was African; we know this because the expedition recorded in the temple carvings was manifestly a scientific one, sent out to bring back specimens of the flora and fauna of Punt for the botanical and zoological gardens of the Pharaoh.

From the centuries immediately before 2000 B.C., a remarkable series of monuments have survived along the coasts of Europe. Throughout the islands and along the shores of the Mediterranean, they take the form of large communal tomb chambers, built in courses of stone, topped by a domed roof and approached by a long passageway, the whole covered by a mound of earth or stones. Along the Atlantic coasts, in Spain and Portugal, northwestern France, western England, Ireland, the Western Isles of Scotland and the Orkneys, north Germany and Denmark, and south Norway and Sweden, precisely the same type of burial chamber and mound is found, to the number of several thousands. But in these countries they are built of massive upright stones, capped by equally massive roof slabs. The resemblance between these passage graves, scattered along five thousand miles of coastline within a span of at most two hundred years, is so close that no prehistorian has ventured to doubt that they are related to each other—the outward signs of some community of interest along the shores of Europe four thousand years ago. There is little reason to doubt that they are the visible evidence of a religion, or at least of a common belief in existence after death, which began in the eastern Mediterranean about 2400 B.C. and was spread by small bands of men who traveled by sea westward and northward around Europe in the course of the next two centuries. Certain it is that the passage graves are rarely found more than a day's journey from the sea, except where an isthmus can be crossed from

The labyrinth motif, originating in the eastern Mediterranean in the early Bronze Age, turned up a few hundred years later as a traditional design on a Cretan coin (above) and on the Etruscan Tragliatella vase (right). Its appearance in Ireland, on the famous Hollywood stone (below), indicates an active sea trade between the Mediterranean and Atlantic countries during the Bronze Age.

sea to sea, as from the Mediterranean to the Atlantic.

The Beaker movement is a different proposition in every way, though equally significant from our point of view. Built some two hundred years after the passage graves, the small burial mounds of the Beaker people are found dotted thinly over Europe, from Spain to Poland and from Italy to Ireland. In England they are very numerous, bearing witness to an occupation of the country by Beaker folk, but elsewhere they are sparse intrusions among the regular inhabitants. Everywhere the artifacts buried in these graves are identical: bronze daggers, barbed arrowheads, archers' wrist guards, large buttons of jet or amber—and beakers. These bell-shaped drinking vessels have given their name to the people who used them, and their shape and ornament are so uniform, wherever the Beaker folk are found, that one is tempted to think of mass production.

Where the passage-grave builders traveled by sea, the Beaker people traveled by land, spreading out, it would appear, from Spain in small parties over the length and breadth of Europe. That they were archers is clear. The fact that, with their coming, bronze implements and ornaments first appear among populations that previously used only flint suggests that the Beaker people's primary concern was bronze-trading and tinkering.

There is other evidence of early trade in Europe, and again the distances are vast. The primary sources of amber in Europe are the Baltic and the North Sea coasts of Denmark. During the late Stone Age in northern Europe, from about 2600 to 1600 B.C., amber was exceedingly common. Huge necklaces, comprising hundreds of amber beads, and buttons as large as a clenched fist have been found in graves and the ruins of settlements. But with the onset of the Bronze Age, about 1600 B.C., the amount of amber placed in graves diminished sharply. At the same time amber began to appear in the Near East. Clearly trade was in operation here, and discoveries along the Elbe and the Oder show that at least some of the trade routes followed the rivers running north and south across Europe. But the discovery of identical gold-mounted amber ornaments in Crete and in Britain suggests that other routes followed the seaways around the coasts of Europe, the routes opened up by the passage-grave people. And the discovery of carvings, on the sarsens of Stonehenge, of a dagger and axes that resemble the types used about 1500 B.C. by the Mycenaeans of Greece, suggests that visitors, perhaps architects, had come to southern England from the eastern Mediterranean at the time when Stonehenge was erected in its present form.

The occurrence of faïence beads tells an even clearer story. Faïence, a fused and glazed quartz, was the first type of glass ever made. As early as 4000 B.C. it was used for small figurines and beads in Mesopotamia and in Egypt, and for the next two thousand years and more it was confined to the eastern Mediterranean, to Mesopotamia, and to the Indus valley. But about 1500 B.C. the picture changes. Around this time faïence beads, particularly of a star-shaped and a segmented variety, appeared over a truly vast area. They have been found in large numbers in England, on the trans-European trade routes, in France, Czechoslovakia, and Poland, as far north as Scandinavia, as far south as Kenya in central Africa, and as far east as Siberia. All are of the same type, and clearly they are not of local manufacture. They are the clearest possible evidence of trade emanating from Egypt, or thereabouts, and following partly the sea route around the coasts of Europe and partly the river routes across Africa, Asia, and Europe.

This abundant evidence of trade by land and sea in the years between 2500 and 1500 B.C. has an interesting corollary in the far north. On the smooth slabs of the rock outcrops to the east of Oslo Fiord, in southern Norway and central Sweden, the people of the Bronze Age, about 1500 B.C., suddenly developed the custom of carving pictures. It is agreed that these pictures are mainly portrayals of religious festivals and sacred symbols, but even so they give a variegated picture of the life of the times. Here we find pictures of ritual plowing with teams of oxen, representations of oxcarts, horses, and chariots. But one subject predominates: seafaring. Over and over again are portrayed ships, ships singly and in huge fleets, ships with high prows and sterns, ships with sails and with oars, up to twenty oars a side. There can be little doubt that these people of the coastal regions of Scandinavia, at the time of the *Argo* or a little before, were seamen first and only secondarily farmers. The ships portrayed are no small vessels designed for coastal travel; they are as large as the vessels which, two thousand years later, regularly sailed from the same region to Iceland, Greenland, and the coasts of Maine.

These, then, are some of the factors which we must take into account in any assessment of man's knowledge of his world in the days before the Argonauts. They add up to a broad picture very different from that which the early Greek writers and the chronicles of the later Assyrian and Egyptian kings might have led us to expect. Apparently, from about the middle of the Third Millennium to about the middle of the Second Millennium B.C., a very large area of the world was continuously known and traversed. The civilized portion of the world was small, comprising little more than Greece, Crete and Asia Minor, Egypt and Palestine, Syria and Mesopotamia. But from this circumscribed area traders, missionaries, and, perhaps, even casual tourists went out, journeying over incredible distances, and doing this so habitually that there can be no doubt that the traffic was regular, safe—and profitable.

Nor must we imagine a one-way traffic from the Near East to savage lands below the horizon. We have seen the evidence for Indian merchants in Mesopotamia and for amber export from the "perimeter" to the Mediterranean. There were large ocean-going fleets based in Norway and Sweden, and it may well be that not only was the trade reciprocal—as trade must always be—but that much of it was in the hands of seamen and shipowners from the "fringe" areas. Trade was not entirely radial—that is, outward from and inward to the Near East. The Beaker folk sent their caravans across the direction of the main trade routes, from one peripheral area to others, while Irish gold in Scandinavia and Scandinavian amber in England and in Spain tell the same story.

Thus the picture is nearly filled in. From approximately 2500 B.C. to 1500 B.C. the whole world west of the Urals and the Ganges valley was an organized mercantile unity—and we have only negative evidence that the area of unity was not even larger.

What are the reasons for this? And, perhaps more important, why did the horizons of knowledge again narrow almost to the vanishing point by about 1000 B.C.?

The answer must be sought, partly at least, in the technology of the period. The period 2500–1500 B.C. was the height of the Middle Eastern Bronze Age and of the spread of bronze to the uttermost parts of Europe. Tools and weapons and ornaments were of bronze; the ubiquitous objects that literally hold a civilization together—nails and rivets and brooches and safety pins—were of bronze. The whole fabric of culture depended upon plentiful supplies of bronze. And bronze is an alloy of two comparatively rare metals, copper and tin. The search for and exploitation of these two metals is sufficient to explain the initial impetus to trade. And, once started, trade was self-perpetuating. The familiar pattern of reciprocal trading developed, raw materials moving in one direction and manufactured articles in the other. Manufactured articles, previously unknown and undemanded in the primary producing countries, became first luxuries and then necessities, and other raw materials, such as amber and jet and lapis lazuli, previously unknown in the manufacturing countries, were exported to pay for them. An expanding economy necessitated expanding markets, and the trade routes stretched ever farther.

And yet it ended. In the course of a few centuries, most of the world reverted to a subsistence economy, the trade routes dead and forgotten.

It would seem that what happened resulted from a combination of economic weaknesses, a technological innovation, widespread warfare, and, perhaps, climatic changes.

An expanding economy bears the seed of its own destruction, and its growth can be followed in the story of Bronze Age Denmark. Denmark was distant from the main centers of bronze manufacture and far from the trade lines of the Beaker bronzesmiths. Yet, from as early as 2400 B.C., the first copper and bronze articles, small ornaments such as rings and pendants, have survived in very small numbers from an otherwise purely Stone Age economy. Gradually, over the next eight hundred years, as the export of amber was organized, the number of imported bronzes increased, and they became more utilitarian; in addition to the ornaments, objects such as axes and daggers appeared in increasing numbers. But the economy was still essentially Stone Age, based on flint as the raw material for the tools of everyday life, and therefore basically self-sufficient. It was only about 1600 B.C. that bronze became the usual material for almost all tools and weapons and the Bronze Age proper began in Denmark. Bronze had ceased to be a luxury and had become a necessity.

But the corollary followed immediately. A country that exports raw materials and imports manufactured articles is vulnerable as soon as the manufactured articles become essential to its economy. Denmark rapidly established its own manufacture of bronzes, possibly aided by the equivalent of a preferential tariff system. Shortly, Danish bronzes were competing on the export market, not only in countries still farther distant from the original exporters but even in the countries lying between Denmark and the Near East.

It is probable that this growth of manufacturing industries in lands previously exploited as markets hastened regional self-sufficiency and, in consequence, the collapse of organized long-distance trade. But the process was aggravated by the spread of a new metal, iron. It was about 1400 B.C. that new smelting techniques produced the high temperatures which at last could produce an iron superior in strength to bronze. This development seems to have occurred in northeastern Turkey, and the process spread over Europe considerably more rapidly than had the art of processing bronze. Partly this was due to the fact that the spreading agency was war and the movements of peoples (which may in themselves have tended to disrupt trading relations), but chiefly it was because iron ore occurred more widely than copper or tin. Iron was in fact available for smelting in almost every land; it could even be extracted from peat bogs when there were no natural ore deposits. In effect, iron-forging offered every country the prospect of economic self-sufficiency.

It was eagerly seized upon—and the bottom fell out of the bronze market. Trade stagnated, ships were laid up, the recession set in. For a century or so the struggle went on, with competition more and more fierce for the contracting markets. Too literal a search for "the Trojan War's economic causes" has rightly been ridiculed, but commercial rivalry may well have acerbated the quarrel over the abducted queen. After the sack of Troy there were no more sailings to the world's end. But when Homer came to compose the stories of his country's heroic past, there were still traditions current of great ships which had sailed out to traffic for the riches of the lands below the horizon. If the *Argo* indeed existed, then its voyage must have been one of the last of the Bronze Age trading ventures, the end of the great period of exploration that preceded our own.

Geoffrey Bibby, a British archaeologist, heads the Department of Oriental Antiquities at the Prehistoric Museum, Aarhus, Denmark. For the past twelve years he has participated in an expedition to ancient sites along the Persian Gulf.

THE OLD WORLD'S PECULIAR INSTITUTION

The Greeks and Romans

practiced slavery and condoned it—for war,

for luxury, and for business—

but even then they knew it to be evil

By M. I. FINLEY

A stele celebrates an ancient slave trader

Aulus Kapreilius Timotheus does not appear in any history book. There is no reason why he should, but an accident of archaeology makes him a figure of some curiosity if not importance. He was a slave in the first century of our era who obtained his freedom and turned to slave dealing, an occupation in which he prospered enough to have an expensive, finely decorated marble tombstone seven feet high (see photograph above). The stone was found twenty-six years ago at the site of the ancient Greek city of Amphipolis on the Strymon River, sixty-odd miles east of Salonika on the road to the Turkish border—and nothing like it exists on any other surviving Greek or Roman tombstone, though by now their number must be a hundred thousand or more. The stone has three sculptured panels: a typical funeral banquet scene at the top, a work scene in the middle, and a third showing eight slaves chained together at the neck, being led along in a file, accompanied by two women and two children who are not chained and preceded by a man who is obviously in charge, perhaps Timotheus himself for all we know. The inscription in Greek reads simply: "Aulus Kapreilius Timotheus, freedman of Aulus, slave trader."

It is not his occupation that makes Timotheus a rare figure, but his publicly expressed pride in it. The ancient world was not altogether unlike the southern United States in this respect. After the Civil War a southern judge wrote: "In the South the calling of a slave trader was always hateful, odious, even among the slaveholders themselves. This is curious, but it is so." More than two thousand years earlier a character in Xenophon's *Symposium* said to Socrates: "It

56

is poverty that compels some to steal, others to burgle, and others to become slavers." In neither case was the moral judgment quite so simple or so universally accepted as these statements might seem to suggest, nor was it carried to any practical conclusion, for the most respectable people depended on these same "hateful" men to provide them with the slaves without whom they could not imagine a civilized existence to be possible.

Yet contempt of the slaver was not uncommon, and this suggests that slavery itself was a little problematical, morally, even when it was taken most for granted. On this score ancient and modern slavery cannot be wholly equated. There were special circumstances in the southern states, pulling in contradictory directions. On one hand slavery was "*the* peculiar institution" and few southerners could have been unaware of the fact that most of the civilized world had abolished the practice and did not like it; whereas Greeks and Romans had no such external voice of conscience to contend with. On the other hand southern slaveowners found comfort in the racial factor and in its concomitant, the belief in the natural inferiority of black men—a defense mechanism of which the ancients could make relatively little use. The Negro in the old South could never lose the stigma of slavery, not even when, as an exception, he was freed nor, as was often the case, when he had some white ancestry. But the descendants of an Aulus Kapreilius Timotheus could become ordinary free inhabitants of the Roman Empire, wholly indistinguishable from millions of others.

We have no clue to Timotheus's nationality. His first two

A minor stylized figure of sixth-century B.C. *design, this slave crouches on the east pediment of the Siphnian Treasury, built at Delphi to house tribute to the oracle there.*

names, Aulus Kapreilius, were those of his master, which he took upon receiving his freedom, according to the regular Roman practice. Timotheus was his name as a slave—a common Greek name that tells us nothing about him, since slaves rarely bore their "own" names but those given them by their masters. In more primitive times the Romans usually called their slaves Marcipor and Lucipor and the like —that is, "Marcus's boy" or "Lucius's boy"—but soon they became too numerous and required individual names so that Marcus's slaves could be distinguished from one another. When that happened there was no limit to the possibilities. The choice was a matter of fashion or of personal whim, though one rough rule of thumb was applied with some consistency. As Roman power spread to the east, the Empire was divided into a Greek-speaking half and a Latin-speaking half, and the naming of slaves tended to follow this division. It is more likely therefore that Timotheus came from the lower Danube, or the south Russian steppes, or perhaps the highlands of eastern Anatolia, than from Germany or North Africa.

To a buyer this question of nationality was important. It was generally believed that some nationalities made better slaves than others, temperamentally and vocationally. Prices varied accordingly, and Roman law (and probably Greek law, too) required the seller to state his chattel's origin specifically and accurately.

One example is worth looking at. In the year A.D. 151 a Greek from Alexandria purchased a girl in the market in Side, a city on the south coast of Anatolia (about two hundred miles west of Tarsus) that had a long tradition and notoriety as a center of slaving activity. He took the girl back to Egypt with him, and also the bill of sale—a bilingual document in Greek and Latin, written on papyrus, which was found in legible condition at the end of the nineteenth century. The girl is described in this way: "Sambatis, changed to Athenais, or by whatever other name she may be called, by nationality a Phrygian, about twelve years of age . . . in good health as required by ordinance, not subject to any legal charge, neither a wanderer nor a fugitive, free from the sacred disease [epilepsy]." The seller guaranteed all this under oath to the gods Hermes and Hephaestus, and under penalty of returning the price twice over should any of it be untrue. The phrase "or by whatever other name she may be called" is a typical lawyer's escape clause; in fact, the girl was born free and given a good Phrygian name, Sambatis, which was replaced by the Greek name Athenais when she was enslaved. How this happened cannot be determined, but it was well known in antiquity that Phrygians often sold their own children into captivity, a practice they continued even after Phrygia was incorporated into the Roman Empire. It is also not stated whether the buyer and seller were professional slave dealers, but Side was a long way to come from Egypt merely to purchase one little girl for oneself.

Bills of sale were usually written on perishable material, so that it is only by accident that a handful, written on papyrus or wax tablets, has survived. This is a pity, because there is no other evidence from which to build a statistical

The Romans, whose military monuments often depict enslaved captives, were quick to turn a profit from their prisoners-of-war. The chained Gaul (left) appears on an arch built at Carpentras, France, about 15 B.C. A detail from the column of Marcus Aurelius (right) shows prisoners and cattle from Germany on their way to market, and in a scene from the Arch of Septimus Severus (far right) a Roman soldier has seized his prize, no doubt during the campaigns in Asia minor, A.D. 194–197. The slave badge (right, above) is a token of less rigorous times: in the fourth century A.D. such metal tags replaced branding as a means of identification. It reads: "Hold me lest I escape, and return me to my master Viventius on the estate of Callistus."

picture of the racial and national composition of the large slave populations of the ancient world. But the broad contours of the picture are clear enough, and they shifted with the times. The crucial point was that there were no specifically slave races or nationalities. Literally anyone and everyone might be enslaved, and which groups predominated at one time or another depended on politics and war. Greeks enslaved Greeks when they could, Romans enslaved Greeks, and they both enslaved anyone else they could lay their hands on by capture or trade.

The majority of slaves, however, were always "uncivilized" from the point of view of the Greeks and Romans. Inevitably the attempt was made, therefore, to justify slavery as an institution on the ground of the natural inferiority of the slaves. The attempt failed: it had to for several reasons. In the first place, there was too large a minority that could not be squeezed into the theory. For example, after the Romans defeated the Carthaginians under Hannibal, they turned east and conquered the Greek world, bringing back to Italy in the course of the next two centuries hundreds of thousands of captives. Among the effects of this involuntary Greek invasion was a cultural revolution. "Captive Greece made captive her rude conqueror," said the Roman poet Horace, and it was manifestly impossible to maintain the doctrine of natural inferiority (which might do for Gauls or Germans) against a people who provided the bulk of the teachers and who introduced philosophy and the drama and the best sculpture and architecture into a society whose virtues had not previously lain in those directions.

In the second place, it was a common practice in antiquity to free one's slaves as a reward for faithful service, most often, perhaps, on one's deathbed. There were no rules about this, but some idea of the proportions that were sometimes reached can be gathered from one of the laws passed by the first of the Roman emperors, Augustus. He tried to put a brake on deathbed manumissions, probably to protect the interest of the heirs, and so he established maxima on a sliding scale, according to which no one man was allowed to free more than one hundred slaves in his will. After centuries of continuing manumission, who could distinguish the "naturally superior" from the "naturally inferior" among the inhabitants of Greek and Roman cities (especially in the absence of any distinction in skin color)?

Human nature being what it is, many individual slave-owners no doubt went right on wrapping themselves in their preordained superiority. But as an ideology the notion was abandoned, and in its place there developed one of the most remarkable contradictions in all history. "Slavery," wrote the Roman jurist Florentinus, "is an institution of the law of all nations whereby someone is subject to another *contrary to nature*." That definition became official: we find it enshrined in the great codification of the law by the emperor Justinian, a Christian emperor, early in the sixth century. Yet no one, at least no one of consequence, drew the seemingly obvious conclusion that what was contrary to nature was wrong and ought to be abolished.

War was the key to the whole operation. The ancient

ALINARI

world was one of unceasing warfare, and the accepted rule was that the victor had absolute rights over the persons and property of his captives, without distinction between soldiers and civilians. This right was not always exercised in full measure; sometimes tactical considerations or pure magnanimity intervened, and sometimes more money could be raised by ransom than by sale into slavery. But the decision was the victor's alone, and a graph would show no more than occasional downward dips in the curve, never a long period (say fifty years) in which fairly large numbers of captives were not thrown onto the slave market. No total figures are available, but there can be no doubt that in the thousand years between 600 B.C. and A.D. 400, the Greeks and Romans between them disposed of several million men, women, and children in this way.

This is not to say that wars were normally undertaken simply as slave raids, though some surely were—as when Alexander the Great's father, King Philip II of Macedon, deliberately undertook an expedition into the Scythian regions north of the Black Sea in order to replenish his depleted treasury in 339 B.C. He is said to have brought back 20,000 women and children along with much other wealth. Granted that this was not a typical affair and that wars usually had other causes, it remains true that the prospect of booty, among which slaves bulked large, was never absent from the calculations—partly to help maintain the army in the field, always a difficult problem in antiquity, but chiefly to enrich both the state and the individual commanders and soldiers. Caesar went off to Gaul an impoverished

nobleman; he died a multimillionaire, and Gallic captives played no small part in bringing about this change of fortune. When he took the town of the Aduatuci, he himself reported that 53,000 were sold off; and after the battle of Alesia in 52 B.C. he gave one captive to each of his legionnaires as booty. Yet Caesar did not plunder to the limit; he often tried conciliatory tactics in the hope of dividing the Gallic tribes, as he did after Alesia when he restored 20,000 captives to the Aedui and Arverni. Half a century earlier, the Roman general Marius, with no reason to be generous to the Germanic Cimbri and Teutones who had penetrated to the south of France, sold all the captives taken at the decisive battle of Arausio (now Orange). The figure we are given on that occasion is 150,000.

That may be an exaggerated number, but human plunder even in quantities only half that size created problems for an army on the march. It could become completely bogged down, and sometimes in fact it was. In 218 B.C. King Philip V of Macedon invaded Elis in the northwestern Peloponnesus and soon found himself so overburdened with booty, which included more than 5,000 captives and masses of cattle, that his army, in the words of the historian Polybius, was rendered "useless for service." He therefore had to change his plans and march through difficult terrain to Heraea in Arcadia, where he was able to auction off the booty.

This case is not typical. If it were, the military and therefore the political history of the ancient world would have been an altogether different one. Normally preparations were made beforehand for booty disposal, and they con-

sisted above all in seeing to it that a crowd of peddlers and merchants came along, equipped with ready cash and means of transport. The booty was assembled at a designated spot and auctioned off (the Spartans, with their characteristic bluntness, gave the responsible officers the title of "booty-sellers"). What happened thereafter was the sole concern of the buyers, and the army was free to continue on its way, enriched by the proceeds.

Possibly the scene on the tombstone of Aulus Kapreilius Timotheus represents just such a situation, the removal on foot of slaves he had bought at an army sale. Certainly this would have been a very profitable business (providing the wherewithal for an expensive marble memorial), for slaves and other booty must have been extremely cheap to buy under such conditions. The only flaw was that war, for all its frequency, was nevertheless irregular and could not guarantee a steady flow of merchandise, and other sources had to be tapped as well. One of these was "piracy," an unfortunate label because it evokes the image of isolated Captain Kidds, whereas the reality was altogether different in scale and character: a continuous, organized activity, illegal yet (like rumrunning) not unwelcome to many of its ultimate beneficiaries, the consumers. Among the Greeks even in classical times this was a traditional occupation in certain areas, especially in the western part of the Greek peninsula.

But that was small stuff compared with the later upsurge in the Roman Republic, beginning about 150 B.C. Then there arose in the eastern Mediterranean a complex business network of pirates, kidnappers, and slave dealers, with its headquarters apparently at Side and its main emporium on the island of Delos (whose docks were rebuilt and extended so that it was possible to turn over as many as 10,000 slaves in a day). The main impetus to this traffic was the rise in Italy and Sicily of the notorious latifundia, large estates or ranches owned by absentee landlords and worked by slave gangs. The profit-side of the trade left a mark on Delos that is still visible today in the excavated remains of the rich houses of the Italian traders.

Direct consequences of the trade were the two greatest slave revolts in antiquity, both in Sicily—the first beginning about 135 B.C., the second a generation later at the same time as the invasion of Gaul by the Cimbri and Teutones. To meet that invasion, Marius was authorized to levy auxiliary troops wherever he could. When he appealed to Nicomedes of Bithynia (along the southwestern shore of the Black Sea), a "client-king" under Roman suzerainty, Nicomedes replied that he had no men to spare because most of his subjects had been carried off into slavery by Roman tax collectors. The Senate was alarmed (by the Germans, not by the complaint) and ordered provincial governors to release any "allied" subjects whom they found in slavery in their districts. Eight hundred were accordingly freed in Sicily, but this was an isolated action that hardly scratched the surface of the problem.

The needs of the latifundia owners were comparatively simple: quantity rather than quality of labor was what they were after. But important as they were, they were not the only consumers. In 54 B.C. Cicero wrote to his friend Atticus

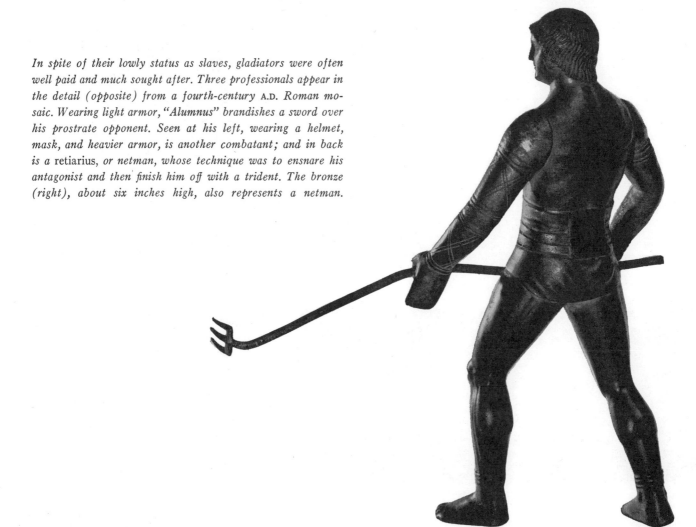

that Caesar's second expedition to Britain was causing concern in Rome. Among other things, it was now clear that there was no silver on the island and "no hope for booty other than slaves, among whom I believe you cannot expect any instructed in literature or music." The sneer need not be taken too seriously, but it does point to still another aspect of the slave procurement problem, the demand for specialist skills.

Slaves could be trained, of course, especially if they were bought young. All vocational training in antiquity was accomplished by the apprenticeship system, and slave boys or girls were often so taught alongside their free contemporaries. Gladiators were specially trained for their profession and obviously had to be, since no one was normally brought up from childhood with that aim in view. They were an exceptional group, requiring exceptional techniques that were developed in schools established for the purpose. Probably the earliest was in Capua, and it is no coincidence that Capua was the center from which the gladiator Spartacus organized the third greatest—and the most famous—of ancient slave revolts (73–71 B.C.).

There were limits to the training of slaves, however, quite apart from strictly economic considerations. The right raw material was a necessary precondition: in the case of gladiators, Celts, Germans, and Thracians were sought, rather than Greeks or Syrians. Or in the case of the Athenian silver mines, the preference was for men with mining experience (Thracians and Paphlagonians), and the scale of the prob-

lem is shown by the fact that in the fourth century B.C. the concentration of slaves in these mines reached a peak of perhaps 30,000. What happened, then, if in any given decade war and piracy together slacked off or turned up mostly women and children?

In the year 477 B.C. or thereabouts the Athenians established a police force of 300 Scythian slaves, owned by the state and housed originally in tents in the public square—the Agora—and later on the Acropolis. The system lasted for a hundred years, and the number of men may eventually have been increased to a thousand. Now Scythians were famous as bowmen, an art little practiced among the Greeks, and they were sometimes employed in this capacity as mercenary troops. But the Athenians did not hire their Scythian policemen, they bought them. How on earth did they get this curious idea? And how could they count on regular replacements to keep the force up to par?

The answer is that there was already in existence by 500 B.C. a regular trade in "barbarians," who were bought from their own chieftains—captives in their own wars, children, human levies, and the like—exactly as most Negro slaves were obtained in more modern times. This trade had nothing to do with Greek or Roman military activity or with piracy. It was a purely private business carried on by traders who had their personal connections and methods in the various regions outside the Greco-Roman world proper. To return to Aulus Kapreilius Timotheus once more, it is likely that this was how he operated. Certainly the place where his tombstone was found was a main debouching

61

point for traffic coming from the regions of the lower Danube into the Aegean Sea. Had he lived five hundred years earlier, the Athenian state could confidently have placed an order with him to supply fresh stock for its police force whenever needed.

As a commodity slaves created peculiar problems for the merchant. Apparently in the larger cities there were a few shops where slaves could be bought: in Rome in Nero's time they were concentrated near the temple of Castor in the Forum. But they were the exception. One could not keep on hand, like so much merchandise on the shelves, a supply of gladiators, pedagogues, musicians, skilled craftsmen, miners, young children, women for brothels or concubinage. The slave trade has always been conducted in a special way, and the ancient world was no exception. On the one hand there were the main slave markets where, probably on fixed dates, dealers and agents could count on large supplies being put up for sale. Some of the centers were the obvious larger towns, such as Byzantium or Ephesus or Chios, but there were important lesser markets, too, like Tithorea in central Greece where there was a slave sale twice a year on the occasion of the semiannual festival in honor of the goddess Isis. On the other hand itinerant traders went with their slaves wherever there were potential customers, to garrison towns, country fairs, and what not.

The actual sale was normally by auction. The only surviving pictorial representations are on tombstones again, to be exact on two—one from Capua (see above) and the other from Arles—with substantially similar scenes. On the Arles stone the slave stands on a rotating platform while a man, presumably a possible buyer, lifts his single garment to reveal his very muscular legs and buttocks, and the auctioneer stands nearby in a characteristic pose with his arm outstretched. As the stoic philosopher Seneca observed, "When you buy a horse, you order its blanket to be removed; so, too, you pull the garments off a slave."

Seneca was one of the wealthiest men of his day, in an age (the first century A.D.) of enormous fortunes and luxurious living, and of course he possessed his quota of slaves. In one of his *Moral Epistles* he insists that a slave is a man with a soul like every free man; like you and me, he says. From this he concludes that one should live on familiar terms with one's slaves, dine with them, converse with them, inspire respect in them rather than fear—everything but free them.

Seneca was a Roman, but his attitude was more Greek than Roman. To the Greeks, as Nietzsche once remarked epigrammatically, both labor and slavery were "a necessary disgrace, of which one feels *ashamed*, as a disgrace and as a necessity at the same time." It would be more correct to say that the shame was generally subconscious; one sign was the almost complete silence of ancient writers about what was surely the ugliest side of the institution, the slave trade itself. The occasional exception usually has a special twist to it. Thus Herodotus tells a story about a dealer from Chios named Panionion, who specialized in handsome young boys whom he castrated and then sold, through the markets at

Two small bas-reliefs of the imperial period (left) give an idea of the tasks assigned to slaves in a Roman home. The young slave in the upper relief holds an abacus, no doubt to assist his master and mistress with their accounts. The four girls below are helping their mistress to dress: two arrange her hair, one holds a mirror, one (nearly effaced) holds a jug. Far left, a tombstone from Capua describes an auction: the naked slave on the block is flanked by the auctioneer, in Greek robes at left, and by a man in a toga who may be the Roman buyer. The fragment (right) depicts the ceremony of manumission, through which thousands passed to freedom. The master touches the kneeling slave with a rod, ending his bondage, and as a pledge of good faith, he shakes hands with a man newly set free. WAROCQUE COLLECTION; MARIEMONT, BELGIUM

Ephesus and Sardis, to the Persian court and other Eastern customers. One of his victims became the favorite eunuch of King Xerxes; when the opportunity fell his way, he took the appropriate revenge on Panionion and his four sons. Herodotus applauded, for in his view Panionion "gained his livelihood from the most impious of occupations," by which he meant not the slave trade as such but the traffic in eunuchs.

This may seem a hairsplitting distinction, but distinctions have to be drawn. The ancient world was in many respects a brutal one by modern standards. The gladiatorial shows were surely among the most repellent of its habits—as the Greeks would have agreed until they, too, were finally corrupted by the Romans—yet there is abundant evidence that gladiators were proud of their successes and that not a few free men voluntarily joined their ranks. This, it can reasonably be argued, merely proves how deep the brutalization went. But what about the Paphlagonian named Atotas in the Athenian silver mines, who claimed descent from one of the Trojan heroes and whose tomb inscription included the boast, "No one could match me in skill"? The skill and artistry of slaves was to be seen everywhere, for they were not used only as crude labor in the fields but were employed in the potteries and textile mills, on temples and other public buildings, to perform the most delicate work. The psychology of the slave in the ancient world was obviously more complicated than mere sullen resentment, at least under "normal" conditions.

Even the slave trade had its shadings, so that it can serve as a barometer of the state of the society itself. It is no coincidence that the last century of the Roman Republic, a period in which moral and social values broke down badly, was the period of the most reckless slave hunting and of the great slave revolts. Then came the relatively quiet centuries of the early Roman Empire, followed by the long period in which ancient society itself finally dissolved. One incident is symptomatic: when the Goths achieved a massive breakthrough into Thrace in A.D. 376, the Roman armies were badly handicapped because many of their officers were more interested in the profits of slaving than in resisting the barbarians. But by then slavery itself was a declining institution, not because a higher morality was finally in the ascendant, but because serfdom, a different kind of unfreedom, was replacing it.

Slavery did not altogether disappear, of course. The word "slave" itself is a medieval term that entered the languages of Europe when the Slavs became a main source of chattels, many of them sold to the Moslems across the Mediterranean. And farther ahead in the future lay the vast traffic in African slaves. Yet throughout these ups and downs in the history of the institution, the slave trader seems never to have changed significantly, either in his methods or in his ill repute in polite society.

M. I. Finley is Reader in Ancient Social and Economic History at Cambridge University. Among his recent books are The Ancient Greeks *and* The World of Odysseus. *Earlier in this volume he provides a backward glance at "The Year One."*

In this sixteenth-century Persian miniature, Alexander appears as a Timurid horseman. The head on the facing page may be a Roman copy of a statue done by Leochares in Alexander's lifetime.

THE TWO WORLDS OF ALEXANDER

SOMEWHERE ALONG THE ROUTE OF HIS ASIAN CONQUESTS THE YOUNG HERO DISCOVERED A VISION OF WORLD UNITY WHICH FOREVER CHANGED THE DESTINIES OF WESTERN MEN

By C. A. ROBINSON, JR.

Alexander passed across Asia like a flash, and since he never lost a battle and was young, handsome, and personally dramatic, he stirred the imagination of men as few have ever done. He was, as Napoleon said, the greatest general who ever lived. But his real significance, in the history of Western civilization, goes beyond his military genius to his conception of a world state based on the equality and co-operation of all peoples. This political vision, so strangely found in a young and prideful conqueror, outlasted his life and his empire to inspire men in every age from his day to ours.

So dazzling was Alexander's military conquest that for centuries it almost obscured his real nature. In fact, medieval Europe and the Orient of all periods completely forgot the true Alexander. They knew only the Alexander of legend and romance, embedded in an amazing body of literature that began to form soon after his death and ultimately circulated, in eighty versions and in twenty-four languages, from Iceland to Malaya.

Even today chieftains in remote parts of Turkestan claim descent from Alexander, while their ordinary folk are said to be sprung from his soldiers and their horses from Bucephalus. The early Christians portrayed Jesus in Alexander's likeness, the Jews looked upon Alexander as a propagandist of the Most High, and the Koran calls him Dulcarnain, the Lord of Two Horns. Alexander, or Iskander as he has generally been known to Asia, was supposed to have built a gate to exclude Gog and Magog, who were later equated with the Ten Tribes of Israel and then with barbarism itself. As geographical knowledge expanded, the mythical gate was moved from the Caucasus to the Great Wall of China and finally to the Arctic Circle. Still other stories brought the conqueror of the known civilized world to the Blue Nile and to Britain—and then, as if that were not enough, to the heavens and on to the Land of Darkness and even farther to the end of the world, where one finds the Well of Life.

The net of legend extended back to include Alexander's father, King Philip of Macedon, and his mother, Olympias, an Epirote princess of fiery, passionate nature. Ancient historians, for example, say that Philip met this imaginative and terrible woman when both were initiated into the mysteries of Samothrace. During religious celebrations, it seems, Olympias was always more deeply affected than other women and used to supply the reveling companies with great tame serpents, which would often lift their heads from out of the ivy or coil themselves about the garlands of the women, thus terrifying the men. At any rate, according to the story, she and Philip fell in love with each other on sight.

Some time after their marriage, the story continues, Philip dreamed that he was putting a seal upon his wife's womb; and the device of the seal, as he thought, was the figure of a lion. Some seers said that Philip should keep a closer watch upon his young wife, but Aristander, the best of all seers, maintained that the woman was pregnant, since no seal was put upon what was empty, and pregnant with a son whose nature would be bold and lionlike.

Moreover, it was commonly believed in antiquity that the temple of Artemis at Ephesus burned to the ground on the night of Alexander's birth. One witness made a remark frigid enough to extinguish the flames, to the effect that it was little wonder that the temple had burned because the goddess was busy bringing Alexander into the world. Since the ancient Greeks loved coincidences, it is probable that they moved the month of Alexander's birth back to midsummer (356 B.C.) in order that Philip, who had just taken a large Greek city, might receive three messages simultaneously: that Parmenio, his chief general, had conquered the Illyrians in a great battle; that his race horse had won a victory at the Olympic games; and that Alexander III, as he was later called, had been born at Pella, the capital of Macedonia. The seers added to Philip's delight by saying that the son whose birth coincided with three victories would always be victorious.

Philip was a practical man and military genius with the savage appetites and passions of his mountaineer ancestors. For the sake of honor and renown, as his bitter Athenian opponent, the orator Demosthenes, declared, he was ready to let his eye be gouged out, his collarbone broken, his hand and his leg disabled. Personally ambitious, urbane, and friendly, Philip lacked moral scruples and was ready at any time to lie, to break a treaty, to buy friends, or to bribe statesmen. He seemed to feel that a diplomatic victory was as good as one on the battlefield, and he had the ability to lull states to a sense of security until the time arrived for striking the fatal blow. "Taken all in all," concluded a contemporary, "Europe has not yet produced such a man as Philip, the son of Amyntas."

It is a safe guess that Alexander inherited his military skill and cold rationalism from his father. But the son's own inner being, his mysticism and romanticism and impetuousness, came from his mother, Olympias. Perhaps from her, too, came the ability to kindle the imagination of multitudes by a single act—as when, desiring to rally the Greeks wholeheartedly to his cause at the outset of his expedition against the Persian Empire, he visited Troy and stirred in the breast of every Greek glorious memories and the picture of a new Trojan War against the Asiatic foe.

The great structure of legend that grew up around the birth of Alexander finds reflection in this fifteenth-century French miniature. It was said that the air changed color, that thunder and lightning shook the earth, that animals shivered with fear and everything trembled at Alexander's birth because he would conquer and rule all things. It was said that wise men gathered to discuss the strange portents. It was said, too, that when Olympias delivered her baby, thirty other princes were born in Greece and surrounding countries—Alexander's future officers. Later it was even said that his father was not Philip of Macedon, whose image is shown on the contemporary coin at left, but the god Zeus.

67

For three years, Aristotle (above) tutored Alexander and some of his companions at Mieza, near Pella. There they studied letters, including grammar, rhetoric, and dialectic; arithmetic, geometry, and astronomy; gymnastics, for Aristotle believed in the merits of a sound body as well as a trained mind; drawing and music. Alexander used to say that he loved Aristotle more than his father, for the one had given him life but the other had taught him the noble life. The relationship of Alexander and Aristotle gave medieval writers and artists an occasion to remind their fourteenth-century monarchs of the importance of encouraging scholarship and of surrounding themselves with learned men.

At the age of thirteen, Alexander had the philosopher Aristotle as a teacher, and during three impressionable years his keen mind became thoroughly Greek in character, while his romantic imagination developed a love for Homer and his supposed ancestors Heracles and Achilles. On his expedition to Asia, Alexander took along a text of the *Iliad*, which Aristotle had edited for him, and kept it with his dagger under his pillow at night. It seems clear that Aristotle implanted in the youth a love of learning of encyclopedic scope, with a special interest in scientific investigation and medicine. Moreover, Alexander learned from the philosopher that moderation is necessary in government —a virtue he was not likely to get from Olympias—and he also learned, or rather was taught, that all barbarians (i.e., non-Greeks) were slaves by nature, especially those of Asia.

Alexander's admiration for Greek culture was tempered by the simple, vital, active life of Macedonia. This was a narrow coastal strip, with a mountainous interior, along the Aegean Sea in northern Greece. Though the Macedonians were Greeks, the proud citizens of Old Greece southward despised them as a semicivilized people with a veneer of Greek culture.

These Macedonians, who were destined to remake the world, formed the first nation in European history. Rough and simple though they were, they looked upon themselves as one people, and not, in Greek fashion, as the citizens of this city or that. In the time of Philip and Alexander, the Greeks themselves were caught up in a deep crisis. Were they to continue to insist on the sovereignty of their city-state, or had the time come for a fundamental change in their thinking, for a reconciliation of autonomy with a wider union? A century earlier, in the days of Periclean Athens, they had reached a summit of civilization never before attained by the human race. Now—despite great men such as Praxiteles, Plato, and Aristotle, who lived amongst them—they were torn by fratricidal warfare, an economic depression, and the interference by the Great King of the predatory Persian Empire in their internal affairs. How much attention, therefore, should they pay to certain orators who were urging them to unite under the Macedonian monarchy in a war against Persia, the traditional foe?

The sharp division in Greek thought exactly suited Philip's personal ambitions. By 338 B.C. he found that Athens and Thebes were the only city-states remaining that would fight effectively on behalf of Greek freedom. Without much difficulty he defeated them at Chaeronea in a battle that ended forever the ability of Greek city-states to dominate the peninsula's politics. And then he called together at Corinth representatives of most of the states in Greece and joined them in a federation known as the League of Corinth.

The chief action of the League was to appoint Philip commander in chief of a Panhellenic war of revenge against Persia, to punish her for her invasion of Greece a century and a half earlier. Doubtless, Philip planned no more than an expedition against Asia Minor, for the empire of the Persians stretched 2,700 miles from the Hellespont (or Dardanelles) across Asia Minor through Syria, Palestine, and Egypt, and then eastward through Mesopotamia and Iran to India. It was a rich and mighty state, well-governed and able to dispose large armies of disciplined, courageous men. In Asia Minor alone there were 20,000 superb Persian cavalry; and of the various other troops, 20,000 obstinate Greek mercenaries formed the empire's chief hope as heavy infantry.

Philip delayed his departure two years, during which time he gave himself alternately to state business and carousals. Then, suddenly, he was murdered. At the age of twenty, Alexander fell heir to his kingdom, his army, his plan of the Asiatic expedition, and the command of the Corinthian League.

If Alexander is famous for incredible speed of action, he should also be known for his caution at almost every point in his career. Instead of rashly setting off for Asia in what could only have been another in a long line of interminable wars, this youth spent the next two years insuring that his lines of communication would not be cut while he was absent from Greece. This required long marches through trackless forests, over high mountain ranges, and across the Danube to what is today Bulgaria, Rumania, and eastern Yugoslavia, striking such fear into the hearts of the inhabitants that they did not stir during his absence.

The expedition against Asia, when at last it was ready to set out, had an air of permanence about it. Artists, poets, philosophers, and historians went along with Alexander, just as in later days they were to accompany Napoleon. There were also surveyors and engineers, geographers, hydrographers, geologists, botanists, and other scientists to study the phenomena of Asia and perhaps to send back to Aristotle specimens for further observation. One person deserves special mention: Aristotle's nephew, the historian Callisthenes. He was implicated in a plot against Alexander's life in Central Asia, was arrested and executed. Aristotle hated Alexander for this, and so powerful was Aristotle's influence that, when the generation that knew Alexander died out, not a favorable biography of him was written for three centuries. Instead there was created the familiar picture of the bloodthirsty, lucky despot, which it has been the task of modern scholarship to study and correct.

Alexander's army of Macedonians and Greek allies consisted of about 30,000 infantry and 5,000 cavalry. These troops rarely fought as a body, but even when only small contingents were engaged, Alexander combined the various arms. This practice, and especially the close union of light troops and cavalry with the phalanx, largely explains the invincibility of the Macedonian military machine. Moreover, Alexander invariably pursued the enemy with the aim of destroying him utterly, a policy which the Prussian strategist Von Clausewitz has termed "the strategy of defeat."

In a pitched battle, Alexander's army was likely to line up as follows: in the center, intended as a firm anchor, was

Amid the flowering hills and mists of Delphi, the oracle proclaimed Alexander invincible. These prophetic words caused the young chosen Macedonian king to rejoice, for at twenty he was to lead his armies into the depths of lands yet unexplored by Europeans.

*S*traight *toward the Persian king, his lance piercing a foe, rides Alexander (left) at the Battle of Issus in 333* B.C. *Mounted on his horse, Bucephalas, Alexander wears a breastplate with the head of the mythical Medusa whose face had turned all who saw it to stone. Darius, standing high in his chariot, is distinguished by his tiara, the symbol of kingship.*

In this damaged Roman mosaic, discovered as a pavement at the House of the Faun in Pompeii in 1831, the two kings are shown in much closer proximity than they actually ever were. The mosaic, which dates from the first century A.D., *is a copy of a painting done by a contemporary of Alexander. The Romans became widely acquainted with the exploits of Alexander through the* Parallel Lives *of Plutarch who, as a Greek living within the Roman Empire, wanted to demonstrate that the Greeks had their full share of heroes long before Rome achieved its glory.*

the phalanx—9,000 heavily armed infantrymen, formed in a mobile rectangle eight or more men in depth, with three feet between every two men. This demanded soldiers who were highly trained and disciplined, who would not huddle together for safety, but it also meant that rough ground or momentary shocks from the enemy would not disarrange the mass. To the right of the phalanx came Alexander and his magnificent Companion cavalry—the real striking arm —with lancers, javelin men, and archers thrown out to their right as flankers and skirmishers. To the left were other cavalry and light troops. Parmenio, the second in command, was in charge of the left wing. As an able and cautious tactician he was especially suited for this post, since in the oblique order of battle (the favorite also of Frederick the Great of Prussia) it was the duty of the left wing to hold firm, while Alexander, choosing the decisive moment, charged from the right and rolled the enemy in upon the spears of his slowly advancing infantry.

Alexander varied these arrangements as circumstances dictated. As for tactics, he once said that this was merely a matter of using his brains; his success, he added, was due to never putting anything off. His men worshiped him, and though obviously he was not a reckless adventurer, they had no doubt about his lucky star.

71

Alexander's organizing ability manifested itself in the siege train, which was far superior to anything of its kind elsewhere. There were siege towers, placed on rollers or wheels and covered with hides to protect them from fires; they might be over 150 feet high, with many stories, so that the top of any part of an enemy wall could be reached. Boarding bridges were used at Tyre for the first time in history. It was possible to undermine the enemy's walls by tunneling or to knock them down with battering rams, which had huge beams over 100 feet long with metallic heads. The besiegers themselves were protected by movable sheds, known in later days as tortoises. But the greatest military invention of antiquity, used for the first time at Tyre by Alexander, was the torsion catapult, which could fire huge arrows accurately for 200 yards as well as stones weighing fifty or sixty pounds. Alexander never employed

catapults as field artillery in a pitched battle, but he used them in irregular warfare, in sieges, mounted on ships as at Tyre, and to clear a river's bank of the enemy.

Over this army, infused with a proud professional spirit, stood Alexander, commander in chief of the League of Corinth, and as king of Macedon responsible to no one but himself in military matters and (subject to certain checks of the army assembly) in civil affairs as well. By his side he had seven bodyguards, a staff of what we might describe as general officers, and also a group of eighty to one hundred influential officers, known simply as Companions. These men formed his council, as it were, and provided military and civil officers as needed.

The Grand Army was destined to march under Alexander many thousands of miles during eleven long years, often at terrific speed; it was not unusual for a contingent to cover

MAP BY DAVID GREENSPAN; DRAWINGS BY EMMA LANDAU

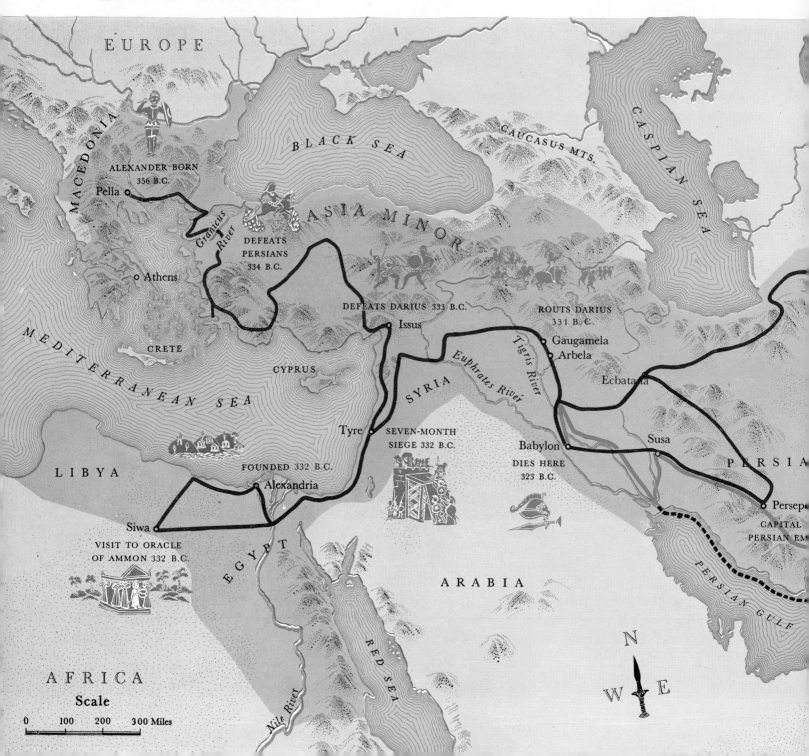

forty or fifty miles a day with him for several days. Events frequently proved his bravery and self-discipline. He was often wounded—on the neck, head, shoulder, and in the thigh; in Turkestan, the fibula of his leg was broken; thrice he was wounded in Afghanistan; in India an arrow pierced his lung; and besides he suffered attacks of fever and dysentery. Every inch of the march was new, yet his reinforcements reached him regularly, over 60,000 in the first eight years alone. And every inch of the way he met opposition, save in Egypt. He fought four pitched battles: three with Persia, and another with an Indian rajah in the Punjab, where he encountered for the first time large numbers of terrifying elephants who barred his passage of a great river.

In addition to the disciplined armies of the ancient East, which greatly outnumbered his own, Alexander had also to fight fierce mountain tribes. There were deserts to over-come, and a long guerrilla warfare with its utterly strange tactics awaited him in eastern Iran. There were, too, strong cities to besiege, the island city of Tyre alone requiring seven months and all his tenacity.

Alexander's plan was probably to conquer as much of the Persian Empire as possible and hold on to it, but his every success opened up further vistas until the possession of the entire empire was his. The conquests confronted him with enormous problems of administration, for he now had an empire of his own that contained not only many different races but peoples in all stages of civilization. Greater still, since his ambitions developed in this direction, was the task of giving a sense of unity to a world state.

It was in the spring of 334 B.C. that Alexander, then twenty-two years of age, began the march. Many portents from heaven were reported; it was said, for example, that

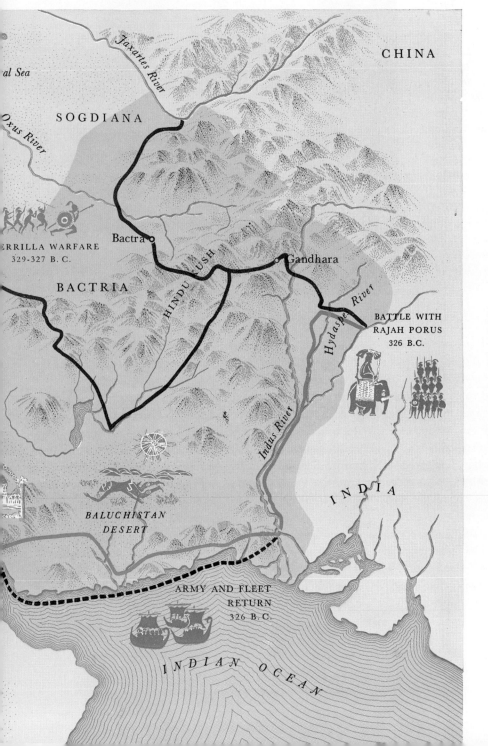

THE ROUTE OF ALEXANDER

ROUTE OF MARCH	━━━
RETURN ROUTE	━━━
ROUTE OF NEARCHUS	▄▄▄▄

In The Family of Darius Before Alexander by Paolo Veronese, the painter bestowed upon the Macedonian the favorable verdict of the sixteenth-century Italian Renaissance scholars, who found in the newly translated editions of the Greek historians Arrian and Plutarch an Alexander of nobility and compassion. An elegant Venetian square surrounded by Palladian archways has here become the setting for the famous incident which followed the Battle of Issus. Darius' mother, Sisygambis, having first knelt before Hephaestion, thinking he was the King, has discovered her mistake and now turns in humiliation to Alexander. But the King, gesturing toward his friend, assures the Queen that Hephaestion too is Alexander. The conqueror's honorable treatment of Statira, Darius' wife, and the daughter Barsine, whom he later married, was the model of Renaissance social conduct extolled by Castiglione in The Courtier. "Have continence," he advised, "as did Alexander the Great towards the very beautiful women of Darius—an enemy and a vanquished one at that."

the wooden statue of Orpheus sweated profusely. Most people feared the sign, but Aristander, the reliable seer, bade Alexander be of good cheer and assured him that he was to perform deeds worthy of song and story that would cost poets and musicians much toil and sweat to celebrate. Thus, amid great excitement, the army set out for Asia under a leader who was destined never to return.

Darius III, the Great King of Persia, considered it beneath his dignity to bother personally with yet one more intruder from Greece. This he left to his satraps in Asia Minor; but when they were decisively defeated at the Granicus River, **he** began to bestir himself and collected an army of perhaps 100,000 men. Alexander was now at Tarsus, with all of Asia Minor successfully behind him. He knew that Darius and his vast host were somewhere in the broad Syrian plains: he feigned sickness, hoping to entice

Darius into the narrow plain of Cilicia. This was the only time in his life that his intelligence service broke down, for it happened that either king tired of waiting for the other, and Alexander crossed the Amanus Mountains in search of Darius the very night that Darius crossed the same range by a different pass in search of him.

Alexander found himself with his lines of communication cut, a hostile empire all around him, and Darius between him and home. Immediately he retraced his steps and at Issus overwhelmed the Persians. Darius, who was a coward as well as a despot, promptly fled and despite the rapid pursuit managed to escape.

On his return to camp that night, Alexander found that his men had picked out for him the tent of Darius, which was full to overflowing with gorgeous servitors and many treasures. Straightway, then, according to Plutarch (the

biographer of the first century A.D.), Alexander put off his armor and went to his bath, saying, "Let us go and wash off the sweat of battle in the bath of Darius." "No, indeed," said a Companion, "but rather in that of Alexander." And when he saw the basins and pitchers and tubs and caskets, all of gold and curiously wrought, while the apartment was marvelously fragrant with spices and unguents, he turned his eyes upon his Companions and said, "This, as it would seem, is to be a king."

As Alexander was going to supper, someone told him that among the prisoners were the mother, the wife, and two unmarried daughters of Darius whom they believed dead. He sent word to them that Darius was alive and that they need have no fear of Alexander, for it was upon Darius that he was waging war for supremacy; they should have everything that they had thought their due when

Darius was undisputed king. Such are the statements of two historians who were present at the time.

Another report says that on the following day Alexander himself, accompanied only by his bosom friend, Hephaestion, visited Darius' mother. She was in doubt which of them was the king, for they were both dressed in the same way, and went up to Hephaestion, who appeared the taller of the two, prostrating herself before him. When he drew back and one of her attendants pointed out Alexander, saying he was the king, she was ashamed of her mistake and wanted to withdraw. But Alexander told her she had made no mistake, for Hephaestion was also Alexander.

Alexander actually never laid eyes on the wife of Darius, who was reputedly the most beautiful woman in Asia. Years later, though, he married one of her daughters. As for the other captive women, seeing that they were surpassingly stately and beautiful, he merely said jestingly that Persian women were torments to the eyes. According to the Royal Journal, or Diary—the "official" truth and as close to the real truth as we shall ever be able to come—Alexander never had a mistress. Moreover, he drank but rarely, and then it was generally a deliberate action, enabling him to associate freely with comrades from whom his new position was slowly isolating him. His self-restraint and moderation he ascribed to the belief that it was more kingly to conquer himself than others, though his temper always remained his worst enemy. Probably his boastfulness was annoying chiefly to his close associates.

Alexander had come to Asia with a fleet made up of Athenian ships and in part a hostage for Athens' good behavior during his absence. He quickly saw that it was no match for the Phoenician fleet of the Persians, and to avoid the loss of prestige that would follow upon defeat, he disbanded it. After Issus, however, when it might have been advantageous to continue the pursuit of Darius, Alexander realized that he could not leave the Phoenician coast in the hands of the enemy, with their own fleet free to raid Greece. He resolved, therefore, to take the home bases of their fleet and thus bring it over to his side.

It turned out exactly as he expected, though he could not have foreseen the difficulty of taking Tyre, a heavily fortified island half a mile offshore. By building his own fleet as well as a mole to the island, Alexander eventually took Tyre and totally destroyed it. It was a great crime, as great a one as his destruction of rebellious Thebes shortly before his departure from Greece. If, however, a man is to be judged by the standards of morality of his own day, we should add that the destruction of cities was common contemporary practice. Plutarch says that Alexander waged war according to usage and like a king; while Arrian—the second century A.D. historian whose account is the best we have, since it drew from the soundest contemporary sources —remarks that Alexander was the only one of the ancient kings who, from nobility of character, repented the errors he had committed.

Egypt fell to Alexander without a blow, for she hated Persian misrule. On the coast he planned a great city, the first of the seventy-odd cities Alexander founded on his march. His purpose was to give the eastern Mediterranean a commercial and administrative center that might also act, if circumstances warranted, as a link between East and West. Meanwhile, it was essential to provide a commercial substitute for ruined Tyre. The site of Alexandria was chosen with consummate skill, for it was west of the westernmost mouth of the Nile and therefore, thanks to the currents of the Mediterranean, free from the river's silt.

While the army was laying out the city, Alexander and a few friends made a dramatic trip across the Libyan Desert to the oasis of Siwa, to see the oracle of Zeus Ammon, which in Greek eyes was second in importance only to Delphi. It

was a youthful stunt, and Alexander, we must remember, was never anything but young. There was a purpose in it, too, as there generally was with Alexander. He had crossed the Danube a few years earlier to insure his communications. Now he wished to confirm that the desert actually existed and would serve as a natural boundary. Also he could bribe the priests to police the desert for him and, en route, accept the surrender of envoys from Cyrene to the west.

So great was the impression that Alexander made on men's minds that a story soon grew up that Alexander had gone to the oracle to ask about his birth, and that, in fact, he was greeted as the son of Zeus. The story has no foundation in history, and Alexander left Egypt without hearing it. He was intent on finding Darius.

The two kings met for the last time east of the Tigris River at Gaugamela, though the battle popularly takes its name from Arbela, a town nearby. Darius kept his men under arms the entire night before the battle, suspecting a surprise attack, a fact that not only lowered their vitality but added to their natural fear. Alexander, however, followed his usual custom and ordered his soldiers to take dinner and rest themselves. While his Macedonians slept, he himself passed the night in front of his tent with his seer Aristander, celebrating certain mysterious sacred rites and sacrificing to the god Fear. And it is said that the older of his Companions, and particularly Parmenio, when they saw the plain and mountains all lighted up with barbarian fires and heard the sound of voices arising from the enemy camp as if from a vast ocean, were astonished at their multitude and argued that it would be difficult to repel such a tide of war in broad daylight. They therefore came to Alexander's tent after he had finished his sacrifices, and on their behalf Parmenio urged him to make a night attack upon the Persians. But Alexander, realizing the hazards of a battle in the dark, gave them the celebrated reply, "I will not steal my victory."

It was October 1, 331 B.C. The Persian army did not even approach the 1,000,000 infantry and 40,000 cavalry of later legend, but it was larger than the one at Issus—so much larger than Alexander's, indeed, that it extended well beyond his flanks. Alexander's infantry still stood at 30,000 men; the cavalry perhaps had grown to 7,000. As the battle progressed, Darius was again seized with terror and was the first to turn and flee. He hoped to raise a rebellion in eastern Iran, but some months later he was murdered in the Parthian Desert by his cousin, a remarkable prince of Bactria named Bessus. Alexander gave the body a fitting burial.

It is not difficult to imagine Alexander's thoughts as he passed through the lands and capitals of the ancient East, Babylon, Susa, and Persepolis. The hereditary foe of Greece had been utterly defeated, and he was now the ruler of the largest empire the world had ever seen. When he took his seat for the first time under the golden canopy on the royal throne at Persepolis, his old friend, Demaratus of Corinth, burst into tears and declared that those Greeks were deprived of great pleasure who had died before seeing Alexander seated on the throne of Darius. Acting against Parmenio's advice, Alexander deliberately set fire to the palace, in order that the world might clearly understand that one regime had given way to another. Legend created from this the fanciful story of Thais, the Athenian courtesan who incited the banqueters to the act and thus punished the Persians for their evil deeds. But the cold fact was that the rule of the Persians had come to an end; so, too, had the war of revenge.

The death of Darius confirmed what the sword had already proclaimed, that Alexander was in fact the Great King of the former Persian Empire. Determined to hold and organize his conquests, he recognized the necessity of examining and possessing his state. He probably considered this a relatively easy task, though the flight of Bessus, Darius' murderer, to Bactria (northern Afghanistan) had its own implications. Bactria was an extensive and solid area of Iranian rule, where the Indo-Europeans preserved much of their early vigor and vitality; still, Alexander had no way of guessing that nationalism in eastern Iran would give him the longest and stiffest resistance in his career.

In the course of the march to Bactria and Sogdiana (Russian Turkestan) there occurred one of the great tragedies of Alexander's life. This was the conspiracy of Philotas. Philotas' family was ancient and proud and had fought nobly for Philip and Alexander. Parmenio, his father, had recently been brushed aside by Alexander and left at Ecbatana; two of his brothers had died during the expedition. Moreover, Alexander's endless marches into an utterly unknown world were preventing the conquerors from settling down to the enjoyment of their gains. Most important of all, perhaps, was the fact that in Macedonia the king was little better than the nobles, and yet here was Alexander grown powerful and aloof, often acting and thinking strangely. Had not the time come, thought Philotas, for the Macedonian nobles to take things into their own hands?

When the plot against Alexander was discovered, Philotas was brought before the army, as Macedonian law required. He confessed and was killed by the soldiers with their javelins. Alexander then sent orders to the generals at Ecbatana to put Parmenio to death also—an action, it has always been said, that marks the darkest moment in his life; in later eyes, it was plain murder. Yet an ancient Macedonian law decreed that relatives of a conspirator against the king must also die. The execution of Parmenio was judicial, although it is difficult to believe that Alexander, had he wished, could not have persuaded the army to a different action in the case of a man to whom he owed so much. Probably he decided to let the famous general pay the penalty of the law in order to break the Macedonian opposition to him.

Alexander had indeed been displaying dramatically strange ideas and actions ever since he first set foot in Asia. It is quite impossible, at this point in his career, to put a label on them and say what he had in mind, but the end result was one of the greatest revolutions in the history of thought. Alexander had acquired, it should be remembered, the Greek point of view toward barbarians (non-Greeks). Plato had held that all barbarians were enemies of the Greeks by nature; and Aristotle, as we have already remarked, said that all barbarians were slaves by nature, especially those of Asia. Now let us observe Alexander's extraordinary capacity for rapid growth along many lines.

Alexander had come to Asia Minor in a dual capacity, as king of Macedon and commander in chief of the League of Corinth. Soon he became the ally of the Greek cities along the Asia Minor coast, the adopted son of a native queen, Ada of Caria, and the Great King at least in the interior districts. This latter title became his in actual fact not much later, and before his death he was also the suzerain of Indian rajahs, and a god in both Greece and Egypt. In working out his position in the state, his solution was to take over the existing forms of government and to assume a different relation to the various sections of the empire, much in the manner of the British monarch of a later day. More extraordinary than his allowing the queen of a barbarian people to adopt him—to show that he had come as *their* king, too—was his appointment of two barbarians as governors of provinces in Asia Minor. Then, he asserted his independence of the Corinthian league by not punishing Darius' captured Greek mercenaries, but adding them to his own army. Finally, he began a significant improvement on the Persian administrative system by separating the military, civil, and financial powers of the provincial governors. All this he did in eighteen months, during which

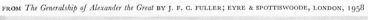

FROM *The Generalship of Alexander the Great* BY J. F. C. FULLER; EYRE & SPOTTISWOODE, LONDON, 1958

The last encounter between Alexander and Darius occurred at Gaugamela and continued the next day on the plains of Arbela, seen stretching out beyond the mound of Keramlais, east of the Tigris in Iraq. The site was especially chosen by the Persian king since the flat land would facilitate the swift attacks of his charging cavalry.

time he had also won two pitched battles with the Persians and overcome various strong cities and mountain tribes.

The conclusion of the war of revenge, which the burning of the palace at Persepolis helped to signalize, meant also the end of Alexander's reliance on his Greek allies. Not much later, therefore, he dismissed them all and allowed those who wished (as most of them did) to re-enlist in his imperial army. Was this an indication of a rapidly growing personal dominion, or was it his way of showing the vast barbarian world that the Greeks were not to occupy a privileged position, that all peoples were to be treated equally? A clue may be found in Alexander's adoption of Persian dress for occasional wear at this time, though once again we have the hostile gossip to the effect that Alexander was giving himself up more and more to Oriental luxury and indeed, that he had a retinue of concubines.

The actual question that Alexander was confronting was simply whether he was to substitute Greek despotism for Oriental—that is, whether it was to be the same old world, or whether a new state could be formed along very different lines. We learn from Plutarch that Alexander considered it his kingly business to mix all men as in a loving cup. Alexander had been able to test Greek smugness by contact with barbarians, on the battlefield and off, and experience had convinced him of the essential sameness of all people. It was in Egypt, Plutarch continues, that Alexander accepted the teaching of the philosopher Psammon, that all mankind is under the kingship of God. Still more philosophical, Plutarch adds, was Alexander's own opinion that although God is indeed a common father of all mankind, still, He makes peculiarly His own the noblest and best of men.

To give concrete expression to these ideas, to create a common bond within his world state, was Alexander's hardest task. For the moment, at least, his founding of cities had to suffice. Usually these were not wholly new cities, as is generally supposed, but rather existing settlements to which he added old or wounded soldiers. They were located at strategic points and were intended to police the countryside and guard communications. But, of course, the soldiers were Greeks and Macedonians (the distinction between the

"Alexander's Entry Into Babylon"

abylon Today

*I*n triumph Alexander entered Babylon, a winter capital of the Persian kings, barely three years after he had crossed into Asia. Quintus Curtius describes the scene: "A great part of the Babylonians had taken their places on the walls . . . Bagophanes, guardian of the citadel and of the royal funds, had strewn the whole road with flowers and garlands and had placed here and there on both sides silver altars which he had piled high, not only with frankincense but with perfumes of all kinds." At dusk the citizens spread the streets with the "naptha" which oozed from their oil-rich land, then set it afire to light the sky and amaze the conqueror.

This splendid scene was painted by Charles Lebrun for the splendor-loving king of France, Louis XIV. The court of Versailles might have pondered in it the transitory nature of earthly glory. For after Alexander left Babylon for eight years of hard campaigning, he returned to it only in time to die. And Babylon itself, in succeeding centuries, vanished beneath the surface of the earth. At left is all that remains today of what Plutarch called "this richest of cities."

ALEXANDER M DARIVM VII T. SVPERAT
CA SIS IN ACIL PERSAR. PEDIT CM.EQVIT
VERO X M INTERFECTIS, MATRE Q OOVE
CONIVGE LIBERIS DARII REG CVM M.HAVD
AMPLIVS EQVIT IB. FVGA DILAPSI.CAPTIS.

"This day," said Darius, "will establish or end the greatest empire any age has seen." The battle fought that day—October 1, 331 B.C.—on the plain of Arbela has been depicted by Albrecht Altdorfer in a painting which, for intricacy of detail, is without parallel in the history of art. Out of his imagination the sixteenth-century German artist created a vast landscape of plain, mountain, sea and sky, castles and cities, the Persian camp and the battling armies. The Greeks, surging across the scene from the right, have

just broken the Persian line. Darius, in a chariot drawn by three white horses, races for the mountain refuge, pursued by Alexander in golden armor, with poised lance. Symbolic darkness closes over the Persian horde while the rays of the sun fall upon the victorious army, and a legend in the sky proclaims: "Alexander the Great finally defeats Darius, killing 100,000 Persian infantry and 10,000 cavalry on the field of battle, and capturing the mother, the wife, and children of King Darius, who escaped with only 1,000 horsemen."

two peoples was soon forgotten) and from these islands of Hellenism, or Greek culture, there spread a knowledge of Greek ways which, as Alexander hoped, helped to unite the peoples of his empire. The Hellenization of Hither Asia, as it turned out, was the most important specific result of Alexander's life.

These, then, were the chief "strange" ideas that Alexander had held up to the time of Parmenio's execution. It is little wonder that he should exclaim that Hephaestion was the only friend to understand and approve his plans of empire.

In the spring of 329 B.C. Alexander crossed the Hindu Kush into Bactria by the Khawak Pass. Almost at once his most important body of Greek cavalry, which had been under the executed Parmenio, rebelled and was sent home. The resentment of these men at the death of their beloved commander and their subsequent dismissal presented Alexander with the greatest crisis in his life. Should he himself also return? Obviously he could not find more Greeks and Macedonians at a moment's notice, and yet his entire expedition might end in disaster at this point. There was only one thing to do: to take a chance and, for the first time, to incorporate large numbers of Asiatics in his army.

Alexander's willingness to trust his own personal safety and the success of his expedition to barbarians must be placed at the top of the extraordinary ideas that now rapidly took form and unfolded to the world. And their motivation was the immediate need for survival.

The new Asiatic troops proved invaluable to Alexander during the two years in Bactria-Sogdiana. It was a time of guerrilla warfare, of constant marching, ambushes and treachery, of wounds and sickness. The opposition of the Macedonian nobility, moreover, remained; and one night at a banquet Alexander was taunted about his great debt to Philip and Philip's men. Finally, thoroughly drunk as he was this evening, he let his terrible temper get the better of him, and he murdered Clitus "the Black," as he was called, a friend since boyhood who had saved the King's life at the Battle of Granicus in 334 B.C.

Somehow or other during these same two years, as we have said, Alexander found time to think. If the Asiatic troops were so loyal, could not some gesture be made to placate eastern Iran and bring the guerrilla warfare to an end? His solution was to marry Roxane, the captive daughter of a Bactrian prince, whom the soldiers pronounced the most beautiful of all the women they had seen in Asia,

with the single exception of Darius' wife. Legend turned it into a love affair, but it was a political marriage, the beginning of a real effort to take Asia into full partnership with him. This, and the desire to legitimize his rule, led him in the year before his death also to marry Barsine, Darius' daughter. At that time, most of his friends took barbarian wives, and gifts were distributed to those soldiers, 10,000 in number, who in the course of all the marching had taken up more or less permanently with Asiatic girls.

Alexander's idea of a fusion of races did not mean that he planned a deliberate Hellenization of the East or a barbarization of the Greeks and Macedonians. Those who wished were free to pursue their own national life—and they represented the overwhelming majority—but at the same time there was to develop a new life based on an interchange and mixture of customs and blood. This new attitude toward the world was to be the driving and unifying force of his empire. As part of this program, he now ordered that 30,000 native youths should be taught the Greek language and trained in the use of Macedonian weapons. And to leave no doubt that these ideas were to be applied on an immense scale, he revealed his intention, once he had finished with the East, of marching against the

On the hot, dry plain of eastern Persia the ruins of Persepolis still stand against the sky as they have stood for more than two thousand years since Alexander put this conquered city to the torch. Beyond the columns of the Apadana, or audience hall, may be seen the remnants of the royal palace, built by the early Achaemenid kings, Darius I and his son Xerxes I, predecessors of Darius III whom Alexander defeated. Here the Persian monarchs exercised their double powers as temporal kings and as earthly vicars of the great divinity Ahura Mazda. It was to break this double power, some historians theorize, that Alexander, acting for himself and Zeus, ordered the city burned. "Such," we are told, "was the end of the capital of the entire Orient from which so many nations previously sought jurisdiction, the birthplace of so many kings, once the special terror of Greece . . . And not even in the long age that followed its destruction did it rise again."

West, to Italy and beyond. This was one of the first manifestations, surely, of a growing megalomania.

But what to do about an uncertain officer corps, as represented by the Macedonian opposition? Here was an immediate military problem, deserving treatment as drastic as that meted out to the mutiny of his cavalry. Alexander reached the decision to abandon the comradely relationship with his officers that had long characterized the Macedonian monarchy, and to put an end to wavering support and possible plots by becoming an autocrat. Or better, to put it in Greek terms, he decided, in this century which had already raised living men to divine status, to become a god.

The plan fell through for the moment, but when we look at Alexander's extraordinary ideas—on world conquest and his own relation to the state, on the use of barbarians in administration and army, the foundation of cities, a common culture, personal deification—we must conclude that there was no way to realize them except by autocratic action. Ideas, however, have a way of growing. In the year before his death, during a banquet of reconciliation with his men after another brief mutiny, Alexander prayed for partnership in the empire and for unity and concord in a joint commonwealth where all peoples were to be partners rather than subjects. It was this prayer, it has been said, that marks a revolution in human thought. It was picked up, first by Zeno, whose Stoicism preached the brotherhood of man, and then by Saint Paul in his stirring vision of a world in which there shall be "neither Greek nor Jew, barbarian nor Scythian, bond nor free."

When the time came to leave eastern Iran, Alexander

This highly romantic version of The Marriage of Roxane and Alexander *by the Renaissance artist Il Sodoma, bears little relation to the fact that this was a political union intended to end the guerrilla resistance of the eastern Iranian tribesmen. The painting is based on a description given by Lucian, a rhetorician of the second century* A.D., *of a painting on the same theme done by the Greek painter Aëtion, a contemporary of Alexander. Of the original painting, Lucian wrote: "A splendid bridal bed is seen on which Roxane, in the sweet flower of her youth, shy and coy sits, in front of Alexander standing. Smiling cupids hover around her. One pulls off one of her stockings; one removes her veil from behind as if to show her to her spouse. Another kindly unlaces her sandal, whilst yet another, laughing, is pulling Alexander towards her by a flap of his coat. The king is seen offering a crown to the maid." In Il Sodoma's painting, Roxane's attendants have just finished the ceremonial ablutions and prepare to withdraw. On the right bearing a torch, Alexander's friend and best man, Hephaestion, stands with Hymen, the god of marriage, gazing wistfully at the royal couple.*

recrossed the Hindu Kush by the Kaoshan Pass and continued down the Khyber Pass to India. This ancient land, with its ascetics and Brahmans, its marvels and curious customs, filled the Greeks with awe. But Alexander hurried on, for, being wholly ignorant of the size of India and even of the existence of China, he thought that Ocean—the great sea, so men believed, that ringed the inhabited land—lay not much farther east. A few years earlier, standing beside the Caspian Sea, he believed it to be a northern gulf of Ocean and organized an exploring expedition to find out. Now he thought he was near the eastern and natural limit of his empire, where great cities and harbors of his creation would produce a wonderful prosperity and serve to tie together in an economic whole the various sections of the state.

As Alexander traversed the Punjab, however, the great Indian rajah Porus opposed his crossing of the Hydaspes River, now known as the Jhelum. Alexander won a victory over him at great cost; but when, not much later, his men stood upon the high bank of the Hyphasis and gazed across the interminable plains extending to the horizon, their spirits sank. The rumor of more enemies, of men larger and braver than the other Indians, and of countless elephants, unsettled a morale that had already been weakened by the recent fighting. During the past eight and a half years Alexander's men had marched over 11,000 miles. Fatigued mentally and physically, they could not see the purpose of further marching and fighting in unknown lands. When Alexander learned that the army would go no farther and insisted upon returning home, he retired to his tent for three days—like Achilles—and hoped that the men would change their minds. But it was of no avail.

It had been a curious mutiny, for it had never occurred to the army to depose Alexander, the only man who could bring them safely home. To mark the farthest point of his advance Alexander erected twelve tremendous altars to the Olympian gods and offered sacrifice upon them, and celebrated gymnastic and cavalry contests. He also prepared armor that was larger than usual, and stalls for horses that were higher and bits that were heavier than those in common use, and left them scattered up and down to impress later generations with the manner of men who had come that way.

Alexander's men won their point, but it was he who chose the route home. In November, 326 B.C., the army, aboard ship and on foot, began the descent of the Indus river system. Indescribable slaughter followed their progress, but in July of the following year the Indian Ocean was reached. Alexander's joy at seeing the southern limit of the inhabited world was great. All that now remained was to explore the route by land and sea between the Indus and Mesopotamia, and the empire would be a well-knit and self-sufficient whole.

Alexander knew something of the difficulties that lay ahead, for he had already sent westward, by a different route, many of his troops, most of his baggage, and his elephants. (He was too good a general to use the beasts in battle, for he recognized their unreliability, but he did employ them for transport and in hunting.) He had no real conception, however, of the torrid, arid wastes awaiting him, especially the 150 terrible desert miles in Baluchistan. His journey became one of the greatest marches in military history. His commissariat, for the only time in the expedition, failed him, and he was unable to keep in touch with the fleet under Nearchus. Most of the camp followers died, but he got his army of 15,000 men back safely to Persepolis early in 324 B.C., almost exactly six years after his first triumphant entry.

Plans of further conquest, of the administration of his empire, of the exploration of Arabia, now filled Alexander's mind. But it was too much for him. His ceaseless mental and physical activity, the immense responsibilities of state, his long marches and dangerous wounds had so lowered his vitality that he was unable to throw off a fever. On June 13, 323 B.C., Alexander died at Babylon, not yet thirty-three years of age, after a reign of twelve years and eight months.

The world was never again to be the same. Gone forever, at least as a force in politics, was the small democratic city-state of the Greeks; gone, too, was the homogeneous civilization concentrated around the Aegean Sea. The high standards of taste, the freedom, responsibility, and intensity of Periclean life became things of the past. The world now belonged to the large monarchic state.

Nothing could be further from the truth than to imagine that, because Alexander's empire upon his death broke up

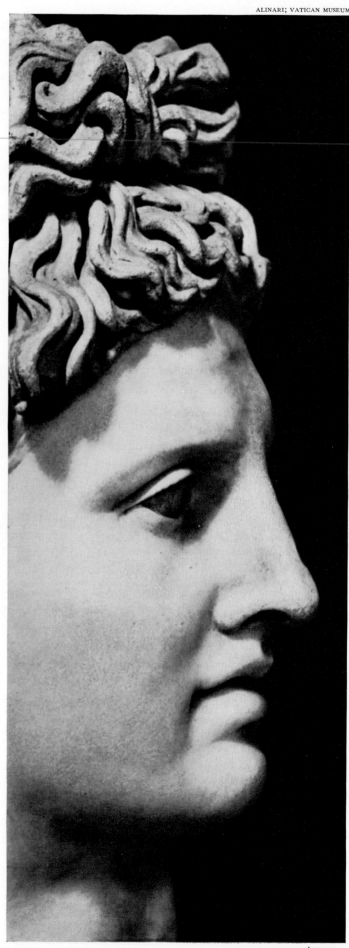

APOLLO

FROM APOLLO TO BUDDHA

*O*ne strange and lasting result of Alexander's march to the East was the image of Buddha. Before the Greeks arrived in Asia, Buddha was never represented in painting or sculpture. His horse might be shown—riderless—or his throne—vacant—but no Oriental artist ventured to carve or draw his sacred person. The Greeks who followed Alexander into India took with them statues of their gods, which became the inspiration of sculptors in the northern frontier province of Gandhara. There in the second century A.D. appear the first images of Buddha, clearly modeled on Apollo. The native sculptors kept the Greek profile and topknot but gave Buddha a more contemplative expression and added the Oriental feature of a third "eye" in the forehead. Gradually, over the centuries, the image spread eastward and was metamorphosed into a purely Oriental figure, in both features and dress. As shown below, the Gandhara sculptors modeled the Buddha's dress on the Greek himation, but made it soft and clinging, as if changing the fabric from Greek wool to Indian silk; later the lines of the himation disappear altogether. But the Apollonian topknot remains to this day to mark the Western origin of the Buddha image.

SOPHOCLES IN A HIMATION

GANDHARA SCULPTURE

LATER CHINESE BUDDHA

BUDDHA

into three or four large states, his conquests came to naught. The new kingdoms that resulted were ruled by Macedonians and Greeks for three centuries along Western lines, until the coming of Rome. The most striking fact about the Hellenistic age—as we term those extraordinary centuries after Alexander's death, when Hellenism was adopted by non-Greeks—is the unity of the large world that had been opened by his expedition.

Macedonians and Greeks who had been left behind in Bactria eventually mustered enough strength to march again across the Hindu Kush and conquer India as far as Calcutta. In the region of the Khyber Pass known as Gandhara, they created an art that was an extraordinary mixture of East and West. Hitherto Buddha had been merely an abstraction in art, but the only way Greek sculptors knew how to represent a god was in the form of a man. Thus when Chinese pilgrims to Buddha's birthplace passed through Gandhara, they brought back with them the new conception of Buddha. Except for this, however, the Farther East would be exactly the same today had Alexander and his men never existed.

It was distinctly otherwise westward. If some of Alexander's dreams took root slowly, such as that of co-operation between peoples, nevertheless his idea of the *oikoumenē*, the "inhabited world," found immediate acceptance. In the

---

Alexander in his own defense

In answer to Hermolaus, whom he later put to death for conspiring against his life, Alexander said:

He says, the Persians, whom we have conquered, are in high honour with me! In my opinion at least, the surest indication of my moderation is that I do not rule even the vanquished tyrannically. For I came into Asia, not in order to overthrow nations and make a desert of a half part of the world, but in order that those whom I had subdued in war might not regret my victory. . . .

That possession is not lasting of which we are made owners by the sword; the gratitude for acts of kindness is everlasting. If we wish to hold Asia, not merely to pass through it, our clemency must be shared with its people, their faith in us will make a stable and lasting empire. . . .

I see in many nations things which we should not blush to imitate; and so great an empire cannot fitly be ruled without contributing some things to the vanquished and learning from them. . . . Would that the people of India may believe me to be a god. For wars depend upon reputation, and often even what has been falsely believed has gained the place of truth.

Do you think it was to gratify my luxury that I adorned your arms with gold and silver? I wished to show to those who are accustomed to nothing cheaper than those metals that the Macedonians, who are invincible in other things, cannot be outdone even in gold. It is this glory, parricide that you are, that you wished to interrupt and to deliver the Macedonians to the conquered nations by killing their king!

Hellenistic age man thought of himself more and more as a member of a world society, a society in which there might be (and were) sharp differences, but in which a common culture nevertheless acted as a natural bond. The new culture was different from that of Periclean days, for it was affected by the rapid rise of the ordinary man and by close contact with Orientalism. There could be no more vivid illustration of the unity of the world than the fact that the New Testament was written in Greek.

It was the culture of the Hellenistic age that civilized Rome and facilitated her creation of her own world state and then Christianity's conquest of that state. Only a mighty historical force could have brought that state into being. As such it is Alexander's monument; while his dreams have been, and still are, a challenge to humanity to substitute the idea of universalism, of solidarity of the world and co-operation between peoples, for narrowness of race and outlook.

C. A. Robinson, Jr., Professor of Classics at Brown University, is one of the world's leading experts on Alexander. His latest book, The History of Alexander the Great, *is a study of surviving historical material on Alexander's life. His other works on Alexander include* The Ephemerides of Alexander's Expedition *and a popular narrative biography,* Alexander the Great.

THE
YEAR
ONE

A big date in retrospect, yes—but merely 754 to Romans then,

3761 to Jews now, and very likely not anno Domini *at all*

This panel from the Ara Pacis proclaims the peace and plenty of the Augustan Age

Decisive years, like decisive battles, are an old favorite with historians. Some—1492, 1776, 1914—are pretty obvious: knowledgeable contemporaries could not have escaped the feeling that something big was up, even though they could not have foreseen all the consequences. More often, however, great historical processes begin altogether invisibly, and only much later, looking back, is it possible to pin the critical date down. Such a year is the Year One. Indeed, of all the great years in history it is the oddest because no one alive at the time, or for centuries thereafter, had any idea that this was the Year One at all. If they ever used such a date, they would have meant by it the year in which the world was created, not what we mean by A.D. 1.

How, for example, was a birth certificate, a marriage contract, a business agreement, dated in the Year One? There is no single answer to such a question since for most of the purposes of ordinary living, local dates were used. In Rome

By M. I. FINLEY

a contract would be dated "in the consulship of C. Caesar son of Augustus and L. Aemilius Paulus son of Paulus." Elsewhere there were regnal years, or years of local officials, or of priesthoods. This may look like chaos to us, habituated as we are to a continuous, fixed calendar in use more or less all over the world, but it worked well enough. Only the learned were troubled, the men who wanted an exact answer to the question "How long ago?" or who wished to synchronize events in Greek and Roman history. A number of systems had been invented for their use. In Rome scholars commonly dated events from the legendary foundation of the city by Romulus in the year we call 753 B.C.; in Greece they used four-year units, Olympiads, beginning with the first Olympic Games in 776 B.C. In those two systems the Year One was, respectively, 754 A.U.C. (*ab urbe condita*) and the first year of the 195th Olympiad. No system was official: every scholar and historian was free to choose whichever he preferred, singly or in combination.

It is therefore hardly surprising that it took the Christians a long time to think up and introduce a scheme of their own. The honor goes to an eastern Greek-speaking monk, Dionysius Exiguus, who lived in Rome in the first half of the sixth century. He calculated that Christ was born in 754 A.U.C., called that the first "year of our Lord," *anno Domini,* and counted everything that preceded it as so many years *ante Christum,* "before Christ." His calculation was slightly inaccurate. The only real evidence is in two of the four Gospels, and unfortunately that is conflicting and irreconcilable. If Matthew is right in the way he dates the flight into Egypt, then Jesus was born in or shortly before the last year of the reign of King Herod the Great, who died in 4 B.C. But if Luke is right in linking the Nativity with a census— "And all went to enrol themselves, everyone to his own city" —then the date must be A.D. 6 or even 7. On neither account is A.D. 1 possible. Nevertheless, Dionysius's chronological scheme spread gradually, first in the West, more slowly in the East, until it achieved near universality. The Year One— whatever it really was—became a great year, for many the greatest year in all history.

If A.D. 6 is the right date, then Jesus was born in the newly established Roman province of Judaea. In that year the Romans deposed Herod's son Archelaus, took over Judaea, and sent in Syria's governor, Quirinius, with instructions to conduct the first census there. Galilee, on the other hand, was allowed to continue under the family of Herod for another generation. This rather confusing political situation was not untypical of districts on the eastern frontier of the Roman Empire, where imperial policy fluctuated between backing local client-kings and ruling directly. After all, Palestine was a long way from Rome. Problems much nearer home were pressing: large forces were just then occupied with trying to incorporate the German territory between the Rhine and the Elbe. They were wiped out in A.D. 9 in a treacherous ambush by Arminius (Hermann), a German chieftain who had earlier

served in the Roman auxiliary forces and been rewarded with Roman citizenship. That disaster in the Teutoburg Forest effectively froze the northern frontier of the Empire on the Rhine-Danube line, subject to various later adjustments, including the conquest of Britain. The western frontier was the Atlantic Ocean; the southern was the Atlas Mountains, the Sahara, and the cataracts of the Nile— though parts of northern Africa had the same shifting political history as Judaea.

The Roman Empire was an empire in the strictest possible sense. The "Roman people"—that is, Roman citizens who were concentrated very largely in Rome and central or northern Italy—ruled all the rest as subjects. The Empire outside Italy was divided into what were called *provinciae,* which were not provinces in the way Ontario is now a province of Canada, but rather colonies in the way India or Nigeria were British colonies before they obtained their independence. The total area of the Empire in A.D. 1 was nearly 1,250,000 square miles, the population perhaps sixty million. Whether anyone, in or out of government, actually knew the latter figure is much to be doubted. Although censuses were taken, they were irregular, and they came at different times in different provinces. Their sole purpose was to bring the tax rolls up to date: the tax collector, along with the soldier, was the most obvious and ubiquitous link between the provinces and Rome.

Rome had begun to acquire provinces as far back as the third century B.C., and the process never stopped until the second century of the Christian Era. Imperial expansion is usually deceptive in its motivation because defense and strategy can so plausibly be adduced as the excuse: the farther the frontiers are extended, the farther the menaces—real or imaginary—are pushed back. But in antiquity in general, and among the Romans in particular, there seems to have been much less effort than in modern times to disguise or deny the exploitational purposes of empire. Whatever the reasons piously given for their conquest and incorporation in each individual instance, the right to profit directly from conquered lands was freely recognized. That meant not only taxes—in goods, services, and money—for the state, but often great personal income, legal or illegal, for high officials and members of the tax-farming corporations. It was also in the interests of Rome that her empire be pacific and orderly, as well as reasonably well administered locally. To achieve the latter aim she depended chiefly on the local ruling classes, for she lacked the manpower to do otherwise, and they normally played the part assigned to them as a pro-Roman counterweight in what could well have become a rebellious situation.

From the days when Rome first began to expand, her rulers had also adopted a policy of as much non-interference as possible in social and cultural institutions, although not so much from a broad theory or principle of toleration as from the much more elementary consideration, Why bother? Rome had no "mission"—that myth was imposed retrospec-

PAUL RONALD—EDITIONS ARTHAUD, PARIS

The statue of Augustus below, carved about 20 B.C., embodies all the superb authority with which he ruled the Empire. Like many great men, he was less successful at home. His third marriage, to Livia (left), lasted fifty-two years but gave him no heirs. His only child, Julia (right), was finally banished by her father—who had no choice but to obey one of his own laws—for immorality. In the relief above from the Altar of Peace, her second husband, Agrippa, is at far left and Julia, right foreground.

VATICAN MUSEUM—ANDERSON; ABOVE LEFT: LOUVRE—GIRAUDON; ABOVE RIGHT: BIBLIOTHEQUE NATIONALE—SERVICE PHOTOGRAPHIQUE

Parthia

Armenia

Egypt

Augustus was an accomplished propagandist. He issued the coins above to proclaim the submission of three eastern territories to Roman power: Egypt in 30 B.C., Parthia and Armenia both in 20 B.C. He also had the foresight to compose his own obituary, so that posterity would keep the record straight. The most complete copy extant is the one in Ankara, Turkey (above), with texts in both Latin and Greek. In all this empire-building, it was the conquest of venerable Egypt that excited the popular imagination. An example of this interest can be seen in the detail opposite from a first-century mosaic at Palestrina, near Rome: it shows the conquering Roman legionaries amidst the floods and temples and crocodiles of the Nile.

tively much later. She wished to rule successfully, and it was repeatedly demonstrated to her that minimum interference paid off—even though the Roman provincial governor retained virtually absolute power and did not hesitate to use it when he felt the need, including the imposition of the death penalty. Under normal conditions the upshot was that in their daily lives very large numbers of people were touched lightly indeed by Roman rule. That was particularly true in the eastern parts of the Empire which had had a high civilization of their own long before the Romans came. These areas remained very diverse, both among themselves and from the West—about as diverse as they had been in their days of independence. Latin was of course the official language of the Roman state. But it was not the language spoken in the East or even in some western regions such as Sicily and Libya. There the ruling classes and the intellectuals tended to speak and write and think in Greek, the rest in their native tongues —in some places Greek, in others Aramaic or Egyptian or whatever. Educated Romans were more or less fluent in Greek, but their counterparts in the eastern provinces rarely troubled to know Latin equally well. When Josephus— Joseph ben Matthias, member of a Jewish priestly family, highly educated, born and bred in Judaea—wrote his *Jewish War,* a pro-Roman eyewitness account of the Roman capture of rebel Jerusalem and the destruction of the Temple in A.D. 70, his first version was in Aramaic, his second in Greek.

Josephus was a Pharisee, for whom the villains among his own people were the Zealots, who stirred up and led the revolt against Rome. His favorite word for the rebels is "bandits," so that bandits, Zealots, and lower classes are virtually synonymous in his books. The mighty Romans needed four years to quell the Jewish uprising—precisely because social revolt, the desire for independence, and sectarian religious conflict were closely intertwined. This was an age of lavish living among relatively few men at one end of the scale, and extreme poverty among the many at the other end. The Gargantuan banquet given by the freedman Trimalchio in the *Satyricon* of Petronius is funny in the way it exaggerates; the account caricatures, but it does not invent out of whole cloth. The wealth of Herod the Great was a subject for never-ending comment by Josephus. But the linen weavers of Tarsus, skilled free craftsmen whose products were sought after throughout the Empire, could never afford the small fees charged for the acquisition of local citizenship in their own city.

Outside Judaea serious revolt was rare, for whatever reason. There was much unhappiness and much grumbling, but it takes more than that to make a lasting mark on the record: history tends to be the history of the winners, with the losers assigned the passive, largely unvoiced, faceless role of the people on whom the winners operated. Romans in the Year One were able to contemplate their position with much satisfaction. Not only were they the rulers of what they chose to believe was the civilized world, but they had emerged successfully from a long, desperately violent, and dangerous

period of civil war. The republican machinery of government, led by the exclusive, oligarchical Senate—which had sent victorious Roman armies east, west, north, and south and had carved out the greatest empire yet known—had broken down badly by the end of the second century B.C. Various attempts to mend it had failed, until Julius Caesar's nephew and adopted son, Octavian, finally replaced the old system by a monarchy—although the explicit terminology of kingship was carefully avoided and a republican façade reconstructed, with Senate, popular assembly, consuls, praetors, and so on. But a façade is just that: its function is to conceal the reality behind it. In January of 27 B.C. the Senate formally ratified the position Octavian had won by arms and conferred on him a new name, Augustus, by which he has been known ever since. At the same time a euphemistic title was chosen for him, Princeps—before this a common Latin word which the dictionary defines as "the first, chief, principal, most distinguished person," hence lacking any of the undesirable overtones of *rex* (king). He was also Imperator, a military title he used often because it affirmed his special relationship with the base and guarantee of his power: the standing army which numbered about 300,000 men.

Twenty-seven years later Augustus was firmly in control of an empire which he had considerably enlarged. Small stirrings of anti-monarchical sentiment were crushed, all lingering misunderstandings about the real nature of his rule removed. In 2 B.C. he had been given the title *pater patriae*, Father of the Nation, which recalled to Roman citizens the despotic authority of the Roman *pater* at least as much as paternal benevolence. He lived on to A.D. 14, with only one new honor to look forward to: his formal deification upon his death (like Julius Caesar before him). As important as these titular acquisitions, were his open maneuverings to establish a royal dynasty: Augustus and no one else was going to choose his successor, and in the process he trampled on some of the most deeply rooted of Roman traditions. His two grandsons (and sons by adoption), Gaius and Lucius, were designated consuls at the age of fifteen—in 5 B.C. and 2 B.C., respectively—although they could not actually assume office until they were twenty. Each was entitled "Princeps of the Youth." This rigmarole was pure Crown-princedom. In the Year One, Gaius, having become twenty, was duly elected consul along with his sister's husband, L. Aemilius Paulus. Then Augustus's luck ran out: Lucius died the next year, Gaius in A.D. 4. The sick, aging Emperor proceeded to adopt Tiberius, making it quite plain that he did so joylessly, and it was Tiberius who eventually succeeded him.

That Tiberius was able to take over smoothly and peacefully is a measure of the full extent of Augustus's success. Historians commonly and rightly call Augustus the "architect of the Roman Empire." In the days when imperialism was still a virtue and Roman imperialism the accepted model, he was regularly referred to with unmixed adulation. The

pendulum has now swung back, though less for some, perhaps, than for others—E. M. Forster calls Augustus "one of the most odious of the world's successful men." It is hard to imagine anyone today reading without discomfort these lines from Virgil's *Aeneid* (in C. Day Lewis's translation):

> *And here, here is the man, the promised one you know of—*
> *Caesar Augustus, son of a god, destined to rule*
> *Where Saturn ruled of old in Latium, and there*
> *Bring back the age of gold: his empire shall expand*
> *Past Garamants and Indians to a land beyond the zodiac.*

Virgil and Horace were the towering figures in the literary circle patronized by one of Augustus's closest and richest friends, Maecenas. (It was not for nothing that the very name of Maecenas became a common word in the languages of Europe.) Augustus thought of everything: public opinion was not to be neglected any more than finance, dynastic arrangements, food supply, or the army. Even the coinage was harnessed. When he was given the title *pater patriae*, for example, his chief mint, at Lugdunum (Lyons), began to issue silver coins carrying his portrait with the legend *pater patriae* on the obverse; on the reverse were his two young grandsons in togas, with emblems of priesthood and the legend, "Gaius and Lucius Caesar, sons [by adoption] of Augustus, consuls-designate, *principes* of the youth." Coins circulate rapidly, and public response was not slow. Poets picked up the theme; so did individuals and communities in dedicatory inscriptions on monuments.

Yet it would be a mistake to speak cynically of prostituted art. Neither Virgil nor Horace, who died in 19 and 8 B.C., respectively, nor the historian Livy, who in the Year One was still writing away on his vast epic history of Rome, had been bought in any real sense. Horace was the son of a rich ex-slave, while Virgil and Livy came from the propertied middle classes of northern Italy. These classes had suffered heavily in the civil wars, but now there was peace again— the *pax Augusta*—and great hope for the future, both for Rome and for the Empire. With renewed greatness would come moral regeneration. This last was a favorite theme of Augustus, expressed in a stream of legislation designed to curb excessively wasteful personal living, licentiousness, and depravity in the upper classes. They were to be called back, these upper classes—not to the freedom and power they had had in the Republic, but to responsible participation in the army and the civil administration under the Princeps.

Moral crusades are never easy to judge: standards, motives, and realities are too much like icebergs. Certainly the visible part of contemporary behavior looked rotten enough, even allowing for differences between ancient and modern values. In the same year in which he became *pater patriae* (2 B.C.) Augustus banished his own daughter Julia, mother of Gaius and Lucius, for sexual depravity, and a number of men of high rank were exiled as her accomplices. Ten years

There was no religious orthodoxy in Rome: where there are already so many gods, it is always easy to accommodate one more (the Christians were persecuted for political rather than theological reasons). In Pompeii, for example, Venus was worshiped as the tutelary goddess of the city, and a shop sign from there (upper left) shows her in a chariot drawn by elephants. A painting from nearby Herculaneum (upper right) depicts a ritual of Isis—suggesting that her cult had a strong hold there, as it did elsewhere in the Empire. An important element in many of these religions was augury—attempting to divine the future, as the priest in the relief at the left is doing by examining the entrails of a bull. At first glance the children in the fresco below look like a group of Christian choirboys, but they are actually taking part in a ceremony honoring the goddess Diana.

later her daughter, also called Julia—wife of the L. Aemilius Paulus who had been the second consul in the Year One—was exiled to a barren island on similar charges. Aemilius was executed, either at that time or earlier, and there is something altogether mysterious about both affairs. There is no particular reason to whitewash either of the Julias, but it is hard to avoid the implication that dynastic palace plotting was a more important element in the picture. Conspiracy was henceforth endemic in the Empire, and it is not unimportant that it touched the heart of the regime as early as the reign of the founder himself.

One of the younger Julia's co-victims was the poet Ovid, sent off to Tomi (now Constanta) on the Black Sea, where he was forced to live out the remaining ten years of his life, grumbling, whining, and begging in the most toadying terms for a reprieve which never came. In a sense Ovid sums up in his own career the great paradox of the Rome of his day. What had he done to warrant such severe punishment? As far as we know, nothing—or at worst something trifling. But ten years earlier he had written the *Art of Love,* and throughout his brilliant career—he was enormously popular —he belonged to a circle of poets and intellectuals who gave only lip service to the glories of the new reign while they exulted in their own individuality and, sin of sins, in the delights of love when the Emperor was demanding moral regeneration. The *pax Augusta* was enforced by a military despotism; the literary renaissance was expected to stay pretty much in line; the rule of law could be broken at the ruler's whim.

It was not the brutality that disturbed anyone. This was a brutal world at all levels. The list of Augustus's massive philanthropies, which he himself compiled for posthumous publication (see page 92), included the sponsorship of eight monster exhibitions in which about ten thousand gladiators fought, the largest number on record. These were now the most popular type of public show in the Empire: men and women of every class came by the tens of thousands to relish the slaughter of men by men, and of men by wild beasts. If the theatre was the characteristic secular building of classical Greek civilization, the amphitheatre was its Roman counterpart. What critics of the imperial system (the few whose voices we hear) attacked was not its brutality but the arbitrariness and the sycophancy it bred, the inevitable conspiratorial atmosphere.

Yet there *was* a great cultural renaissance under Augustus. And there was peace throughout the Empire most of the time, peace without political freedom as the Greeks had once understood it, even without freedom in the more limited sense men had experienced in republican Rome, but more continuous peace than the Mediterranean world had perhaps ever known. The Roman and Italian response is well documented in literature and sculptured monuments, and is not hard to understand. But what of the "provincials," the subjects, and

particularly what of the great mass of them who were not local magnates supporting Rome in return for benefits received? Part of the answer, for the East in particular, is that they began to worship Augustus as Saviour, Benefactor, and God Manifest (Epiphanes), just as they had deified a succession of Ptolemies, Seleucids, and other rulers in the preceding centuries. Among the Romans themselves divinity had to wait until his death; in the meantime only his genius or daemon, the immortal spirit within him, could have an altar. But the East, with a different tradition, built temples to Augustus the god.

This ruler-cult should neither be underestimated nor misunderstood. It was cult in the strict sense, difficult as that may be to grasp today. At the same time it did not prove the existence of widespread popular enthusiasm for the ruler as a person, or of anything more positive than a recognition of the facts of life. Power had to be worshiped, that was self-evident: the power of natural forces, Fate or Fortune, the many gods and goddesses in their multiple attributes, and the great power on earth. To do otherwise was stupid and brought certain punishment, even though rewards for proper veneration were unfortunately far from guaranteed, at least not in this life. In so one-sided a relationship, in a world in which there was little hope of material success for the majority of the free population (let alone the slaves), and in which the earthly power was now pretty close to despotism, fear rather than love was often the dominating emotion behind worship.

However complicated the psychology, emperor worship was a binding force in the Empire. The first manifestations were more or less spontaneous, but it would be naïve to imagine that Augustus or his advisers and successors were unaware of the value of the institution. Particularly zealous to foster it were the petty tyrants and client-kings who depended on Roman arms for their very existence, among them King Herod of Judaea (who also, significantly, introduced the amphitheatre and gladiators into his realm). Herod thereby set off a delayed chain reaction with the most far-reaching consequences. Where there were already many gods, to add the emperor to the pantheon was easy. The polytheistic religions of the eastern Mediterranean had been adding, combining, and altering their divinities and their rituals for millennia. A small minority of intellectuals rationalized the system into one or another kind of universal religion, in which the individual gods and their cults were all manifestations of one God. Everyone else was more literal-minded, with a take-it-or-leave-it approach that permitted one to pick and choose. It was physically impossible for anyone to participate in the observances of all the divinities. A policy of *laissez faire* prevailed, provided only that no one blasphemed against anyone else's gods and that cult did not become entangled with political opposition or create an excessive amount of vicious public immorality.

The Jews stood apart. Many now lived outside Judaea:

Augustus built an impressive mausoleum (right) for himself and his family, and he was buried there in A.D. 14 as he had planned. He could hardly have anticipated, however, that in succeeding centuries his tomb would be used as a fortress, garden, bull ring, theatre, and open-air concert hall. By 1938 it was excavated and restored. Time has dealt even more roughly with the Roman Forum and its Basilica Aemilia (below, foreground), reconstructed under Augustus. Pliny called the basilica one of the world's three most beautiful buildings.

there were particularly large communities in Egypt and also where in North Africa, smaller ones in Asia Minor and in Rome itself. In the Diaspora they had become very much Hellenized: the Old Testament had been translated into Greek by the middle of the third century B.C. because few could any longer understand Hebrew. In Palestine, by contrast, Hellenization had been relatively negligible, restricted to small aristocratic circles and to certain districts. Yet wherever they were, Greek and other external influences left untouched the fundamental commandments:

> *Thou shalt have no other gods before me. Thou shalt not make unto thee any graven image. . . . Thou shalt not bow down thyself to them, nor serve them: for I the Lord thy God am a jealous God.*

Once before, in the second century B.C., there had been grave trouble over this question: when the Jews under the leadership of the Maccabees had rebelled successfully against Antiochus IV Epiphanes, the Greek ruler of Syria and Babylonia. Now Herod was trying to repeat the same sacrilege. There was an outcry and he quickly backed down, in time to avoid civil war but not an attempt to assassinate him.

In the next generations the Romans were thus faced with a strange and to them distasteful and even unintelligible situation, with a people who would not play the rules of the game as they were understood by everyone else, who worshiped one God, an exclusive, jealous God. Opposition to emperor worship was to the Romans not so much a religious issue as a political offense, *contumacia*, insubordination, civil disobedience. Augustus and Tiberius made no attempt to force matters with the Jews, and under their immediate successors official policy was inconsistent. But Roman officials in the provinces, and the local populations, for reasons of their own, were far less tolerant and cautious; there were flare-ups against the Jews, ostensibly over imperial statues, in Egypt as well as in Palestine. The Jews themselves were right to be nervous about it. Jewish "extremists" played on these fears, and on social unrest, till finally they brought about the great revolt which the emperor Vespasian and his son Titus smashed in A.D. 70.

It is this complicated combination of motives and circumstances that explains why Jewish nationalism emerged and rebelled whereas Egyptian or Syrian or Greek did not, though widespread poverty, imperial taxation, and similar factors were equally present in these other areas. Economic misery and social unrest had long been turning people to religious salvation as the only promise for the future. In this instance religion drove men to political action (as druidism may also have done in Gaul in A.D. 21). To put the whole burden of explanation on emperor worship would be wrong: religious exclusiveness and alienness, in a world which otherwise found room for all varieties of cult and belief, bred misunderstanding, dislike, wild rumors, irrational hate, mob violence. It cannot be doubted that the destruction of Jerusalem was a

Herod the Great of Judaea was no exception among the local client-kings when it came to flattering the Romans in general and Augustus in particular. None of this was very subtle. He called his seaport Caesarea and built there a temple to Rome and Augustus (above). Then he rebuilt the ancient Biblical city of Samaria (below), which had been destroyed in the second century B.C., and renamed it Sebaste—Greek for Augustus.

popular measure, on the whole, with other peoples of the Empire. Imperial Rome triumphed for the moment, only to discover that she was faced with the same problem under a new name, Christianity—a religion which was just as fiercely monotheistic and exclusive as Judaism, and even more dynamic in its proselytizing zeal. "Render unto Caesar the things that are Caesar's" did not extend worship of Caesar for Christians any more than for the Jews.

Of course there were no Christians in the Year One. Not even a hundred or two hundred years later could anyone have foreseen how radically the balance was going to shift, that the invincible Roman Empire would turn out to be transitory while the still negligible Christian sect would one day bid for universality. To emperors and ordinary non-Christians alike, Christianity was a nuisance and no more. Early in the second century, Pliny the Younger, governor of the province of Bithynia (lying just east of the Bosporus), wrote to the emperor Trajan for advice on how to deal with men and women denounced to him for being Christians. Trajan in reply agreed that Christians must be punished, but "they should not be hunted out." Roman emperors never took so casual a view of problems they regarded as really serious.

Trajan, incidentally, was the last Roman expansionist. He conquered Dacia, roughly modern Transylvania in the loop of the lower Danube, and created a new province there. Then he embarked on an absurd campaign against the Parthian Empire, the heirs of the Persians east of the Euphrates River. He had fleeting success, but Hadrian—who followed him on the throne—immediately and unavoidably gave up the new eastern gains. All in all, the frontiers of the Year One were not far from the absolute limits of the Roman world, except for adjustments, a few conquests, and the final elimination of client-kingdoms as in Judaea. Roman contacts through trade were something else again. Luxury goods moved back and forth across vast distances, and with the products some information and more misinformation. Even though silk came overland from China (the middlemen living in what is now Chinese Turkestan), it may safely be doubted that anyone within the Roman Empire had ever heard of the early Han dynasty or that it was about to come to an end just then (actually in A.D. 8). Trade with India and even Ceylon was more direct and on a considerably larger scale, chiefly by sea from Egypt. Indo-Roman trading stations existed as far away as Pondicherry; there was a drain of Roman coins to India and still farther east. Yet the knowledge of Indian life and civilization scattered in Roman literature is thin and unreliable, showing little advance over the reports brought back from the campaigns of Alexander the Great several centuries earlier. Similarly, there was trans-Sahara trade, especially for ivory, but almost total ignorance of the African continent below the desert.

The peoples the Romans knew best were of course their neighbors, the Armenians and Parthians immediately to the east, and, more important, the Germans beyond the Rhine and Danube. The latter were illiterate, organized in loose tribal federations rather than in more advanced political systems, and constantly on the move, both because their relatively primitive agricultural techniques exhausted the soil rapidly and because from time to time they were driven by invaders, such as the later Huns, who swept across the eastern and central European plains. Germans and Romans were in constant contact, sometimes hostile but more often neutral or even friendly, exchanging goods and occasionally ideas. It is hardly surprising that these less advanced peoples envied the superior Roman material standards and tried to share them, which meant trying to come into the Empire.

Whatever the cultural influences going out—and they are visible in such far-flung places as Taxila in the Punjab, or among the Celts of Britain—it is easy (and sometimes too tempting) to exaggerate the reverse process, except in religion. Astrology from Babylon, the god Mithra, and the old Zoroastrian dual principle of Light and Darkness from Persia spread rapidly through the Empire. Again one must not exaggerate: apart from these examples, the great matrix of religious innovation was *within* the Empire, in its eastern regions: Egypt, Syria and Palestine, Asia Minor. And, of course, in the end the triumphant contribution from that area in this period was Christianity.

All this outruns the Year One by centuries, and it must be confessed that it was a decisive year only by convention, thanks to the slight error committed by Dionysius Exiguus. Nevertheless, the victory of Augustus and the birth of Christ between them marked out paths for the future, the impact of which cannot possibly be overstated. It is a commonplace to say that European civilization (and therefore American, too) has three roots, Greek, Roman, and Judaeo-Christian. But it has become a commonplace because it is so obviously true. The Romanization of western Europe, for which the Augustan imperial settlement was essential, was one factor that eventually made the idea of Europe possible. The eastern half of the Empire was fundamentally not Romanized, and in the end it broke away, from Rome and from Europe; but it produced and exported to Europe a second binding factor, a common and exclusive religion. These were not the only factors in subsequent European history, to be sure. In history, unlike biology, one must not ask too much of roots. They cannot explain everything. It is enough to understand how deep down they go and what they have contributed.

Classicist Finley, who also contributed the article on slavery in antiquity, pages 56–63 of this volume, has most recently edited the complete works of Flavius Josephus, a first-century Jewish historian under emperors Vespasian and Titus.

THE EMPEROR CLAUDIUS: IDEALIZED VERSION
(For the real Claudius see page 104)

The High Art of Portraiture on

ROMAN COINS

Changing modes of depicting the Caesars mirror the fortunes of the Empire

After the downfall of the initial, spectacular, Roman imperial dynasty, which began with Augustus and ended disastrously with Nero, the first emperor to establish himself successfully, a year or two later, was Vespasian. He was—and wanted to be—a very different sort of man from his glorious or melodramatic predecessors. Augustus had, it is true, started as middle-class, but he and his dynasty rapidly became the last word in aristocracy. Vespasian, on the other hand, was and remained thoroughly and deliberately bourgeois—not least in appearance and expression. Imagine the problem this presented to the designers of the superb Roman coinage. Were they to endow their emperor with as homely and unpretentious an appearance as he possessed, and was indeed proud to possess? Should they, in this way, impress his distinctive personality upon the population of the Empire, or might they, alter-

VESPASIAN: REAL

The rough features of the middle-class emperor appear on this gold aureus, minted at Rome about
A.D. *75 with the inscription* IMP CAESAR VESPASIANVS AVG *(Imperator Caesar Vespasianus Augustus).*

natively, iron out his knobbly features into a more idealized, heroic shape?

There were precedents for both courses of action. And both of them were now adopted simultaneously. One can bring together today two contemporary coins of Vespasian—or portrait busts, for that matter—on which he looks like two quite different men, his rugged self on one, and the approximation of an ideal warrior-monarch on the other (see above and opposite). So it is with the rest of the Roman rulers, too; and as one brilliant artist after another portrays them with great variety on a coinage of incomparable richness and abundance, the whole course of Roman history passes before our eyes, reflected in this medium.

These imperial heads deserve some attention, for several reasons. First, because Roman coin portraiture is extraordinarily good—one of the great arts of antiquity and perhaps, despite its necessarily miniature character, of all time. It is a sobering thought that our own vastly improved technical processes have produced nothing as brilliant; and it is, I think, time to recall the attention of artists and art critics to this remarkable quality, which was amply appreciated by Italians of the Renaissance but is less well-known today. These Roman coin portraits also re-

mind us that we of the twentieth century are not the first to have thought long and carefully about publicity methods. In spite of the absence, in his day, of modern scientific media of communication, there was not much the average Roman emperor failed to understand about publicity. The problem, as he saw it, was to ensure that his regime should be favorably impressed on men's minds, and willingly accepted, from the Atlantic coasts to the mountains of Armenia. It did not escape him, for all the republican frills under which, at first, the imperial regime was concealed, that its greatest potential asset was his own personality —if suitably presented. Accordingly, a multitude of talented sculptors were employed to design the official versions of the portrait busts that were displayed in every township of the vast Roman Empire. These sculptors were mostly non-Roman. It has been said that they were for the most part Greek, but more probably the majority were non-Greek Asians with Hellenized backgrounds and training. Behind them was a tradition of vivid Hellenistic portraiture, of the idealistic conceptions of classical Greece, and in the remote past (how much they knew about it is doubtful) of some masterly heads, massive and miniature alike, of Egyptians and Sumerians from around the Persian Gulf, going back to the third millennium B.C.

VESPASIAN: IDEAL

This heroic depiction of the warrior-monarch circulated during the same period. The coin, also an aureus, is about the size of a dime and contains gold worth about $8.25 in today's market.

Now, under Rome, even these marble busts did not penetrate the Empire so thoroughly as did coins. Every illiterate village and hovel could house the emperor's features on his currency. That fact, added to the economic need for a comprehensive series of issues, explains how, from the beginnings of the Empire, we see the beginnings of a new art form: imperial Roman coin portraiture. And just as the sculptors represented their rulers in a variety of guises intended to correspond with the differing needs and aspects of the Empire and its diverse communities, so the coin engravers used varied techniques—partly on purpose, and partly because they were always prepared to experiment.

Sometimes, the emperor appears in good old unpretentious simplicity, and sometimes with the sophisticated grandeur of Hellenistic Alexander-style monarchy. This variety of interpretations was not unparalleled; in sculpture and coin portraiture alike, there had already been for some centuries, first in Greek lands and then in Italy, a more or less recurrent tug of war between the style that made a man look as he really was and the conception that made him look a quasi-human reflection of the gods. In late republican Rome, after a series of more or less imaginative coin heads of remote ancestors (whose death masks were cherished in the family galleries), Caesar, Brutus, and

Antony had started the fashion for portraits of living men on their coinage. With the possible exception of the Brutus coin—which caught Michelangelo's attention—these portraits, though of great historical interest, do not successfully represent either style or achieve a blend between them. It remained for imperial Rome to exploit their every nuance by all the impressive means at its disposal.

The medium was now an enormous coinage in four metals, of which the most imposing constituents are large pieces made of brass; the emperors had revised and improved the coinage, adding to the customary silver, and more recent gold, a token series of brass and copper (see the note on coinage on pages 106–107). The Roman public had usually suspected a cheat when token coinages were tried upon it, but this experiment succeeded—partly, perhaps, because of the spectacular golden yellow of the brass and the fine deep red of the copper, both more handsome in appearance than the traditional dull-brown bronze.

In general the portrait engravers could interpret their task in two different ways. A ruler could be displayed in ideal guise —as a Hellenistic hero-monarch, or a grand old Roman, or a mixture of the two—or he could be represented "veristically,"

THE JULIAN EMPERORS

AUGUSTUS

To help establish his authority the first emperor stamped coins with his own image —at this time a fairly conventional one.

TIBERIUS

The able, misanthropic second emperor is depicted early in his reign, before he became, if he did, the vile old man described by Tacitus.

CLAUDIUS

This truthful portrait belies the idealized Claudius on page 101. His ungainly appearance concealed a scholarly, if eccentric, mind.

THE HAPPY YEARS

TRAJAN

Statesman and soldier, he pushed the Empire to its farthest boundaries, ushered in what Gibbon considered the happiest age in history.

HADRIAN

Traveling constantly through a prosperous empire, he founded cities, encouraged the arts, ruled the world with wisdom and moderation.

MARCUS AURELIUS

Archetype of the philosopher-king, he lived by the wisdom of his own Meditations. *But his indulgence of his son Commodus led to ruin.*

THE LAST REAL PORTRAITS

DECIUS

An Illyrian of noble descent who claimed to restore the ancient Roman virtues, he was killed in battle by the Goths on the Danube frontier.

GALLIENUS

Nature fitted him for the soft pursuits of philosophy and poetry, but History required him to resist an avalanche of barbarian invasions.

AURELIAN

After stemming the barbarian tide, he staged a glittering triumph in Rome, with Queen Zenobia of Palmyra as his fairest captive.

The Stern Successors

NERO

It took a brilliant artist to convey this image of royal opulence without losing the gross, cruel, sensual aspect of the young monster.

GALBA

A hard-bitten commander, he led the army revolt against Nero, thus ending the Julian line. His severity and greed led to his assassination.

DOMITIAN

Son of Vespasian, scheming brother of the kindly Titus, he tortured flies and senators with equal relish. He, too, was assassinated.

The Gathering Storm

CARACALLA

After murdering his brother in their mother's arms, he went on to wholesale massacre. His image reflects the return of evil times.

MAXIMINUS I

The son of a barbarian peasant, he ruled more as a savage chief than a civilized emperor. He could break a horse's leg with his fist.

PHILIP THE ARAB

A professional robber in his native Arabia, he led an army revolt that made him emperor. He celebrated the 1000th anniversary of Rome in 248.

The Freezing Image

DIOCLETIAN

He halted Rome's decline but assumed the diadem, ritual, and mien of an Oriental monarch. Visitors had to kiss the hem of his robe.

CONSTANTIUS I

A kindly man, the husband of Saint Helena and the father of Constantine, he is shown on this ceremonial piece as the stony-faced reconqueror of Britain.

MAXIMINUS II DAZA

Little human character remains in the image of this emperor, who ruled briefly in Asia Minor before he was overthrown by Licinius in A.D. 313.

FAUSTINA THE ELDER
Ladies of the court appear on coins of the second century. Faustina was the beloved, perhaps unfaithful, wife of Antoninus Pius.

FAUSTINA THE YOUNGER
A great beauty, she was the wife of Marcus Aurelius, who philosophically ignored the constant rumors about her infidelity.

JULIA DOMNA
The power-loving mother of Caracalla, she was one of two Syrian sisters whose influence did much to orientalize the Roman Empire.

with all his peculiarities of feature or personality faithfully delineated or even, in an effort to make him a clear-cut person to his subjects, exaggerated. In the reign of Augustus's grand-nephew Claudius (A.D. 41–54) the conflict between these aims began to be noticeable. On the one hand, this emperor's eccentric, grotesque appearance (as described by Suetonius) cannot even be guessed at from the dignified rejuvenated portrait on his Roman coinages; whereas a more realistic and unflattering portrayal is attempted by the designer of his silver pieces intended for circulation in Asia Minor (compare the versions shown on pages 101 and 104).

The next emperor, Nero, possessed heavy baroque features which inspired his artists to achieve a spectacular synthesis between the two trends. The brass and copper issues of the last four years of his reign (A.D. 64–68) represent a climactic stage in the iconography of the Roman Empire, and indeed of all time. There is a dashing over-all conception, a grand panache owing much to the Hellenistic culture of which the Emperor was a devotee. Yet there is no face lifting of his gross, thick flesh (much too thick for a youth of twenty-six), his small hard mouth, his heavy chin and jowl. Even the Greek naturalistic profusion of his hair is modified by the set and crimped frontal fringe which he adopted in keeping with his popular role as a charioteer. We can never tell *who* designed this or that Roman coin; but it is a fair guess that Nero himself, to the Senate's dismay decidedly artistic, took a hand in approving his own portraits.

A particularly splendid period of coin portraiture was now under way. With Nero's successors, however, designers did not again achieve the same fairly uniform synthesis of ideas about their rulers' features. Galba's stern, old Roman, reaction against Nero's foreign extravagances is mirrored—even in his short reign of a few months (A.D. 68–69)—by interpretations varying between ideal and realistic, conceived with a virtuosity that was greatly to attract Renaissance designers. During the months of

Vitellius's rule, in A.D. 69, some artists presented his gluttonous, degraded features unflinchingly, whereas others made attempts to transform them. And then, in the last period of this outstanding decade of numismatic art, the same contrasted treatment is lavished, as noted earlier, upon Vespasian.

His son Domitian (A.D. 81–96) is generally represented with a somewhat grandiose impersonality, though certain exceptions hint at his morbidly despotic character; and then follows a century in which the great rulers—Trajan, Hadrian, Antoninus Pius, Marcus Aurelius—are almost always invested with an impersonal dignity suited to their roles of untiring, philosophic, benevolent fathers and defenders of their country. Contemporary sculptors follow the same bent. Only rarely is there an endeavor to hint at the nervous, self-torturing restlessness of Hadrian.

In the days of the Antonines, children and youths began to

A NOTE ON THE COINAGE

AUREUS
Gold (worth 25 denarii)

DENARIUS
Silver (worth 4 sestertii)

The emperor Augustus established a bimetallic system with a gold-silver ratio of about 12½ to one. In terms of its silver content, the denarius was worth about 15 cents, but its purchasing power, measured by the price of wheat in the early years of the Empire, was about five times that amount. A legionary's daily pay, in Julius Caesar's time, was ten asses. Values, size, and metallic content of

JULIA MAESA
By intrigue with the army she foisted on Rome her young grandson, a perfumed boy-priest of Baal who became the emperor Elagabalus.

ANNIUS VERUS
Marcus Aurelius struck a special piece with portraits of his handsome sons on the two sides. Annius, the younger, died in childhood.

COMMODUS
The elder boy grew up to break his father's heart and become a brutal emperor whose pleasure was fighting lions in the Colosseum.

appear on statues, coins, and the splendid commemorative medallions which the Roman emperors were now beginning to issue (see above). On one such brass medallion Marcus Aurelius depicts his young sons (the elder of whom, Commodus, was to grow up into a horror). These attractive studies show that children had graduated, in art, from being merely miniature adults—as they were in Greek statuary, even in its last original achievements such as the Laocöon. Now they have a fully realized, if somewhat sentimental, life of their own.

Another attractive and unfamiliar aspect of Roman coin portraiture—one with a great future—was the portrayal not only of the emperor and his male relatives and dependents but, on occasion, of the women of the imperial house. Thus the coinage of the deranged emperor Caligula produces a memorable head of an indomitable lady of the family, his mother, Agrippina the elder.

SESTERTIUS
Bronze (worth 4 asses)

AS
Bronze (worth 4 quadrantes)

all the coins varied over the course of the centuries. The four shown above were minted during the time of Tiberius and are reproduced in their actual size. These are the reverse sides, showing, left to right, the Emperor in a chariot; a figure of Peace or Justice; the deified Augustus; and a rudder superimposed on a round world, symbolizing the vastness of Roman power on land and sea.

Under Vespasian's dynasty some exquisite court ladies, contrasting with their battered-looking males, were displayed with a new fluent sensibility. Then under Trajan we see the severe elderly ladies of his warlike court, Plotina, Marciana, and Matidia, whose only visible extravagance was their monstrously elaborate coiffures. (Did they sleep in their hair?) There are noble posthumous heads of Antoninus Pius's wife Faustina the elder; and her daughter of the same name, the wife of Marcus Aurelius, whatever the truth about her allegedly bad morals, was a beauty. On some coins her feminine expression is as lovingly delineated as her enterprising and constantly changing hair styles (which were imitated in Napoleon's Empire). Certain statues of Roman women had removable tops to their heads, so that a change in fashion did not mean commissioning a whole new statue.

At the turn of the first century and shortly thereafter two Syrian sisters, Julia Domna and Julia Maesa, attained an unprecedented degree of political importance. Domna, wife of the north African Septimius Severus, took to a strange coiffure of rigid waves descending in a heavy lappet over her ears and surmounted by the crescent diadem symbolic of the goddess Diana. Maesa, who had the nerve to place her degenerate grandson Elagabalus on the throne and then to acquiesce (or take the lead) in his forcible replacement by her grandnephew, is plainer, but her features are sharper and no less formidable.

Domna's son Caracalla (A.D. 211–217) is represented, as befitted his revolutionary, pro-army policy, with a more brutal, swashbuckling *élan* than the previous century had witnessed. His portraits are executed with a skill which is a reminder that incipient economic and political collapse made it all the more necessary for emperors and usurpers to master the best possible methods of presenting their features to their dubiously loyal subjects. The result was a new and perhaps uniquely brilliant period of portraiture, in which the struggling military rulers are dramatically displayed in their rapid succession. We see the for-

CONSTANTINE: THE HELLENIC ECHO

On some of his coins the first Christian emperor is still depicted in realistic style, though now with an otherworldly gaze. This is a gold solidus which he minted to replace the devalued aureus.

bidding Thracian strong man Maximinus I (in both an ideal and a realistic version); the fat, bickering Balbinus; Philip the Arab, who amid growing chaos celebrated the millennium of Rome in A.D. 248; Decius, whose scapegoat for disaster was Christianity; his bulletheaded son Hostilian; and the careworn Trebonianus Gallus. Gone are the flowing locks of peaceful monarchy. These —as can also be seen from their remarkable portrait sculpture— are men of close-cropped hair and unshaven jowls, constantly in uniform and on the watch, anxious, and (officially at least) not forgetful of ancient Roman austerity.

With the aid of technical changes (such as the chiseling of the eye's pupil, habitual since the Antonines) the mid third century A.D., quite as much as the first century, is one of portraiture's finest epochs. Gallienus (253–268), at a time of utter disaster and fragmentation, even leads a sort of neo-Hellenic cultural Renaissance, clearly perceptible from his pose (see page 104). It remained for the Illyrian emperor Aurelian, by superhuman efforts, to re-establish unity. And, as he did so, he imprinted upon his coinage one of the very last interpretations of a ruler's persona—except perhaps that of a usurper in Britain, Carausius, a

few years later—in which the impenetrable iron of imperial grandeur is still to some extent modified by human individuality.

A change had come over life in the Empire; the relatively peaceful days of the second century were gone forever. According to Gibbon, that had been the happiest time in world history, and it is at least true that the benefits of the Pax Romana had percolated fairly far down through society. But in the following century the price of survival, and of continuous civil war and invasion, was crushing taxes and ruthless regimentation; and so people looked for solace to other worlds, to pagan mysticism and Christianity. These two factors—grinding autocracy and spiritual otherworldliness—radically affected imperial art. Aurelian began to institute a rigid, orientalized court ceremonial stressing the ruler's remoteness; and this new formalism was soon reflected on the coinage. A great gold medallion of Constantius I, struck in 293 to commemorate his reconquest of Britain from Carausius's successor Allectus, demonstrates that the third-century picture of the hard-bitten military monarch had entered upon a new and more "dead-pan" phase. This was the time when Diocletian standardized the Oriental hierarchy along lines clearly foreshadowing Byzantium, and he and other

CONSTANTINE: THE BYZANTINE FREEZE

On other coins, all mortal expression is gone from the Emperor's countenance. The free portraiture of the classical coinage has now given way, in the changed Empire, to an iconlike formalism.

princes, such as Maximinus II Daza, appear concealed behind an almost expressionless mask of superhuman omnipotence. Maximinus II was one of the last persecutors of the Christians. The stress on austere, formal symbolism reached its climax, and its most carefully thought-out expression, under Constantine the Great (306–337), who made Rome Christian and founded a new Christian capital on the Bosphorus.

Some of his coin portraits infuse a touch of dying Hellenism into the new conception (above opposite); on another the face, flat and non-plastic, is seen frontally (above). Such frontal or three-quarter-face poses had been few and far between since classical Greek days, but now they served to achieve the startling but scarcely mortal intensity which the engraver wished to convey. The human strain of the third century has given place to an ecstatic inhumanity. Hollow, staring eyes tell of the vanity and insignificance of human effort—and of the emperor's inaccessibility to such trivia. This was the spirit in which Constantine's son Constantius II, as he ceremonially entered the former capital city of Rome, sat fixedly aloft in his ceremonial carriage, looking neither to the right nor to the left and raising not so much as a finger to acknowledge the salutations of the crowd. So the pecul-

iar but very un-Roman charms of Byzantine art now prevailed.

There were one or two last blows struck for individualism of a sort, as under Magnentius (350–353). But there was no place left for the vigorous, subtle variations between the real and the ideal which Roman coin portraiture had so fully probed. In doing so, it had set up models for future engravers. It had also set them a standard which none—apart from some Renaissance medalists—have so far been able to exceed, and which modern engravers, with very few exceptions, conspicuously fail to equal.

Michael Grant, a leading scholar of the Roman era, is President and Vice-Chancellor of the Queen's University of Belfast, Northern Ireland. Two of his most recent books are titled The World of Rome *and* Myths of the Greeks and Romans.

Special credit is due the American Numismatic Society in New York City, whose collections provided most of the coins shown in these pages, and to Miss Joan Fagerlie, Assistant Curator of Roman and Byzantine Coins at the Society. Other coins and medallions are from the Bibliothèque Nationale, the Musée d'Arras, the Ashmolean Museum, and the Boston Museum of Fine Arts.

GISLEBERTUS HOC

By FERNAND AUBERJONOIS

FECIT

"Gislebertus made this." Thus, in an age when most artists were anonymous, a medieval sculptor proudly "signed" his lofty tympanum at Autun. Yet only now have experts come to value the full range of his work and his artistry

In November the flood of sightseers drawn to the old Burgundian town of Autun by the famous Romanesque sculptures of its cathedral of St. Lazare has begun to ebb. The pace of life and labor slackens in the surrounding fields and orchards. There is more time then for diligent observation of one's neighbors' actions.

On a gray November day in 1948, Abbé Denis Grivot, choirmaster of St. Lazare, was seen carrying a heavy bundle from the Musée Rolin, a small local museum of assorted antiquities, to the cathedral a hundred yards away. What followed caused astonishment among watchers peering from kitchen windows.

Having stopped outside the main portal, the Abbé took out from the cloth wrapping a head of Christ carved of stone and weighing a good forty pounds. Propped against the cathedral's west entrance was a ladder. With the Savior's head tucked under his arm the choirmaster began a cautious ascent toward the tympanum of sculptured figures above the great doors (illustrated at left). Reaching the top rung, he stood on the same level with a giant, headless, central figure. He lifted the stone head, and the ladder swayed. The priest whispered a short prayer and kept his balance. At last, raising the head above his own, he placed it on the shrouded shoulders.

Abbé Grivot's hunch was right. The head fit perfectly on this tympanum figure of Christ—and thus belonged here rather than in the museum from which he had borrowed it that afternoon for his experiment. Of the many visitors familiar with Autun's art treasures, two art historians had already suggested a possible relationship between head and body. But it had remained for the choirmaster to put his own guess to the practical test.

This was the first hesitant step toward a goal vastly more ambitious than any onlooker outside the cathedral that day could have suspected. It was an adventure in rediscovering and reassembling the phenomenal wealth of St. Lazare's twelfth-century sculpture—figures on the capitals of tall piers, in lofty niches of the apse or tympanum, many of them out of reach of everyday sight and some long since fragmented or dispersed—with the result of identifying one particular sculptor, by name Gislebertus, as the creator of virtually all of this. So distinctive is his style, so powerful and original are the concepts embodied in the hundreds of stone figures at St. Lazare when seen together and at close hand, that this Gislebertus—working in a time when cathedral builders and sculptors were all but anonymous—has now

Christ presiding at the Last Judgment is the subject of the theological panorama above the main portal of Autun Cathedral; Gislebertus's "signature" is carved directly below the Savior's feet. Recently restored, this work has given the clue to his others.

been hailed in France as that country's earliest major artist of name in terms of time, and as the greatest single master to have worked in the entire Romanesque era.

To be sure, Gislebertus himself had signed his crowning work, the St. Lazare tympanum—a vast theological panorama depicting the joys and punishments of the Last Judgment—with the proud inscription, *"Gislebertus hoc Fecit"* ("Gislebertus made this"). Never before had the clergy permitted a master carver to take up so much prominent space for self-glorification. But until Abbé Grivot set out to determine the true scope of Gislebertus's work, no thought had been given to the hypothesis that a single artist had conceived almost all the statuary of the great cathedral, inside as well as out.

The more the Abbé looked at the surviving carvings throughout his edifice, the more he had become impressed with similarities in their style, composition, and facial expression. Everywhere he found the Gislebertus touch—an approach marked not only by striking elongation of the body but by extraordinary freedom of movement and expression, by drapery that reveals the human form, whereas in other works of the time, it conceals it, and by dramatic, open handling of space at variance with the crowded clusters of shapes one usually finds in Romanesque art.

It took Grivot twelve years to complete his search for clues—for lost stones, for scattered heads and angels' wings among the dust and rubble. Over the generations bits of human and animal anatomy had been scattered from St. Lazare in all directions, one angel from its north portal coming to rest as far away as the Cloisters of New York City's Metropolitan Museum. As his studies grew, an enterprising British publisher, Arnold Fawcus, conceived the idea of a definitive study of Gislebertus's work. Fawcus in turn brought in one of Europe's foremost experts on medieval church art, Professor George Zarnecki of the Courtauld Institute of London University, who joined with the Abbé to produce the richly illustrated monograph, *Gislebertus: Sculpteur d'Autun*. The photographs accompanying this article are taken from the American edition of this work, which was recently published in the United States by the Orion Press.

Grivot, the modest Burgundian priest, and Zarnecki, the Polish-born London professor (a graduate of Kraków University and a veteran of the Polish army in World War II), combined to offer a mass of evidence presenting Gislebertus as the most imaginative and productive sculptor of his era; and it was this evidence, when made the subject of an official French exhibition in 1960 of great impact upon the art world, that prompted André Malraux, President De Gaulle's Minister of Culture, to describe Gislebertus as *"le Cézanne du Moyen Age."*

But who was Gislebertus? And why was his art, now belatedly come into renown, so long forgotten or obscure? Who, furthermore, in times past undertook to destroy it—covering up his whole masterful tympanum with plaster, for instance, and chopping off the head of Christ when it still emerged?

Of Gislebertus, or Gillebert, the man, next to nothing is known. But with some knowledge of Romanesque art we may attempt a portrait. He lived in Burgundy long enough for fellow Burgundians like Abbé Grivot to claim him as a native son. He is believed to have worked at Autun from 1125 to 1135. He may have received his early training in one of the rock quarries that were then the focal points of the building trade, and where a skilled mason supervised a number of apprentices. There were, of course, no art or architectural schools then. Gislebertus, like his fellow carvers, started on simple figures and low-relief foliage, then progressed to deep carving. His apprenticeship over, he is believed to have worked on the decoration of the Benedictine abbey of Cluny and, later, the church of La Madeleine at Vézelay.

He is not thought to have been a monk, but as a close associate of churchmen, he may have received a fairly thorough education. We do not know whether Gislebertus, like some of his colleagues, belonged to the guild of *Mortelliers et Tailleurs de Pierre*, or whether he used the quaint title of *Doctor Latomorum* —doctor in stone carving.

Dr. Zarnecki suggests that Gislebertus may have been a member of the team that created Vézelay's great tympanum, from 1120 to 1125. If so, his supervisor was the unnamed "Master of the Tympanum," regarded as Cluny's most important sculptor as well. Again, the only clues are stone fragments from Cluny and Vézelay which bear the imprint of Gislebertus's talent.

Assuming that Gislebertus was intimately associated with these most ambitious architectural ventures of his time and of the region in which he lived—Cluny and Vézelay—what is known of his one-man effort at Autun?

It was in about the year 1120 that Hugues II, duke of Burgundy, and Bishop Etienne de Bâgé undertook the building of a

TEXT CONTINUED ON PAGE 121

Gislebertus, Master of Autun: A Portfolio

Both inside and out, the twelfth-century Romanesque cathedral of St. Lazare (left) in the Burgundian countryside is ornamented with sculptures now found to have been carved by one man of stirring originality and power. The following eight pages present major examples of his work, some of it long dispersed or obscured from view. At right, crowning a column where nave and crossing meet, is his relief of God interrogating Cain ("Where is Abel, thy brother?"). On the following spread, another capital portrays the sleep of the Magi after their journey to the new-born Christ and God's warning to them in a dream not to return to Herod.

112

PORTFOLIO PHOTOGRAPHS ARE FROM *Gislebertus, Sculptor of Autun*, PUBLISHED 1961 BY THE ORION PRESS, NEW YORK, AND TRIANON PRESS; PHOTOGRAPHED BY FRANCHESCHI (PAGES 116–117) AND HERB (PAGES 118–119)

At left, at the top of an interior column, Gislebertus portrays Judas hanged from a tree in punishment for his betrayal, flanked by grimacing devils. Above, finely-wrought forms represent signs of the zodiac (Pisces and Scorpio) in the molding of the tympanum over the main portal; below, in the lintel at the base of the same (see pages 110–111) a mortal is seized by a demon's hands.

117

TEXT CONTINUED FROM PAGE 112

new cathedral at Autun. Both men must have had great respect and possibly friendship for the sculptor whom they now engaged to provide ornaments for its portals outside and its piers within. Today a visitor to the cathedral of St. Lazare is bound to wonder how any one man, in the space of only ten years, could have accomplished so much. There are, in Autun's own Bible of stone, four hundred figures. Among them, Jesus is portrayed sixteen times, Peter six times, Judas once (hanging by the neck), all the Apostles, thirty angels busy with a variety of chores, eighteen devils, sixty leading characters of the Old and New Testaments, thirty lesser personages—eighty-six figures in the tympanum alone. Also there are seventy animals, wild and domestic, and twelve monsters serving Satan.

Stone carving is and always has been a time consuming art. To those who doubt Gislebertus's tour de force, Dr. Zarnecki says, "At the St. Isidorus cloister of León, Spain, I met a stone carver who, without formal training and with tools as crude as those used by Gislebertus, could turn out a high-relief capital in a week. Gislebertus could have done it."

When Gislebertus went to work at Autun in 1125, stone carving was no longer done in the quarry. He may have had his own "studio," a shed near the construction site, with a level area of sand on which to assemble the twenty-nine blocks of the tympanum—three times as many as at Vézelay. Fitting them together required superior skill. Assistants prepared the blocks and carved the simpler ornamental patterns, such as leaves and conventional designs, for the highest pillars. But with the exception of two scenes attributed to his pupils, Messrs. Zarnecki and Grivot hold that he did all the carving himself.

He started with the capitals for the apse, nave, and choir. Later he concentrated on portal decorations. He must have worked ceaselessly. By 1135 he had finished, although the cathedral itself was not completed. Eleven years after his departure, in fact, builders were still working on it.

We do not know where Gislebertus went from there, or what he did thereafter. His trace is lost; only his work remains—though, unfortunately, not all of it.

During the French Revolution anticlerical fanatics carried out wholesale desecration of religious sculpture. Yet not all the spoliation that overtook medieval devotional art can be attributed to them. Shortly after the mid-eighteenth century, and a full generation before the Revolution, the Church itself did considerable artistic "house cleaning" of its own, replacing Romanesque carvings then looked on as barbaric with ornaments more suited to the era's new-found Greco-Roman taste. Thus at the great pilgrimage church of Conques in the Dordogne, the polychrome twelfth-century tympanum was plastered over; at St. Denis, whole sculptures were removed. Such, also, was the case of St. Lazare, where in 1766 the clergy had mortar spread over the Gislebertus tympanum of the west front, and in the process removed the head of Christ because it projected too far forward to be covered up. One of the three archivolts above the tympanum, showing a procession of twenty-four Patriarchs and Prophets, at the same time was completely chiseled away.

The north portal of St. Lazare suffered even more grievous harm. Here Gislebertus had portrayed the resurrection of Lazarus, as well as Satan, Adam, and a magnificent Eve whose gesture at the moment she picks the fatal apple is an unrivaled example of absent-minded detachment (see pages 118–119). Of the main figures that adorned this entrance, only Eve has survived. She disappeared for years, having been carted down to the foot of the hill where the large stone on which she is carved served as building material for a house constructed in 1769. There she remained hidden for a century until that dwelling in turn was torn down. Today she has become the prize exhibit of the local Musée Rolin, and Abbé Grivot still hopes to find a companion Adam in the walls or foundations of some other building of Autun. His search has been narrowed down to a few likely sites, the owners of which are co-operative—more so than the butcher, in a town farther south, who chased Dr. Zarnecki with a meat cleaver when the visiting professor asked to see medieval sculptures embedded in the wall of his cellar.

Although it was the classicizing eighteenth century that set out to mask or dismantle such work as Gislebertus's, it is well to recall that a reaction against the vivid, sometimes all-too-vivid imagery it exemplified had set in centuries earlier—even in Gislebertus's own day. In 1125, when his work at St. Lazare was just beginning, his renowned fellow Burgundian, St. Bernard, abbot of Clairvaux, wrote in a celebrated letter: "The Church inlays the stones of cathedrals with gold but leaves her sons naked. . . . Why, in an age when so many of our brothers can read, such ridiculous monsters, such abhorrent deformities? What are they doing here—these revolting apes, ferocious lions, centaurs, spotted tigers, and horn-blowing hunters . . . everywhere a variety of shapes so astonishing that the worshipper finds it more entertaining to read stones than books. Great God! Even if no sense of shame surges at the sight of such futility, why not at least deplore the high cost of it all."

The canons of St. Lazare who, six hundred years later, objected to Romanesque sculptures because they found them obscure, alien, apocalyptic, or simply sacrilegious, were less eloquent than St. Bernard. But they caused more damage.

Nevertheless, the Autun tympanum survived the ordeal. In 1837 archaeologists, guided by early descriptions of the west portal in its original condition, probed the mortar and discovered Gislebertus's Last Judgment. By that time, no one in Autun remembered or had even heard of the hidden treasure, though it had been masked for only seventy years. The tympanum, with its giant enthroned Christ presiding over the weighing of souls, was restored by Viollet-le-Duc in 1858, who replaced a number of damaged pieces by copies but left the Christ itself headless. So it has remained for a Burgundian priest, a Polish art historian, and a British publisher in our own day to complete the work of uncovering the triumphs of one of the West's greatest sculptural masters of all time.

Fernand Auberjonois, London correspondent for the Toledo Blade, reports frequently on art finds on the Continent.

Preceding spread: In one of his most brilliant Autun sculptures (recovered from rubble and now preserved in the local museum, for the north portal that bore it was stripped of its figures two centuries ago) Gislebertus represents Eve plucking the fatal apple with an absent-mindedness that suggests a James Thurber drawing. Opposite, a capital gives the master the occasion to carve his tender portrait of the Holy Family's escape into Egypt.

121

Met in bloody war for the Holy Land, the champions of Christendom

and Islam gave the medieval world a lesson in the honor of kings

By ALFRED DUGGAN

On June 8, 1191, King Richard Coeur de Lion joined the besiegers of Acre, who were themselves besieged by the great army of Saladin. He was thirty-three years old and already a veteran; since he was sixteen he had led armies. He was not only a brave knight but also a skilled commander, especially expert in siegecraft and in the dull business of looking after supplies. He was tall and fair and amazingly handsome; he was as well known for his poetry as for his courage, and he loved beauty in every form. He could inspire in his followers a lifelong devotion. But there were weaknesses in his character. His witty poet's tongue could say unforgivable things; in any company he must be first; he was stern, unyielding, truculent, and avaricious.

For two years he had been king of England, but his throne was not secure; John, his younger brother, would displace him if he could. Nonetheless, he and King Philip of France had sworn to reclaim the Holy Land together. After a winter spent in Sicily, and a detour by Richard to Cyprus (a conquest that later proved to be one of his shrewdest moves), they moved on separately to join the Third Crusade already in progress in Outremer on the Palestine coast.

On the European continent, France and England had been quarreling for a generation. Recently Richard had made matters worse by refusing to marry Philip's sister Alice, to whom he had been betrothed since childhood, giving as reason the rumors that she had been his father's mistress. To clinch the matter, Richard's mother brought Princess Berengaria of Navarre down to Sicily, and Richard married her on the island of Cyprus.

Relations between the two monarchs could scarcely have

been worse. And although Richard had brought to Acre a finer body of troops and a larger sum of money than Philip, he could not command an army that contained the king of France because, as duke of Aquitaine, he had previously done homage to Philip. So Richard's intention was to clear up the mess in Outremer and get home as soon as possible, before trouble broke out in England.

However, the mess in Outremer presented many complications. Almost one hundred years earlier, in 1095, Pope Urban II had called upon Christian Europe to rescue the Holy Land from the infidels. In that First Crusade groups of Frankish and Norman knights had assembled large retinues, crossed Europe, fought their way through Asia Minor, and finally managed to wrest Jerusalem from its Egyptian rulers.

But these restless, ambitious adventurers had come to make their own fortunes as much as to restore the Holy Places. Each knight seized and secured what he could for himself, warring constantly with his Christian neighbors. Thus the Christian community was scarcely unified. It consisted principally of the kingdom of Jerusalem, which stretched from the Egyptian border to Beirut, and three associated states of Antioch, Tripoli, and Edessa, covering what is now Syria, Lebanon, and southeast Turkey. Edessa was retaken by the Moslems in 1144; its fall occasioned a second and wholly unsuccessful crusade.

Each of the remaining states was governed by hereditary descendants of the original knights, who carried on the feuds of their forebears. Toward the end of the twelfth century the king of Jerusalem, a leper, died childless, leaving two sisters whose marriages assumed supreme political importance. Sibylla, the elder sister, married Guy de Lusignan, a native of France, and they became king and queen of Jerusalem. Her teen-age half sister, Isabella, married Humphrey of Toron, the son of a native baron.

King Guy was heartily disliked by all of the local seigneurs because he was both ineffectual and a foreigner. The ensuing quarrels so weakened the Christian community that in 1187 Saladin, sultan of Egypt and Syria, marched upon the Christians at Hattin, captured King Guy, and destroyed most of the Christian forces. The Moslems then swept through Judaea, taking the Holy City and many castles of the hill country. When news of this disaster reached Europe, the Pope called for a third crusade.

By the end of the year, the Christians held only the seaport of Tyre, and that had been preserved by a strange stroke of luck. Its frightened defenders had already asked for terms when Conrad of Montferrat, arriving from Constantinople, rallied the city to hold out until reinforcements could save it. Conrad became thereby a local hero. Most of the lay barons through Outremer rallied to him, and it was suggested that he marry Princess Isabella, which would at least give him a rival claim to the throne of Guy and Sibylla.

Conrad was said to have left one wife in Italy and another in Constantinople; and Isabella's marriage to Humphrey of Toron was annulled rather against her will. She liked the gentle, charming young man who had been kind to her, and she did not at all fancy the rough old soldier. (Humphrey, who had homosexual leanings, had neglected to consummate the marriage. Later he and Richard, who was rumored to be too fond of handsome young men, became close friends, which did not help matters.)

When King Philip of France reached Acre in April, 1191, six weeks before Richard, he encountered a strong movement to displace King Guy and make Conrad king of Jerusalem. The barons of the kingdom, sprung from French families, treated Philip as their natural lord; he in turn willingly supported their favorite, Conrad. Richard, upon arrival, backed Guy, partly because he refused to accept any of Philip's notions and partly because King Guy came from Richard's French domain of Poitou. Shortly thereafter a compromise was made whereby Guy would retain the crown during his lifetime (Sibylla had died without surviving issue), and Conrad would then assume the throne. This decision pleased no one and lasted only eight months.

Richard had other enemies. Because his sister Matilda was married to Henry the Lion, a hated foe of the Hohenstaufen emperors, the German Crusaders who preceded both the French and the English at Acre also distrusted him. Thus Richard went into battle with the French, most of the native barons, and the Germans all hostile to him for different reasons. His was not an enviable position.

But Saladin, encamped behind the besiegers of Acre, saw only that the Christian army had been reinforced by a mighty warrior. He made even greater efforts to relieve his blockaded city, for a great defeat might destroy his power. Saladin was a self-made sultan. He lacked the prestige of hereditary rule, and unless he led his men to victory and

A herald wearing the combined coat-of-arms of France and England welcomes two ladies to Sicily in 1190, where Richard and Philip spent the winter before journeying to the Holy Land. The women may be Richard's mother and his betrothed, Berengaria of Navarre.

The immediate cause of the Third Crusade was the fall of Jerusalem in 1187. Here Saladin, bedecked with crown and scepter, supervises the siege of the city walls. These illustrations from a French manuscript are based on the chronicles of the Christian crusader William of Tyre.

plunder they would desert him. His horsemen were Turks or Kurds (he was himself a Kurd); his foot, Sudanese; and his indispensable sappers and miners, Egyptian. All his soldiers hated the climate of the unhealthy coast, ravaged and stinking after four years of war. They would not stay unless they were paid punctually, and the money to pay them could come only from Egypt.

In 1191 Saladin was fifty-three and in poor health. But the Holy War was the great object of his life and, when his doctors warned him that a long stay in the hot plain would be fatal, he answered with a proverb: "Kill me and Malek, kill Malek with me." That had been spoken long ago by an Arab champion, struggling wounded on the ground with the leader of the enemy. Perhaps it had a more topical application, for in Arabic *el Malek* means "the King." Sixty years later, during the Crusade of St. Louis, Saracens would still say to a restive horse: "Do you think *el Malek* is after you?" They did not mean King Philip or King Guy; to Moslems *el Malek* could be no one but Richard, king of England.

Saladin had won his dominions in war, but he did not charge at the head of his troops. In battle his station was with the reserve; there is no record that he ever used his sword, save to kill unarmed prisoners after victory. Yet he was fearless, and if his army seemed to be beaten he would hold his ground to the last.

In every respect he was the pattern of a Moslem ruler. Though he never found time amid the cares of state to make the pilgrimage to Mecca, he said his prayers regularly and kept the Fast of Ramadan. He loved to listen to readings from the holy books, even while he rode down the front of a hostile army.

His almsgiving was so generous that when he died only one gold dinar remained in his treasury. To his subjects he was just, and even to Christians he kept his given word. His mercy was famous; but it was a Moslem mercy, not to be judged by Christian standards. When Jerusalem surrendered to him there were 60,000 Christian refugees in the town, and he set their ransom at the moderate figure of ten dinars a man. The money in the city treasury was reckoned toward this ransom, though Saladin might have claimed it as booty; to please his brother Saphadin, he freed a thousand captives and permitted the patriarch to beg off another seven hundred. Yet so many slaves remained that a pair of old shoes would buy a man.

While he lay before Acre, a Christian woman came from the crusaders' camp seeking audience with the sultan; she begged him to return her baby girl, stolen by Saracen soldiers. Saladin found the child, restored her to her mother, and returned both to the Christian camp—although he himself had organized this corps of Arab marauders.

As a young man he had served in the Egyptian civil wars alongside the army of Christian Jerusalem; it was said that he had been knighted by old Humphrey of Toron, grandfather of young Humphrey. He knew the type of behavior expected from Christian knights and, though he was not habitually chivalrous, he could answer chivalry in kind. When, in 1183, he suddenly attacked Kerak, that remote castle southeast of the Dead Sea was full of guests come to

Brutality was familiar to both Moslems and Christians during the fighting. Saladin's sense of honor did not prevent him from severing the head of Reynald of Châtillon with a stroke of his sword after that undisciplined lord had raided a rich Arab desert caravan.

Such cruelty was outdone by Richard, who calmly watched the slaughter of 2,700 Moslem survivors in Acre after the city had been won by the Christians in the summer of 1191. The decapitated prisoners in their white robes are stacked beneath the wooden gallows.

124

the wedding of Humphrey of Toron and Princess Isabella. With cheerful defiance the chatelaine announced that since the great sultan had come to the wedding he must share in the feast; she sent out her servants with the best dishes and the best wine. In return Saladin gave orders that the tower which sheltered bride and bridegroom must not be bombarded.

We know nothing of Saladin's married life; but he had seventeen sons and at least one daughter, and took pains to bring them up properly. When the boys wished to join in a massacre of Christian prisoners he forbade it, explaining to his puzzled councilors that the children were too young to understand the true religion; if they were encouraged to kill helpless Christians, they might think it right to kill helpless Moslems.

When Richard reached the camp before Acre in June, 1191, the Moslem and Christian armies had been in close contact for three years, and truces were frequent, official or unofficial. It was natural that Richard, as soon as he arrived, should send envoys to Saladin; he was eager to meet the champion of Islam, who in a single battle had overthrown a kingdom. His first request was merely for an interview. Saladin answered that kings should not meet while they were at war, though if peace came he would be delighted to see him. Though Richard returned to this project more than once, the two leaders never met save on the battlefield, and never in single combat.

Richard was madly curious to learn more about his great antagonist. Again he sent his envoy, a Moroccan noble who had long been a captive in Christian hands (trustworthy interpreters were always hard to find). This time his mission was frivolous in the extreme. The envoy announced that Richard had some fine hawks that he would like to send as a present to Saladin; but the hawks were sick, and in the besieged camp of the besiegers of Acre they could not get the fresh food they needed. Would Saladin please send them some chickens?

Saladin willingly sent the poultry, though he said with a laugh that he knew Richard would eat them. He added a suggestion that any further envoys should be sent to Saphadin, his brother and the second lord in his dominions. Saladin may have been genuinely busy, or this may have been a barbed reminder that, while King Philip lay before Acre, Richard was only the second lord in the Christian army. Richard then asked if he might meet Saphadin. This request was granted, and a three-day truce was arranged to cover the interview. But Richard fell sick, like most other newcomers to the unhealthy coastal plain, and for the time being the project was abandoned.

Throughout July envoys passed to and fro. Richard sent the hawks and other Western curiosities; Saladin in return sent fruit and snow, precious luxuries in the blockaded camp. There was a sound political reason for these contacts.

The Moslem leaders in Acre were preparing to surrender, and Richard wished to make sure that Saladin knew it.

The surrender took place on July 12. King Philip promptly went home three weeks later to snatch at Richard's French holdings (and, some say, to intrigue with his brother John). In the tangled negotiations that followed, Richard spoke for the whole Christian army. The Moslems in Acre had offered to buy their lives by handing over three things which were not theirs to give: a large sum of money, the True Cross (captured at Hattin), and a hundred named Christian knights. Saladin eagerly collected the money; he was reluctant to hand over the True Cross, though he would probably have done so under pressure; but he failed to produce the named prisoners. On August 11 Richard's envoys refused to accept the money alone, though tempting sacks of gold were actually brought to their tent. On the twentieth, recognizing that the agreed ransom would never be handed over, Richard killed the Saracen soldiers in the surrendered garrison, along with their wives and children, to the number of 2,700, though a few wealthy emirs bought their lives by the offer of large individual ransoms. It is worth noting that, although modern historians reproach Richard, Saladin continued to negotiate and thought none the worse of him.

Having gained one impressive victory, Richard decided to march sixty miles south to Jaffa, which had fallen to the Moslems after Hattin. On September 5, during the march, Richard himself went out to Saphadin under a flag of truce. He offered to go home and leave the Moslems in peace— if Saladin would evacuate the whole kingdom of Jerusalem. He cannot have expected that his proposal would be accepted; but perhaps that was merely a convenient way of publishing his maximum demand on the eve of a great battle that he hoped would be decisive.

The Battle of Arsuf, on September 7, was indeed a Christian victory, although the Moslems were more frightened than hurt; the Turkish horse fled so fast that few were killed. But to Saladin it was a heavy blow. He ruled these men only because he led them to victory; if he made a habit of being beaten, as he had been beaten at Acre and Arsuf, they would find another sultan. Grimly he prepared to stand a siege in Jerusalem; for if he retired from that great conquest his army would desert him.

Richard delayed in Jaffa to secure a base of operations where he could receive supplies from his fleet. Also, he had been talking with the knights of his army, and it must suddenly have been brought home to him that he could not win the war. Every pilgrim was eager to assault the Holy City; but every pilgrim would go home as soon as he had prayed in the Holy Sepulchre. Jerusalem could not be held by the barons of the kingdom, split between Conrad and Guy, and their allies from Europe would not stay to help them. Richard, strong in the prestige of Arsuf, sat down to think out the best terms such prestige would bring him.

Wearing their crowns, King Philip II of France (left) and King Richard I of England (right) set out from Vézélay on July 4, 1189, with their knights and infantry. This unity of purpose temporarily halted the royal feuds that had kept France and England at war.

He chose a good envoy: Humphrey of Toron, the brave, epicene warrior whose grandfather had bestowed on the youthful Saladin the girdle of knighthood. Humphrey spoke Arabic well and needed no interpreter; Saphadin knew and liked him, and Saphadin was nearby at Lydda.

To Saphadin, Humphrey propounded a reasonable compromise. Let Saladin retire from Jerusalem and the western half of the kingdom, as far as the line of the Jordan; and the True Cross, of no value to Saladin, should be returned. Saladin also had been thinking things over. The coastal plain was deadly, not only to himself but to his army; he began to see that he would never conquer the Christian ports. In his answer to Richard, Saladin said that he would never yield Jerusalem. (Perhaps he managed to convey that he dared not, lest such a retreat should cost him his throne.) Though one day he might return the True Cross, the great

prize must be dearly bought. Yet he still wished for peace. Could Richard make another offer?

Richard answered with a plan for the neutralization of the Holy Places, a plan quite unmedieval in its practical forethought. But since this was still the twelfth century, the foundation of the scheme was a royal marriage. Richard had with him in Jaffa his sister Joan, the widowed queen of Sicily. He offered to make over to her his conquests in Outremer, the strip of land he had conquered between Tyre and Ascalon. Let Saladin give his brother the whole of Palestine; then Joan should marry Saphadin. The plan was worked out in elaborate detail. The royal pair would reign in Jerusalem, which would be open to pilgrims of every faith; in each town there would be separate Moslem and Christian quarters; all prisoners held by either side should be freed without ransom; the Templars and Hospitallers would return to their castles, so that Christians would have armed protection.

As a scheme for the government of Palestine the plan had great merits. In the proposed realm of King Saphadin and Queen Joan, Arab peasants, both Christian and Moslem, would till their fields in peace, as they do in Jordan today; Christian pilgrims would visit Jerusalem and go home again; in the ports, Italian traders would do business under an alien government, as in Alexandria and other Moslem markets. Turkish emirs and the knights of the military orders would keep the peace in open country.

But the plan was in advance of public opinion. When the Crusaders heard of it they were deeply shocked, so shocked that the loyal English compiler of the *Itinerarium Regis Ricardi* does not mention it. Joan, furious, announced that she would never marry a Moslem. Then Richard asked Saphadin whether he would consider turning Christian and got the answer he must have expected. Saladin chuckled to see the champion of the Cross in such a false position. He at once made things more difficult by giving his solemn assent, and then sat back to see how Richard would extricate himself.

To save his darling project, Richard offered his niece Eleanor of Brittany in place of Joan, but Saphadin would accept no substitute. The scheme was buried. Richard advanced to Beit-Nuba, within twelve miles of Jerusalem, but changed his mind and marched south to Ascalon. That gave him a valuable bargaining counter; a Christian army at Ascalon could cut the road between Syria and Egypt, severing Saladin's recruiting ground from his principal source of revenue.

Therefore, at the end of March, Saladin for the first time made overtures for peace, instead of waiting for Richard's envoys. Saphadin came down to Ascalon with an offer: the Franks might have all the coast cities they had conquered and in addition the harbor of Beirut; they would enjoy free access to the Holy Sepulchre, and as a bonus, the True Cross would be returned. For a fortnight Saphadin was entertained as Richard's guest, and during the festivities Richard knighted his son. But the negotiations petered out.

Reports had reached Richard of his brother's constant encroachment in England. But before he could leave the Holy Land, he had to settle the rivalry between King Guy and Conrad. King Guy consented to abdicate, taking Cyprus as compensation; then Conrad, the unanimous choice of the barons, was murdered by Assassins (the followers of the Old Man of the Mountain whose motive for the crime is still obscure). Eventually a compromise candidate was found, nephew to both King Richard and King Philip. When Henry of Champagne was proclaimed king of Jerusalem, Richard at last had the support of every Frank in Outremer. To cement his claim Henry married Isabella,

then twenty-one, seven days after her husband's death.

In June, Richard led his united army for the second time to Beit-Nuba, only to learn that the wells between Beit-Nuba and Jerusalem had been destroyed. His army could not live without water, so in July he retired to Jaffa. From thence he sent envoys to Saladin; at last the long negotiation seemed to be leading to a settlement.

If Richard would evacuate Ascalon, Saladin offered not only peace but friendship with the new King Henry: the Franks might dwell undisturbed on the coast and their priests could minister in the Holy Places. Richard still argued, hoping to gain these terms and keep Ascalon too, but peace seemed so near that he moved north two weeks later to Acre, planning to embark for Europe.

Suddenly Saladin swooped on weakly held Jaffa, marching down from Jerusalem in one day, July 27. Since Arsuf, in the previous September, he had been on the defensive, and Richard was taken unawares. Within three days the Moslems breached the town wall, and the small garrison retreated to the castle. But Richard hastened to the rescue.

In the chapter of accidents that followed, Saladin was an eyewitness to the deeds of the Christian hero, though still the two leaders never met in a parley. Richard left Acre by sea, while his army marched south by the coast road. When he was delayed by contrary winds his army, not wishing to fight without him, loitered on the march. On the thirty-first he reached Jaffa, only to see Moslem banners on the town wall. He thought he had come too late, but a brave priest swam out from the beleaguered castle and explained the situation. Richard had with him only eighty dismounted knights, a handful of crossbows, and the Italian sailors of his ships. He waded ashore, and with this small force drove the Moslems from Jaffa.

Next morning Saladin sent his chamberlain to seek peace, still offering large concessions in return for Ascalon. Abu Bekr found Richard joking with some captured emirs, explaining that Jaffa had been guaranteed to hold out for three months—yet Saladin had taken it in three days and he, Richard, had won it back in three hours. He had hurried so fast to the fight that he had charged still wearing his boating slippers.

Richard would not yield Ascalon, but he offered to hold it as a fief under Saladin. This might have worked if there had been a genuine peace: there was no compelling reason why Christian knights should not fight for Saladin against his Moslem enemies. But Saladin did not trust feudal tenures, and the offer was refused.

Richard and his escort encamped outside the walls of Jaffa, for the town was littered with unburied dead. The Moslems, while killing the unarmed citizens, had also killed all the pigs, and fragments of pork had been deliberately

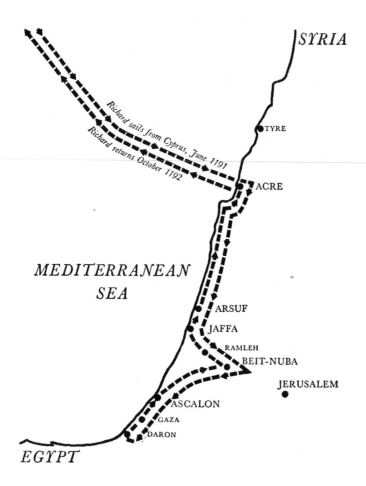

SYRIA

MEDITERRANEAN
SEA

TYRE

ACRE

ARSUF

JAFFA

RAMLEH

BEIT-NUBA

JERUSALEM

ASCALON

GAZA

DARON

EGYPT

Richard sails from Cyprus, June 1191

Richard returns October 1192

Richard's route in the Holy Land mainly followed the coastline to the south. His only moves inland were to Ramleh and Beit-Nuba, where he was stopped by the Moslems in two unsuccessful attempts to reach Jerusalem. This failure eventually forced him to sign a peace treaty with Saladin and make his way back to Acre, where he withdrew from Palestine sixteen months after his arrival at that same port.

mingled with fragments of Christians; so burial was a slow process. The Frankish army had still not arrived when, on August 5, Saladin made a sudden assault on the unwalled bivouac.

Richard had about 2,000 men, and only fifteen horses. With this force he withstood the attack of 7,000 Turkish cavalry. In the afternoon Saladin, watching from his usual post with the reserve, saw Richard counterattack. Then suddenly the King of England was down, his horse killed under him. Overwhelmed by such a display of courage, Saladin made the noblest gesture of his life. Through the thick of battle he sent a groom, leading two horses as a gift to his brave enemy. At the end of the day the Moslems marched back in good order to Jerusalem.

Negotiations began again. The usual presents were exchanged: fruit and snow for Western hawks and hounds. In the end Richard agreed to evacuate Ascalon, after dismantling its fortifications. In return Saladin promised five years of peace. Pilgrims would be welcome in Jerusalem and Latin priests might serve in the Holy Places, Nazareth and Bethlehem as well as the Sepulchre. Most important of all,

because Outremer needed the ships and trade of Italian merchants, Moslems would be free to trade with the Christian ports.

The treaty was signed on September 2. At once a crowd of Western Crusaders visited the Sepulchre and then took the next ship home; Moslem emirs visited Jaffa to spend their pay on Western trinkets, and then returned to Saladin. That had been from the beginning Richard's handicap; his men would go home when they had fulfilled the pilgrimage, but Saladin's men were already at home.

Richard refused the humiliation of an unarmed visit to Jerusalem; on October 9 he embarked. Before leaving he sent a last message to Saladin, boasting that when the five years of peace were over he would come back to storm the Holy City. Saladin answered courteously that he would do his best to hold it, but that if God willed otherwise, Richard was the man most worthy to conquer it.

Saladin had retained his conquests at the cost of his life. He died on March 4, 1193, in his fifty-fifth year, worn out by his exertions. His heirs were his seventeen sons; but by 1201, Saphadin, that experienced, cosmopolitan diplomatist, had displaced them all and ruled over Syria and Egypt.

As king of England Richard was a failure; only in Outremer did he show himself a statesman. His plan for a neutral kingdom of Jerusalem might have satisfied all parties if he could have persuaded his sister to marry a Moslem. He perceived that military victory was within his reach and that military victory would dissolve his army. Then he perceived that Ascalon would be a standing threat to Saladin. To the end he bargained boldly and saved what could be saved—a thin strip ninety miles long and less than ten miles wide. But because he had given it an indispensable base in Cyprus, the kingdom of Jerusalem endured for another century. Of how many statesmen can it be said that their gains endure for a hundred years? And besides his achievements as a diplomatist and general, Richard was personally the best warrior in his army.

Saladin was no warrior. But he could recognize gallantry in others, and his gesture to Richard outside Jaffa is something in which both Christian and Moslem may take pride. In all these lengthy negotiations neither was ever accused of double-dealing; neither broke his pledged word. What is more, neither tried to convert the other. Islam and Christendom must always be foes, but wise men may fix up a local truce on a disputed boundary. As we watch the gyrations of those who wish to settle the whole Cold War at one conference, we should remember that long ago two brave soldiers brought peace to a patch of land. Because they agreed to differ on essentials, they managed to work out a limited local compromise.

The late Alfred Duggan, one of England's leading historical novelists, wrote of Richard's medieval England in Devil's Brood *and* My Life for My Sheep, *of the First Crusade in* Knight With Armour.

THE EDUCATION OF
RENAISSANCE
MAN

In his pioneer school in Mantua, Vittorino da Feltre
taught classical learning and bodily graces and bred
a line of enlightened princes and patrons who sought
to embody his ardent ideal of the "complete citizen"

*Some of the intellectual rigor of Humanist education is suggested by Vincenzo Foppa's fresco
of a very youthful scholar reading Cicero (whose initials M. T. C. appear on the bench behind).*

By IRIS ORIGO

Under Vittorino da Feltre's guidance Ludovico Gonzaga, Marquis of Mantua, had acquired the taste and wisdom that made him one of the great princes of Italy. In this Mantegna fresco he is seated at left, speaking to a secretary. Between him and his wife are their two youngest children, and behind them two older sons: Federigo and Gianfrancesco. The fresh-faced young woman at right center is Federigo's wife. The others are courtiers.

In the little dominion of Mantua, in the year 1423, an experiment in education began, of which the results were more far-reaching than its founder could ever, in his most hopeful moments, have foreseen. His name was Vittorino da Feltre, and his school was called La Giocosa. The pupils schooled there, and later on their children and grandchildren, grew up to form little centers of civilization as complete as the world has ever seen—the courts of Mantua and Urbino, of Ferrara and Milan—and the ideas underlying that civilization are still under active debate today. After five hundred years, the famous "Renaissance Man" still seems rather larger than life-size—not only a scholar but an athlete, a captain of armies, a wise ruler, and a patron of all the arts. Were these claims indeed justified? If they were, it is surely still pertinent to inquire by what process it was that such a man was shaped.

Let us look first at the man who founded this school and directed it for twenty-three years: Vittorino Rambaldoni, generally known, from his little native city in the Venetian Alps, as Vittorino da Feltre. His appearance, according to the two portraits remaining of him and the accounts of his contemporaries, was unimpressive—a man small and slight in stature, with an ascetic yet kindly face, a quiet voice, and a gentle and unemphatic manner, who was always dressed in a plain dark scholar's gown and rough sandals. Yet so high was this little schoolmaster's reputation that when, on a visit to Pope Eugenius IV, he knelt at the Pontiff's feet, the Pope raised him up, exclaiming, "How great a soul is lodged in this little body! Had my position allowed it, it is I who would have liked to rise, as he came in."

When Gianfrancesco Gonzaga, Marquis of Mantua, invited Vittorino to his court as preceptor to his sons, the teacher—who had had schools of his own in Padua and Venice—hesitated greatly before accepting, and then did so on two conditions: that his employer should never require anything of him "unworthy of either of us," and that, in the management of the boys and the household, he should be given as free a hand "as if he were the boys' own father." Gianfrancesco agreed; and

Medal of Vittorino da Feltre by Pisanello

Vittorino, without even inquiring what his salary was to be, took up his new post.

The house which was assigned to him and his pupils was a fine villa on the outskirts of Mantua. Built in 1388 by Gianfrancesco's predecessor as a pleasure house, it stood in the midst of wide meadows sloping down to the river Mincio and was bordered by broad, shady avenues, while the interior was decorated with frescoes of beasts, birds, and children at play. Vittorino started by stripping it of every luxury: fine hangings and draperies, silver and gold plates and ornaments. Then he turned to the daily life of his pupils. The young Gonzagas—of whom the two elder, Ludovico and Carlo, at once came into his charge, the younger children later on— were not at first sight prepossessing pupils. Ludovico was a fat, phlegmatic boy with a great belly and dragging steps, who spent his days in eating, drinking, and sleeping; Carlo, while tall and active, was rickety and nervous. (Both boys were soon restored to health by their preceptor's wise diet.) Their companions, the sons of the Mantuan nobles, were a set of spoiled and lawless boys dressed in fine silks and brocades adorned with jewels, heavily scented and pomaded, who came to school whenever they pleased and spent much of their time there with acrobats and jesters.

To all this Vittorino swiftly put an end. After a short period of patient inaction, during which he quietly observed each pupil, he firmly dismissed a few whom he considered incorrigible, and those servants who had encouraged their bad habits. He placed a reliable porter at the gate, so that no one could come in or go out without his permission. He obtained the Marquis' permission to summon a few of his former pupils from Venice, to appoint competent teachers for every branch of learning, and to award scholarships to some poor boys of outstanding gifts, who were received at La Giocosa (as they had been in his previous school in Padua) "for the love of God." Then he set to work.

The object of his training was, in his own words, the full development of each of the principal elements of man's nature: "the mind, the body, and the heart." The first two parts of this formula were, of course, based on the familiar Platonic principle: "gymnastic for the body and music for the mind." The rest of it was based on the teachings of Christianity. And it was the combination of both, the harmonious blending of the ideals of Humanism and of Christianity, which gave to Vittorino's school its particular flavor.

In returning to the classical conception of the equal development of body and mind, Vittorino swept aside many centuries of medieval prejudice, according to which the body represented only the lower part of our nature. It is true that at the medieval courts young knights had been taught to ride, joust, and hunt, but never had it been admitted that, as Plato had taught, the perfect man could only be formed by a harmonious balance between mind and body. But now Vittorino turned La Giocosa into a true classical gymnasium. His pupils

were taught to run, to wrestle, to play football, to hunt, to swim and fish in the waters of the Mincio, and to learn the arts of javelin-throwing, archery, and dancing. In summer they were even taken mountain-climbing (then a most unusual pursuit) in the Venetian Alps. And so much attention was paid to dignity of carriage that if Vittorino saw a boy standing about awkwardly or slouching, he would chalk a circle around the place where the boy stood and require him to remain there motionless for a specified time, in the presence of his companions in a correct posture.

All the sports of La Giocosa must have made the school a paradise for active boys, compared to the almost wholly sedentary lives of the pupils of the monastic orders, but for Vittorino their real purpose was training in hardihood and self-restraint. Just as he abolished any corporal punishment, so he required his pupils to show their own respect for their

Mantua today wears the same profile that it did in its golden age under the Gonzagas. Dominating the sky line is the dome of Sant' Andrea, the basilica that Alberti designed for Ludovico Gonzaga. Just beneath it is the Palazzo Ducale, while just above the bridge is the Castel San Giorgio—both belonging to the group of palaces, gardens, and courtyards now known collectively as the Castello dei Gonzaga. The square tower to the right of the dome is the Torre della Gabbia, where criminals were exposed to the elements in an outdoor cage.

bodies by the greatest moderation in eating, drinking, and sleeping; by regular exercise in all seasons; and by denying themselves any self-indulgence, such as wearing gloves or furs or fine linen or sleeping in featherbeds, or even allowing themselves a small fire on the coldest, most misty days of the Mantuan winter. "Clap your hands or stamp your feet," he would say to his boys when they were cold, "or say a fine poem, to stir the sluggish blood in your veins." He himself, even when visibly numb with cold, was never seen to stand before a fire.

So much for one side of education at La Giocosa. What was the academic training? Vergerius, who taught in the University of Padua when Vittorino was there, defined "liberal studies" as "those worthy of being studied by free men, to promote virtue and knowledge." The approved subjects included first, of course, the classics; then philosophy and history, mathe-

matics, and, with some reservations, music and dancing. Indeed the only major subjects excluded were medicine, theology, and the law, which were university subjects in any case. Vittorino, however, always maintained that it was not fair to expect every pupil to show the same tastes and talents. "Whatever our own predilections may be, we recognize that we must follow nature's lead." He declared that "everyone has some gift, if only one can discover it," and he therefore bestowed especial pains upon the dullest boys, trying to find some subject or skill to meet their needs.

Such individual attention was all the more remarkable when we consider that his school contained sixty or seventy pupils of the most various ages (the Gonzaga children entered at the age of five, but Sassuolo da Prato only at twenty-one). We are told that—in the belief that five hours of sleep were enough for a keen scholar—Vittorino would walk about the school in the dark on early winter mornings with a candle in one hand and a book in the other, rousing the ablest scholars from their sleep, to work with them for an extra hour, "and encourage them with grave and earnest words to high endeavor."

The youngest children learned to read by playing games with colored letter cards. Arithmetic, too, was at first taught as a game; for, like Quintilian, Vittorino believed that "the first thing to be avoided is, that a child should begin by feeling aversion for the studies he cannot yet love." History and mythology, too, were told as exciting and ennobling stories. By the time the child was six or seven he was ready to begin his serious studies in *grammatica*, the foundation of all knowledge, for this word comprised not only the study of Greek and Latin grammar (both languages being started together) but the reading of the great classical authors. A great deal of the teaching was oral: in the grammar lesson the master would dictate the list of words to be learned by heart and their declensions, commenting on any grammatical difficulty as it arose. When the time came for reading the Greek or Latin text itself, the master would first read a passage aloud, explaining and commenting, followed by each pupil reading the same passage in turn, until not only his translation but his enunciation and expression were considered perfect. Finally each passage was learned by heart. Every child was taught to read aloud agreeably and clearly, "not muttering in his teeth," and without uncouth gestures or making faces. And Vittorino was always especially pleased when any of them asked questions, saying that a passive acceptance of instruction was an infallible sign of an inattentive, dull, or lazy mind.

In the choice of authors, the principle was that laid down by Vergerius: "Begin with the best." Virgil, Homer, Cicero, and Demosthenes were the four authors on whom the teaching at La Giocosa was based. Only after these had been thoroughly mastered were the pupils allowed to pass on to Lucan and Ovid (in extracts, to "form an elegiac taste"), as well as to Xenophon and Herodotus. Terence, Plautus, Horace, and Juvenal were permitted only to the older boys, whose characters were considered to be already formed. In Greek the advanced students were allowed to read first Aeschylus and then Euripides and Sophocles, as well as Pindar, Theocritus, and some parts of Aristophanes. Vittorino thought it very important to learn Greek at the same time as Latin, and, since he considered himself only a mediocre Greek scholar, he engaged two renowned Greek teachers for La Giocosa, both recommended by the great Humanist Francesco Filelfo—George of Trebizond and the celebrated grammarian Theodore Gaza.

All the pupils were expected to write Greek and Latin verses and to compose speeches in these languages, which they recited to their companions or to distinguished guests. One boy composed such an oration to thank his fellow students for having saved him from drowning. Gianlucido Gonzaga, at fourteen, recited two hundred Latin hexameters of his own composition, celebrating the arrival of the Emperor Sigismund in Mantua, to an illustrious visitor, the Abbot Ambrogio of Camaldoli, "with so much grace," according to his hearer, "that I think Virgil spoke no better when he recited the sixth book of the *Aeneid* to Augustus." And he added that on the same day Gianlucido's sister of ten, Cecilia, wrote for him in Greek and Latin "with so much elegance as to put me to shame, considering that among my own pupils I could scarcely find one capable of doing the same." In these orations Vittorino advised his pupils to use a clear, straightforward style, avoiding archaisms and any excessive display of learning; and indeed it is plain that he was well aware of the dangers, as well as the advantages, of too great a skill in rhetoric. "There is," he said, "nothing that may eventually do greater harm to a city than eloquence, for . . . when it is possessed by evil men, they may use it to stir up trouble and to corrupt public manners."

As for the other subjects, history was confined to that of Greece and Rome, ignoring both medieval and contemporary history, and was entirely uncritical. Vittorino, for instance, whose favorite historian was Livy, indignantly repudiated any suggestion that so great a man could ever have been inaccurate. Equally, the study of philosophy was limited to ethics—that is, to the study of precepts from Cicero, Aristotle, Seneca, and Boethius, with illustrations from Plutarch, and at La Giocosa (though not in most other schools), of some of the Fathers of the Church, particularly Saint Jerome. Mathematics was given an important place and included geometry and astronomy. Vittorino also added the study of natural history (in a very rudimentary form) but discarded and despised astrology, in spite of its general popularity. As to music, many Humanists still regarded it, as the Middle Ages had done, with a considerable amount of distrust, declaring that too many young men "lose all vigor of mind and of character in their absorption in unworthy harmonies." But Vittorino, like Plato, held that it was necessary to the formation of a "complete" man; at La Giocosa both singing and playing the lyre and the lute were taught, and even dancing to music was approved.

In this connection a word must be said—since it was in this, too, that Humanist education broke new ground—about Vittorino's views on the education of women. His only girl pupils were the two Gonzaga daughters, Cecilia and Margherita, but other little bluestockings were being formed at much the same time in other parts of Italy. In Verona, Guarino's two pupils, Isotta and Ginevra Nogarola, were given a sound classical education. In Florence, when Poliziano fell in love with his beautiful pupil Alessandra Scala, it was in Greek verses that they corresponded. "You bring me, Alessandra, sweet violets—but I would taste the fruit."

There are, however, several prevalent misconceptions about the Humanist education of women. The first is that up to that time no girls had received any education at all: little Minervas, learned and wise, had sprung full-armed from the brains of Vittorino, Guarino, or Poliziano. Yet there is, for instance, the description given by the Tuscan chronicler Giovanni Morelli of his sister Mea, a whole century before the emergence of the young ladies of the Renaissance. This young lady, who had "hands of ivory, so well-shaped that they seemed to have been drawn by Giotto," was "delicate and pleasant in her speech, modest and measured in her gestures, yet a valiant, frank woman with a virile soul. She read and wrote as well as any man, she danced and sang perfectly, she was skilled in the arts of housekeeping, guiding her family with good advice and good habits, and living cheerfully and

No one owed more to Vittorino's inspired teaching than Federigo da Montefeltro, Duke of Urbino and among the most cultivated of Renaissance princes. This portrait—possibly by Justus van Ghent, more probably by Pedro Berruguete—shows him reading to his son Guidobaldo. On his left leg the Duke wears the Order of the Garter, awarded him by Edward IV of England. The richly dressed boy, about five years of age, is holding his father's sceptre.

gaily." This is, surely, a woman as highly civilized (except for a knowledge of Latin and Greek) as any daughter of the Renaissance. Moreover, it is also not entirely true that Vittorino, or indeed any other Humanist, advocated the *same* education for girls as for their brothers. Cecilia and Margherita Gonzaga did indeed study the classics. They were encouraged to know something of history, to practice the arts of agreeable conversation, to ride and dance and sing and play the lute, and above all, to appreciate poetry; since, according to the first treatise on education dedicated to a woman (written by Leonardo Bruni for Battista Malatesta), "anyone ignorant of and indifferent to so valuable an aid to knowledge and so ennobling a source of pleasure can by no means be entitled to be called educated." But arithmetic and geometry were wholly omitted from their curriculum, and also rhetoric, as "absolutely outside a woman's province." And the *first* place in a woman's education (in this all teachers agreed) was to be given to "the whole field of religion and morals, as a subject peculiarly her own."

And now we come to the third and most important part of Vittorino's method: the formation of what he called "the heart" and we should call character. Since he well knew that it can be formed only by example, he spent every hour of the day with his pupils, bearing a silent witness by his own life to the virtues he most valued: self-restraint, modesty, truthfulness, and kindness. His gentle equanimity, we are told, was the result of a stern self-discipline, by which he had conquered the sensuality and quick temper of his youth—at La Giocosa he led a life as dedicated as any monk's. His generosity was as spontaneous as his gentle smile: not only did many penniless students owe him their education, but his purse was always open to the poor. At his death, in spite of the handsome yearly salary of 240 gold florins awarded him by the Gonzagas, it was found that there was nothing left for his heirs but a little farm not far from Mantua, on the very site (and this must have delighted him) which was believed to be that of Virgil's birthplace. He was generous, too, with what he valued more than money: his fine collection of books, lending them freely, but becoming so angry when they were taken without leave that a law was passed in Mantua declaring the unauthorized borrowing of a book to be a punishable misdemeanor, like any other theft.

A poet in his youth, he finally destroyed the few poems he had kept and wrote very little else; all his energy went into his studies and his teaching. A devout Christian, he never required of his boys an austerity equal to his own (he lived on the most frugal of diets and scourged himself daily), but he did demand a daily attendance at Mass, confession once a month, and, above all, a deep reverence in word and deed. The only occasion when, breaking his own rule, he inflicted a corporal punishment was when he overheard Carlo Gonzaga blaspheme in the heat of a quarrel, and gave him, in the presence of the whole school, a sound box on the ear.

But the punishment that his pupils most dreaded was merely his displeasure and, in cases of cruelty or deceit, his glance of contempt and refusal to speak for several days to the offender. This was the more marked because at all other times his relationship with the boys was easy and affectionate, sharing their sports, delighting in their successes. Abbot Ambrogio has left us a charming description of him at the Gonzaga castle of Goito in the hills, where he had taken some of his younger pupils to escape from the summer heat: the children clustering round "on the happiest terms with him" to take part in the talk and show off their accomplishments, and then, when the guest left, riding with him for some distance to speed him on his way.

It should always be remembered that Vittorino considered Humanist education to be, above all, a *practical* preparation for life. His aim, he said, was not the formation of a great scholar but of a complete citizen. "Not everyone is obliged to excel in philosophy, medicine, or the law, nor are all equally favored by nature; but all are destined to live in society and to practice virtue." (By society he meant, of course, not only the world of the courts, but the community of men.) It was for this reason that, in spite of his personal interest in the clever poor students whom he himself had brought to the school, he attached an especial importance to the training of young noblemen, realizing that it was they who would become the model for all their subjects. It is in this sense only that La Giocosa can be considered, like the public schools of England, a school for the formation of a ruling class. But it was certainly, in its emphasis on the fusion of virtue and knowledge, a school for an elite—in Vergerius' words, for "free men."

And now we may inquire, what indeed were the fruits of this education? The Milky Way that led from La Giocosa across the skies of the Renaissance is full of minor stars: grammarians and versifiers, mathematicians, learned bishops, a musician and a *condottiere*. But we know that the formation of able scholars, or indeed of specialists of any kind, was not Vittorino's purpose. Did he then succeed in his ultimate aim, that of forming some "complete" human beings? The answer is, I think, both yes and no. The moral climate of the courts was a very different one from that inculcated on the playing fields of La Giocosa, and the violence, cruelty, and treachery which underlay the civilization of the Renaissance inevitably tainted the lives and characters of many of his pupils—except those who, like the brilliant and gentle Cecilia Gonzaga, forsook the life of the world for a convent. The rest had to deal with the society of their time as they found it—a world in which their old master's lessons of truthfulness, mildness, and forbearance held little place. Where Vittorino was entirely successful, however, was in the transmission of a certain fineness of *taste*—in life as well as in art. Ferrara under Lionello d'Este and his bride Margherita Gonzaga; Mantua under Ludovico Gonzaga and his son Federigo, and again in

Guidobaldo da Montefeltro, Federigo's sensitive and scholarly son (upper left), married Elisabetta Gonzaga (above), the gentle granddaughter of Ludovico of Mantua. Together they presided over the court of Urbino, which attracted the best artists and scholars in Italy. Among them were Baldassare Castiglione (left), who described the life at Urbino in one of the most delightful books of the Renaissance, The Courtier *(for an excerpt, see page 143). In it, Castiglione set up his model of what Chaucer would have called "a verray parfit gentle knight," Lord Chesterfield a gentleman, and still later generations a man of the world. Vittoria Colonna wrote to him, "I do not wonder that you have depicted the perfect courtier, for you had only to hold a mirror before you, and set down what you saw there." The attribution of Guidobaldo's portrait is uncertain; Castiglione's is by Raphael, and Elisabetta's probably by Mantegna.*

the next generation, under Federigo's son Francesco, who brought home Isabella d'Este as his bride; Urbino under Federigo da Montefeltro and his son Guidobaldo, who married Ludovico Gonzaga's granddaughter Elisabetta; and finally, Milan under the rule of Beatrice d'Este (Isabella's sister) and her husband Ludovico Sforza—these four courts showed, under the influence of Vittorino's pupils or their descendants, a remarkably fine flowering of the human spirit, an exquisite pattern of civilized life. If their members did not all, in Vittorino's sense, "practice virtue," they certainly had learned to perfection how "to live in society." Indeed, all other societies before and since, with perhaps the exception of eleventh-century Japan, seem by comparison a little graceless, a little coarse.

Two men, both pupils of Vittorino's, stand out as the dominating figures of two of these courts: Ludovico Gonzaga, Marquis of Mantua, and Federigo da Montefeltro, Duke of Urbino. Both were skillful and intrepid *condottieri;* both were also wise rulers; both made their courts centers of learning and of the arts.

The temperaments of these two men, however, were widely dissimilar. From early youth Federigo (in spite of his illegitimate birth) had seemed marked for success. *"Tu quoque Caesar eris"* (You also will be Caesar), Vittorino would remind him in his school days, and it is said that his pupil's promise sometimes caused him to shed tears of joy. Ludovico, on the other hand, had so many obstacles to overcome that one may doubt whether he would ever have become a great man without the early help of his master. It was Vittorino's training that, in his boyhood, enabled him to conquer his ill-health and his tendency to corpulence and apathy; and it was also Vittorino's intercession that at last obtained his father's forgiveness when, having despaired of ever being able to rival his handsome, gifted younger brother Carlo at home, he took service under Filippo Maria Visconti in Milan and spent long, bitter years abroad in exile. Yet it may well have been these years spent earning his spurs as a *condottiere* that fortified and matured him, for when he inherited the state of Mantua, Ludovico at once showed himself a wise and provident ruler. He built dikes and banks to stem the floods of the river Po and a canal (designed by Brunelleschi) to irrigate the Mantuan plain, assigning the land to anyone who was prepared to farm it properly; he paved the city streets, built a hospital, and set up a printing press. He summoned the great architect Alberti to design two new churches, that of San Sebastiano and the Basilica of Sant' Andrea; the mathematician Bartolomeo Manfredi to make the clock for his great new belfry; and Andrea Mantegna to decorate his palace, declaring that Mantegna's little toe was dearer to him than the whole body of most of his subjects.

Under Vittorino's guidance Ludovico enriched his library with rare manuscripts. (It included not only a fine collection of Greek and Latin authors and of medieval manuscripts, but a few books in the Vulgar, among them one thus described in the inventory: "INCIPIT, *nel mezo del camin di nostra vita,* ET FINIT, *l'amor che move il sole e l'altre stelle,*" CONTINET CARTAS 74.) He seized every pretext—a birth or a wedding or a foreign prince's visit—for great feasts and banquets; he offered constant hospitality to scholars such as Filelfo and Pico della Mirandola, and such poets as Poliziano, whose *Orpheus* was written and performed in Mantua. And if at the end of all this the Mantuan coffers were empty, he was not ashamed to ask one of his artists to wait a little longer for full payment, since, he said, at the moment the Gonzaga jewels were in pawn! Yet the portraits of him that have come down to us are not those of a happy man. They show the face of a ruler who has achieved power and security, but on whom the years of struggle and anxiety have left their mark—a man always on his guard, never forgetful of the motto on the family crest, CAUTIUS, "live cautiously."

It is to the other of Vittorino's most famous pupils, Federigo da Montefeltro, that we must turn to see not only the qualities of the mind, but also of the heart, that La Giocosa sought to form; for here indeed we are close to finding Vittorino's "complete man." Although he was not entirely free, as a *condottiere,* from the cruelty of other soldiers of fortune, Federigo was almost unique in his faithfulness to his word and to his friends, in defeat as in victory. As a ruler his generosity and friendliness, and a total absence of the suspicion and arrogance of almost all other princes of his times, endeared him to all his subjects. Accounts by his contemporaries describe him as spending a part of each day, alone and unguarded, in the market place or in the shops of his artisans. "To one he would say, 'How is your old father?' to another, 'How does your trade thrive?' or 'Have you got a wife yet?' . . . One he took by the hand, he put his hand on another's shoulder, and spoke to all uncovered, so that men would say, when anyone was very busy, 'Why, you have more to do than Federigo's berretta!' "

One morning, meeting a wedding procession, Federigo dismounted to join the escort that was honoring the bride; and on a winter's day, when the monastery of San Bernardino, outside the city, was snowed in, he himself set off at the head of his men to cut a path through the snow to feed the hungry monks. In times of famine he distributed corn free from his private estate in Apulia. Whenever possible, he answered petitions on the same day he received them. It is hardly surprising that, as he walked through the streets, people would kneel down, crying, "God keep you, *signore!*"

At the same time Federigo displayed to the full, with the fruits of his successful wars, the magnificence expected of a Renaissance prince. Life in the great palace designed for him by Laurana was on a truly royal scale. His household counted "500 mouths," which included—besides knights, men-at-arms, grooms, and servants—four teachers of grammar, philosophy, and rhetoric, five architects and engineers, a German

The Gonzagas maintained the intellectual and artistic splendor of Mantua through the reigns of Ludovico, his son Federigo, and his grandson Francesco. The latter brought home a dazzling wife, Isabella d'Este, who surrounded herself with writers, architects, and painters. Among the works she commissioned is the curious picture above, one of five "allegories" she ordered for the decoration of her private apartments in the Gonzaga palace. Lorenzo Costa painted it according to her precise instructions, which included the peremptory order: "It is forbidden to you to add anything whatever of your own." It has been given various titles and interpretations over the centuries, for the allegory is anything but clear. It probably glorifies the triumph of poetry and music, and it is likely that Isabella herself is the lady being crowned with laurel by a cherub. These were the imaginary realms into which this brilliant, grasping woman, who wished to see and to learn and to possess everything, escaped —a retreat from the cruelty and intrigue around her into an ideal world of "luxe, calme, et volupté."

139

astrologer, five "readers aloud at meals," four "elderly and staid gentlemen" for his wife's court, four transcribers of manuscripts, the keeper of the bloodhounds, and the keeper of the giraffe. His stables held three hundred horses; his library, the rarest and most complete collection of manuscripts and books in Europe. His own tastes remained those formed at La Giocosa. Livy and Saint Augustine were read aloud to him at meals, and in the afternoons, if he was not watching a joust or some boys practicing gymnastics on the wide meadow of San Francesco, he would attend a classical lecture, or discuss theology, through a grating, with the learned Abbess of the Convent of Santa Chiara.

His son Guidobaldo followed in his father's footsteps. At a very early age he showed a passion for the classics and for geography and history, as well as for the gymnastics and knightly sports which greatly injured his already fragile health. After his marriage at sixteen to Ludovico Gonzaga's granddaughter Elisabetta, their court became a magnet for the best scholars and artists in Italy. The scholar Pietro Bembo came for a few days' visit, and stayed for six years; Castiglione came and wrote *Il Cortigiano*. The artists at Guidobaldo's court were Piero della Francesca, Francesco di Giorgio, Justus van Ghent, Ambrogio da Milano, Giovanni Sanzi (who was also the court chronicler), and above all, Sanzi's son, "the divine Raphael," who later on, in his famous *School of Athens* in the Vatican, reproduced the very quintessence of the Renaissance view of the classical world.

The days were spent in hunting, jousting, and riding; the evenings in singing to the harpsichord or the lute, or in parlor games, and especially, under the guidance of the gentle Duchess and her brilliant sister-in-law, Emilia Pia, in long philosophic debates: Was it indeed true that matter was masculine and form feminine? What were the qualities required of the perfect courtier? And of the ideal woman? And what was the true nature of love? "It is," said Bembo, "nought but a desire to enjoy beauty, and since one can only desire what one knows, so knowledge must precede desire." But the highest love, he maintained, the Platonic, "is an emanation of the divine goodness . . . shining over all created things, like the sun's light." So, night after night, they talked, until the candles burned low and the ladies, in their stiff brocades and high, heavy headdresses, dispersed to bed, and the Duke went down to his great library, where the portrait of his father's old schoolmaster—placed beside the greatest classical philosophers and the Fathers of the Church—bore witness to the influence he had exerted, and to his pupil's gratitude: "Federigo to Vittorino da Feltre, his revered master, who by word and example instructed him in all human excellence."

Iris Origo's books include biographies of the poet Leopardi and of Byron's daughter Allegra; The Last Attachment, *about Byron's affair with Teresa Guiccioli; and* The World of San Bernardino, *a vivid reconstruction of fifteenth-century Italy.*

VITTORINO'S GREATEST PUPIL AND HIS LADY:

THE URBINO DIPTYCH

Piero della Francesca

A major patron of the arts whose tastes had been shaped in Vittorino da Feltre's school, Federigo da Montefeltro is himself the subject of one of the most arresting portraits of the Renaissance (opposite). This is one half of the famous diptych painted by Piero della Francesca; the other is a portrait of Federigo's wife, Battista Sforza (page 142). They are paired so that husband and wife face each other, Federigo on the right and Battista on the left.

Commanding, virile, grave, Duke Federigo of Urbino is set like a monument against the idealized landscape. His extraordinary profile is the result of a jousting accident in which he lost an eye and had his nose broken.

Battista's portrait, like her personality, is in a fainter tone. She appears to have had a most thorough education as a little Humanist aristocrat (at the age of four she delivered a Latin oration in public), and possessed, besides, a natural sedateness and wisdom that enabled her to act as her husband's regent during his absences in time of war. She was his second wife, married when she was only fourteen; and she presented him with six daughters (one of them, Agnesina, became the mother of the famous Vittoria Colonna). She died giving birth to her only son, Guidobaldo.

The precise date of these portraits is not certain. Most critics think it was about 1465, but Lionello Venturi dates them 1472, the year Battista died.

142

A MIRROR OF RENAISSANCE MAN

It was through Petrarch, as much as any one man, that Italy moved from the medieval world onto the threshold of the Renaissance. He was quite aware of this, and in 1352 commented wryly on his role in the revival of learning:

Is it then true that this disease of writing, like other malignant disorders, is, as the Satirist claims, incurable, and, as I begin to fear, contagious as well? How many, do you reckon, have caught it from me? Within our memory, it was rare enough for people to write verses. But now there is no one who does not write them; few indeed write anything else. . . . Even carpenters, fullers, and ploughmen leave the implements of their calling to talk of Apollo and the Muses. I cannot say how far the plague, which lately was confined to a few, has now spread.

From *Petrarch, the First Modern Scholar and Man of Letters,* J. H. Robinson and H. W. Rolfe, Putnam 1898

Leon Battista Alberti, who was called to Mantua to design the basilica of Sant' Andrea for Ludovico Gonzaga, left behind him a famous portrait of the educated "universal man." It may be somewhat disconcerting to discover that the man he was actually describing was Leon Battista Alberti (himself). But false modesty was not among the Renaissance ideals, of which this remains an accurate catalogue:

His genius was so versatile that you might almost judge all the fine arts to be his. . . . He played ball, hurled the javelin, ran, leaped, wrestled, and above all delighted in the steep ascent of mountains. . . . As a youth he excelled in warlike games. With his feet together, he could leap over the shoulders of men standing by. . . . With his left foot lifted from the ground to the wall of a church, he could throw an apple into the air so high that it would go far beyond the top of the highest roofs. . . . Strange and marvellous! that the most spirited horses and those most impatient of riders would, when he first mounted them, tremble violently and shudder as if in great fear. He learned music without teachers, and his compositions were approved by learned musicians. . . . But in truth, because he could not live without letters, at the age of twenty-four he turned to physics and the mathematical arts. . . . When he heard that a learned man of any kind had arrived, he would at once work his way into a position of familiarity with him and thus from any source whatsoever he began to learn what he was ignorant of. . . . When

his favourite dog died he wrote a funeral oration for him.

Whatever was done by man with genius and with a certain grace, he held to be almost divine; and he so respected anything achieved that he insisted even poor writers were worthy of praise. The sight of gems, flowers, and especially pleasant places more than once restored him from illness to good health.

From *The Viking Portable Renaissance Reader,* translated by James Bruce Ross

Vittorino's pupil, Federigo da Montefeltro, seemed even to his contemporaries the ideal man of the age. So he appears to the Humanist scholar Marsilio Ficino, writing in 1492 to Paul of Middelburg:

For this century, like a golden age, has restored to light the liberal arts, which were almost extinct: grammar, poetry, rhetoric, painting, sculpture, architecture, music, the ancient singing of songs to the Orphic lyre, and all this in Florence. Achieving what had been honored among the ancients, but almost forgotten since, the age has joined wisdom with eloquence, and prudence with the military art, and this most strikingly in Federigo, Duke of Urbino, as if proclaimed in the presence of Pallas herself, and it has made his son and his brother the heirs of his virtue.

From *The Viking Portable Renaissance Reader,* translated by Mary Martin McLaughlin

The perfect handbook of Renaissance conduct was eventually written by Baldassare Castiglione. In describing the polished manners and intellectual ardor that characterized the court of Guidobaldo da Montefeltro at Urbino, he projected an image of the ideal courtier:

I would have him more than passably learned in letters, at least in those studies which we call the humanities. Let him be conversant not only with the Latin language, but with Greek as well, because of the abundance and variety of things that are so divinely written therein. Let him be versed in the poets, as well as in the orators and historians, and let him be practiced also in writing verse and prose, especially in our own vernacular; for, besides the personal satisfaction he will take in this, in this way he will never want for pleasant entertainment with the ladies, who are usually fond of such things.

From *The Book of the Courtier,* translated by Charles S. Singleton, Doubleday Anchor Books

The
Bad Bishop's
Book of
Love Songs

This illuminated songbook, made about 1470 for a worldly French cleric named Jean de Montchenu, is now one of the treasures of the Bibliothèque Nationale. Although it is known that there was a vogue for heart-shaped illuminated manuscripts during the latter half of the fifteenth century, they are rare, and this one is unique, the only known surviving manuscript that is in the shape of a single heart when closed and of two joined hearts when open.

The songs in the book are light and popular—the "Some Enchanted Evening"s of the early Renaissance. Fifteen are in Italian (with spelling errors that identify the scribe as a Frenchman), and the rest are in old French. According to manuscript experts, the illuminator was either French or Flemish, and the artist who painted the two delicate miniatures that enhance the book was—judging from the ladies' costumes—French. The name Burgundian has been attached to the style of music represented in this songbook. The dukes of Burgundy were then the

The capriciousness of love seems to be the subject of the first of the songbook's two miniatures. Fortune is represented by the lady balanced on a wheel—a fair-faced creature who has a monstrously evil side, symbolized by sword and batwing. The wheel suggests Dame Fortune's instability and the speed with which she can change her aspect. Above her head, floating on a blue cloud, a blindfolded Cupid has just dispatched an arrow toward the young lady at the right. She, in turn, perhaps refusing to believe that anyone so elegant and beautiful as herself could possibly come to grief, casts her eyes down meekly and allows the arrow to fly home. At the bottom of the page, two angels display the Montchenu family crest. Above them reposes a black cap of the type that Montchenu wore when he was a prothonotary of the Church. The decorative border is typical of Franco-Flemish manuscript illumination of the period, and is composed of motifs and figures that have no association with the subject of the manuscript.

greatest music patrons in Europe, and anyone who could write a chanson tried to go to their court. Burgundian songs are usually love songs, set to music that expresses tender melancholy and sensual longing. They are written for three voices moving within a fairly narrow range (normally not exceeding a tenth), with one predominating voice carrying the melody. The three voices are distinct, however, and move with a certain amount of independence, so that the whole has a transparent texture. The charm of the melodies, the miniature proportions, and the over-all delicacy of the chansons find their visual equivalents in the songbook itself. These songs continued as a popular musical form long after the dukes of Burgundy ceased to be music patrons, and were often the starting points for more serious works. One of the greatest of Renaissance composers, Josquin des Prez, used his own and other composers' chansons as the basis for masses.

Jean de Montchenu, to whom this charming *chansonnier* owes its existence,

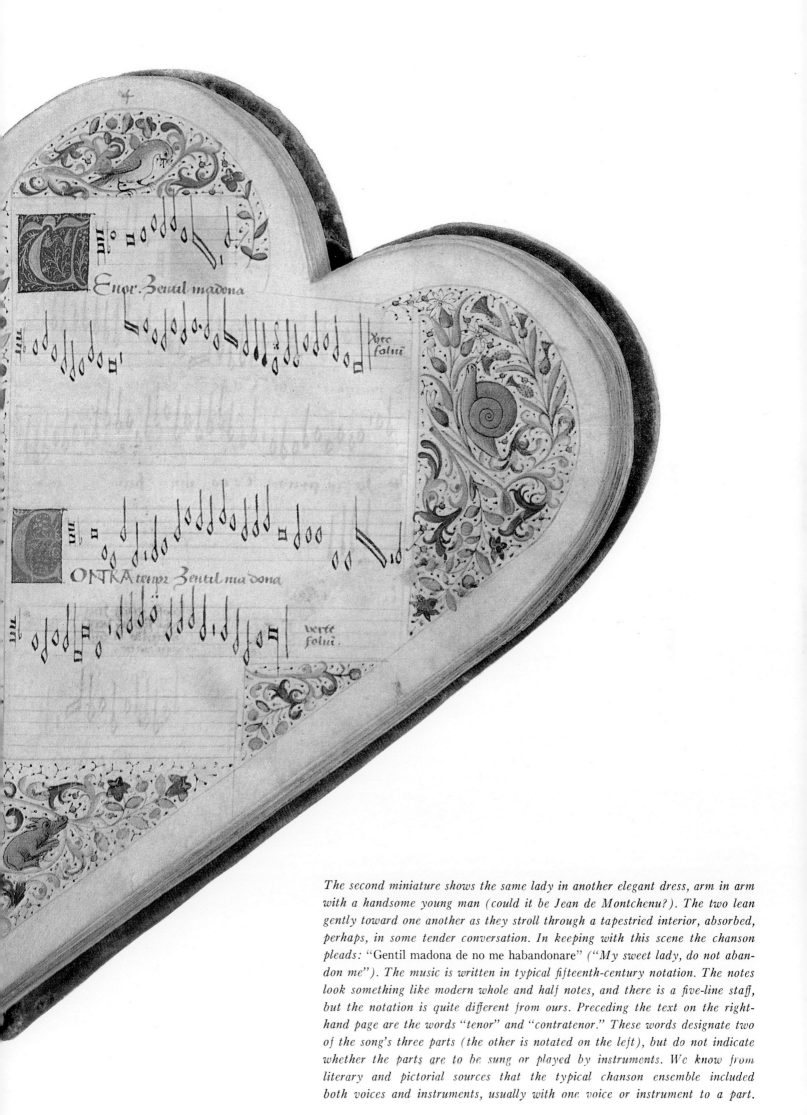

The second miniature shows the same lady in another elegant dress, arm in arm with a handsome young man (could it be Jean de Montchenu?). The two lean gently toward one another as they stroll through a tapestried interior, absorbed, perhaps, in some tender conversation. In keeping with this scene the chanson pleads: "Gentil madona de no me habandonare" ("My sweet lady, do not abandon me"). The music is written in typical fifteenth-century notation. The notes look something like modern whole and half notes, and there is a five-line staff, but the notation is quite different from ours. Preceding the text on the right-hand page are the words "tenor" and "contratenor." These words designate two of the song's three parts (the other is notated on the left), but do not indicate whether the parts are to be sung or played by instruments. We know from literary and pictorial sources that the typical chanson ensemble included both voices and instruments, usually with one voice or instrument to a part.

is described in a contemporary chronicle as "a great scoundrel, of shameful conduct, lewd, detestable, dissolute, full of vices." Born of a noble family, he took holy orders at an early age, and in 1460 was assigned to the fairly important position of apostolic prothonotary. Ten years later he became head of an abbey in Piedmont, a lucrative post that probably enabled him to afford this songbook. He involved himself in political intrigues: first supporting Burgundy against France, and later supporting France against Burgundy. As a secret agent for Louis XI, he connived to eliminate Burgundian influence at the Court of Savoy. (His methods were not particularly subtle: he had the Burgundian secret agent dragged out of bed, bound hand and foot, and carried off to France.) He seems to have managed to stay in favor with Louis XI for the rest of his life, and in 1477 the pope made him a bishop. But *ars longa, vita brevis:* all that remains of the bad bishop is his excellent songbook.

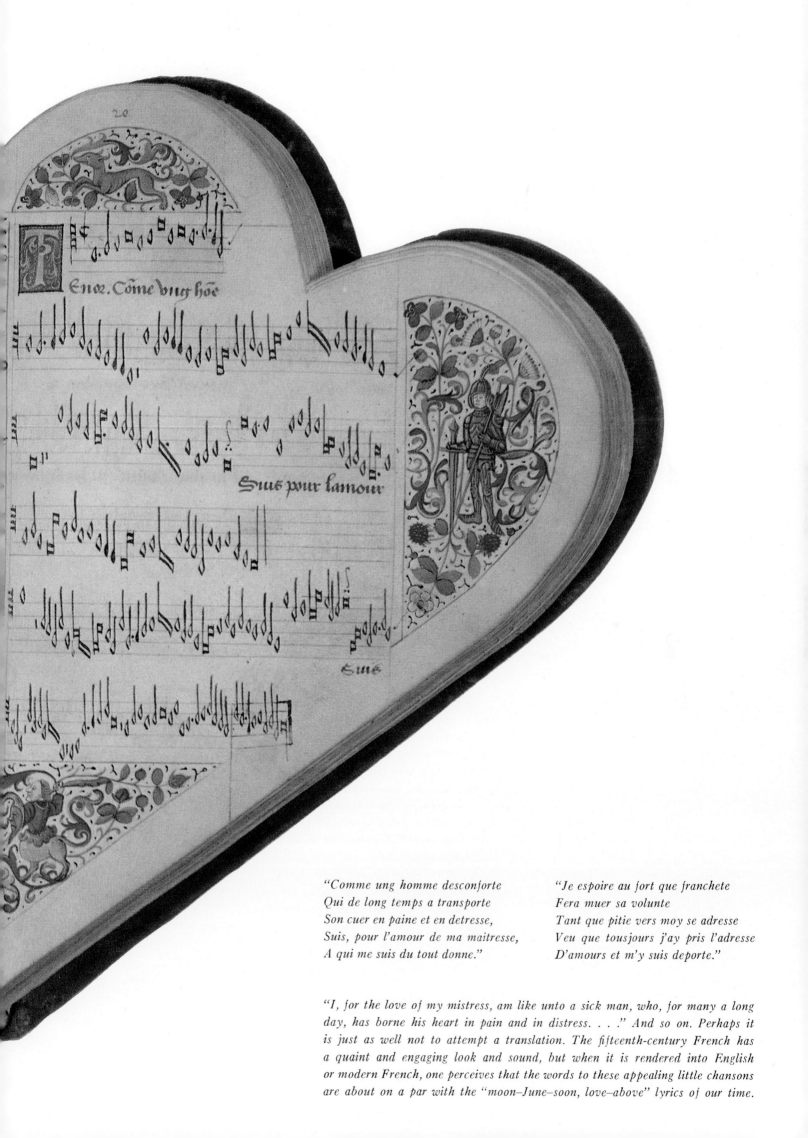

"Comme ung homme desconforte
Qui de long temps a transporte
Son cuer en paine et en detresse,
Suis, pour l'amour de ma maitresse,
A qui me suis du tout donne."

"Je espoire au fort que franchete
Fera muer sa volunte
Tant que pitie vers moy se adresse
Veu que tousjours j'ay pris l'adresse
D'amours et m'y suis deporte."

"I, for the love of my mistress, am like unto a sick man, who, for many a long day, has borne his heart in pain and in distress. . . ." And so on. Perhaps it is just as well not to attempt a translation. The fifteenth-century French has a quaint and engaging look and sound, but when it is rendered into English or modern French, one perceives that the words to these appealing little chansons are about on a par with the "moon–June–soon, love–above" lyrics of our time.

Pascal

He had one of the best minds of all time, but it was at war with itself. One half

of it he gave to God; with the other he laid the foundations of the Age of Reason

Blaise Pascal lived a scant thirty-nine years,
but if one is a prodigy, as he was,
that is time enough to earn immortality. At
nineteen he invented his pascaline,
the first real calculating machine (opposite).
Although it won him early fame (but
little money), he is remembered today chiefly
for his later scientific discoveries,
Pascal's Law, and two books: the Provincial
Letters *and the* Pensées. *His greatest*
celebrity did not come until after he died,
in 1662; except for one quick sketch
from life, all his portraits—including the one
from which this engraving was made—
are posthumous and based on his death mask.

By MORRIS BISHOP   *Photographs by* ERICH LESSING—MAGNUM

On the slopes of the Puy de Dôme, above his native Clermont-Ferrand, a tube of mercury recalls the experiment by which Pascal proved that air has weight. He had his brother-in-law carry two such tubes up the mountain. As they ascended into the thinner atmosphere, the column of mercury fell in the tube; it rose again on the descent into the valley. Aside from the larger implications of this discovery, it gave us the barometer. Pascal was twenty-five at the time, and had not yet undergone the spiritual crisis that eventually caused him to seek the austere solitude of a cell at the convent of Port-Royal des Champs (at right).

Every now and then humanity produces an intellectual sport, a genius, a mental monster. We expect the great mind to serve us, and so, usually, it does. But with its higher order of values it is likely to dismiss our own and to perceive and pursue aims that astonish our earthliness. Thus Isaac Newton abandoned science to spend his incomparable mind on unriddling the prophecies of Daniel. Thus Joseph Priestley, the discoverer of oxygen, came to America and settled in frontier Pennsylvania, to write twenty-five volumes of unreadable, or at least unread, theology. Thus also Blaise Pascal.

What made the great mind? The genes, of course, or if you prefer, God. But notice Pascal's background and development. He was born in Clermont-Ferrand, in the center of France, in 1623. His mother died when he was three. His father, a civil servant and amateur scientist, recognized that he had fathered a prodigy and resigned his post to devote himself entirely to the education of Blaise and his two remarkable sisters. The father's views were unorthodox. He believed that the need of knowledge must precede knowledge, that reason and judgment must precede formal study. He taught the experimental method: observe, classify, generalize. Thus Blaise, at eleven, noticed that a china dish struck with a knife hums until silenced by a touch of the hand. "Why?" he said, like any child. Unlike any child, he found the answers unsatisfactory and made a series of experiments on sound and wrote a treatise much applauded by his elders. Having been kept in ignorance of geometry, he invented, at twelve, his own, and was discovered doing his version of Euclid's thirty-second proposition on the kitchen floor. At sixteen he printed some remarks on conic sections that herald our projective geometry.

Thus he was trained to originality, to genius. He never knew the orthodoxies and subjections of a school, nor the group spirit and rivalries of a school; he was destined for lonely apartness. Nor did he ever play, or build his body in sports and games. Nature shook her head and sighed.

When Blaise was sixteen his father was appointed collector of internal revenue in Rouen. The post was an exacting one; Blaise was drafted to aid in the endless calculations. Promptly bored by drudgery, he wondered if the mechanical work could not be done by a machine. Characteristically, he proceeded from the problem to its practical solution. He created the first calculating machine.

His initial, momentous idea was to conceive the digits of a number as arranged in wheels; each wheel, after making a complete revolution, should turn its left-hand neighbor a fraction of a revolution. (Look at your speedometer.)

One machine preserved in the Paris Musée des Arts et Métiers is a polished brass box, about fourteen by five by three inches (see page 151). On the top, or working surface, we see a row of eight movable dials. The right-hand dial, twelve-slotted, represents deniers, or pence; the next dial, twenty-slotted, represents sous, or shillings; the remainder, ten-slotted, are for livres, or pounds. At the back of the box is a series of windows in which numbers, on drums, appear.

The dials are actuated by a stylus. To perform a simple addition, for example 9 pounds 6 shillings and sevenpence plus 10 pounds 15 shillings and eightpence, one begins at the right, inserts the stylus in the seventh slot, and revolves

153

*Determined to stamp out Jansenism, Louis XIV
forcibly removed the nuns from Port-
Royal des Champs in 1709 and razed it the following year. Today nothing is left
of the convent where Pascal wrote his* Pensées
*but the farm buildings and a well-
windlass he is thought to have designed. By
a simple set of reduction gears it
raises a barrel of water weighing 270 pounds
while an empty barrel descends.*

the wheel clockwise, like a telephone dial, to the stop which catches the stylus. The proper figures appear in the windows. Begin again with the second sum. We read the total in the windows: 20 pounds 2 shillings and threepence. To subtract: push back the brass strip at the back of the box, disclosing a second set of windows. Dial the minuend and the subtrahend; the remainder appears in the windows. Multiplication and division (which are only abridged additions and subtractions) take longer.

It was an extraordinary mechanical achievement. "Pascal knew how to animate copper and give wit to brass," said an admiring friend. Pascal made at least fifty machines and built on them great hopes of gain. But the *pascaline* did not sell. Since accurate gear-cutting was impossible, the mechanism was forever getting out of order, and only Pascal or one of his workmen could fix it. And it was too expensive. Though it could do the work of half a dozen men, the half-dozen men were still cheaper than the machine. Technology had to wait for economics to catch up.

In mathematics Pascal's work is known to every professional. He created the theory of probability, gave Leibniz the hint that became his infinitesimal calculus, and—as a diversion from a toothache—solved the problem of the cycloid. Most of his mathematical work is too technical for exposition here. But physics, or the world we live in, is everybody's business. We are all physicists, or we would be dead.

In Pascal's time there was much learned talk of the vacuum, or the void, which was identified by verbal habit with *nihil*, nothing. Philosophers argued that nature abhors a vacuum, that a Nothing cannot be a Something. But Pascal was impressed by reports of Torricelli's famous experiment, today a high-school commonplace. A forty-inch glass tube is filled with mercury, then turned smartly upside down, with the open end in a bowl of mercury. The mercury in the tube sinks to a height of about thirty inches, leaving a ten-inch gap at the sealed top of the tube. What is in the gap and how does it get there? Pascal concluded that it is a real vacuum, that the weight of mercury in the tube balances the weight of air on the mercury in the bowl. He developed his thesis with a sensational series of experiments. He had, for instance, forty-six-foot glass tubes made, a triumph of glass

155

blowing. He bound them to ships' masts, pivoted in the middle. He filled the tubes with water, wine, or oil, reversed them so that the open ends sat in tubs of liquid, removed the stoppers, and saw the fluids fall and create measurable vacuums.

If air has weight, he argued, there should be less at the top of a mountain than at its foot; hence the measure of mercury in a Torricellian tube should vary with the altitude. The Puy de Dôme stands conveniently four thousand feet above his native city of Clermont. He commissioned his brother-in-law, Florin Périer, to make the great experiment. Two Torricellian tubes were borne by a party of enthusiastic amateurs to the summit. The mercury dropped about three inches, and rose again on the return journey. Meanwhile control tubes set up in the city had remained unchanged. Thus the weight of air was not only demonstrated but measured. And thus Pascal propounded the principle of the aneroid barometer.

Pascal continued with important work on hydrostatics, or the equilibrium and pressure of liquids. He enunciated the general rule of the transmission of pressure in fluids, now known as Pascal's law. He proposed the hydraulic press. He stated, apparently for the first time, the principle of the elasticity of gases. He tried to relate the behavior of fluids and gases in corresponding formulas. And he wrote some precious analyses of scientific method and of the scientific mind.

But science palled. He wrote: "I had passed a long time in the study of the abstract sciences; and the limited number with whom one can treat thereof had disgusted me with them. When I began the study of man I saw that these abstract sciences are not proper to man and that I was straying farther from my natural state in penetrating them than others were in their ignorance of them, but I thought at least to find many companions in the study of man, and that this was the true study proper to him. I was mistaken; there are still fewer who study man than geometry."

He plunged into the study of man in society, or social psychology, with a scientist's thoroughness. He had his entree at court, in literary salons, in the high bourgeoisie of Paris. He attended the theatre, and gambled like a gentleman. Did he know love? Very likely; but if so, most of the evidence was carefully suppressed after his death.

His father died; his beloved sister Jacqueline became a nun at Port-Royal; his married sister Gilberte was far away in Clermont. He was alone, sick, wretched. Science and man had failed him. He turned to God.

His God was the God of Jansenism. This was a movement within the Catholic Church, proposing a rigorous, fundamentalist interpretation of sacred texts and of the early Fathers. Its doctrine was grim, dwelling all on man's guilt, from which he can be redeemed only by God's rare predestined grace. The chief enemies of the Jansenists were the Jesuits, who had developed a more modernist theology, more kindly toward errant man.

The headquarters of Jansenism were the convents of Port-Royal de Paris and Port-Royal des Champs. The Paris convent is now the Hôpital de la Maternité, on the Boulevard de Port-Royal. The nuns' choir has become a laundry, and

When Pascal's body was laid out for burial, two discoveries were made:
that he wore next his skin a spiked wire belt to mortify
the flesh, and that sewn into the lining of his coat was the record
of a great mystical experience. On a sheet of paper
dated November 23, 1654, he had written, in part: "From about half
past ten in the evening until about half past twelve,
FIRE. Certitude, certitude, feeling, joy, peace. . . . Joy, joy, joy,
tears of joy. . . . Jesus Christ. I have been separated
from him; I have fled him, renounced him, crucified him. Let me never
be separated from him. . . . Renunciation, total and sweet."

in the cells consecrated to virginity the poor women of Paris suffer the pains of childbirth. Port-Royal des Champs stood fifteen miles southwest of Paris, in the lovely valley of the Chevreuse. It was razed by angry old Louis XIV in 1710; it is now marked only by a votive museum and by the farm buildings, Les Granges. About the two Port-Royals clustered a group of adherents, the *solitaires,* mostly men of distinction fleeing the void of their world, seeking to fill the vacuum in their hearts. They devoted themselves to the meanest of labors in the service of the nuns, their Ladies.

To this center Pascal turned, in disgust with the world. And on the evening of November 23, 1654, from half past ten to half past twelve, God came in fire to give him a mystic revelation. This was the capital experience of Pascal's life. His record of that fiery vision, of the coming of certitude, joy, peace, and grace, he wrote on a sheet of paper, which is now one of the treasures of the Bibliothèque Nationale (see page 159). We call it his Memorial, for during the rest of his life he carried it always with him, sewed in the lining of his coat. It was discovered only when his body was laid out for burial.

Was it God who spoke to him? Or was he victim of a hallucination? Abnormal psychology can give of his experience a description that has no need of God. But abnormal psychology can never prove anything to a mystic. He smiles, and says: "I was there. I know."

After his night of fire Pascal abandoned the world and science to devote himself to the care of his soul. "What would you say of a leper who, indifferent to his gnawing disease, would talk of botany or astronomy to his doctor?" He made long retreats at Port-Royal des Champs, living with the solitaries at the Granges, doing his own housework, delighting in the earthen dish and wooden spoon which, his sister in religion told him, are the gold and precious stones of Christianity. He is said to have designed, during one of his visits, the well-windlass, still in operation (see pages 154–155). The ascription of the device to Pascal rests only on an old tradition first recorded in 1723, but there is nothing unlikely about it. His habit was always to pass from the recognition of a need to its satisfaction. Visiting Port-Royal's Little Schools, he was annoyed by the illogicality of the traditional system of teaching reading. He devised a new method, that which became standard throughout the Western world. And even in little things: irritated by waiting for sedan-chair bearers, the taxis of the time, he established in Paris the first omnibus company. Annoyed at fishing for his watch, he amazed his friends by strapping it to his wrist.

Jansenism was under attack in those days, and Pascal was summoned to aid its defense. He did so in his *Provincial Letters,* a series of polemics addressed to the general public. These turned from defense to offense, to a savage attack on Jesuit theology and practice, particularly on casuistry and on the relaxation of moral principle by comforting concessions to man's weakness. To reach the large public Pascal found an easy, colloquial style, based on speech, which determined the form of French prose even to our own time. The effect of the *Provincial Letters* on Western man's common fund of ideas has been immense. They seem to render theology so clear and easy that every man felt himself competent to argue with the doctors. They broadcast the legend of Jesuit duplicity for all the world to read. The weapon forged against the Jesuits fell into the hands of Catholicism's enemies, and soon into those of Christianity's enemies. Read as they are in every French school, they still provide knowing pupils with anticlerical arguments and examples, remembered their lives long. What a fate for Pascal, the champion of Catholic faith!

The *Provincial Letters* angered rather than convinced the high churchmen. The pope condemned Jansenist theology and forbade the order to propagandize or to recruit new members. Pascal then turned to a new and greater task—the defense of the Christian doctrine by purely rational means, an Apology for Christianity.

As his health steadily grew worse he could no longer trust his clouding memory. "Escaped thought, I wished to write it; I write instead that it escaped me." He jotted down his thoughts as they came to him, now in an illegible invalid's scribble, now in a clear, confident hand. When too weak to write he would dictate the scheme of an idea or a few happy phrases. He would return from church with a suggestion scratched on his fingernails with a pin.

These notes are the *Pensées* of Pascal, as we possess them today. Some are incomprehensible; some are commonplace memoranda; some are fragments of dialogue, imaginary conversations with objectors; some are careful developments, pages long; some are lyric outbursts, forever memorable and unforgotten. The *Pensées* make one of the great books of

French literature, of all literature. They are admitted to every Five-foot Shelf, to every collection of Great Books. They are the comfort of soldiers, the companions of exiles, night voices to fevered men, songs in solitary hearts.

One can construct from the *Pensées* the general scheme of his unwritten *Apology for Christianity*. Let me string together some of his thoughts on a connecting thread:

Look first at the natural state of man. What is man in nature? A nullity in relation to infinity, an all in relation to nullity, a mid-point between nothing and everything. . . . Forever uncertain and drifting, we sail on a vast middle sea, impelled from one shore to another. To whatever fixed point we think to tie and cling, it quakes and fails us; and if we follow it, it escapes our clutch, slips away and flees us in eternal flight. Nothing stops for us. This is the state which is natural to us, and yet the most unwelcome to us; we burn with the desire to find a firm footing, a last constant base whereon to build a tower rising to infinity; but all our foundation cracks, and the earth opens, down to the abyss. . . . "The eternal silence of infinite space terrifies me."

Man is worse than weak, ignorant, and vain; he is evil. His actions are determined by self-interest, a marvelous instrument for putting out our own eyes agreeably. We would do anything for the applause we love. We even lose our life joyfully, if only people will talk about it. We hate the truth and those who tell it to us; we are only disguise, falsehood, and hypocrisy. All men naturally hate each other. What a sink is the heart of man, how full of ordure!

But look more closely; something noble peers from the eyes of that ogreish face. The creature thinks; he is not utterly a stone or a brute. Visibly he is made to think; that is all his dignity and his merit. Man is only a reed, the weakest in nature; but he is a thinking reed. There is no need that the whole universe arm itself to crush him; a vapor, a drop of water, is enough to kill him. But even if the universe should crush him, man would still be nobler than that which kills him, because he knows he dies; and of the advantage the universe has over him the universe knows not at all. By thought man has learned the truth; by it he conceives a possible nobility. He knows himself to be wretched; a tree, a ruined house, does not know itself to be wretched. Man's very wretchedness proves his grandeur, for his are the woes of a great lord, a king unthroned.

This is man—part misery, part grandeur—two opposites which cannot be resolved. What a monster is man, judge of all things, witless worm; casket of truth, sewer of incertitude and error; glory and refuse of the universe!

Of man's duality God has given us a lucid and convincing explanation. Man was once perfect and has become corrupt through sin. His misery is natural to his present condition; his grandeur indicates his lost perfection.

Christianity offers a means of rescue from this parlous state. A sensible man will test the proposition that the Christian God exists. You could bet on that proposition. If you bet that God exists, and win, you win everything; if you lose, you lose nothing.

You will examine the overwhelming proofs of Christianity's truth, the miracles, the fulfillment of prophecies, the persistence of the faith. But in the end you will have no need of proofs based on fallible human reason. The heart has its reasons that reason does not know. It is by the heart that we know the first principles, and reason must rest on the perceptions of the heart and of instinct. There is nothing so conformant to reason as the disavowal of reason. Christianity, so rich in proofs, miracles, witnesses, signs and wisdom, dismisses them all and declares to you that none of these can change us and make us capable of knowing and loving God, but only the virtue of the folly of the cross, without wisdom and signs.

Thus in the end Pascal surrenders all his proofs, to rest on man's need to love his God.

As Pascal meditated and wrote, his health continued to fail. Modern diagnoses are insecure, but there is some agreement on peritoneal tuberculosis, accompanied by an evil growth in the brain. He was tortured by frightful headaches, but he blessed God for his sufferings, regarding them as a fire burning away his sins little by little by a daily sacrifice. Sickness, he said, is the natural state of Christians.

He hurried the end of his sufferings by austerities. He refused any concession to appetite. He made secretly a wire belt, with sharp points turning inward against the flesh, and when he felt any stirring of pleasure or vanity he would rub his elbows against it, to wound his spirit through the body. He tortured also his sisters, forbidding any show of affection toward him, forbidding even Gilberte's children to embrace their mother: "Jesus shakes off his disciples to enter his agony. We must shake off our nearest and dearest to imitate him."

Blaise Pascal died in the summer of 1662, aged thirty-nine. The direct cause was a hemorrhage of the brain. The great mind was poisoned by the corruption of the blood, the corruption of life.

He was as authentic a genius as our world has produced. But the logic of genius would not permit him to rest satisfied with the reasonable work of genius, the service of human knowledge. He was trying, by force of will, to pass from what he called the order of minds to the higher order of charity. He was attempting sainthood, attempting to take the heavenly city by storm. He tried to surpass and abandon humanity; he succeeded only, in pain and misery, in abandoning himself. We commonplace men and women, content with our humanity, must regard him with wonder and pity, recognizing in him a victim of the curse of genius.

Morris Bishop is a teacher (Cornell), a translator (Eight Plays of Molière), a biographer (Petrarch, Pascal, La Rochefoucauld), and a writer of light verse (A Bowl of Bishop).

By H. R. TREVOR-ROPER

It was not the medieval world
that produced the witchcraft delusion.
It was the age of the Renaissance
and the Enlightenment. An English
historian examines the forces that nurtured it
and the forces that finally overcame it.

THE PERSECUTION OF WITCHES

Three witches are burned, and two confederates executed, in Germany in 1555

The Dark Ages were not all that dark. They were sensible about witches. To believe in witches or werewolves, said Saint Boniface in the eighth century, was unchristian. In the tenth century a Church dignitary declared night-flying a hallucination, and his declaration was accepted into the canon law. In the eleventh, the laws of King Coloman of Hungary refused to notice witches "since they do not exist." Of course, shepherds and peasant women continued to talk of them, as they had done in pagan times: we find sympathetic magic in Theocritus, werewolves in Petronius, anointment and night-flying in Apuleius; and Saint Augustine, with his African credulity, did his best to preserve these peasant superstitions and fit them into his gigantic system. But in general the Church, as the civilizer of nations, disdained such old wives' tales. They were the rubbish of paganism which the light of the Gospel had dispelled. Even the Devil, in the Middles Ages, sank through familiarity into contempt. The Prince of Darkness became a village hobgoblin, dismissible with a formula.

And then, with the end of the Middle Ages, what a change! In the sixteenth century, the century of the Renaissance, and the seventeenth century, the century of the

New Science, all Europe seemed given over to witches. Scotland and Hungary, where they had hitherto been unknown, were suddenly found to be swarming with them. By their own confession, thousands of old women every night anointed themselves with "devil's grease," slipped through cracks and keyholes and up chimneys, and flew off to the witches' Sabbath. There they worshiped the Devil in the form of a stinking goat, danced around him amid macabre music, kissed him solemnly under the tail, and feasted on such viands as tempted their national imagination. In Germany these

The Devil's converts (as shown in a tract of 1626) enter into a pact with him by stamping on the Cross.

were sliced turnips, parodies of the Host; in Spain, exhumed corpses, preferably of kinsfolk; in England, more sensibly, roast beef and beer. When not thus engaged, these old ladies, it seemed, were busy suckling familiar spirits in the form of weasels, moles, bats, toads, or other convenient creatures; they were compassing the death of their neighbors or their neighbors' pigs; they were raising tempests, causing blights, or procuring impotence in bridegrooms; and as a pledge of their servitude they were constantly having sexual intercourse with the Devil, who appeared (since even he abhors unnatural vice) to she-witches as an incubus, to he-witches as a succubus.

What Gibbon called "the chaste severity of the Fathers" was much exercised by this last subject, and no detail escaped their learned scrutiny. They established that as a lover the Devil was of "freezing coldness" to the touch, and certain items were lacking in his equipment; but there was no frigidity in the technical sense: his attentions were of formidable, even oppressive,

solidity. That he could generate on witches was agreed by nearly all (how else, asked the Catholic doctors, could the birth of Luther be explained?); but was that power the Devil's own, as a Franciscan specialist maintained ("under correction from our holy Mother Church"), or did he, being neuter, operate with borrowed matter? Some important theologians conjectured that the Devil equipped himself by squeezing the organs of the dead; others had other theories, more profound than decent; but on the whole holy Mother Church followed the magisterial ruling of the Angelic Doctor, Saint Thomas Aquinas. The Devil, she ruled, could only discharge as incubus what he had previously absorbed as succubus: he therefore nimbly alternated between these postures. It seems surprising that the Roman Church, which has never renounced these beliefs, should not have recalled them to prove the diabolical nature of artificial insemination donors.

What was the Church to do when faced with this alarming epidemic of witches? What indeed except discover, test, and destroy them? To discover them, village hatreds must be exploited, German schoolboys trained to denounce, confessors supplied with elaborate questionnaires. To test them, there were certain reliable evidences, or *indicia*. Unless one was lucky enough to discover "a pot full of human limbs, sacred things, hosts, etc.," which, as an inquisitor sagely observed, "is a grave *indicium*," one had to be content with circumstantial tests. Of these, fortunately, there were plenty: a mole or wart, by which the familiar spirit was suckled; an insensitive spot that did not bleed when pricked; a capacity to float in water; an incapacity to shed tears; or even the mere aspect of a witch—old, ugly, or smelly. And then there were certain professions that were automatically suspect. It was well known, for instance, that midwives were ordered by the Devil to destroy newborn infants. If anything went wrong at childbirth, that too must be a grave *indicium*.

When the witch was thus identified, the next thing was to make her confess. On the Continent, and in Scotland, this was easy. There were the torturer and the questionnaire. Witchcraft being *crimen exceptum,* there was no limit to the torture, and many and various were the instruments and re-

finements used. There were the *grésillons*, which crushed the tips of fingers and toes in a vice; the *échelle*, or rack, for stretching the body, the *tortillon* for squeezing its tender parts at the same time; and the *estrapade*, or pulley for jerking it violently in mid-air. All these were used liberally in Lorraine. In Scotland, the legs of the suspect were broken, even into fragments, in the boot, or grilled on the *caschielawis*; the thumb was screwed in the *pilliwinckes*; the fingernails were pulled off with the *turkas*, or pincers, and needles were driven up to their heads into the quick. Elsewhere the ingenuity of the torturers had contrived other exquisite devices. As for the questionnaire, that made confession simple: the learned details were ready to hand, and the victim had only to say yes. Hence the detailed identity of witches' confessions. If the witch did confess, her guilt was held to be proved and clerical science confirmed; but she was expected, of course, to name all those neighbors and kinsfolk whom she had seen at the Sabbath. Even without torture, there were many self-accusing exhibitionists who were only too glad to give this "special evidence." In this way whole villages were decimated, and even judges sometimes took fright at the ever-expanding complicity. If the suspect did not confess, her guilt and her torture were both increased. To be a witch and deny it, and deny it even under torture, was evidence of the blackest guilt: such courage, it was agreed, could only proceed from hardened wickedness and the help of the Devil. In either case, whether she confessed or not, the witch was sent to the flames—unless, as a special "grace" from the bishop or abbot or secular lord, she was merely torn with red-hot pincers and beheaded.

In England, it is fair to add, the methods were milder. There was no Holy Inquisition in England. Also there was no torture in English common law, only discomfort (though the distinction could sometimes be blurred). Moreover, in England condemned witches were hanged not burned. When Oliver Cromwell conquered Scotland and introduced English justice, persecution almost ceased, much to the indignation of the Presbyterian clergy. Nor was the doctrine so fully developed in England as on the Continent. The "witch-mark," the insensitive spot which revealed the witch—and which sometimes gathered four surgeons with long needles round a Continental suspect, pricking, till mere paralysis procured the necessary insensitivity—was not recognized in England.

How can such lunacy have possessed humanity for two centuries? It seems inconceivable, and yet, though the numbers have often been greatly exaggerated, the facts are not in doubt. Now, with the republication of the unfinished work of the great American historian H. C. Lea, we can trace the whole history of the craze and the persecution. It was his work on *The History of the Inquisition*—that monument of liberal scholarship—that led Lea, in his last years, to turn his mind to the closely related subject of witchcraft. Unfortunately, he died when he had merely collected the materials. But the materials alone, with his commentary, are a magnificent historical work. Arranged and published half a century after the author's death, they enable us better than any other work to trace the causes and history of the European witch mania: a history of collective cruelty and credulity instituted, inflamed, and prolonged (though not always controlled) by organized religion.

For there can be no doubt that the witch craze was organized, and received its final organization late in the fifteenth century, by the medieval Church. Little by little, in the later Middle Ages, the Church had equated witchcraft with the more serious crimes of sorcery and heresy, and the Schoolmen had systematized, embellished, and condemned those hitherto disregarded superstitions and hallucinations that spring, at bottom, from rural poverty. By such attentions they had built up and advertised a grotesque new mythology for which the inquisitors afterwards, by their torture and their questionnaires, obtained massive confirmation.

For it is quite clear that witchcraft, as a systematic cult, was not discovered; it was invented by the inquisitors. We can trace the movement in all its stages by dates and places. Everywhere it is the same: first the persecutors, then the heresy. It was the inquisitors who discovered the first witches in Hungary and Scotland and who spread the epidemic over Germany. Elsewhere half the details to which thousands of witches readily and unanimously confessed had been quite

unknown in their districts until the inquisitors had arrived with their books and pincers. And the crucial date can be pinpointed. In 1484 the Dominican inquisitors in the bigoted Alpine valleys, where they had long been burning witches, sought to increase their power, extend their field, and silence their critics by calling in papal help. So they solicited from Pope Innocent VIII the first general Witch-Bull, the Bull *Summis Desiderantes Affectibus*. Two years later the same inquisitors, as if in response to the Bull, advertised the disease they were now armed and authorized to cure. They published the first great encyclopedia of the subject, *Malleus Maleficarum*, the Hammer of Witches. From that date the delusion began its fabulous course. From the Swiss valleys papal authority sent it out over all Europe. The disease was created by its pretended remedy.

At first the educated laity were contemptuous of this clerical nonsense. How could lawyers, scholars, philosophers, in the age of Erasmus, swallow these Alpine credulities, this monkish phantasmagoria? The

In homage to their new master, the initiates offer the Devil black candles and kneel to kiss his buttocks.

European humanists, putting (as the clergy sourly complained) human reason before divine theology, poured eloquent scorn on yet another instance of barbarous folly. Witchcraft, said the great Italian scientist Girolamo Cardano, in 1550, was merely an illusion of minds distorted by poverty and undernourishment, and confessions were therefore worthless. But against massive, systematic propaganda who can hold out? Clerical machinery was organized; lay intelligence was not. Moreover, the clergy controlled education. So, as encyclopedia

followed encyclopedia, as commentator quoted commentator, as confession echoed confession, the sheer weight of documented rubbish ultimately overwhelmed even the most rational mind. In Catholic countries the clergy, having survived the Protestant threat, redoubled their control over all departments of life. The result was the *sacrificio dell' intelletto*, the sacrifice of the intellect: a sacrifice made easier by that other phenomenon, which we also know, *la trahison des clercs,* the treason of the intellectuals.

Such was the Catholic Counter Reformation. Nor did the Protestant Reformation help—as yet. Luther was as credulous as any Schoolman; and the Swiss Reformers, in addition, breathed the same Alpine bigotry as the Catholic inquisitors. Indeed, it was in consequence of their resort to Geneva and Basel and other purified "schools of Christ" that the Marian exiles carried the craze back to Elizabethan England, to Calvinist Scotland, and to New England. Besides, there was that phrase in the Bible, their Bible: "thou shalt not suffer a witch to live." "The Bible," said Calvin firmly, preaching to the Elect about the Witch of Endor, "teaches that there are witches and that they must be slain. . . . God expressly commands that all witches and enchantresses shall be put to death; and this law of God is an universal law."

So in Geneva, which before had been free from witch trials, Calvin introduced a new reign of terror: in the sixty years after his coming, one hundred and fifty witches were burned. Moreover, in Protestant as in Catholic lands, the rules of evidence were now quietly changed. There was to be no nonsense about proof of material damage: to *be* a witch, even a harmless witch, was enough. In Calvinist Scotland, in the Lutheran and then Calvinist Palatinate, in Lutheran Saxony, the law was adjusted accordingly. Witches must be destroyed, declared the Elector of Saxony, "even if their sorcery has harmed nobody." In England the law preserved the old distinction, and the Anglican Church preserved an honorable record of sanity and moderation; but if the Calvinist clergy had had their way, it would have been changed. "Death," declared the oracle of Cambridge Puritanism William Perkins, "is the just and deserved punishment" even "of the good witch." And

Perkins, who also advocated the introduction of torture into England for such cases, was "our Perkins," the revered teacher of the Founding Fathers of New England.

Thus, as the sixteenth century went on, all Europe, Catholic and Protestant alike, was infected. The clergy vied with each other in ferocious absurdity, the lawyers followed obediently in their wake, and the laws were duly tightened up. Even the intellectuals surrendered. By 1580 Jean Bodin, one of the greatest of French thinkers, had joined the hue and cry. Himself a judge and burner of witches, he attacked his king as their defender, argued that judges who spared them should themselves be executed, and approved anonymous denunciation and lynch law. In Lorraine Nicolas Rémy, *procureur-général* of the duchy, a cultivated scholar, historian, and poet, sent two or three thousand victims to the stake and even so thought the laws too mild. By law, children who were said to have attended their mother at the Sabbath were merely flogged in front of the fire in which their mother was burning; Rémy would have had the whole seed of witches exterminated, and he pointed (to show that Catholics too could quote the Old Testament) to the irreverent children whom Elisha so properly caused to be devoured by bears. In Germany, in the next century, Benedict Carpzov was regarded as the greatest jurist of his time. He was a devout Lutheran and his handbook on witches was honored as the *Malleus* of Protestantism. Reflecting on his meritorious career, he boasted that he had read the Bible from cover to cover fifty-three times, taken the Holy Sacrament every week, greatly intensified the efficacy of torture, and procured the death of twenty thousand witches. In England the most liberal of judges, Sir Matthew Hale, an enlightened natural scientist and humane reformer of the law, hanged an old woman on the evidence of a wart; Joseph Glanvill, a Baconian scientist and Fellow of the Royal Society, devoted his intellectual energy to the confutation of the "Sadducees" who disbelieved in witches; and the Cambridge Platonist and rational theologian Henry More was perfectly ready to believe not only that his own urine smelt of violets but also that an old man had sailed over Shelford steeple by night and torn his breeches on the weathercock.

No doubt there were skeptics, too; but who would dare to express skepticism where the churches had power and the lawyers, as usual, conformed? "It is rating our conjectures high," wrote the discreet Montaigne, after witnessing the trial and confession of a batch of witches at the court of some petty prince, "to roast other people alive for them"; but even that discretion was silenced as Montaigne joined all other

The witches are now prepared to practice their evil powers. Houses, at their whim, are consumed by flames.

critics of the witch mania on the Roman Index. Others, as they were more explicit, suffered more directly. In 1589 Dietrich Flade, rector of the university and chief judge of the electoral court at Trier, found himself unconvinced by the confessions, under torture, of the old women who were brought before him. He therefore judged them with leniency. At once the Prince-Archbishop had him arrested, accused of witchcraft, tortured till he confessed whatever was put to him, strangled, and burnt.

A generation later the German Jesuit Friedrich von Spee was converted by his own experiences as a confessor of condemned witches. "Torture," he declared roundly in 1631, "fills our Germany with witches and unheard-of wickedness, and not only Germany but any nation that tries it. . . . If all of us have not confessed ourselves witches, that is only because we have not all been tortured." And who, he asked, were the men who demanded these tortures? Jurists in search of gain, credulous villagers, and "those theologians and prelates who quietly enjoy their speculations and know nothing of the squalor of prisons, the weight of chains, the implements of torture, the lamentations of the poor—things

far beneath their dignity."

Spee's book, *Cautio Criminalis*, is one of the most eloquent protests against the witch craze in Germany: it has earned him more lasting fame than his poetry and caused him to be called "saint and martyr by a higher canonization than that of the Church." But what fury it caused in his Order! For in many places the Jesuits, as the paladins of orthodoxy, led the hunt. To escape the wrath of his colleagues, Spee's book was published anonymously, without the knowledge of his superiors, in the relative freedom of a Protestant city.

Even in England, in the days of Puritan influence, one had to be careful. Under Queen Elizabeth, Reginald Scot, a country gentleman, boldly attacked the belief in witches. At once the king of Scotland rushed to its defense. He was a firm believer and fancied himself as a demonologist—indeed, he claimed to have been personally inconvenienced by a storm at sea raised by the co-operation of Scottish and Norwegian witches. Naturally he was enraged by Scot's skepticism. Moreover, since he was heir to the English throne, his rage could be disagreeable. Twenty years later, when he came into his new kingdom, his adversary was safely dead, but the impious book was seized and burned by the hangman. After that, although "the frequency of forged possessions" converted King James himself to sense, his less privileged subjects took no risks. Even Sir Francis Bacon and John Selden, two of the greatest lay minds in England, were careful to frame their undoubted skepticism in discreet, orthodox terms.

Meanwhile, the persecution abroad went on. Torture, of course, was the basis of it. "Now my dearest child," a burgomaster of Bamberg wrote to his daughter in 1628, after having publicly confessed that he had renounced God, given himself to the Devil, and met his fellow officials of Bamberg at a witches' Sabbath, "you have here all my acts and confessions, for which I must die. It is all falsehood and invention, so help me God. . . . They never cease to torture until one says something. . . . If God sends no means of bringing the truth to light, our whole kindred will be burnt." And indeed he said no more than the truth. As the rage for denunciation spread, whole families were exterminated, whole parishes depopulated. In Trier, in 1585, when the Archbishop had aroused himself, two villages were left with only one female inhabitant apiece. And as the population shrank, so the executioner swelled in prosperity and social status. At Trier he was seen to ride abroad on a fine horse, "like a nobleman of the court, dressed in silver and gold, while his wife vied with noble ladies in dress and luxury." At Schongau in Bavaria he rode about in state with his wife, two servants, and a supply of needles to prick as witches ever more and more victims.

But if, as Spee wrote, it was torture that filled Europe with witches, it would be idle to pretend that all denunciations or confessions came from torture alone. Many witches were undoubtedly impelled by exhibitionism. This was largely true of young girls, some of whom were cured by finding real lovers instead of imaginary incubi. Others genuinely believed their own confessions. After all, they might say, who were they to judge? Old and feeble, undernourished and half-demented, these poor women hated their neighbors with peasant rancor and were hated by them in turn. They lived in a world of malice and delusion, wished to cast spells, dreamed of night-flying and the Devil, and would gladly have served Antichrist, if he existed, to oppose the Christian society which they felt was mobilized against them. When the highest and most learned authorities gravely assured them that all these things were real and could be proved out of books, who were they to dissent? They allowed clergymen and judges to give form and detail to their vague hankerings, their half-felt experiences. And so, even without torture, they confessed. But their confessions rested ultimately on torture all the same. It was because thousands had been tortured into saying they were witches, that the mythology had been built up and now seemed so certain that other thousands, without torture, confessed in tune.

Torture and mythology, the pincers and the book, these were the essential machinery of the European witch craze. Out of hallucination and suggestion they created a terrible empire of darkness which then acquired a life and momentum of its own, independent of outside forces. By the mid-seventeenth century the documentation was so immense, the evidence so complete, the authorities so confident in their mutual corroboration, the penalties of nonconformity so great, that the return to sanity might well have seemed impossible. A new church had been established, more universal than Catholicism or Protestantism, and all the forces of tradition, custom, discipline, and vested interest joined to sustain it. How could skepticism or sense prevail against so powerful a system? Even a challenge seemed impossible. The thing, it must have seemed, was final. It had come to stay.

So weak men must have argued. So they always do, against any prevalent folly. And yet, as it happened, they were wrong. Even in the hour of triumph the monstrous system began to crumble; now here, now there, the opening cracks appeared. It was in the 1640's that the persecution reached its height in England. Those were the days when Matthew Hopkins, the notorious "witch-finder general," spread terror all through East Anglia, and the greatest holocaust of witches ever known in England—twenty-nine in a batch—took place at the Chelmsford Assizes. And yet within a few

Thunder and lightning, hail and rain are stirred into a wild tempest by a witch riding on a galloping goat.

years the reaction set in. Quite suddenly the tide began to ebb: the few English executions between 1660 and 1685 are trivial last exceptions to a new rule. In France it is the same: witch burning was already in decline when Colbert, in 1673, abolished the charge of *sorcellerie sabbatique*. In Geneva, once so ferocious, the last witch was executed in 1652. The aristocratic cities were emancipated first: popular prejudices were less easy to conquer, especially in rural areas. In the early 1660's there were new outbreaks in backward countries: in Sweden, released from royal control; in Scotland and Lorraine, released from English and French occupation. In all three countries the old clergy—Lutheran, Calvinist, and Catholic—had suddenly recovered power. But their victories were short-lived. In general, throughout Europe, the climate of opinion has changed. The old laws may remain on the statute book, the old beliefs linger in school and cloister, but the old power has gone. Even in Germany, where the prince-bishops burned away in corners for another century, the scale of operation is insignificant: the Archbishop of Salzburg's bonfire of ninety-seven witches, in 1679, is the last of the great burnings. The empire of darkness has begun to rot inwardly. The clergy are on the defensive, and there is something hysterical in their last, despairing cries: the cry of the odious Bishop Bossuet in France, protesting that an army of 180,000 witches is threatening all Europe—"I wish they could all be put in one body, all burned at once in one fire"; the protest of the Scottish ministers, in 1736, against that "national sin," the repeal of the witch laws by parliament "contrary to the express laws of God"; the lament, in England, of John Wesley that "the infidels have hooted witchcraft out of the world." Well might they lament. They were defeated. The laity had won. The Enlightenment was at hand.

How did it happen? How does it happen that a closed ideological system, seemingly watertight, self-preserving and self-perpetuating, and fortified with multiple interests, suddenly weakens and crumbles? The question is of obvious general interest. It is of particular interest today, when such systems have been newly built up among us, have become the orthodoxy of the learned, the piety of the devout, and have led, in once civilized countries, to wholesale purges for crimes scarcely less ridiculous than those once analyzed and defined by Rémy and Del Rio, Carpzov and Perkins. In order to answer this question it may be well to consider first the forces that worked against the witch mania, even at its height. For even then there were restraints that prevented it from further expansion. These were of two kinds. First, there was internal discipline, the discipline of the clergy. Secondly, there was external doubt, the doubt of the laity.

The discipline was effective first. At first, indeed, it was the most that could be hoped for. And the only force that could discipline the persecution was the same force that had originally launched it: the Inquisition. It was in Italy and Spain, the centers of the Roman and Spanish Inquisition, that the monstrous doctrines had been formulated; it was there too that they were most firmly controlled. In a memorable chapter of his *History of the Inquisition in Spain,* Lea himself pointed out how that hideous engine of intellectual and racial tyranny yet, by its "wisdom and firmness," held the witch mania down. In this as in other respects it kept Spain in the ignorance and bliss of the tenth century. In Italy the Roman Inquisition was only a little behind. The phenomena were the same as elsewhere, but the attitude of authority was different. Not only was the Inquisition stricter in its definition of witchcraft: sometimes it also tamed the heresy by incorporating it into orthodoxy. The Roman Church has always known how to do this. In the Dark Ages it converted pagan gods into Christian saints; in the Middle Ages it converted its radicals, its enthusiasts, into new orders of monks or friars; and now it did much the same with sorcery. In the Mediterranean lands those who supposed themselves levitated into the air were not burned as witches but canonized as saints. Of course this did not mean that the mythology was discredited; far from it. The Catholic Church clung fast to the belief in witches. But action at least was regulated. Perhaps it is no accident that the period of English history when the persecution, though not intellectually undermined, was most firmly controlled, was the period of "Arminian" government under Charles I and Archbishop Laud—the nearest Protestant England ever came to an Inquisition.

Thus something was owed to clerical discipline. The Inquisition burnt scholars, saints, and Jews, but it was scrupulous about old women. And yet in the long run this leads us nowhere. At best, clerical discipline could only have limited the persecution to "true witches." The intellectual foundations of the persecution remained intact. To end it, it must be proved that there were no true witches, and this meant an intellectual revolution. It did not, of course, mean a Protestant revolution: for the Prot-

estant clergy, as we have seen, were just as bad as the Catholic, the Calvinist ministers as the Dominican friars. What was needed was an anticlerical revolution, a revolt of lay reason against the new cosmology of the Church. But such a revolution was in fact easier in Protestant than in Catholic countries, because in Protestant countries the clergy, in general, had less power. The Reformation had owed its original success to lay support; and where it had prevailed, and where there was an educated middle class to consolidate its victory, the laity saw to it that the new clergy never obtained quite the power of the old. Moreover, in Protestant countries there were no religious orders—those formidable religious armies which, while they evangelized among the masses, could also mobilize the prejudices of the masses against the occasional liberalism even of popes and bishops. Thus the educated laity, if they existed, were far stronger, far freer in Protestant than in Catholic countries. Being free, they could accept intellectual revolutions which their own clergy resisted. They could accept the revolution against Aristotle, the revolution of Copernicus and Galileo. They could also accept the revolution against witches, the revolution of the "Sadducees." The revolu-

Unsuspecting victims are first put to sleep with devilish potions and later poisoned by well-dressed witches.

tionaries themselves might be Catholics, as Copernicus and Galileo were, but that made no difference. The base even of their revolution had to be found in Protestant, unclerical lands. So the work of Galileo, condemned in Rome, was published in Protestant Strasbourg. Thus it was in Protestant Holland, the first country to abandon witch trials and witch burnings, that the under-

lying theory itself, long secretly doubted, was first publicly overthrown. It was overthrown by Balthasar Bekker who, in 1691, "struck at the roots of the terror by doubting the Devil himself."

So in the days of its expansion the witch craze ran up against a double movement of restraint. In the south, clerical discipline pressed on its surface; in the north, lay reason undermined its heart. The importance of these restraints is clear if we look, for a moment, at areas where neither was effective: where the clergy had power but not discipline and where the laity lacked education and social strength. Such conditions can be found in both Catholic and Protestant lands: in Catholic lands without centralized church law, in Protestant lands without a strong, educated middle class.

In Catholic lands the obvious instance is the region north of the Alps. There customary law gave all power to local rulers and those rulers were Catholics without restraint. So Lorraine and Burgundy, Bavaria and the Rhineland, the prince-bishoprics of Germany and the Catholic cantons of Switzerland were the classic lands of witchcraft. There the greatest persecutions took place, there the great encyclopedias were published, thence the successive waves of hatred and fear rolled out over Europe. On this geographical fact all were agreed, believers and unbelievers alike. It is notorious, wrote Spee, that witches abound in Germany above all other countries. In Burgundy, protested the magistrates of a clerical enclave, "the evil grows daily and this wretched breed multiplies everywhere." It was in Germany, said Bossuet, that the whole population was kept busy burning witches, in Switzerland that villages were entirely depopulated by executions, in Lorraine that the traveler could see "thousands and thousands of stakes," the only means of keeping down this pest "that multiplies on the earth like caterpillars in our gardens." Clerical power, lack of legal centralization, absence of an educated middle class, and torture—all the conditions were fulfilled to make these old "prince-bishoprics" the last stronghold of the European witch mania.

In Protestant lands the classic examples come from the Calvinist theocracies in those two underdeveloped countries, Stuart Scotland and colonial New England. The

Scottish clergy enjoyed their last great witch hunt in the 1660's; their New England brethren a whole generation later, in 1692. But the basic elements are the same. New England society was a society without, as yet, a strong educated laity; its clergy, the Calvinist oligarchy, was sufficiently powerful to dictate orthodoxy and fan hatred, but it lacked the centralized machinery of law to control the passions aroused; and if there was no legal torture, at least there were equivalent inducements: "hardships and torments" for those who would not confess, life and liberty for those who would. So, when the witch craze broke out at Salem, there was much to extend it, little to stop it. The clerical leaders, delighted by the evidence produced by a few hysterical girls for their own theories, first beat the drum ecclesiastic and then failed to control their followers. "I have set myself," wrote the Reverend Cotton Mather complacently, "to countermine the whole plot of the Devil against New England, in every branch of it." No doubt, he admitted, evil spirits would be exasperated by his words, just as the Jewish Sadducees had been by those of Christ; but he would not stop his crusade for that. Nor did he. In the end, when two hundred people had been accused, one hundred and fifty imprisoned, and twenty-nine executed on the "spectral evidence" of their demented neighbors who claimed to have seen them at the Sabbath, even he took alarm. But still he reserved his real hatred not for the executions but for a "vile volume" produced by "a very wicked sort of Sadducee": a volume which his father, the respected president of Harvard College, caused to be burned in the college yard. This vile volume was the protest of a layman, the merchant Robert Calef, who, with his fellow-merchant, Thomas Brattle, deserves to be remembered as the herald of lay reason in America; and it had been published safely outside clerical control, in London.

Thus, after two centuries, the lay spirit triumphed again, and belief in witchcraft, intellectually discredited, deprived of its organization and sanctions, no longer sure of the assent of rulers and judges, sank back again into its original, its permanent character: it remained, and remains, what it had been in antiquity and the Dark Ages, a congeries of peasant superstitions. By the

eighteenth century the clergy, Catholic and Protestant alike (all but their lunatic fringe), quietly forgot the doctrines they still did not dare to disown. For the clergy too, by the eighteenth century, had become laicized. Their extremists—the Dominicans, the Calvinists—had fought hard. Where they had held power, where the laity had been weak or uneducated, and the traditional rulers—princes, bishops, or town governors—had been dependent on them, there they had prevailed. But where they had been weak or divided, as in Protestant Holland and England, and even in Catholic France (which was also, to its intellectual salvation, Jansenist France), there lay reason had found a base, the "Sadducees" had

Compendium Maleficarum, GUAZZO, LONDON 1929

The burned remains of hanged disinterred corpses provide the powerful fuel to propel a witch's flying stick.

published their books, and the forces of orthodoxy had been gradually divided. Even within the clerical body there had appeared "liberal" clergy, allies of the laity and strong by that alliance, the heirs of the old humanist, Erasmian clergy who, in the sixteenth century, had been so remorselessly snuffed out. Once that division had happened, what a prospect opened! Having found a base, the rot spread. Iron curtains could not keep it back; for it is impossible, in a prosperous, competitive, literate world, to keep even a clergy, even a bureaucracy, even a praetorian guard permanently divorced from the laity—provided the laity have equal opportunities of self-support and independent education.

And this, it seems to me, is the ultimate comfort in this squalid story of collective, organized lunacy and cruelty. The theorists of power maintain that by creating a separate caste in society—a Party, or the Elect

—and arming it with a doctrine, an ideology, they can make both slavery and nonsense permanent. "I am persuaded," Bertrand Russell, our greatest rationalist once sadly confessed, "that there is absolutely no limit to the absurdities that can, by government action, come to be generally believed. Give me an adequate army, with power to provide it with more pay and better food than falls to the lot of the average man, and I will undertake, within thirty years, to make the majority of the population believe that two and two are three, that water freezes when it gets hot and boils when it gets cold, or any other nonsense that might seem to serve the interest of the State." The history of the European witch craze shows that this can indeed be done—for a time. When we read of men like Bodin and Rémy—by all accounts liberal, humane, learned men—hanging and burning old women with the conscientious zeal of saviors of society, we realize how completely an artificial system of nonsense, once established, can take possession even of thinking, rational men; and we are tempted to wonder whether perhaps today our minds may not be equally imprisoned, though in other prisons, from which only the cranks whom we persecute will ultimately save us. For it is not only churches that manufacture myths and win assent to them: bureaucracies, political parties, general staffs can do the same. On the other hand, the history of the witch craze also shows the limitations of delusion. Perhaps in an economically undeveloped country isolated from the outer world and absolutely controlled by the priests of the myth, it may be possible to fool all the people all the time. But if political power requires economic development and economic development requires an educated laity, able to listen to ideas from outside, and if there is an outside world where different ideas can find a base, then ultimately the solidarity even of such a party can be rotted; lay reason will infiltrate even into the clergy; sense will prevail.

H. R. Trevor-Roper, Regius Professor of Modern History at Christ Church, Oxford, has written Men and Events, *a collection of historical essays, and recently edited* Blitzkrieg to Defeat: Hitler's War Directives.

TERTIVS C PLATONE PHILOSOPHIÆ PRINCEPS

Alone and strangely out of place in his own world, would he be more at home in ours? It is, after all, the product of his scientific method

FRANCIS BACON

By LOREN EISELEY

In January of 1561 a son was born to Nicholas Bacon, Lord Keeper to Elizabeth I. In twelve years this bright, grave child, Francis, would be called by Elizabeth her little Lord Keeper, but all his life she would deny him great office (as one denies, yet counsels with, a wizard), and all his life poverty and ill fortune would dog him in the midst of luxury. Yet it is this man who first fully visualized in all its splendor the "invention of inventions"—the experimental method which would unlock the riches of the modern world.

The most curious aspect of the technological environment which surrounds us today is one we rarely think about—namely, that it exists. How did it arise and why? We define ourselves vaguely as *Homo sapiens*, the wise, and we assume, if we think about our surroundings at all, that man's innate wisdom has, in the course of time, automatically produced the scientific world we know. Yet the archaeologist would be forced to tell us that several great civilizations have arisen and vanished without the benefit of a scientific philosophy. Similarly, Western society, down to the last three centuries or so, betrays but feeble traces of that type of thinking known today as "scientific," with its emphasis upon experiment and dispassionate observation of the natural world.

There is only one great exception in Western thought—Greek philosophy and Greek science before that tiny but enlightened world was destroyed by internecine conflict and the expanding power of the Roman Empire. In other words, we are faced with the problem that this wise creature, man, has rarely shown any penchant for science and would

From a 1640 edition of The Advancement of Learning, *Bacon's revolutionary discourse on the scientific method, comes this portrait of the author in his study.*

much rather be left to his uninhibited dreams and fantasies.

Scientific thought demands some kind of unique soil in which to flourish. It has about it the rarity of a fungus springing up in a forest glade only to perish before nightfall. Perhaps, indeed, its own dynamism contains its doom. Perhaps the tendency of science to fragment and crumble also partakes of the qualities of the mushroom. This much at least we know: science among us is an *invented* cultural institution, an institution not present in all societies, and not one that may be counted upon to arise from human instinct.

Science is as capable of decay and death as any other human activity, such as a religion or a system of government. It cannot be equated with individual thought or the unique observations of genius, even though it partakes of these things. As a way of life it has rules which have to be learned, and practices and techniques which have to be transmitted from generation to generation by the formal process of education. Neither is it technology, although technology may contribute to science, or science to technology. Many lost civilizations—Roman, Mayan, Egyptian—had great builders, whether of roads, aqueducts, temples, or pyramids. Their remains show enormous experience of transmitted and improved techniques, but still we are not precisely within the true domain of science.

Science exists only within a tradition of constant experimental investigation of the natural world. It demands that every hypothesis we formulate be subject to proof, whether in nature or in the laboratory, before we can accept its validity. Men, even scientists, find this type of thinking extremely difficult to sustain. In this sense science is not natural to man at all. It has to be learned, consciously practiced, stripped out of the sea of emotions, prejudices, and wishes in which our daily lives are steeped. No man can long endure such rarefied heights without descending to common earth. Even the professional scientist frequently confines such activity to a specific discipline, and outside of it indulges his illogical prejudices.

To introduce the concept of the scientific method into the world at large as a way of life, therefore, is a more arduous and difficult task than merely to conceive of its philosophical possibility. Even today, when scientific achievements surround us on every hand and the textbooks of our schools bulge with illustrative experiments, men are, in the mass, still emotional and resistant to fact, particularly in their political and social thinking. We are always more willing to accept mechanical changes in an automobile than to revise, or even to examine our racial prejudices, to use just one painful example. We are more willing to swallow a pill that we hope will relax our tensions than to make the sustained, conscious effort necessary to alter our daily living habits.

The interest and significance of Francis Bacon, the little boy born at Elizabeth's court, lies in this: he played a powerful role in getting English society to swallow, figuratively, a pill—the pill of science. It took fifty years of his life and the patient endurance of the court's and the world's contempt, before, a generation or so later, society finally gulped down its medicine and turned to look in the mirror.

Since the dawn of the scientific world is a strangely unique, almost unnatural one, the life and times of the great statesman who played a major part in the half-light of that spectral

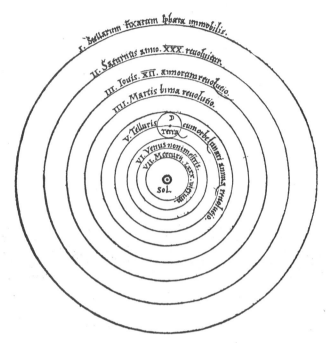

Bacon's inductive method was born in a lively era for science: Copernicus issued his concept of the solar system in 1543.

morning will be of perennial interest so long as science and its world endure. Of all those who dreamed in secret, experimented but confined their endeavors, Francis Bacon alone walked to the doorway of the future, flung it wide, and said to his trembling and laggard audience, "Look. There is tomorrow. Take it with charity lest it destroy you."

*T*ime dulls the horrors of the past. A traditional monarchy like that of Britain has much in its history which both subjects and later monarchs desire to forget. We remember Elizabeth as an adept ruler of men; we remember her sea rovers and the destruction of the Spanish Armada. As the centuries recede the screams of tortured men sound faraway; the fall of the headsman's axe is no longer heard upon the block. But to understand the Elizabethan world in which Francis Bacon rose to a Lord Chancellorship we must know the realities of that world.

Its bloody legacy came straight from Henry VIII. It was a world in which the English language was still being shaped into the vehicle of great literature. It was also a world of terror, corrupted by absolute power. A world where the throne defined treason and where to rise was also to invite one's fall, a world where rulers expected to be struck in the dark and where the logical paranoid act was to strike first. "Every public man in the England of the Tudors and the Stuarts," writes one historian, "entered on his career with the familiar expectation of possibly closing it on the scaffold."

Spies and informers swarmed everywhere. *Agents provocateurs* promoted treason for pay. Bestial crowds swarmed to torturings and hangings in public. The heads of executed men withered on the city gates as object lessons. Withal, this was Shakespeare's world and Francis Bacon's. It was the latter who was to write of himself and his generation as wearing out days few and evil. It was he who was to say, in weariness, that his soul had been a stranger to his pilgrimage. It was he, the last great Elizabethan, who was to murmur when they came to summon him back to the court of Charles I, "I have had enough of that vanity."

*A*ll along the way he had done the will of princes, had been a true servant of the state. Why was disgrace his reward? The world forgives his treasonous, intemperate patron, Essex, who died under the axe. The world remembers with favor the great freebooter, Raleigh, who ate his heart out in the Tower and could not believe his age was dead until he had tried the seas once more. These men were truly Elizabethans. They died bloodily as their age demanded, and were understood.

Francis Bacon, by contrast, walks masked and cool through this age of violence. Traps snap on either side, associates perish, he remains. Even when he is caught between parliament and king, and a powerful enemy demands his imprisonment in the Tower—even then, he goes free, though robbed by a strange combination of events of his personal honor, his fortune, and his place at court.

Yet among all these plots and subplots a curious mythology lives on: that Francis Bacon "took a bribe"—a not very respectable thing for a judge to do, a thing to moralize upon in the safe seclusion of a modern study. Only yesterday the charge was raised again in conversation as a new legal book, heaping invective upon him, came up for discussion. Though Francis Bacon valued his good name and left it, when he knew the worst had come upon him, "to the next ages and to foreign nations," it is doubtful that he, or the callous favorite Villiers, or James I could have foreseen how close that charge would stick after three hundred years.

The men of violence have been forgiven. A romantic halo envelops them. But the man who outlived the violence and who husbanded his power of survival in order to communicate a great secret, our age finds it oddly difficult to forgive. One wonders why. Perhaps it is because he was truly a stranger in his own age—a civilized man out of his time and place, dealing with barbarians and barely evading the rack and gallows in the process. It affronts our sense of dignity to see him bowing painfully to titled fools and rapacious upstarts, while presenting his books hopefully to learned men who scornfully fling them aside. He walks hesitantly toward

us through history as though he could see our century but not reach it; he is out of place.

In a grim moment he whispers in *The Advancement of Learning* that one must consider how one's nature suits the state of the times. If one is out of place then one must walk "close and reserved." This is all we ever learn of the man except that he had one burning passion: to change the world through thought, through an "engine" he had devised. Otherwise there is nothing of himself; nothing, that is, save the cry of the painter Nicholas Hilliard, who wished he could have painted Bacon's mind, and the words of Ben Jonson, who spoke of his eloquence, and of another who remarked upon his generosity.

Bacon died, appropriately enough, in the midst of an experiment. He had gone out in a carriage on a winter day and decided suddenly to investigate the effects of cold in delaying putrefaction. He stopped his carriage, bought a hen from a cottage woman, and stuffed it full of snow. Immediately aware of having taken a chill himself, he sought the hospitality of a friend who lived nearby, and in that house he died.

It is symbolic that Bacon died in a borrowed bed. The century in which he found himself was equally borrowed, and he had no genuine place within it. One might say, if one were a student of literature, that here was Everyman engaged in that great pilgrimage which runs through the centuries. Perhaps this is why he repulses us. He is Faust and something more. In some fashion he is ourselves, and we project upon Bacon the fear we have of what he has brought to us. His work is not a gift that can be recalled, and the more we come to fear the gift, the more hatred we extend to the giver of it. Before we can understand and therefore for-

Vesalius's Fabrica, *of 1543, introduced to anatomy the kind of direct observation that Bacon later sought to methodize.*

Among philosophers affected by techniques of science, Hobbes was an extremist; his Leviathan *posits a mechanistic world.*

give the giver, we must understand the intention of his gift.

Rumor has it that Francis Bacon, his father's favorite child, the boy whose courtesy had caught the eye of the queen, played alone a great deal. Once he was found investigating the nature of echoes in some rocky spot, the story goes, and a likely enough incident it is, for what boy has not shouted into a well or bounced experimental sounds in reverberating places? But it is also likely that his intent, listening ear caught sounds not heard by ordinary, boisterous children. In the fey mind of this solitary, gifted youth it might have seemed as though fate whispered, or an echo sounded from some yet distant century. For Bacon, at least in his adult years, was to show an uncanny sensitivity to time.

In 1573 Francis, along with his brother Anthony, went to Cambridge. He was just twelve, unusually young even for that day of early university training. Cambridge, at the time, had sunk to a low intellectual level and Bacon did not linger long. The school was given over to bitter theological disputes. "Men of sharp wits," Bacon was later to describe his tutors, "shut up in the cells of a few authors, chiefly Aristotle, their Dictator." A strong admiration for the lost classic literature could not conceal the fact that at Cambridge learning was largely pretense, that all was of the past. Men endlessly wove and rewove a spider web of ideas derived from Greek and Roman sources.

At the age of fifteen the youth returned home, indifferent to his abandoned degree. In 1575 he turned, as was natural in a legal family, to Gray's Inn and began to study for the law. The next year, however, he was sent abroad by his father in the company of the English ambassador to France.

For nearly three years Bacon experienced not only events at the foreign court of Henry III but the enormous stimulus of a society in which letters were honored. It was the time of the French Renaissance. Montaigne was being read, the great poet Pierre de Ronsard was writing his autumnal verses. It is likely that in this morally corrupt but brilliant society Francis Bacon received much of the literary stimulus that was to haunt his strangely divided career in the less literate circle of the English court.

In the winter of 1579 Francis had a strange dream. He saw his father's house "plastered all over with black mortar." The dream was prophetic: three days later Lord Keeper Nicholas Bacon was dead.

*F*rancis, the youngest of the several children of two marriages, received only a pittance from the divided estate. His father's unexpected death had left him unprovided for. The student, the man of dreams, was never again to be totally free of financial insecurity. By birth and training he had been fitted for a life far beyond his financial station. And now, where others could be independent, he must humble himself to petition. He was doomed to strive impatiently after what others, securely entrenched, might confidently expect the stream of time to bring to them.

Yet, seen in the afterlight of history, perhaps his misfortune contained a secret blessing. Until the near close of his career he possessed no estates worth confiscating, nothing likely to strike the covetous eyes of kings or their favorites. His chief danger—in spite of his recognition of the necessity of going masked, so to speak—would be a certain stiff-necked, aristocratic pride showing through in unexplainable odd moments, in books, in Parliament.

"I have taken all knowledge to be my province," he once wrote in importuning aid from his uncle, Lord Burghley, the Secretary of State. Burghley, that sturdy, imperturbable minister, must have shuddered. His nephew talked as though from a place beyond the century, while at the same time he revealed a vaulting ambition likely to cause an experienced courtier to frown. Bacon was eager, and like all bright youths, occasionally uncertain and gauche in his impetuous demand for place. Burghley would give the young man little aid. He was intent on furthering the career of his own son, Robert Cecil, and held the Bacons—Francis and his brother Anthony —at arm's length.

All through the reign of Elizabeth—and even though his cause had been promoted by the Earl of Essex who had become his patron—Bacon was denied everything but crumbs. There was one exception: Elizabeth's lease-gift of the pleasant country residence of Twickenham Lodge in 1595. It was evident that the Cecil faction would never tolerate Bacon's accession to any post of power. Essex's brief rise to royal favor, and his sudden fall, brought Bacon nothing but danger and the animus of powerful foes.

All of the more able biographers of Bacon repudiate the

canard that he aided in the fall of Essex and ungratefully abandoned him. In vain Francis had given Essex sound advice and had pleaded with the frustrated man to abandon the course which led to his downfall. But the hotheaded, impetuous courtier, full of the proud violence of a sea dog's age, had run headlong into revolt and his own death by the axe. Surveying his career today, one might suspect that Essex was not totally sound, mentally. Yet he was a brave man and a generous one, and the way his life ended tore many hearts.

Elizabeth herself was never the same afterward; for days at a time, it is said, she would brood motionless, or else suddenly drive a sword into tapestries and hangings, as if in fear of lurking assassins. Bacon was ordered to draw up a state paper explaining the treason of the Earl and his accomplices to the restless populace, who had adored Essex. Painfully he did so. His affection for his old patron made the document too lenient for the Queen's taste. Those who accuse Bacon of ingratitude might well examine Elizabeth's sharp reaction to Bacon's document: "It is my Lord of Essex, my Lord of Essex on every page; you can't forget your old respect for the traitor; strike it out; make it Essex. . . ."

Until the death of Elizabeth, Bacon's life was largely lived in the shadows where he wrote state political tracts and advised the Queen as a "Counsel Extraordinary." One of his biographers, John Nichol, has commented that "no man ever proposed to enter upon public life with more reason to expect rapid advancement, and very few have had to wait longer for it." The reason is quite plain: in a mercenary age he lacked the means to buy advancement, and the only faction which could have helped him—that of Burghley and, later, Robert Cecil, his cousin—regarded him with distaste. His very brilliance was anathema to them.

As for Elizabeth, Bacon once remarked, not unfondly, to her successor, James I, "My good old Mistress was wont to call me her watch-candle, because it pleased her to say I did continually burn and yet she suffered me to waste almost to nothing." At another time he had spoken bitterly of the way in which he was forced to trudge after small favors like a child pursuing a pretty bird that hops away. Elizabeth could be parsimonious and fickle. As long as Robert Cecil, Bacon's secret enemy, lived, the shadow of that cunning little hunchback would fall across Bacon's path. And when that shadow lifted, Bacon's last great elevation spelled his doom even as he walked into the full sunlight of eminence. He learned what it was to hold power without personal wealth under a king without greatness.

Elizabeth died in 1603 leaving no heirs, or at least none acknowledged. In her final illness, men—swept like sea birds before a rising storm—had posted hard up the great north way to the court of James in Edinburgh: by remote lines of descent he was now heir to the English throne; courtiers had to look to their fortunes. James was not Elizabeth. Essex had favored him. The wheel was turning. "By the mutability

of fortune and favor," as the old Elizabethan documents would put it, Bacon's hour would seem to have struck. The Scottish king was reputed to be a learned man. Bacon sought his favor.

The first results were inauspicious: the King had not recognized Bacon, and his former office was not renewed; Robert Cecil, by contrast, remained Secretary of State. The new king intended to knight several hundred people, and Francis —after some correspondence with his cousin Cecil—was one of those selected. But the honor, done hastily to a large body of people, was a small one. A little pension was given him in remembrance of his late brother Anthony's services as an intelligence messenger between Essex and James. He was made a "King's Counsel." The term meant little: there was a plethora of counselors. There is evidence that Bacon was in despair and contemplated withdrawing from court life to become a recluse and scholar.

It is here, while Bacon's star seems waning, that we may seize the opportunity to examine the intellectual life of this man who was so long entangled with the practical affairs of state. As always, a babble of conflicting voices assails us. Some insist that his scholarly abilities were such that he should never have stooped to politics; others maintain that his talents as a statesman held off the Puritan revolution for a generation and might have prevented it altogether, had those he served taken his advice.

One thing seems clear: Bacon himself, so far as we are allowed to penetrate that aloof mask, preferred the cloister. He had, however, one trait which would never have suited the life of a recluse: he was a man of action. By family and tradition he had been bred to serve the state. Moreover, he was a reformer more than he was a philosopher. Reserved and shy though he appeared, he was eloquent. In Parliament he could sway men. He was honored there. Curiously, it was this, and neither his vast learning nor his dreams, that finally caused James's eye to fall upon him.

In the meantime, however, in the period between Elizabeth's death and the aroused interest of James, Bacon had little to do. He turned vigorously to the completion of a book—a book destined to be one of the great books of all time, even though it was finished in haste in the hope of interesting the learned James. By no means Bacon's first venture into scholarship (his equally well-known volume of *Essays* having appeared in 1597), *The Advancement of Learning* contains the essence of his inner life and his long-frustrated hopes for man.

It is incredible, now, to realize that this great statesman of science was sneered at as a fool by many of his literate fellows in law, government, and the universities. In despair, he had all his works put into Latin because, in that barbaric time, he feared that the rapidly altering English tongue would not survive. Time-conscious as no other man of his era, he viewed books as boats with precious cargoes launched on the great sea of time. One can catch the quality of this time sense, as deep and brooding as that of a modern archaeologist, when he writes:

But howsoever the works of wisdom are among human things the most excellent, yet they too have their periods and closes. For so it is that after kingdoms and commonwealths have flourished for a time, there arise perturbations and seditions and wars; amid the disturbances of which, first the laws are put to silence, and then men return to the depraved conditions of their nature, and desolation is seen in the fields and cities. And if such troubles last, it is not long before letters also and philosophy are so torn in pieces that no traces of them can be found but a few fragments, scattered here and there like planks from a shipwreck; and then a season of barbarism sets in, the waters of Helicon being sunk under the ground, until, according to the appointed vicissitude of things, they break out and issue forth again, perhaps among other nations and not in the places where they were before.

Through all his trials Bacon's faith in his books, even as lost and bobbing "planks" in the wreckage of time, never faltered. "I have lost much time with this age," he wrote a friend as if, from some high place, his eye spanned centuries. And though he regarded Latin as a more certain medium for survival, it is also known that he promoted the English translation of works that might encourage learning.

We of today have difficulty in realizing that the world of Bacon and Shakespeare was only semiliterate, steeped in religious contention, with its gaze turned backward in wonder upon the Greco-Roman past. Oswald Spengler justly remarks that human choice is only possible within the limitations and idea-forms of a given age. More than three hundred years ago, Francis Bacon would have understood him. Bacon's world horribly constricted his ability to exert his will upon it. At the same time he would have had a slight reservation. "Send out your little book upon the waters," he would have countered, "and hope. Your will may be worked beyond you in another and more favorable age."

For a man whose personal life had been disappointing, Bacon was singularly sure of his destiny. All that he wrote of it has come to pass. The men who destroyed him are remembered, if at all, only because of their perfidious roles in the life of a man whose name now stands with Shakespeare's as the light of the Elizabethan Age.

Other men of Bacon's period were beginning to grope with the tools of science. Only he, however, would clearly perceive its role and the changes and dangers it would introduce into the life of man. In the years left to him, and particularly after his fall from office in 1621, a flood of works poured from his pen. It was almost as if he foresaw that this would be his last chance to speak "to the next ages."

There is no doubt that his concentration upon philosophy contributed to his political downfall. It closed his ears to signs of public danger; it closed his eyes to the machinations of his enemies. His single-minded devotion to duty, his curious ebullience of temperament, would make him the easy

TEXT CONTINUED ON PAGE 179

174

The course of philosophy in 1620 ventured past the Pillars of Hercules—the limits of the old Aristotelian world—and into the bold, tough-minded new age of science. Bacon piloted the ship, and placed this grand metaphor on the title page (opposite) of his Instauratio Magna.

The Great Instauration followed a century of immense activity in the sciences, after discoveries in astronomy by Copernicus, Tycho Brahe, Kepler, and Galileo; after Gilbert's experiments with magnetism; and after Vesalius introduced scientific disciplines to the study of anatomy. And the new discoveries caused the Aristotelian authority to totter in the sixteenth century: the old system could not encompass the new science. In the 1580's Michel Eyquem de Montaigne's Essays *began—unsystematically but energetically— to demolish the last vestiges of Aristotle's influence.*

It was left to two men, Francis Bacon and René Descartes, to raise a new philosophical structure suited to the new discoveries. Bacon provided a methodology of empiricism; Descartes offered mathematical reasoning, rationalism. For the next few centuries, philosophers would struggle to reconcile Bacon and Descartes; and, although Cartesian philosophy overshadowed Bacon throughout the seventeenth century (even to the extent that previous philosophers like Montaigne were reinterpreted as rationalists), our own age is decidedly Baconian.

The following portfolio of frontispieces recalls three of the books that prepared the way for The Great Instauration: *Brahe's correspondence on astronomical instruments, Kepler's statement of the three laws of planetary motion, Montaigne's* Essays.

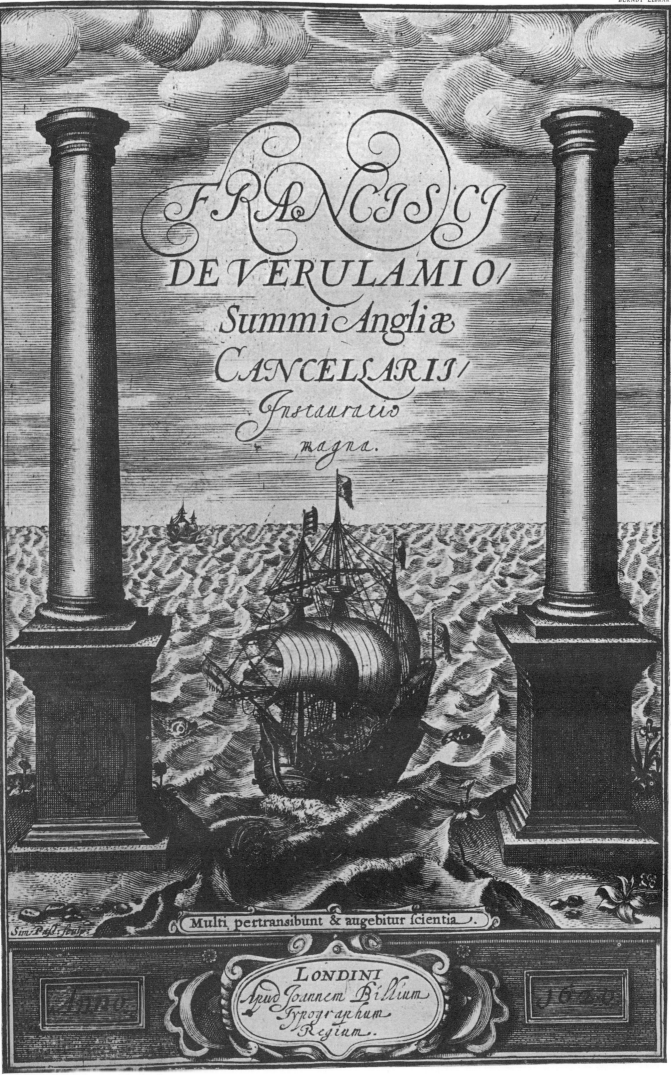

FRANCISCI

DE VERULAMIO/

Summi Angliæ

CANCELARIJ/

Instauratio

magna.

Multi pertransibunt & augebitur scientia.

LONDINI
Apud Joannem Billium
Typographum
Regium.

Anno

1620

The frontispiece of Epistolarum, *which Tycho Brahe published himself in 1596, shows the famous mural quadrant used for his observations*

Kepler's Third Law, published in 1619, had a dedication page with figures to whom Kepler felt he owed some scientific debt

THE
ESSAYES
OR
MORALL, POLITIKE,
AND MILITARIE
Difcourfes
of
Lo: Michael de Montaigne,
Knight
Of the noble Order of S. Michael, and
one of the Gentlemen in Ordinary of the French
Kings Chamber.

THE THIRD EDITION
Wherunto is now newly added an Index
of the principall Matters & perfonages
Mentioned in this Booke

LONDON.
Printed by M. flesher for Rich: Royston
in Iuie-lane next the exchequer Office
M DCXXXII.

Martin Dr. fculpfit.

The title page of the 1632 English edition of Montaigne's Essays bore an aura of the rationalism then dominating philosophy

victim of a political ambush. Nevertheless, the forces that brought about Bacon's fall might well have achieved their purpose even against a more unscrupulous and cunning man.

The times were running against the King, and Bacon was expendable. In a weird way he would be trapped in a portion of his own political philosophy. But of that, more later. Here let us examine the essence of that remarkable book, *The Advancement of Learning,* along with those works which bear upon his significance as a harbinger of the modern age.

"This is the foundation of all," wrote Bacon in his masterpiece, "for we are not to imagine or suppose, but to *discover,* what nature does or may be made to do." Bacon's gift for condensation is so remarkable that it is easy, three hundred years later, in a different intellectual climate, to overlook the significance of his words.

The remark just quoted lies at the root of the modern scientific method. Distilled into one brief phrase, it is the very essence of science as we know it today. We would search unavailingly among the practical experimenters of Bacon's time—even the greatest of them—for any comparable analysis of science throughout the whole range of its activity. In a breath he had chained the imagination to reality, but at the same time had left it free to explore "the dark crooks and crannies" of nature.

*W*e must enter into the intellectual life of Bacon's period if we are fully to grasp the enormity of the task that confronted him, or his challenge to his epoch. I have said that science does not come easily to men; they must be made to envision its possibilities. This was Bacon's role, and it is sheer folly to dismiss him, as some have sought to do, because he personally made no inventions. He did far more; by eloquence and an unparalleled glimpse of the possibilities contained in the new learning, he forced a backward-oriented culture to contemplate its own future.

The magnitude of his educational vision can be perceived only when we realize that well into the nineteenth century the greatest universities in England were still primarily devoted to the classical education of gentlemen. This fact is both a measure of Bacon's perception and a revelation of the glacial slowness with which ancient institutions are modified. Most of Britain's great scientific contributions in the post-Baconian years had come from members of The Royal Society (an association of scholars which was largely the result of his posthumous stimulus) or from other enlightened amateurs working alone.

"I say without any imposture," wrote Bacon, "that I . . . frail in health, involved in civil studies, coming to the obscurest of all subjects without guide or light, have done enough, if I have constructed the machine itself and the fabric, though I may not have employed or moved it." Before examining the forces that shaped Bacon's thought, let us now consider his mysterious "engine" and see wherein his originality can be said to lie. This is always more difficult to do in the case of a great philosophical thinker than in the relatively simple case of a man who produces a new mechanical invention.

The thinker may range over a wide area, he may reshape old ideas into new and original forms, he may postulate views that are only assimilated or proved long after he is gone. In the end, later comers may either be ignorant of the source of their own thinking or loath to accord to a long-vanished individual credit which might detract from their own originality.

We have to face the fact that the world of scholarship is sometimes a contentious and prickly one. By and large, as the mass of knowledge grows, men devote little attention to the dead. Yet it is the dead who are frequently our pathfinders, and we walk all unconsciously along the roads they have chosen for us. We find what they warned us to look for, and sometimes, also, we are unknowingly entrapped in some half-enchanted circle of ideas woven by a vanished mind. It is a credit to Bacon's perception that, at the very dawn of science, he warned the scholar against this kind of bewitchment, of which the later history of science can provide many instructive examples.

Bacon has long been known as an advocate of inductive reasoning. Indeed, this is a substantial part of his engine for the discovery of the truths of the natural world, the secondary causes which he believed to control all the phenomena of nature. Bacon's emphasis upon induction—that type of logical thinking by which one ascends from specific, observed facts to the establishment of general laws or principles—need not be regarded as original with him, since the classical world was not unaware of the distinctions between inductive and deductive logic.

Bacon, in fact, never claimed such originality. What he did seek to do with his new *use* of induction was to avoid the sterile logic of the Aristotelian schoolmen. Since this type of thought has practically vanished from the modern world, we forget that education, in Bacon's day, was largely confined to metaphysical argument along with the reading of Greek and Roman classics. The techniques of logic, in other words, were being expended upon abstract controversy, while nature itself passed largely unexamined.

Men, to paraphrase Bacon, were spinning webs out of their own substance. To recapture reality it would be necessary to bring speculation into conformity with reality, to ascend from genuine facts to deductions, and to avoid hasty and unsubstantiated theory. As one student of the time has remarked, people "decided all questions not by investigating the observable facts, but by appealing to the infallible authority of Aristotle." Around the scholars of Elizabeth's century lay a natural universe scarcely investigated except for the exploration feats of the often unlettered voyagers.

Bacon was convinced that once man came to understand this unexplored nature about him, he could attain power over it, but that this potential power could be achieved only by

179

the right methods of investigation exerted on a very large scale. "Looking back," says the philosopher C. D. Broad, "we can see that he was right, and we may be tempted to think that it was obvious. But it was not in the least obvious at the time; it was, on the contrary, a most remarkable feat of insight and an act of rational faith in the face of present appearances and past experience."

Bacon's associates in government, such as Elizabeth and James, had been brought up in the traditional learning. James, in particular, prided himself on an antique, pretentious classicism. Neither was impressed by so unconventional an idea as Bacon's and one which, if adopted, would upset the prevailing school system. Both rulers were dancing bewitched in a ring out of which he was powerless to lead them. The more he wrote in the vein of his own convictions, the more warily he was regarded by his political contemporaries.

Experimenters—such as William Harvey, the discoverer of the circulation of the blood—were beginning to appear, but none seems to have had Bacon's total vision of what science and the experimental method could achieve over the centuries. Harvey, in fact, referred amusedly to Bacon as writing of science "like a lord chancellor." His remark is true, but imperceptive. Bacon was the first great statesman of science. He saw its potentiality in the schools; he saw the necessity of multiplying researchers, establishing the continuity of the scientific tradition, and promoting government-supported research for those studies which lay beyond private means and which could not be accomplished "in the hourglass of one man's life."

This vast vision could only have emerged from a mind trained to state affairs, to the management of kingdoms, and withal, a mind equally devoted to discovery. It is ridiculous to bemoan Bacon's practical experience of statecraft; it contributed enormously to his insight. The pity lies in the fact that he came so close to the seats of power without the opportunity to realize his dreams. It is an apt illustration of the degree to which even a great genius can be restricted and made helpless by his time. Yet in justice we must add, not totally so. The prestige of Bacon's final offices gave greater weight to his literary pronouncements, financed his publications, and in other indirect ways, lent wings to his words beyond what would have been possible for an obscure scholar opposed by many of his compatriots.

Another aspect of Bacon's contributions which deserves attention is his conception of the *mundus alter*—"the other world" produced by human culture, a world drawn out of the void and made possible by the arts of man. It is, in a sense, a latent world filled with novelties which man, by his own ingenuity, can bring out of nature. Until the time of Bacon, man had more or less "drifted" in the natural world. His culture, with all its rational and irrational elements, had grown up largely without conscious self-examination or attention to the fact that man might possess the power success-

fully to mold and improve his own society through science.

Bacon, by contrast, was intent to turn man into an actively anticipatory creature rather than a backward-yearning one. In doing this he contended against great obstacles. He fought against the vested interest of the Scholastic teachers indifferent to experiment; he inveighed against the widespread belief that the classical past would never be equalled because the world was far sunk in decay and destined to perish at no very distant date. This last notion, which was widely accepted and promoted, was destructive of initiative and conducive to indifference.

Bacon struggled against this despair with every means at his command. "If we must select some one philosopher as

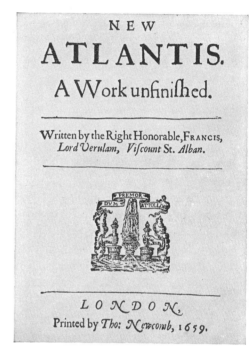

Bacon's New Atlantis, *published posthumously, spoke of a coming utopia of science, an age full of marvelous machines.*

the hero of the revolution in scientific method," said William Whewell, a learned nineteenth-century historian of science, "beyond all doubt Francis Bacon occupies the place of honor." He based his estimate upon Bacon's conception of the dawn of a new era and the shifting of logic from contention to its use in the analysis of experiments. "In catching sight of this principle, and in ascribing to it its due importance," continues Whewell, "Bacon's sagacity wrought unassisted and unequalled." Ungrounded argument, Bacon saw, must be replaced by a logic applied to reality. Only then could man bring his second world into being.

Considering the time at which he wrote, Bacon's numerous insights are phenomenal. For example, although he himself was not a mathematician, he foresaw the necessity for using mathematics in some of the more subtle examinations of nature. The mathematician A. R. Forsyth dwelt upon this aspect of Bacon's thought before the British Association for the Advancement of Science in 1905, and it has not gone unnoted by others.

Similarly, Bacon reveals perceptive insights into biology and anthropology. He raised, in a quite objective way, the question of whether the transmutation of species could occur, and commented that the problem required deep research. He refused the arbitrary abandonment of the idea. He observed that the lower organisms might reveal secrets of life which in the higher organisms "lye more hidden."

His analysis of the "cave of custom" and the necessity for understanding the "Idols" that distort the thinking of the average man are the product of long observation of men under emotional stress. Jonathan Wright, a number of years ago, commented that it is to Bacon that we owe the idea of utilization of controls in scientific experiment.

One could point to many other evidences of Bacon's wide-ranging mind—his early recognition of the value of the history of science, his contention that biography should not be confined to rulers, and last, but not least, his recognition of the value of the division of labor in science. Above all else he dwelt upon science "for the uses of life." He warned that knowledge without charity could be as dangerous as the modern world has finally discovered it to be. In contrast to today's warring nationalisms, Bacon spoke in *The Great Instauration* of bearing a strong love for "the *human republic,* our common country."

If one now asks why science arose when it did, and why at its dawn so great a spokesman should have appeared to spread its doctrines, one would have to pursue innumerable beams of light into that globe of crystal which Bacon termed the human understanding. His own mind serves as a kind of condensing lens in this respect. Analogies in language drawn from the great voyagers dot his pages. It is evident that the geographical discoveries of his time, and the circumnavigation of the earth, had set wise men's statements at nought and promoted the independent examination of the natural world. The historian Merle Curti, commenting upon his influence in pioneer America, remarks, "It was no accident that Francis Bacon's ideas were rediscovered and put to work in an era characterized by the rise of the common man."

Formal theology had been shaken by observations in continents unmentioned in the Bible. A second Book of Revelation, the book regarded as unclouded by human error and confusion—the book of Nature—was becoming increasingly respectable to devout minds. Bacon's mother was under strong Puritan influence. The Puritan desire to rebuild an earthly Paradise, even in the wilds of the New World, was growing. It is no secret that later, in New England, the Puritan clergy promoted the new astronomical discoveries. This is not to equate science with Puritanism alone, but it does suggest that something about the Reformation played a part in the emergence of a full-bodied scientific movement which, a generation or so after Bacon, recognized his significance as the great spokesman for the scientific method itself and all that was to follow in its train.

No single man, of course, can be credited with the creation of modern science. A unique institution had appeared, however, with an equally unique spokesman. One can only repeat that no other figure from that dim light of the scientific morning catches more powerfully at our imagination

The title page of a 1588 nautical manual shows the crude navigational instruments used in the great age of exploration.

than the man who wrote: "I could not be true and constant to the argument I handle, if I were not willing to go beyond others; but yet not more willing than to have others go beyond me again."

Science, he maintained, was "not a belief to be held but a work to be done." He thought of it as "a work for the ages and the peoples. . . ." In that work and its promulgation he had worn out such days as were given him. If he was marked, in any small degree, by the times he lived in, who are we of the century of the mushroom cloud to sit in unrelenting judgment?

*W*e left Bacon's political career at a time of crisis, but with a hint of what was to come. He had desperately hurried forward the completion of *The Advancement of Learning,* in order to impress the new king James. That monarch, whose backward-directed classical learning would find little it could comprehend in the *Advancement,* was eyeing quite another aspect of Bacon's diversified career: his role in Parliament. Bacon was highly respected there.

Bacon had sat in the Commons since the days of Elizabeth; in fact, he had once aroused her fury by opposing a tax requisition which he felt to be inordinate, and which would cause suffering among the poor. For those who conceive of Bacon as an unscrupulous manipulator for favor, his letter to Lord Keeper Puckering on that occasion is worth quoting: "It mought please her sacred Majesty to think what my end should be in those speeches, if it were not duty and duty alone. I am not so simple but I know the common beaten way to please."

In 1603 the problems of Parliament versus the King were to emerge once more in another guise. There were church problems, there was the problem of the political union between England and Scotland. James was a newcomer from a more absolutistic and barbaric land. He needed advice and a trusted statesman who could mediate between the Lords and Commons. Bacon's moderation, his ability to sway audiences, the respect accorded him in the lower house, all fitted the needs of the new regime. It was a time when, in the words of Fulton Anderson, one of the most careful students of Bacon's career: "A wise king would decrease the area of his prerogative and gradually increase the range of his subjects' privileges. For some sixteen years," Anderson records, "Bacon would be trying to make James aware of these things; but the King would prove neither wise nor teachable."

*B*acon assumed his first important administrative post under James as Solicitor General in 1607. It was an exacting office, made more so by Bacon's diverse abilities as a statesman. Frequently he was engaged in carrying out duties that ordinarily would have been assigned to others. For a man of frail health his energies seem almost superhuman. In the midst of difficult affairs of statecraft he still yearns over his "rebirth" of the sciences, and studies ways that Cambridge or Oxford might be encouraged toward the new learning—toward laboratories, "engines, vaults, and furnaces."

All this time the King's Treasury, in the hands of Robert Cecil, was sinking into debt. Taxes and impositions levied upon the public were growing more onerous. Opposition to James and the highhandedness of his favorites was growing in the House of Commons. These events were the first weather signs that were to lead to the Puritan revolution. Bacon could read them, but those around him could not. Blind though he might sometimes be to his personal interests, he was never blind to the interests of the state. A long list of state papers and unheeded advice testifies to his efforts.

He would have been an able replacement as Secretary of State for Robert Cecil, who died in 1612 leaving James's treasury empty. Bacon sought the post, but James, wary of Bacon's association with the now-feared Parliament, turned aside from the one logical candidate. He named instead an inexperienced man with no obligations to the House; Bacon was appointed Attorney General. He would yet be made Lord Keeper in 1617 and rise to the high office of Lord Chancellor of England in 1618.

Meanwhile his new office of Attorney General, as events were to prove, was a far more vulnerable post than his previous one. Ironically, the suspicious James, in spite of not trusting Bacon sufficiently to allow him to succeed Cecil, continued to seek his advice on the financial affairs of the kingdom. Once more, in the words of Professor Anderson: "The courts and the constitution were to be preserved in a continuity through great trials and hazards by one man and one man alone, Francis Bacon. In this regard he became for a period the chief axial officer of the kingdom. He managed, without ill-deserving, to keep the constitution intact . . . to maintain the law and liberty of subjects, and to preserve 'the King's honor,' through wise, skillful, and just resorts."

Only in the reign of James's son Charles I would the great storm of the Puritan revolution finally strike. To Bacon is owed no small credit for delaying that storm by a generation. If James had earlier given heed to Bacon's counsels, if Buckingham and Cecil had been less venal, the interruption of the British monarchy and the sorry death of Charles need never have occurred at all. A people's great tragedy was winding to its conclusion—a tragedy which would not end with Bacon's death but only when James's son would lay his head upon the block in payment for his own and his father's obstinacy.

As part of his monarchial creed, Bacon had once written: "It is well, when nobles are not too great for sovereignty nor for justice, and yet maintained in that height, *as the insolency of inferiors may be broken upon them before it come too fast upon the majesty of kings*." This maxim is practiced even in modern democracies, though generally under less severe conditions. Francis Bacon, the moderate monarchist, Parliament's man, the sensible compromiser, was now to act out in life his own observation.

He had risen to high office. The Lord Chancellorship of England, given to him in 1618 had brought along with it the title of Baron Verulam. In the very year of his tragic fall—1621—he was to receive yet another honor: the investiture as Viscount St. Alban. On January 27, five days after the event of his sixtieth birthday, his new dignity was conferred upon him in full ceremony. In a letter to the King, thanking him for this new advancement as well as the previous ones, Bacon added: "And so I may without superstition be buried in St. Alban's habit or vestment."

He was not to die for five years. But he was to be broken by the mob pressing more and more angrily upon the "majesty" of James. High office could not save him. In Parliament a majority of the members, manipulated by such enemies of Bacon's as the sadistic Sir Edward Coke, would turn against him. In frustration at their inability to vent their rage on the King, or upon his favorite, George Villiers, they would destroy the one man who had sought to temper the royal excesses and preserve the state.

It was not all ingenuous. Old enemies would scurry on black errands, traditional homage would be deliberately redescribed as bribery in order to fit the scene, the lapses of servants would be laid upon the overworked master. Southampton, former conspirator with Essex, would charge Bacon with corruption in office. One has only to consider the way the majority of these men were to end, amidst their own violence and rapacity, to realize the nature of Bacon's judges. James wept; Villiers vacillated. Confronted with the charges, Bacon wrote to Buckingham, "Your Lordship spake of Purgatory. I am now in it, but my mind is in a calm . . . I know I have clean hands and a clean heart; and I hope a clean house for friends or servants. But Job himself, or whosoever was the justest judge, by such hunting matters against him as hath been used against me, may for a time seem foul, specially in a time when greatness is the mark and accusation is the game." He added, "If this is to be a Chancellor, I think if the Great

The frontispiece of Sprat's History of the Royal Society *depicts Bacon, at right, as the society's spiritual founder.*

Seal lay upon Hounslow Heath nobody would take it up."

James did not dare dismiss Parliament; the unscrupulous George Villiers, though obligated to Bacon in the past, was not a man of sentiment. Before Bacon could defend himself, there came a fatal interview with James. James advised him—and to a man in Bacon's position this was a command—to avow his guilt and trust his protection to the Crown.

It was the royal will. When Bacon left the King's presence, he is reputed to have remarked: "I am the first sacrifice; I wish I may be the last." He was face to face with his own dictum that in times of crisis the King's circle was expendable for the protection of the monarch. Without land or title of his own, he had been raised high by James. He owed him much. Bacon bowed to the King's wishes. He must have felt, as Charles Williams, one of his most perceptive biographers has remarked, that he was "on a ship, fantastically laboring on a wild ocean, manned with imbeciles." Having condemned himself, the High Court rendered its judgment: "That the Lord Viscount St. Albans . . . shall undergo fine and ransim of forty thousand pounds. . . . That he shall be imprisoned in the Tower during the King's pleasure. . . . That he shall forever be incapable of any office, place, or employment in the State or Commonwealth. . . . That he shall never sit in Parliament nor come within the verge of the Court."

For more than three centuries the intellectual world has contended, censured, moralized, and probed into a world that is gone. The man behind the mask gives back no answer, the man who took care with his documents, those frail vessels in which he put his final trust, utters to posterity no word of vituperation or defense. He was a man who lived by his code, a servant to his monarch and the state.

The world was changing. Even that monarch, in spite of his avowals and a few protective gestures, did little to alleviate Bacon's lot or clear his name. Neither did Charles after him. A terrible loneliness descended on the dying man, the last and least publicized of the Elizabethan explorers—the stay-at-home discoverer of the New Atlantis, the opener of the great door into the future. "I may truly say," Bacon wrote, "my soul hath been a stranger in the course of my pilgrimage. I seem to have my conversation among the ancients more than among those with whom I live."

About him the storms of a new era were gathering. In a generation men would begin to talk of Bacon again, scientific societies would arise on the plans he and other dreamers had modeled. Men would grow curious about him, but the stain would be there, the ineradicable, terrible stain, unexamined in its time or place or condition, spreading endlessly as his name spread, as it still spreads today.

Strangely, the mask dropped just for a moment after his death. Long ago he had courted the Lady Hatton, who had cast him aside for his old rival, Sir Edward Coke, one of the undoubted contrivers of his downfall. She had grown to hate her overbearing, quarrelsome husband; Bacon had been equally unfortunate in his own marriage.

When the sharp winter airs of which he had complained struck him down at last, there was found in his will an intended gift to Lady Coke. The episode is unexplained to this day. Perhaps Bacon's legacy was dedicated to some lost spring by a man who, rumor says, was cold to the ways of love.

The harsh accusers of his own time have long been silent, but Bacon's ordeal has not ended. What we find in him now may essentially be a measure of the nature of ourselves as individuals. "Bacon's wisdom," said the archbishop Richard Whately, "is like the seven-league boots which would fit the giant or the dwarf, except only that the dwarf cannot take the same stride in them."

Loren Eiseley, who also contributed "The Time of Man," pages 36–43, is author of Francis Bacon and the Modern Dilemma.

Equipages arrive within the gates of Vaux. But when King Louis came for a great fete in 1661, disaster followed.

NICOLAS FOUQUET

Fouquet dared to outdo his king by building France's greatest château, Vaux-le-Vicomte

The Minister's Fatal Showplace

By WILLIAM HARLAN HALE

o give a great party can be a dangerous thing. A few famous balls have become enshrined in history and golden legend—none more so than the Duchess of Richmond's in Brussels on the eve of Waterloo, remembered in the celebrated lines that begin, "There was a sound of revelry by night"—but there have been others whose immortality consists in the fact that their very splendor brought down disaster upon their givers.

The greater the party, sometimes, the greater the fall. In the severe depression winter of 1896–97 in New York, the Bradley Martins of high society threw a fabulous $300,000 ball in the newly completed Waldorf-Astoria Hotel, in the odd belief that the spreading of so much manna would alleviate the condition of the poor—and, when the Martins awoke next morning to find themselves called infamous, they sought permanent refuge in Europe. In the next decade another bemused and lordly New Yorker, the insurance heir James Hazen Hyde, staged an even costlier affair at Sherry's—a court soiree reproducing one of Louis XVI's, with authentic statuary, settings, costumes and liveries, imported for the occasion, along with the actress Réjane—but which also led to Hyde's long disappearance from his homeland, since his spending had helped trigger an investigation as to just what his Equitable Life Assurance Society was doing with its manna.

But perhaps the most self-destructive of all great parties was staged on August 17, 1661, by Nicolas Fouquet, the "Superintendent of Finances" of the France of young King Louis XIV, in order to show off his splendid new château of Vaux-le-Vicomte. The day dawned on a dazzling courtier at the peak of magnificence, with the King and the whole Court about to be his guests. It ended on a decision by Louis that was to strip Fouquet of both his office and his dream castle and to reduce him to disgrace and jail. The fete that misfired had another result: it caused Louis XIV, stricken with envy for his minister's pleasance, to build a greater Vaux-le-Vicomte of his own, and its name was Versailles.

Everyone who knew Fouquet knew that his feast would be very grand; but not even the King knew precisely how grand. In the outdoor theatre there was to be a new play, especially written by Molière, very much the talk of the Court and of the salons since the success of his satirical *Les Précieuses Ridicules* two seasons ago. Indoors, at dinner, France's leading composer, Lully, was to perform new music with his own orchestra. Dinner itself would be cooked and presented by the renowned Vatel. Among the nobles and Crown officials present with their ladies of fashion, the poet La Fontaine would be on hand to celebrate the occasion as its laureate:

ouis overthrew him — and built Versailles

YOUNG LOUIS XIV

Le ciel en fut jaloux. Enfin, figure-toi
Que, lorsqu'on eut tiré les toiles
Tout combattit à Vaux pour le plaisir du Roi,
La musique, les eaux, les lustres, les étoiles.

And there was to be more: perhaps too much more.

The start of the festivities at Vaux, some fifty kilometers southeast of Paris, had been announced for six o'clock, in order to give time for the spectacles and diversions planned by Fouquet to last far into the summer night. If the King was not to delay them, he would have to set out in mid-afternoon from his own château of Fontainebleau thirty kilometers southward, for three hours of coaching across the hills and valleys of the Ile de France in blistering August heat. But young Louis, only twenty-three this summer, had already acquired those habits of punctuality, punctilio, and consideration (to those who merited his consideration) that were to mark his immensely long reign, and his Court was in its carriages, in its perukes and thick lace, promptly at three in order to arrive at M. Fouquet's on time, heat or not.

Accompanied by a troop of Gardes-françaises and musketeers and the usual outriders and pages, the cortege included such august personages as the Queen Mother; Louis's younger brother, Prince Philippe (in French court parlance, simply "Monsieur"); Philippe's recent bride, Princess Henrietta of England, with whom the King was presently romancing ("Madame"); the ranking Prince de Condé ("M. le Prince"); the dukes of Bourbon, Beaufort, Guise, and many others—an extraordinary turnout to be journeying all this distance to the country seat of a man born a commoner. Yet of all the personages of France, there was none who held higher claim to the King's consideration than Nicolas Fouquet, the Anjou lawyer's son who had risen by soaring ambition and extraordinary dexterity to become *vicomte de Melun et de Vaux, ministre d'Etat, surintendant des finances, et procureur général*, a brilliant patron of the arts, the glass of fashion and, since the death of Cardinal Mazarin just three months ago, the most powerful man in France after Louis himself.

The long cavalcade wound on until at length, approaching a high ground, it caught sight of the immense new pleasure dome of the King's favorite. Surmounted by its cupola and gilded lantern, the château of white stone still lay at a middle distance, centered in a vast panorama that extended almost as far as the eye could reach. On either side were rolling woods; but a superb swath had been cut through them, dipping gently from the highway into a river vale and bringing up at the far slope, so that on descending toward the gates one could take in the whole prospect at once—yet in three acts, so to speak.

Nearest, behind a curtain of grilles and a line of heroic sculptured standards that stood like heralds to announce the enclosure, there spread a stately forecourt (see pages 184–185) divided into rectilinear avenues and planted squares, with matching outbuildings and copses on either side and a moat beyond: that could be called Act One, the preparation—a composition of perfect though severe symmetry. Just beyond the moat was Act Two, the dramatic unfolding—the great house of Vaux-le-Vicomte itself, massive but exuberant, rising in a proud profusion of balustrades, classical orders, pediments, *oeils-de-boeuf*, and mansards to a forest of statuary on the eaves and roof tops. Finally, beyond this, the eye could proceed to Act Three, the joyous resolution—Vaux's sparkling and playful gardens with their arabesques, sculptured nymphs, pools, lovers' groves, grottoes, fountains (some fifty in number), and *jets d'eau* (some two hundred) culminating in a grand cascade.

The King was received at the gates by a host twice his age, not equal to him in physical stature, dark-eyed, slight, and compact in contrast to Louis's tall, blue-eyed majesty, yet of a nimbleness and verve of bearing that belied his years and made him seem a worthy peer of so young a king, especially since the latter had grown so very stately when so very young. The radiant host, M. Fouquet, handed down his royal guests from their coaches. First they were shown the outdoor sights, the King being particularly taken with the waterworks, which he pronounced finer than anything at Tivoli or Frascati—without having to add that they were far, far finer than his own at Fontainebleau, since everyone knew that he had little more there than a lake. The gardens as a whole were beyond compare: they had been laid out by the brilliant André Le Nôtre, whom the Crown had first employed to design the Tuileries gardens of the Louvre, but whom Fouquet had since taken into his own service to design something much greater.

Fouquet could point out garden statuary by numerous prominent artists, especially Nicolas Poussin, while ranks of admiring courtiers lined the walks as the King passed between them. (*"Ces courtisans chargés de rubans et de plumes faisaient le plus bel aspect que l'on puisse imaginer,"* one account of the festivity states; *"et c'était une confusion de si belles choses qu'on ne peut l'exprimer."*) Then the King, returning from the fountains, viewed the second, or garden-side, façade of the château—more striking even than that which opened on the forecourt. Here its architect, Louis Le Vau, who had first made his mark with some pavilions for Cardinal Mazarin's château at Vincennes, had outdone himself with a spectacular oval protuberance and dome, breaking all traditions of French château design and infusing new Italian ideas of grandeur into it.

Château indeed! With its magnificence of elevation (its dominating dome rose almost sixty feet above a two-story grand salon of regal width), and with its tiers of grand apartments sweeping out into four tall corners, this was beyond anything yet built in the French countryside by anyone less than a king. Blois, Chenonceaux, Chambord themselves paled beside it, while Louis's own favorite retreat of Fontainebleau was an aged rabbit warren of building and rebuilding, and his late father's hunting lodge at Versailles was still no more than—a hunting lodge.

But Vaux-le-Vicomte's richest splendors remained to be revealed to the King when Fouquet led him through its apartments, some still unfinished in the minister's rush to exhibit the whole establishment without delay. Flanking the Grand Salon—with its pilasters, clerestory lights, caryatid statues, and overhead vault—ran a riot of rooms decked out with tapestries, friezes, garlands, festoons, medallions, cartouches, gilt moldings, shimmering chandeliers and, above all, with swirling murals and ceiling frescoes that represented most of the classical pantheon, each figure chosen with allegorical point.

Thus in the Chambre du Roi (one of a suite of three of his finest rooms that Fouquet had punctiliously decorated for royal use) Jupiter, Mars, Mercury, and Bacchus were depicted on the four walls, evidently with intent to allude to four qualities of the King and his reign: power, valor, vigilance, and abundance, respectively. The lofty Salon des Muses displayed all the Muses, two by two, and also a complex ceiling allegory, "The Triumph of Fidelity," which was to be read as a reminder of Fouquet's loyalty to the King during the recent uprising of nobles called the *Fronde*. But the most triumphant ceiling painting was that in the Salon d'Hercule, which showed the classic hero borne aloft and seated on Olympus beside Jupiter, Diana, and Juno. Who in this instance was Hercules meant to symbolize? To anyone who knew Fouquet, and particularly the motto he had chosen for his armorial bearings, *"Quo non ascendam?"* ("How high can't I rise?"), the answer was readily at hand: Hercules was Fouquet himself.

The King gazed upward and took all this in, as he did the emblem of a cursive F that appeared over and over again in the scrollwork of the salons, very much as the royal initial L had appeared above doorways designed for his own kingly predecessors in the Louvre.* All these paintings and decorations, Louis learned from his host, were due to the third of the trio of extraordinary talents Fouquet had assembled to create Vaux-le-Vicomte—Charles Le Brun, precocious painter, sculptor, master organizer of all arts and crafts; not yet forty, and in command of the thousand-odd artisans who had been working on Vaux, including a whole tapestry factory especially set up in the adjoining village of Maincy.

The diners—there may have been something like five hundred —sat down to Vatel's feast of ortolans, pheasants, quail, partridge, and assorted bisques and ragouts, accompanied by a long list of wines. Lully performed with twenty-four violins supported by other instruments. At one point King Louis admired the dinner service: "What admirable plate."

"Pardon, Sire, it is not plate, it is gold."

The King, reportedly: "We have nothing like this at the Louvre."

Seated not far from him, Mme de La Fayette observed his demeanor amid so much magnificence, and later recalled, "The King was astonished, and Fouquet became aware that he was astonished." Did Fouquet at this moment realize the peril he was courting in daring to outshine his king? But there was no stopping now; the show must go on to its grand finale.

After dinner everyone went outdoors again, and to the open-air theatre. Three knocks sounded. Dark-visaged Molière himself appeared before the footlights, in everyday clothes, putting on the air of a man surprised by this command performance— and indeed he had written and produced in just fifteen days a new masque comedy, *Les Fâcheux* (*The Nuisances*), in which he

* Sometimes, engagingly, Fouquet's F was combined at Vaux with the representation of a squirrel, suggesting that Fouquet had seen an affinity between himself and that quick, vertiginous animal, so deft at supplying its own nest. Whether or not he was playing upon this thought, he was no doubt playing upon the word, since "squirrel," though *écureuil* in French, was also *fouquet* in the old Angevin dialect of the province in which he had been raised.

L̸e Brun (top) was so precocious that he won his first painting commission from Richelieu at fifteen. Employed to celebrate Fouquet's glory, he covered Vaux's ceilings with such allegorical showpieces as "The Triumph of Truth" (above). King Louis himself, though, was just as avid for this sort of grandiose self-celebration and took over Le Brun as premier peintre du Roi, having him execute such stupefying designs as those in Versailles's Galerie des Glaces (below).

was also to play the leading part. After apologizing to his royal guests for his inadequacy, he withdrew to change into costume while a lengthy prologue was delivered, as written for the occasion by another poet in Fouquet's service, Paul Pellisson.

Pour voir en ces beaux lieux le plus grand Roi du monde,
Mortels, je viens à vous de ma grotte profonde . . .

So Pellisson's rhymed obeisance to His Majesty began, followed by the entrance of "numerous dryads, accompanied by fauns and satyrs" from among the surrounding trees and sculptures, to perform a dance as a still further introduction to the play (not by any means one of Molière's best). After three acts and a concluding ballet, at about midnight, came Fouquet's final surprise—an explosion of fireworks such as had never been seen before in France. Hundreds of lanterns had already been lit in Vaux's gardens. Now the Italian Torelli, a master of illuminations, lit up the sky itself with a cascade of rockets of every color, including a blaze of fleurs-de-lis in sparkling white, and then topped even this effect by a smashing discharge of Roman candles from the lantern of Vaux, accompanied by a blast of cannon and a salute of trumpets.

It was distinctly overdone. The King, a master already at covering his displeasure with sovereign correctness, remained briefly for the late-evening supper that followed, but then, disdaining to stay the night in the royal suite prepared for him, coached home with his Court to Fontainebleau, sleeping all the way, we are told, and arriving there about dawn.

It may have been a fitful sleep, for he had a stern resolve to make. He had been concerned for several months at the way his *surintendant* was managing the realm's finances, even though the late Mazarin and many others had conceded that this delightful courtier was a financial wizard. Why was it that the royal treasury remained so bare while Fouquet's own had become so ample? Tonight's spectacle could only confirm the suspicions which Fouquet's enemies, headed by the austere, rising Jean-Baptiste Colbert, had tried to implant in the King's mind: the moment had come to bring down a man who had grown too great.

So, within three weeks, after more evidence had been gathered against him, Fouquet was arrested at Nantes in Brittany by royal warrant on a charge of embezzlement. Vaux-le-Vicomte and his other estates were seized. A long trial followed, resulting in his conviction and the forfeiture of all his property. Meanwhile Louis had determined to show a splendor of his own (with financial assistance from Colbert, who now took over the royal treasury), and set out to build Versailles as a far greater Vaux—the men in charge of the work being none other than Fouquet's own team of Le Brun, Le Vau, and Le Nôtre. Molière, too, passed into the King's service, staging indoor and outdoor theatricals at Versailles after the style at Vaux; so did Vatel, with his dinners; so did Torelli, with his fireworks. In fact, the King was so anxious to turn to his own use all that was best at Vaux that he even had many of its statues transported to his new palace, along with some 1,250 shrubs and trees lately planted in the gardens of the fallen Fouquet.

How could so gifted a man as Nicolas Fouquet, veteran of thirty years' office-holding and of a lifetime's knowledge of Europe's most tortuous court, have set his course for such total disaster? His great miscalculation was not that he mismanaged the King's money but that he misread his mind. Moreover, he had misread the dates on the calendar of Louis's evolution. Until March 8, 1661, Louis was still in the eyes of those around him a stylish but unproven and tame young monarch, captive to the magisterial Mazarin, who had been the lad's preceptor ever since Louis had ascended to the throne at the age of four. Queen Mother Anne of Austria, rid of her feeble and loveless husband Louis XIII, had let Mazarin become her favorite, presumably her lover, and virtual regent of the realm. But on March 9, the very day after Mazarin died, Louis announced that henceforth he would be his own chief minister, obviously glad in his turn to be rid of the presumptuous and avaricious cleric who had oppressed all the years of his youth.

Therewith began Louis XIV's assumption of personal, absolute rule—a regime which over the decades was to prove splendid for France but which in just a few months was to be fatal to Fouquet, the dashing courtier closest to the throne and so dazzled by the hope of becoming the next Mazarin that he failed to realize a virile, pent-up monarch grown into his majority might wish to be every inch a king and brook no rivals.

Fouquet knew much, but was blinded with overweening *hubris*. He knew that Louis particularly resented the great landed nobles who during his youth had staged uprisings against royal authority—an outbreak that at one point had led Paris rioters to invade his very bedroom in the Louvre. The King had plans to put these *Frondeurs* into their place at last; moreover, he was bent on removing his seat of rule from Paris, in order never again to expose himself to such humiliations as he had experienced there, and to make his palace in the countryside the center to which all nobles and placemen must come to bend the knee. Yet now Fouquet himself had built at Vaux the greatest country palace in France—and, as if that were not enough, he had also acquired an island stronghold on the Breton coast, Belle-Isle, which he had proceeded to fortify.

The building of great estates that would reflect new wealth and show off new architecture was then very much the rage in France. The late Cardinal Richelieu had built grandly for himself at Rueil and in Poitou; Mazarin, at Vincennes. Claude de Bullion had a splendid new showplace at Wideville, also by Le Vau; the Comte de Servien, another at Meudon, complete with colossal terraces and grottoes. But Fouquet, fabulously wealthy from his take as *surintendant*, bought and built like a man obsessed. He had acquired two great mansions in Paris; the country seat of Saint-Mandé, not far from Mazarin's own; the seigniory of Maincy, where he would build Vaux; and a number of lesser domains—all this before he went on to Belle-Isle and the completion of the château that was to be his apotheosis or, as he put it to his judges when on trial, "*mon établissement principal . . . où je voulois laisser quelques marques de l'éstat où j'avois esté.*"

Fouquet was rash, vainglorious, and corrupt. Colbert claimed that only one half of the immense tax revenues Fouquet was charged with collecting for the King ever got into the King's hands; and while this was a jealous rival's exaggeration (the state's total revenues from the *taille* (a personal tax), the salt tax, and other imposts and duties then ran to some 140 million livres a year), unquestionably many millions were diverted each year into Fouquet's own pocket. Vaux alone may have cost him more than a million—perhaps the equivalent of $10 million today.

He was also, when he came to build and to patronize the arts, in general a man of superlative taste. Perhaps he was the embodiment of many talents in disarray in a France where new talents could rise quickly. Success dawned early for him: son of a provincial family of legal distinction (what the French called the *noblesse de robe*), he was only sixteen when his father's friend Richelieu gave him his first diplomatic assignment. At twenty-one, as *Maître de Requêtes,* he was a judicial officer of the kingdom; at twenty-seven, the inspector of its armies of the North; and at thirty-eight, under Mazarin's patronage, the *surintendant* who was to rise to such heights before his dramatic and conclusive fall. Two brilliant marriages had established his wealth; then came those dazzling years when as head of the King's treasury he was responsible to no one for his accounts save the King himself, with the result that he mixed up Louis's and his own.

Yet, while making out false returns and signing away his nation's future tax receipts, he lived a many-sided, exuberant life in the arts, patronizing the literary salons of Mlle de Scudéry and Mme du Plessis-Bellière; writing verses of his own; gathering around him and subsidizing a coterie of young spirits ranging from the poets La Fontaine, Scarron, and Pellisson to the playwrights Molière and Corneille; installing in his great house of Saint-Mandé a library of 30,000 volumes ranging from architecture to mathematics; buying Bellinis, Breughels, Veroneses; and finally, at Vaux, assembling the unique team of Le Vau, Le Nôtre, and Le Brun, who made a classic unity of his miscellany of dreams.

The shrewd King had spotted the perfection of Fouquet's taste no less than the man's excess. But in jealously copying and enlarging that taste at Versailles, he doubled and redoubled the excess, with the result that his new palace got quite out of scale, even for a glorious king. Le Vau designed for him façades that went on too long; Le Brun, now *premier peintre du Roi,* covered endless interiors with allegorical scenes that were too many and too alike and that palled courtiers then as they do visitors now; and Le Nôtre, ordered to design gardens several times the size of Vaux's, produced those forbidding vistas that, as Saint-Simon remarked in his celebrated *Mémoires,* "one admired but avoided."

Versailles was Louis's vengeful triumph—an assertion of majesty over Fouquet, over the nobles of France, and over the people of Paris, from whom he had now removed himself into the most haughty isolation. Yet the King's new palace lacked a quality that Fouquet's short-lived one had, ill-advised as it was: exuberance. Versailles was stupendous but dull.

William Harlan Hale is editor of Horizon books *and author of the forthcoming volume* The Horizon History of Ancient Greece.

Soon after he left Vaux between these gates, the envious King Louis set about building Versailles, using Fouquet's artists Le Brun, Le Vau, and Le Nôtre, and much of its fallen owner's property as well. Did he, in turn, build too grandly— as his minister Fouquet had done before him? Many have thought so. Vaux itself was left to a desultory history: returned in a denuded state to the disgraced Fouquet's family, it was bought by a French marshal in 1705, escaped demolition during the French Revolution, deteriorated, and finally came into the hands of another private French owner who set out to restore what was left.

AFRICA: THE FACE BEHIND THE MASK

Its primitive (

By BASIL DAVIDSON

...age profile, modern scholars are discovering, has obscured a rich and cultivated history

Whether in the range of history, archaeology, social anthropology, or the arts, we are in the presence of a major shift in attitude toward the depth and scope of humanity's enterprise in Africa. Almost until the other day it was commonly held and argued that the cultures of that continent—as they were represented, for example, by their sculpture—were the product of a more or less timeless and primitive innocence, possessing value chiefly as tributes to spontaneous emotion or as objects of art that were essentially artless. Here in this mask, it was explained, we may see how Adam experienced fear, or there in that one, baffling by its strangeness, how Eve knew joy. This was the dawn and infancy of mankind. Everything here had stayed motionless in primal bliss and horror. In the words of a former governor of Nigeria, voicing a familiar thought: "For countless centuries, while all the pageant of history swept by, the African remained unmoved—in primitive savagery."

Today it is increasingly seen and written that the truth about old Africa was seldom or never like this, and that the number of surviving peoples of whom this could ever have been said is so small as barely to exist. Perhaps it may be true that the Pygmies of the Congo forest or the Bushmen of the Kalahari desert still live in a society that was fashioned during the Stone Age; so that one may reasonably regard them, or some of them, as little different in their daily life from the men who painted and engraved on rocks through all the centuries of a remote past. Even this is doubtful, since the lives of Pygmies and Bushmen have long been influenced—and, especially with the Bushmen, gravely damaged and distorted—by the presence and pressure of other kinds of people. What at all events we may be sure of is that the vast majority of Africa's populations have walked the wending stones of time and social change, lifting themselves from the primitive to the less primitive, in much the same way as everyone else in the world. The scenery and the methods have been greatly different, but not the general course and destination. One by one our old fixations about Africa go quietly to pieces.

Quietly, no doubt. For none of this has been much noticed in the world at large or, where it has been, readily welcomed and accepted. There is nothing very surprising in this reluctance: what other peoples have thought and often still think about Africans must drag along with it a heavy weight of ancient and accustomed prejudice. The stereotype of "savage Africa" was cast in Elizabethan times, if not earlier, and the mold has grown rock-hard since then. In European judgments of African culture there has been remarkably little advance since Father Cavazzi, to pick a random but characteristic example, gave his views on African dancing in the Congo of three hundred years ago. "Having no object in the skillful talent of displaying the movement of the body or the agility of the feet," he decided, "dancing among these barbarians serves only the vicious satisfaction of a libidinous appetite." With the twist and other joyful exercises in our midst, this description of the samba may be thought a little uncharitable, not to say downright absurd; but

the fact is that Cavazzi was offering a true reflection of the profound contempt that white men have usually felt, then and long afterward, for the moral and intellectual content of the black man's culture.

Contempt grew into a conviction, later on, that the real trouble with Africans was that they had failed to "grow up" and were therefore lacking in some ingredient of the capacity to achieve a mastery over environment, which men have generally recognized as civilization. This paternalistic view of Africans as feckless or retarded children was largely minted by the early explorers. Once an African grows beyond his childhood years, declared Sir Richard Burton, "his mental development is arrested, and thenceforth he grows backwards instead of forwards." The colonizer, according to a Belgian veteran of the Union Minière copper-mining concern in Katanga, "must never lose sight of the fact that the Negroes have the spirits of children." To which a Portuguese authority on Angola added that the "raw native" must be looked on as "an adult with a child's mentality." French records are full of similar opinions.

The reasons for thinking otherwise are many and various. Quite apart from any conclusions that may be drawn from the political evidence of modern Africa, the face behind the mask of traditional Africa now seems altogether different from what we thought it was. Its features may still appear strange and hard to interpret, but the words "primitive" and "childish" are clearly out of place in trying to describe them. Already we can trace the outline of an African "pageant of history" in which the protagonists, far from remaining "unmoved in primitive savagery," have manifestly traveled a long way from their starting point. We can find in traditional African thought, however unexpectedly, a prescientific maturity and sophistication

A "Dark" Continent Finds its History

The Africa shown opposite, newly emerging from the distortions of myth and prejudice, possesses a complex and dynamic history, a past rich in diversity and change. More than two thousand years ago, for example, the knowledge of iron smelting began to spread southward and eastward from the Kushite kingdom of Meroë, altering tribal societies as it went. Contrary to what was once believed the Africans, and not the Phoenicians, built the walled stone city at Zimbabwe in what is now Rhodesia. Within Africa itself were generated the creative energies of the spirited Nok culture, and of its skilled artistic descendants in Ife and Benin. From as far away as China, outside influences have always been at work in Africa, especially through the Islamic eastern coast; and when the gold trade across the Sahara began to thrive, in medieval times, it built the prosperity of the cultivated city-states of the Upper Niger. The arrival of the Europeans was in fact only another chapter in a long story.

PAGE 190: ELIOT ELISOFON—BRITISH MUSEUM; PAGE 199: GUILLEMOT—*Connaissance des Arts*

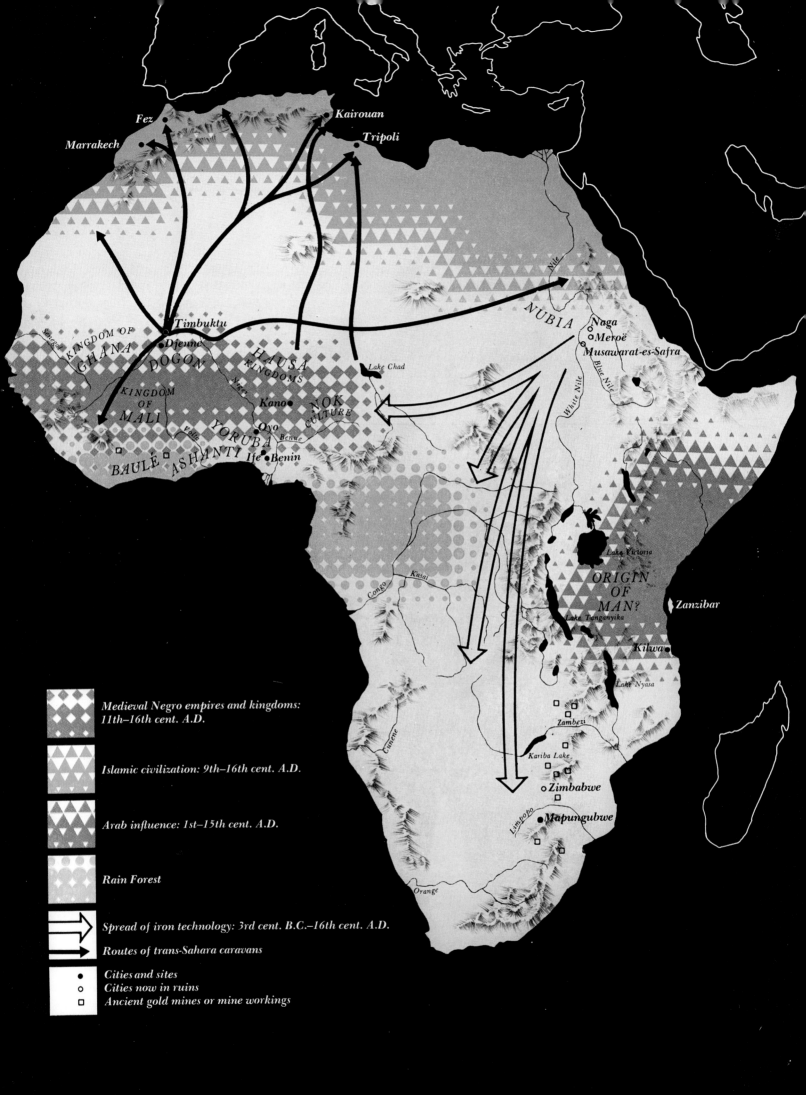

Fez

Marrakech

Kairouan

Tripoli

Nile

NUBIA

Naga

Meroë

Musawarat-es-Safra

Timbuktu

KINGDOM OF GHANA

Djenne

DOGON

HAUSA KINGDOMS

Senegal

KINGDOM OF MALI

Niger

Kano

NOK CULTURE

Lake Chad

White Nile

Blue Nile

Volta

YORUBA

Oyo

Benue

BAULÉ

ASHANTI

Ife

Benin

Kasai

Congo

Lake Victoria

ORIGIN OF MAN?

Zanzibar

Lake Tanganyika

Kilwa

Lake Nyasa

Zambezi

Kariba Lake

Zimbabwe

Cunene

Limpopo

Mapungubwe

Orange

Medieval Negro empires and kingdoms: 11th–16th cent. A.D.

Islamic civilization: 9th–16th cent. A.D.

Arab influence: 1st–15th cent. A.D.

Rain Forest

Spread of iron technology: 3rd cent. B.C.–16th cent. A.D.

Routes of trans-Sahara caravans

● Cities and sites
○ Cities now in ruins
□ Ancient gold mines or mine workings

Awareness of Negro Africa by the ancient Egyptians appears as early as this wall painting (opposite) from the tomb of Huy, or Amenhotep, viceroy in Nubia during the reign of Tutankhamen (c. 1361–1352 B.C.). In it the Nubian princes are shown doing homage—bringing gold, animal skins, and black giraffe tails (the latter were highly prized) to Tutankhamen, while behind them comes a princess in a chariot drawn by oxen, a parasol of ostrich feathers crowning her diadem. In the Nile plain north of Khartoum the ruins still remain of Nubian cities, like Meroë (above) and Naga (top), but far too little excavating has been done to indicate what manner of civilization flourished here—except that it was a rich and powerful one, trading as far afield as India and China, and profoundly influencing the rest of Africa.

that are emphatic in their projection of dynamic and coherent ideas about man and the universe. We can see in many of the arts of Africa, as a distinguished Italian ethnologist has lately written, the impulse of "ancient and elaborate traditions: not works of exuberant youth and still less of childish inexperience, but products of conscious and thoughtful maturity."

These conclusions rest on a large quantity of obscure and detailed work, much of which has been recorded only in specialist journals whose findings seldom reach a wide public. In the past ten or twenty years anthropologists have ceased to measure African skulls for the purpose of speculating on the relative inferiority of African brains—wisely, since the evidence of man-ape fossils proves in this respect distressingly perverse—and have got down to the task of analyzing how Africans have solved or tried to solve their material and moral problems. Archaeologists have begun to sketch an ordered survey of African ruins and remains, and have dug most usefully at several important sites. Historians have embarked on the systematic collection of African social traditions, relating these where possible to the memoirs of travelers and traders from Europe and elsewhere whose writings—often of outstanding value, if sometimes fabulous and almost always needing fresh interpretation —cover a period of more than a thousand years. And the outcome of all this has been so startling as really to deserve the name of a revolution in thought.

It now appears that the earliest types of men, including our own type, were born in Africa possibly as long ago as two million years. All these experiments in evolution except our own were unsuccessful. None of them got beyond the earliest forms of Stone Age culture. They died out, leaving little but a handful of fossils. Our own type adapted itself and slowly multiplied. There is fairly capacious evidence for this in fossils and fragments, dating back some ten thousand years and more to a period when *Homo sapiens* had long since occupied many other parts of the earth. Modern varieties of *Homo sapiens* in Africa begin to turn up, in more or less easily recognizable fossil form, for the period beginning about seven thousand years ago. In the patient centuries that followed, these peoples began painting and engraving on rocks, notably in the Sahara, which was then a green and fertile land. They seem to have lived in many regions of northern, central, and southern Africa but were few and far between. Some of them, certainly those who dwelt in the lower valley of the Nile, had established themselves in semipermanent settlements and were growing food by about 4000 B.C. This New Stone Age, signified by the invention of agriculture, moved gradually across the continent.

So far, so good: most of this, after all, is part of a widely accepted prehistory. Then came a radical change. A few centuries before the Christian era Africa south of the Sahara emerged from the New Stone Age into an age of metals, specifically an Iron Age; and it is with new understanding of the course and spread of this Iron Age that fresh perspectives in thought about ancient Africa begin to appear and take control.

Far from "staying in the Stone Age until the day before yester-day," as the familiar myth would have it, most Africans to the south of the great desert (though the division from North Africa is largely artificial) are now seen to have entered an Iron Age not many centuries after northern Europe. This is the long and complex period, beginning about 200 or 300 B.C., in which most of the traditional societies and cultures of the con-tinent were born.

Techniques of iron smelting and forging induced new kinds of social organization. The technology of iron underlay the early empires of the Western Sudan, shaping the political birth of ancient Ghana, for example, whose central authority seems to have crystallized out of tribal rivalries not long after A.D. 300. Of Ghana an early medieval Arab writer could remark that its warriors made expeditions "with swords and with lances" against neighbors "who know not iron and fight with bars of ebony." But the Iron Age did much more than promote impe-rial systems in the bare grasslands of West Africa: still more tellingly, it also opened routes of southward migration into the dense forests of Central Africa and the upland plains that lay beyond. Use of the iron-pointed spear and the tighter social cohesion that was linked to it ensured easy conquest over Stone Age peoples already in sparse occupation of those lands, gave better defense against dangerous animals, promoted more suc-cessful hunting, and cleared more land for cultivation. By the end of the first millennium A.D., iron-using peoples from west-central Africa had penetrated far across the southern continent. Long before Europe's first large-scale invasion, opening with the settlement of the Cape of Good Hope in 1652, Iron Age peoples whose origin had been far in the north were in strong possession of the central and southern continent almost as far as the Cape itself.

In this way, by wave after wave of migration and settlement through many centuries, inland Africa received the ancestors of most of the peoples who live there today. They advanced in social organization as well as in space. They evolved more complex and efficient forms of government, invented new means of agriculture through irrigation or ingenious tropical farming, developed mining industries wherever valuable ores could be found on or near the surface, split themselves into many com-munities and nations, and gradually established the traditions of a rich and various culture whose special tone and accent ring out clearly even today. And it is this slow but steady spreading of related peoples that explains both the maturity and the un-derlying unity of ideas, beliefs, and customs which have con-trolled men's behavior, and still to some extent control it, throughout much of the continent.

Study of this specifically African culture has lately added or begun to add another new dimension to the picture of Africa's past and present. Here we find, with increasing research, a common stock of philosophical and metaphysical speculation and belief. Not long ago it would have seemed pretentious and perhaps absurd to speak in any such terms of the kind of

"fetish mumbo-jumbo" that pagan Africans were thought to revere. Lately, however, a number of painstaking inquiries into African concepts of God and man and nature have revealed systems of thought that overturn, as the French ethnologist Marcel Griaule pointed out after living with the Dogon of the Western Sudan, "all previous ideas about the mentality of black peoples." Griaule has told how he listened to an old man called Ogotommeli for three and thirty days and found this Dogon sage had laid out for him a conceptual structure about man and the universe that displayed "an internal coherence, a secret wisdom, and an apprehension of realities"—at a prescientific level, needless to say—"equal to that which we Europeans con-ceive ourselves to have attained."

The general source of these ideas is not hard to trace. It is clear that a way of life which comprehended the major human achievement of peopling huge regions of a hot and difficult con-tinent, and was closely linked to kinship settlement and sub-sistence farming, produced in time its own characteristic frame-work of belief. One can see this, to take a single instance, in the so-called "ancestor cult" and its attitudes to land ownership. "I conceive that land belongs to a vast family," commented a Nigerian chief some fifty years ago, "of which many are dead, few are living, and countless members are still unborn." From a number of convictions such as this, jointly held as they are by most communities in Africa south of the Sahara, there has flowed what can reasonably be called a basic unity of culture.

Faced with these unsuspected dimensions of depth of time and breadth of thought, we clearly require a new approach to the arts of Africa. For they in turn will be found to reflect this long-enduring process of migration and settlement over appar-ently limitless plains and forests that the history of the African Iron Age encompasses. They are the works of an age of faith, an age that was pagan and peculiar to itself, severely limited in many ways, yet all-embracing in its imperatives and finally successful in reaching a notable level of moral and material sta-bility. These masks and figures are not, as someone has pene-tratingly observed, points of departure but points of arrival. They do not come from the "beginning of time." They occur at the end of a long development.

I should like to illustrate these various points by referring to the famous sculpture of the old Yoruba state of Ife and of its

Trade had already drawn European attention south of the Sahara by the time the Jewish cartographers of Majorca, in 1375, produced the so-called Catalan atlas of Abraham Cresques, from which the map (opposite) is taken. Though the shape of Spain (upper left) can be seen, the geographical information is too sketchy to be useful—including a nonexistent mountain range (center) bisecting the desert. What interests historians is the Negro king at lower right, Musa Mali of Guinea, of whom the text states: "So abundant is the gold which is found in his country that he is the richest and most noble king in all the land."

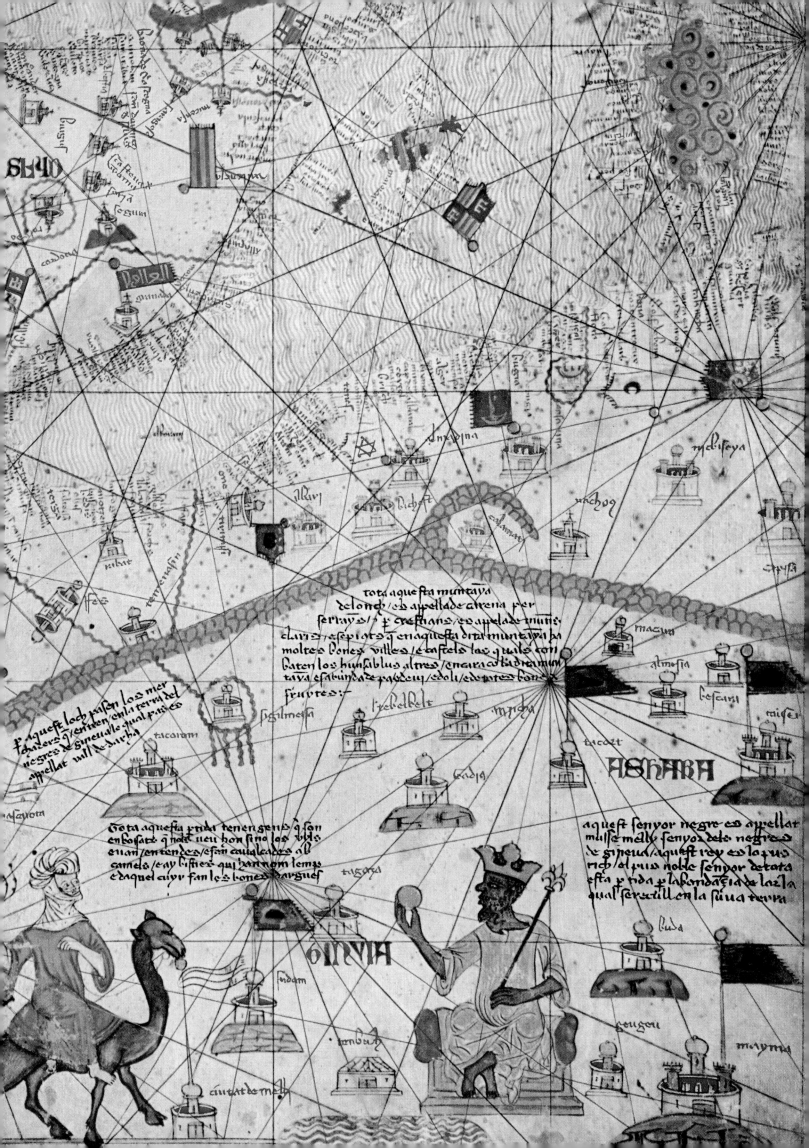

no less well-known successor, Benin. These splendid works have been justly admired, for they are strong and sensitive and beautiful. Yet it is hard to deny that they have owed a good deal of their fame to their anthropomorphic naturalism. Here at last, we have tended to think, is something we can understand—something civilized, classical, or even possibly Renaissance. And so powerfully persuasive has been the myth of the primitive savage that early judgments on this sculpture were unanimous in awarding it a European inspiration. A wandering Italian artist? Perhaps a Greek of ancient times? Or why not a Portuguese? Even today, when it may be shown by historical evidence and latterly by archaeological proof that Ife sculptures are probably older than the Renaissance and certainly much anterior to the arrival of the Portuguese in West Africa, well-intentioned men and women find it difficult to believe these works are truly African.

Nonetheless it is true that the sculpture of Ife and that of Benin stand squarely within the African tradition, being eccentric only to the point that the societies which produced them had developed highly centralized forms of divine kingship and a corresponding requirement from their artists. There is in this respect a most illuminating comparison to be made between the courtly arts of Ife and Benin—ranging from the "pure naturalism" of some of the Ife heads to the hieratic caricatures of decadent Benin—and the wonderfully varied and much more "popular" arts of the peoples over whom the kings and great chiefs ruled. Contrast, for example, a typical chiefly figure of Benin (see page 201) with the superbly stylized leopard now in the Museum of Primitive Art (see page 200). We are obviously in the presence of a most variable and even individual approach; and this impression is repeated and remarkably enlarged by the great diversity of old Nigerian works in metal, such as the Tsoede figures or the group of fine bronzes lately recovered from eastern Nigeria and much else besides, not to mention the parallel achievements of neighboring peoples like the Baulé and Akan.

But let us remain, for the purposes of this essay, with the tradition of Ife and Benin. If completely African, then how and through what diversity of experience did it emerge? Here we enter the realm of speculation, but the speculation begins to be tied persuasively to factual probability and even certainty.

The Yoruba people who built the old empire of Oyo, whose "holy city" was Ife, are now believed to have entered their historical homeland at about the same time that the Normans began casting envious eyes on Anglo-Saxon England. But these newcomers to southern Nigeria were not, if I may quote myself, "the only ancestors of Yoruba civilization, any more than William of Normandy's four thousand knights were the only ancestors of British civilization. They were a relatively small group of travelers, but hard-tried and well-armed: they conquered and settled and were then absorbed among the peoples whom they had found." Yet what kind of people were the "Anglo-Saxons" of southern Nigeria?

TEXT CONTINUED ON PAGE 205

The Acme of African Art

The discovery in northern Nigeria of the two-thousand-year-old Nok culture, of which the head above is a magnificent example, has provided at last a suggestion of whence came, by the thirteenth century, the serene and naturalistic sculptural style of the kingdom of Ife to the south. The terra-cotta head opposite, of a classical simplicity rivaling European efforts at a comparable time, stands at the peak of Ife realism and sophistication. It was disinterred in the latter part of 1957, by ditchdiggers in the environs of Ife who came upon a treasure of four heads in clay and seven in bronze. These were but the latest of numerous discoveries at Ife, which established its preeminence as the Greece of ancient Africa.

Together with Ife, the center of African artistic creativity was the kingdom of Benin, sometimes called "bloody Benin," after the persistence of its brutal sacrificial customs and the massacre of a British expedition that took place there in 1897. Benin bronzes, now world-famous for their authority and skill, include the leopard at left, a symbol of the power of Benin's king, or Oba, who often kept tame leopards in his palace. Among the Oba's possessions, when a punitive British expedition came to chastize him, was the ivory mask at right, bearing European heads around its crown and slits in the forehead, eyelids, and eyes to receive inlaid metal: one of the finest works of art we have from Benin, or elsewhere.

The walls of the palace of Benin's Oba were decorated with bronze bas-relief plaques, of which approximately eight hundred survive. Usually dated from the late sixteenth to the early eighteenth centuries, these were made by the so-called lost wax process, in which a wax model is surrounded by a clay mold, so that the wax can then be melted out and replaced by molten metal. Most of the plaques, like the powerfully shaped example opposite, were representations of the Oba's majesty and aura, displaying a style in which distortion conveys a sense of his somber authority. The figure at center is of course the Oba, wearing the "choker," or necklace, that is the Bini badge of royalty; the attendants who hold up his hands are presumably minor servants, while more substantial courtiers shield him from the African sun. Bronze casting is still practiced at Benin, though as a cultivated handicraft rather than as a necessity of civic ceremonial.

Royal Ease Along the Niger

The most extraordinary work of art ever to come to light in Negro Africa is probably the seated figure (above) first reported in 1921 at Tada, an obscure village on the banks of the Middle Niger. Together with a number of other sculptures, it forms a group known as the Tsoede bronzes, after the semi-legendary Nigerian hero who is said to have been responsible for leaving them in the locations where they were discovered. These figures pose one of the most striking of the many problems confronting the historian of Nigerian art, if only because they include the four largest cast bronzes ever found in Africa, outside the frontiers of Imperial Rome.

It was early in the sixteenth century, according to the traditions of the Nupe and the Igala peoples, that Tsoede, or Edegi, a bastard son of the Ata of Idah, fled up the Niger during a dynastic conflict, taking with him a store of metal heirlooms that included these bronze figures. Before founding the Nupe royal dynasty, he is supposed to have deposited some of them at various stopping places along the river, where they have become sacred insignia of divine kingship. Of these objects, the figures found at Tada, along with two others from twenty-five miles upstream at Jebba, are the most important. It is indeed astonishing to find in a remote riverside village so advanced an example of the spiral in sculptural form, in marked contrast to the rather rigid front view almost universally observed in African art. The posture, in fact, is remarkably close to that known to Orientalists as "royal ease." It could have been made only by a bronze founder of the Ife school, and so may date from the fourteenth century.

WILLIAM FAGG, *Deputy Keeper, Department of Ethnography, British Museum*

203

Cattle were much prized by the Egyptians, as they are today by many Africans, especially the tall Watutsi of Ruanda and Burundi, among whom they serve as a feudal form of wealth. What is remarkable is the extent to which African cattle still resemble the "Hathor" cows of Egyptian bas-reliefs, such as the one (above right) from the temple of the Fourth Dynasty King Khuf-wy. The contemporary cow, with the same long curling horn (right) is one of a breed maintained by the Fulani, a nomadic Moslem people who live scattered across the southern edge of the Sahara from Senegal to northern Nigeria. The Fulani are of Middle Eastern rather than Negro racial inheritance, and may originally have migrated from upper Egypt, bringing their livestock with them. They now do a brisk trade in cattle horns, shipping them to Texas to be sold as souvenirs.

TEXT CONTINUED FROM PAGE 198

Nothing useful could be said about this until a few years ago. Today, thanks initially to accidental discoveries by tin miners in central Nigeria, we know a good deal more about the kind of reply that will eventually be made. These "non-Yoruba ancestors" were the highly artistic and ingenious people of the Nok culture, so called after the name of a village where some of their characteristic terra-cotta figures were first recovered. The diligence and devotion of Bernard Fagg, Nigeria's Federal Director of Antiquities, have brought together at the museum in Jos an astonishing display of Nok heads and figures. What is more, a fairly reliable stratigraphy of the region has linked them to a distant period, while radioactivity tests by the Carbon-14 method have yielded boundary dates of 900 B.C. and A.D. 200. We also know that the Nok people had emerged from the Stone Age. They were smelting iron and forging iron tools and weapons.

Here, excitingly enough, were some of the cultural beginnings of Iron Age society in West Africa. But the Nok discoveries have continued. Nok objects are now being found over an increasingly wide area round the confluence of the rivers Niger and Benue, reaching westward into what is Yorubaland today and what was once the territory of the Yoruba empire of Oyo. Can it be that the arts of Ife have at last found their origin? Parallels of style between Nok and Ife, both in form and content, are often strikingly clear (see pages 198 and 199).

To these material indications the legends of the Yoruba add a persuasive gloss. All the various sections of this nation trace their origin to the city of Ife—the "fabled spot," as one of their historians has written, "where God created man, white and black, and from whence they dispersed all over the earth." With this, indeed, we seem to catch the echo of those early migrations which peopled the central and southern lands of Africa. However that may be, the certain fact is that the Yoruba took over a tradition which they found among the populations with whom they settled; and this, evidently, was a Nok tradition.

But then the Yoruba also have another tradition, parallel but contradictory. They believe that they came "from the East," from the lands of the Nile or even beyond; and for this there is some partial confirmation in a number of their cultural traits. "They seem," one expert has concluded, resuming the evidence, "to have come from the east or the northeast, possibly from Meroë." And with that one may well think hard and think again, for the mention of Meroë in this connection has intriguing possibilities.

Meroë (see page 195) was the capital of the Kushite state that flourished on the Middle Nile between the sixth century B.C. and about A.D. 320, when its last ruler was overthrown by the armies of Abyssinian Axum. Little is known of this Kushite state. Its written language is not yet understood. Its monuments have barely felt the prod of the archaeologist's pick and trowel. Its royal tombs, true enough, have yielded king-lists for an unbroken period of nearly one thousand years, but its far-spread "city mounds" have yet to undergo any systematic in-

KEN HEYMAN—RAPHO-GUILLUMETTE; OVERLEAF: SAME

Traveling up the Blue Nile in 1772, the Scots nobleman James Bruce was astonished to see parading before him a troop of magnificent cavalry, all wearing chain mail. He could see the same today. A common African tradition holds that these suits of interlocked metal rings (not always in perfect repair) come originally from the Crusaders, and have been handed down from soldier to soldier over the centuries. Probably many are of far more recent, if not actually current, manufacture. The horseman above is one of over three thousand who gathered in northern Nigeria in 1959 to celebrate their newly won independence. OVERLEAF: *It is the custom for these riders, many abreast, to come charging up to their ruler, the Sardauna of Sokatu, halting suddenly and saluting him as a pledge of allegiance.*

205

The Lure and Allure of Gold

Africans not only traded gold, by way of the caravans across the desert, they worked in it themselves with high artistry. The three gold ornaments at right, two pendant masks and (center) a scorpion ring, testify to the skill of the Baulé, a tribe of the Ivory Coast that migrated there in the eighteenth century, after some dynastic disagreements in the kingdom of Ashanti, taking their metalworking techniques with them. The height of Ashanti achievement in gold is suggested by the two-thirds life-sized mask (above) of King Kofi Kakari, the sole surviving object from what must once have been an extensive royal treasury in a court of lavish pomp and splendor. Ashanti rulers came to greet the early European explorers so heavily adorned in gold that their region was called "the Gold Coast" until the name was changed to "Ghana" in 1957.

vestigation. All that may be said with confidence is that Meroë was the lavish capital of an important and relatively advanced African civilization which had borrowed much from Egypt, had felt the impact of ideas along the old trading routes from India and Arabia and even China, and had played in its day and age a crucial part in the southward transference of iron-working technology. Arguing from the presence there of large mounds of slag, a British archaeologist of fifty years ago even thought that Meroë deserved to be called—if with some poetic licence—"the Birmingham of ancient Africa."

Readers of the Acts of the Apostles will have heard of Meroë in another connection. There it is recorded how the Deacon Philip met and baptized a certain Ethiopian dignitary on "the way that goeth down from Jerusalem to Gaza." And "behold, a man of Ethiopia, a eunuch of great authority under Candace, queen of the Ethiopians, who had the charge of all her treasure and had come to Jerusalem for to worship, was returning, and sitting in his chariot read Esaias the prophet." But "Ethiopian" was the old Greek word for Kushite, and the queen mentioned in this passage lived not in Abyssinia but almost certainly amid the pillared comfort of Musawarat-es-Safra, whose imposing ruins may still be seen not twenty miles from Meroë, or seventy miles from Khartoum, lying like noble hulks aground in the waste of the Butana desert.

Now if it is true—and it seems to be—that the intrusive ancestors of Yoruba civilization came from the Middle Nile, perhaps in consequence of the disasters of Axumite invasion in the fourth century A.D., may this not be a comprehensive explanation of the many similarities of religious cult that undoubtedly exist? The sanctity of rams, the supernatural power of snakes, the hierarchy of the Yoruba pantheon: are they not the fragments of a culture brought initially from the Nile? It may be so. Yet at this point of inquiry one should guard against any kind of facile diffusionism that would attribute Negro cultural origins, at least on the religious side, to the ancient cultures of the Nile. It is rather a question, on closer examination, of the chicken and the egg.

For even if it is correct that the "Followers of Horus," semi-legendary founders of dynastic Egypt before 3000 B.C., had entered their kingdom from the Middle East—from *outside* Africa—the fact remains that they found other folk in occupation of the land, and these other folk were undoubtedly African and quite possibly Negro. Where had this "oldest" Egyptian population found its cultural beliefs? The notion that the ancestor-wanderers of the Yoruba first brought to West Africa the idea of snake sanctity, for example, or that of anthropomorphic sculpture, falls down as soon as one considers the Nok figures. For the Nok people, it turns out, already possessed these ideas. Had their forefathers received such ideas from Egypt or had they given them to Egypt? At this stage the right conclusion seems to be that we have come upon the scattered survivals of an ancient cultural interplay between the valley of the Nile and continental Africa, linked to Iron Age beginnings but resting

The legendary land of Ophir, where the gold of King Solomon was mined, seemed to have been discovered in Southern Rhodesia when the first white settlers found the region filled with hundreds of abandoned mine workings and many stone ruins, the greatest of them a high-walled fortress (above) called Zimbabwe. The Europeans preferred not to believe that Zimbabwe, with its massively constructed battlements and towers, could have been the work of Negro Africans, and thus they ascribed it to the remote past, so that it could be credited to wandering Sabaeans or Phoenicians. Unhappily for legend, modern archeologists have been at work on Zimbabwe and have given it a radiocarbon date. For the most part they now agree that the site was occupied from about A.D. 500 to A.D. 1750—and the walls built by native Africans alone.

ELIOT ELISOFON

Bronzes played an important role in recording royal succession. Each Oba at his death was memorialized in a ritual head, the manner of portraiture developing from early realism to the highly stylized representation of a nineteenth-century king (left). His elaborate headgear symbolizes in its hanging beads the tradition that Obas do not often show themselves to their people; the broad flange at the base of the collar is studded with tiny sculptures of leopards (the power of the king) and bound and decapitated human bodies (the weakness of his enemies).

on much older African foundations. Here, once again, is the echo of profound unity within the diversity of many cultures.

The same conclusion is likely to emerge from any detailed history of African culture that may be attempted in the future with fuller knowledge: an interweaving of African and non-African ideas both of form and content but also, underlying this, an inexhaustible spring of native originality and creative impulse. Applied to any other great tradition this might seem banal, for where is the major culture that stands uniquely on its own? But with Africa the comment is not banal, or not yet, for we have only begun to give Africa its just weight and value in the balance of cultural give and take. Outside influences have long been recognized, and recent archaeological finds have widened their possible scope and impact. It is easy, for example, to accept the view that Chinese styles in metalware became popular at Meroë, since the Kushites are known to have had many trading ties with the sailors of the Indian Ocean and therefore, in all likelihood, with Han China; while a number of bronze vessels lately recovered in eastern Nigeria have plausibly suggested that the Chinese note may have struck its distant echo even as far as West Africa. Yet, at the same time, we have underestimated the weight on the "native African" side of the scales. "I am more and more inclined," a well-known authority on African sculpture observed the other day, "to think that Egypt owed more to Negro Africa than the other way round."

Unity and maturity are evident, even emphatically so, in the cultural and artistic traditions of many African regions and periods. Along the great rivers of central and western Africa there were peoples whose outstanding skill in the carving of wood produced a wealth of individual styles, which were nonetheless impelled by a broad community of ideas and themes, itself the product, as we have seen, of a common historical experience. Out on the high veld of the central southern plateau, where strong states and empires came to life in medieval times, stone ruins now begin to yield a coherent pattern of development over a prolonged period. The mythical Phoenicians said to have built Zimbabwe (see page 209), greatest of all these many sites, have been banished from the scene: once again the African side of the balance has acquired a new weight. Thus the site of Zimbabwe is now known to have been occupied by a succession of Iron Age peoples through more than a thousand years; and the walls of that strange "temple," as they may be seen today, were built by Africans at about the same time that the *Mayflower* breasted the Atlantic.

These peoples of the high veld were mining gold and selling it to eastern traders as early as the tenth century. They worked extensively in metals, sometimes with remarkable results. Plate-gold fragments of a sceptre and small rhinoceros figures from the site of Mapungubwe in the northern Transvaal are thinner than five-thousandths of an inch, witness to a rare degree of preindustrial skill. Even in the ruined medieval cities of the east coast, where Arabian influence was strong and venerable, Islamic architecture is seen to have acquired a distinctive style of its own. There, too, Swahili poetry touched lyrical and epic greatness.

Today a new Africa confronts the world, independent, resurgent, claiming a place of dignity and due respect in the councils of men. No doubt it may be high time for the rest of us to look at this claim with the eye of understanding, and for that a reassessment of African culture will be essential.

The English novelist and reporter Basil Davidson has himself done much to awaken interest in African history, through books like The Lost Cities of Africa *(1959) and* Black Mother *(1961).*

The Image of the White Man
in the Art of Other Races

A PORTFOLIO
ASSEMBLED AND DESCRIBED BY
JOHN MAASS

The Portuguese traders arriving in Japan after 1542 were greeted with great enthusiasm by the curious populace. In this detail from a seventeenth-century screen, a Portuguese sailor, painted with slightly Oriental features, is playing Go with his Japanese guests on the sterncastle of his ship.

In Seventeenth-Century Japan

An air of excitement hovered over Japanese ports when the black Portuguese carrack arrived on its yearly voyage from Macao. This scene shows Portuguese sailors resting after the journey while Indian deck hands furl the sails. On shore, the Portuguese captain, shaded by a parasol like any Eastern potentate, supervises the unloading of Chinese silks, gold, and trinkets onto a small skiff. A tall Negro in the foreground carries ivory tusks, a precious part of the cargo. Other traders pass a neat row of Japanese textile and porcelain shops,

whose proprietresses peer eagerly at the new wares.

This "Southern Barbarian" screen of the Kano school was painted in the early seventeenth century, when the Portuguese enjoyed a profitable Japanese trade which was soon to end. The screens were so called because the foreigners who first sailed to Japan from the south struck the courteous Japanese as having little refinement. The features of the Portuguese which most impressed the artist were their billowing pantaloons and capes and their fierce black mustaches.

Scenes like this were popular with the Japanese merchants who grew rich from their contacts with the Western traders.

The Portuguese were finally expelled from Japan in 1638 because of the overzealous missionary work of the Jesuits who accompanied them and the resistance of their Christian converts to the power of the shogun. Except for a handful of Dutch traders, the country was tightly closed off from the outside world for more than two hundred years—when Admiral Perry forced the reopening of Japan to the West.

213

In British India

The first settlers to arrive with the East India Company were quick to adopt the customs and delights of the land. The Bengal miniature at left, painted about 1760 by Dip Chand, shows a rather pompous settler smoking a hookah and attended by his servants in the manner of an Indian maharajah. He is thought to be Dr. William Fullarton, a Scot from Ayrshire. Fullarton was second surgeon at Fort William and the bane of company officials, who condemned him for mixing too freely with the Indians.

By 1858, the British had established complete rule in India and a court system with judges appointed by the Crown. In the new Kalighat style of painting, an actual Calcutta murder trial is portrayed (right). A Hindu priest had seduced a pretty Indian girl. Her jealous husband decapitated her and was promptly tried for murder. The detached trunk and head of the girl, still wearing arm jewelry and earrings, lie as evidence before the baby-faced English judge wearing the top hat which the bazaar artists associated with the British. The husband (left foreground), wearing a white dhoti, is held by a local policeman, while the bearded priest tells his story in the witness box. The fate of the unfortunate husband rests on the outcome of the contest being waged between the defense and the prosecuting attorneys behind him.

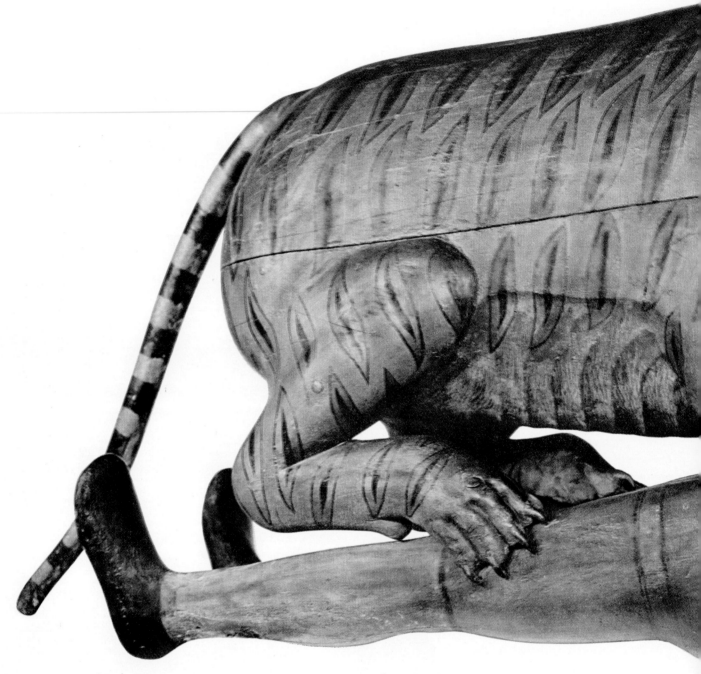

Tipu's Tiger

This Indian tiger gnawing at the neck of a helpless British colonel was the six-foot "toy" of Tipu Sahib, sultan of Mysore. It was captured at Seringapatam in 1799 and dispatched as a trophy of battle to the Court of Directors of the East India Company with the following memorandum: "This piece of Mechanism represents a Royal Tyger in the act of devouring a prostrate European. There are some barrels in imitation of an Organ, within the body of the Tyger, and a row of Keys of natural Notes. The sounds produced by the Organ are intended to ressemble the Cries of a person in distress intermixed with the roar of a Tyger. The machinery is

so contrived that while the Organ is playing, the hand of the European is often lifted up, to express his helpless and deplorable condition."

The owner of this ingenious automaton was the son of Haidar Ali, who made Mysore the strongest state in India and the chief obstacle to the expansion of British rule. The father named his son "Tipu," which means "tiger" in Canarese, and he grew up to sit on a tiger throne and dress his army in striped tiger jackets. "Better to live two weeks as a tiger," Tipu was fond of saying, "than a lifetime as a lamb."

The automaton was built at the time of the Mysore wars,

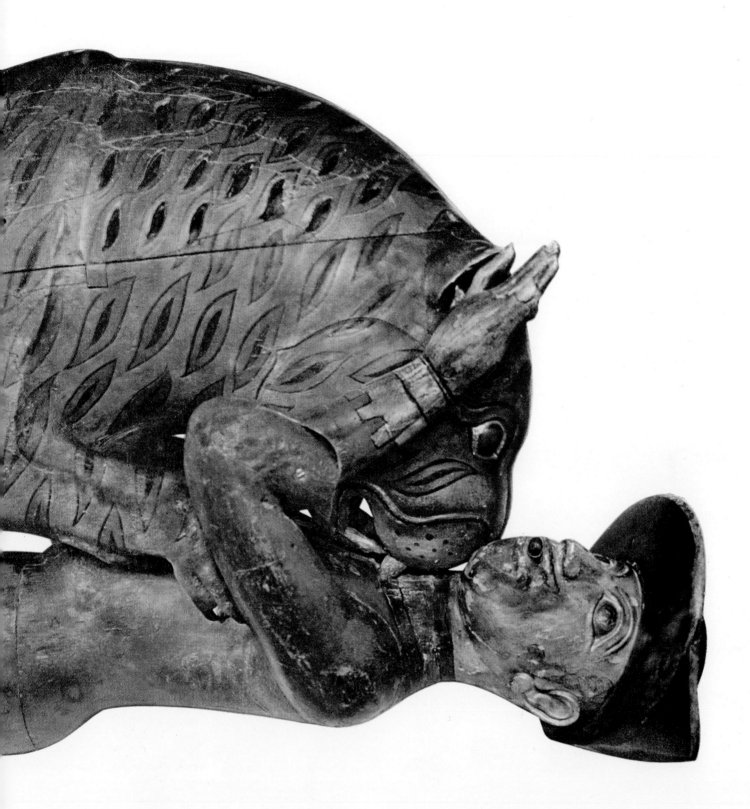

in which the British seized over half of Tipu's realm and held two of his sons as hostages. The interior mechanism, with its semi-mechanical pipe organ, was very likely manufactured by French craftsmen, for the French were Tipu's allies against the British, and automatons were at that time the rage in France. In any case, the musical tiger became the symbol of Tipu's consuming hatred of the British and of his desire for revenge. It is easy to imagine him sitting in the music room of the palace while a servant turned the crank on the tiger's left side, listening with delight to the growls of his favorite animal and the screams of his favorite victim.

Tipu died as he had lived. When a British army under General Sir David Baird stormed his fortress at Seringapatam, he was shot down, sword in hand, at the palace gate. The musical tiger was the chief prize in a shipload of trophies sent back to England. It ended up in the Victoria & Albert Museum where it has delighted generations of visitors, including John Keats. In his satiric poem The Cap and the Bells, Keats describes a visitor to "mid-most Ind" who
"... feared less
A dose of senna-tea or nightmare Gorgon
Than the Emperor when he play'd on his Man-Tiger-Organ."

In Montezuma's Mexico

When the Spanish arrived in the Aztec kingdom in 1519, Montezuma sent artists to record the appearance of the mysterious strangers. The original parchments have since disappeared, but copies of these pictorial histories were made by Spanish priests. The entrance of Cortes is preserved in Codex Vaticanus Latinus 3738 (left) in which he appears as a bearded warrior, carrying the banner of the Holy Spirit in one hand and a long sword in the other. The Indians had never seen a horse, and the strange animal resembles a tall, panting dog with ears of a deer. From his capital of Tenochtitlan, Montezuma's envoy, represented by the feathered headdress glyph of the Aztec chief, brought gifts to bribe Cortes to turn back. When the Spanish refused, Montezuma had no recourse but to welcome them as his guests. A foreigner is already seen within the temple of Tenochtitlan, which is identified by the cactus glyph beneath that of Montezuma. The artist never doubted the intentions of the Spaniards, for below the rear leg of the horse, the shield and arrow glyph of war is clearly drawn.

An episode in the final conquest of the city two years later is told in Codex Az-catitlan (above), which reflects the European influence on the native Aztec style. The Spaniard Pedro de Alvarado fights off an Aztec while the wounded Cortes, who had fallen into one of the canals with other Spaniards, receives aid from a native ally.

In the Americas

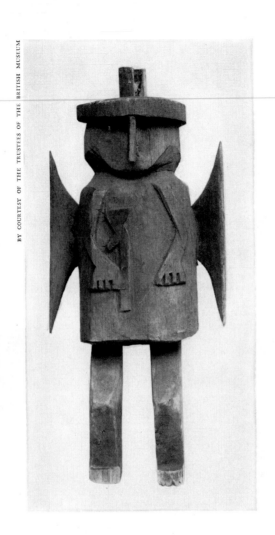

The painted wooden medicine doll of a dour white man (far left) was carved by the Cuna Indians of San Blas, on the old Pirate Coast of Panama, to ward off illness. After the curing ceremony, these uchus *were thrown away.*

The artistic confusion of an angel with a gun (left) was also made by a San Blas carver, who gave it the wings of a Christian heavenly being along with the familiar weapon carried by the ubiquitous white tax collector.

The wishful dream of a North American Indian was drawn in his notebook with crayon colors (below). It shows the Cheyenne brave spearing a United States Cavalry officer. It was later found on his dead body after a fatal skirmish; a bullet had crumpled the right side.

The bearded effigy at right is the low man on a totem pole erected for the Haida Chief Skowl at Kasaan in the North Pacific in the 1880's. It is thought to be a likeness of the Austrian-born, Vincent Baronovich, who on a voyage north married the Chief's daughter.

In China and Japan

Illustrated London News, 1858

此物出在浙江處州府青田縣數十成羣人樂之化為血
水官兵持砲擊之刀箭不能傷現有示諭軍民人等有
能剿除者從重奬賞此怪近日官兵逐急旋即落水逢
人便食真奇怪哉

The hairy monster puffing smoke (left) was a mid-nineteenth-century caricature of a British sailor, meant as a deliberate insult to the Western intruders on Chinese civilization. The billowing cloud might represent tobacco smoke.

In calmer days a century earlier, a Chinese court artist painted on silk a band of musicians accompanying two Western dignitaries (below). Their features and tapering fingernails are Oriental, though their dress is Western. The scene was probably Canton, the only port open to foreign traders, where Chinese hongs, or guild merchants, were appointed "For the continual instruction and guidance of the barbarians, and to repress their pride and profligacy."

After Japan was officially opened in 1854, Yokohama artists recorded the activities and types of foreign sightseers like the American couple on the opposite page viewing a monkey.

John Maass, art director for the City of Philadelphia, is author of The Gingerbread Age.

PRIVATE COLLECTION MR. & MRS. REGINALD PALMER, HURST, ENGLAND

By J. CHRISTOPHER HEROLD

The Pleasures of the Bastille

Servants, fine cuisine, and courteous jailers were the due of the King's incarcerated "guests." There was leisure for music, literature, and love. But one lack of this model prison was that its inmates did not know when, if ever, they would be freed

Historians of all political shades will readily concede that the storming of the Bastille of Paris, on July 14, 1789, was not in itself a glorious action. It was instigated by shady men for shady motives, carried out by a disreputable mob, and abetted by disloyal soldiers. The defenders—a handful of invalid veterans and their officers—capitulated almost without resistance. Despite the terms of capitulation, the mob killed the commandant and two of his officers; a scullion boy, skilled in the art of meat cutting, severed the commandant's head, which was then paraded about on the point of a pike. The total number of prisoners liberated from the huge fortress was seven. Of these, four had been detained for forgery and disappeared immediately. A fifth, a young debauchee held on his family's request, allowed himself to be feted by the revolutionary societies and made

Henri Masers de Latude and a fellow prisoner engineered the Bastille's most famous escape—a feat commemorated in this portrait of him by Antoine Vestier. Latude was recaptured in Amsterdam and locked up for another twenty-eight years, during which he wrote his Memoirs. *Published after his release in 1784, they were an immediate success, went through many editions, and grew more improbable with each.*

speeches announcing the dawn of freedom. The other two, who were madmen, were carried through the streets on the shoulders of their liberators and then hastily locked up in the insane asylum of Charenton.

These facts are well known, and there is no intention, in repeating them here, of "debunking" an action that is commemorated every year as a national holiday in France. Inglorious and unnecessary though it was, the storming of the Bastille is traditionally regarded as the beginning of the French Revolution; the dignity and significance it lacked were conferred on the deed by the generous hopes it stirred, by the tremendous events it set in motion, and by the symbolic significance that attached to the Bastille itself.

Soon after its capture, one hundred and seventy-six years ago, the Bastille was razed. Its destruction was intended to symbolize the destruction of feudalism and tyranny. Yet it would be difficult to name another building of which not a stone has been left for nearly two centuries whose image yet remains as vividly and accurately present to the popular mind. Its outward aspect has been preserved by innumerable prints, reproduced in textbooks, histories, and dictionaries. Its huge, forbidding walls and towers, its outer walls and moats and drawbridge remain engraved in the imagination of

This drawing of the Bastille as it appeared in 1789 is signed (upper right) by Pierre François Palloy, who took charge of demolishing it after its seizure. He used eight hundred men to tear it down, and sold off the locks, keys, and leg irons as souvenirs.

posterity with all the sharpness of the engravings that preserved them. This massive, arrogant anachronism, towering above the nondescript houses of the surrounding districts, seems indeed a permanent act of provocation. What is more, it conjures up an image of grim, dank cells and dungeons, where pale, white-haired, and—needless to say—innocent prisoners, clothed in rags and rattling chains, were kept on bread and water until they died—usually mad.

The truth is that life in the Bastille bore a closer resemblance to comic opera than to Grand-Guignol. It is not suggested that to be an inmate of the Bastille was particularly desirable (though, as will be seen, some inmates found it so), or that the system of arbitrary detention without trial merits defense. But never before or since in history was there a prison quite like the Bastille in the eighteenth century.

The grim exterior of the Bastille and the lurid legends about what went on inside symbolize, though they immensely exaggerate, a certain truth: the fortress *was* an anachronistic survival of the feudal age, and its inmates, though for the most part by no means innocent, were detained arbitrarily and without trial. Yet if there is anything that symbolizes the last years of the *ancien régime*, it is not the medieval façade of the Bastille and the fanciful legends about it, but the bizarre and benign system that prevailed inside it. A prison system often reflects certain features of the society outside. Like the *ancien régime* as a whole, the regime of the Bastille was a patchwork of special and contradictory rules and traditions, an agglomeration of exceptional cases. Individuals were not treated according to an easily ascertainable set of rules of law or equity. Each was treated according to his own status, his means, his connections, and his ability to use his wits. Injustice was administered with a maximum of politeness and humane concern for its victims by jailers of exquisitely refined sensibility. And the humaneness with which the prisoners were treated was jealously hidden from the outside world by a senseless security system which cherished secrecy and mystery for their own sakes.

The Bastille never was a prison in the proper sense of the word. It was a military fortress. Its cornerstone was laid about 1370, but it began to be used as a prison only under Cardinal Richelieu. By the beginning of the eighteenth century it had lost all military significance; its garrison consisted of invalid soldiers, and its sole function became that of a state prison. Yet although its inmates were placed under the authority of the Lieutenant General of Police, the fortress itself remained in theory a military establishment, and the prisoners were guests of the King.

The word "guests" is used advisedly here. The inmates of the Bastille were, with some exceptions, "state prisoners": persons who might, in one sense or another, be considered dangerous to the security of the state if they were left free, but whom the state did not wish to put to trial. (The exceptions were, for the most part, transients who eventually were transferred to other institutions.) To imprison or release a person all that was needed was a royal order, or *lettre de cachet,* countersigned by a minister. The order could originate either with the government or with any private person with the right connections. Its purpose was simply to put an inconvenient person out of the way for a convenient length of time, without the formality of a trial. Indeed there often was no basis for a trial, and even if there was a clear basis, it was deemed undesirable to hold one. A trial might have bared matters which either the government or the prisoner or his family preferred to hush up. Sometimes the reasons for detention were purely preventive or pedagogical; thus a father might have his son locked up to prevent him from fighting a duel, or to induce him to meditate for a few months.

Of course, there were unfortunate cases of men held for many years without anyone's knowing why, and it was at any rate disquieting not to know whether one's imprisonment would last a week, a year, or a lifetime. But nearly everyone in the Bastille had a duke or a minister among his acquaintance, or perhaps the duke's or minister's mistress, or at least his valet or cook: the same system of personal influence which allowed private persons to secure an order of arrest eventually also enabled them to secure an order of release. Most prisoners, had they been bound over for trial, would have suffered a harsher and longer imprisonment, if not worse. And there was an additional advantage in not undergoing trial. Since torture was part of the judicial process, and since by the seventeenth century there was no judicial process at

the Bastille, there also was no torture. Justice and medicine had this in common—that usually a man was better off without the benefit of either.

All the prisoners were the King's guests. Some were paying guests; the others, who could not pay for their upkeep, were his pensioners. The majority were suspected spies or political plotters, indiscreet pamphleteers, religious dissenters (especially Jansenists and Protestants), blackmailers, poisoners, and sorcerers with exalted clienteles, insubordinate or duel-loving officers, indiscreet lovers, counterfeiters, forgers, lunatics with a bent for politics, ladies who ran gambling dens, immoral priests, men of letters who had exercised their wit on the wrong people, spendthrift sons of noble houses, and debauchees. A few, to be sure, were truly innocent victims. To that last category belonged the most famous of the prisoners of the Bastille, the Man with the Iron Mask, whose mask was made of black velvet, whose death certificate bears the name Marchioly, and about whose identity historians and romancers wrote endlessly until it was established with reasonable certainty that his name was indeed Marchioly—or, more accurately, Mattioli. As the secretary of state to the Duke of Mantua, he had double-crossed a scheme of Louis XIV and was kidnapped across the border by the French. Understandably, Louis XIV did not wish to advertise the incident; and he took such elaborate precautions to hide his prisoner's identity that when the prisoner died, not even the authorities of the Bastille could remember who he was, why he was there, or why he had to wear a mask.

The roster of the Bastille's inmates contains such exalted names as the Duc de Richelieu, Voltaire, the Cardinal de Rohan, and the Marquis de Mirabeau. Equally typical, however, were such men as the Abbé Fleur, an ecclesiastic who, at the time of his arrest for forging royal lottery tickets, was domiciled in a bordello; a confidence man named Dubuisson, who had negotiated a loan of 15,000,000 livres from the devil to the Duc d'Olonne, with the soul of the Duc as collateral; the Marquis de Sade; and the Abbé de Moncrif, dean of the Cathedral of Autun, who had debauched two girls, his wards, and got one of them with child, besides being in debt for 70,000 livres, being a party in seventeen simultaneous lawsuits, and having stirred up, while under arrest in an ecclesiastic jail, a rebellion among his fellow inmates and driven his superiors out of their wits by raising chickens and ducks in his quarters.

As a rule, a person against whom a *lettre de cachet* had been issued was arrested by a police officer. There were cases, however, especially in earlier days, when the order to surrender at the Bastille was transmitted directly to the person to be detained. Thus there is the account of the young noble under Louis XIV who received his *lettre de cachet* in the morning, went hunting with the King, and then excused himself to the King, explaining that he had received the King's orders to be at the Bastille at such and such a time.

The legendary "Man in the Iron Mask" was real, but his mask was black velvet and his "crime" a political double cross.

The King graciously gave him permission to leave the hunt.

In the less feudal eighteenth century, the prisoner would be taken to the fortress in a hired cab, with curtains drawn. The cab would stop at the drawbridge and be challenged by the sergeant of the guard. The arresting officer would reply, "Order of the King!" whereupon the sergeant and the other soldiers on sentry duty would execute an about-face, turning their backs on the cab. A bell was rung, the drawbridge lowered, and the cab proceeded to the inner court. The prisoner was then escorted to a large room, called the council chamber, where the governor of the fortress would receive him, sign the *lettre de cachet,* and, after a routine search, have the prisoner conducted to his room.

The guard would politely escort the prisoner to his new quarters, situated in one of the eight large towers of the fortress. The rooms were spacious, with high ceilings and large —though heavily barred—windows and a fireplace. The furniture was austere but adequate. If the prisoner had the means, he could have his own furniture brought in. One abbé's furniture included five armchairs, eight straight chairs, a desk, a small table, three paintings, and two wall tapestries. Some prisoners had harpsichords and other musical instruments. The writer La Beaumelle brought a library of six hundred·volumes. The Marquis de Sade, who wrote a large part of his novels in the Bastille, had his walls covered from end to end with crimson hangings. Prisoners of particularly high rank sometimes were given entire apartments and moved in with a suite of retainers as well as their furniture.

As for food at the Bastille, it was quite adequate. The King's allowance for meals varied from three livres a day for the lowest class of prisoner to thirty-six livres for a marshal of France. A typical three-livre-a-day dinner consisted of *soupe aux croûtes,* beef, sheep's tongue *en ragoût,* and dessert. A ten-livre fare on meatless days might offer crayfish bisque and six courses of fish. One prisoner, who declared that he could not eat butcher's meat, was fed on fowl and venison exclusively. Another, describing the rigor of the Bastille in a pamphlet written after his release, cited the following menu:

Green pea soup, garnished with lettuce and a joint of fowl

Sliced roast beef, garnished with parsley

Meat pie, garnished with sweetbreads, coxcombs, asparagus, mushrooms, and truffles

Sheep's tongue en ragoût

Biscuit, Fruit, Burgundy wine

Distinguished prisoners often were invited to the governor's table. The writer and later revolutionist Linguet accused the authorities of the Bastille of trying to overfeed him in order to poison him. If this was so, the authorities were unsuccessful: Linguet lived on for many years, and the authority that killed him in 1792 was the guillotine.

There is only one recorded instance of a prisoner complaining about his food. On a Friday in October, 1753, at eight in the evening, a prisoner named Danry, alias Latude, who at the time was kept in solitary confinement, could be heard roaring even louder than was his wont. When the jailer hurried to his cell, Danry asked to see the Major (the executive officer) of the Bastille without delay. The Major arrived; Danry declared in a thunderous voice that he ate neither eggs nor artichokes nor spinach, and requested that a man be dispatched immediately to the Halles to buy him fish. The Major pointed out that this was hardly the time for shopping. Flying into another paroxysm of rage, Danry declared that he was short of shirts and linen. The Major pointed out that Danry owned seven shirts, four of them brand-new; Danry responded only with a new fit. Soon afterward, by order of the Lieutenant General of the Police, Danry received, at the King's expense, two dozen shirts at ten dollars apiece and a supply of cambric handkerchiefs.

Danry's passion for shirts and linen seems extraordinary. In his memoirs he declares that at one point during his long imprisonment he owned 162 shirts, twelve dozen pairs of silk stockings, eighteen pairs of socks, and three dozen napkins, all furnished free by the government.

If food and clothing were abundant, drink was no less so for those who desired it. One of the two madmen liberated on July 14, 1789, had consumed in the space of three months twelve bottles of brandy, 121 bottles of beer, and 167 bottles of wine. Indeed, since the prisoners were held in the Bastille as a measure of precaution rather than punishment, the authorities made life as easy for them as they could. Those who could afford it, to be sure, were expected to pay for their food, furnishings, clothing, and servants, but to those who had no money the King gave an ample pension. What they did not spend on their needs, they could keep. Under King Louis XIV this pension was paid directly to the prisoners; later on the system was modified, and the money was paid to the administrators of the Bastille. Still, the prisoners were entitled to an accounting, and if an unspent balance remained at the time of their release, it was paid to them. There are instances of prisoners requesting to stay on in order to increase their nest egg. Many of the prisoners, upon leaving, were indemnified or even granted pensions (as was Voltaire, for instance).

One of the most peculiar features of life at the Bastille was the rule governing personal servants. Prisoners could bring in servants either at their own expense or, by special permission (notably in cases of long confinement), at the King's expense. For a servant's wages the government was willing to spend nine hundred livres a year. But even more peculiar was the provision that if a servant agreed to take employment in the Bastille, he also had to agree to remain there until his master was liberated.

Locked up in 1719, justifiably, for plotting against the Regent, the Duc de Richelieu enjoyed the frequent visits of his two mistresses —one of whom was the Regent's daughter.

Like everything else in the Bastille, prison discipline varied considerably from case to case. As a rule, prisoners were interrogated by the Lieutenant General of the Police within twenty-four hours of their arrival. Interrogation might continue sporadically for days, weeks, or months, and until it was completed a prisoner was held strictly incommunicado. There is every indication that normally the prisoners were questioned politely, without any use or threat of force, though with a great deal of paternal admonition. When this stage was completed, the prisoner might be granted various privileges. If he wished, he might be allowed to share his room with another prisoner, visit with other prisoners, take walks on the platforms of the towers, receive visitors from outside, or leave his room at will in order to walk or play in the courtyard—a privilege called the *liberté de la cour*. To grant or withdraw such privileges, the Governor of the Bastille had to receive special authorization from the Lieutenant General of the Police.

Needless to say, the primary considerations in the granting of special privileges were the rank of the prisoner and the degree of secrecy with which he was to be surrounded. The first of these criteria was fairly clear-cut; all other things being equal, a duke enjoyed more comfort than a barber's apprentice. The security criterion, however, was often of a rather nebulous nature. The Lieutenant General of the Police did not always inform the Governor of the Bastille why a ward of his was regarded as a threat to the state, and sometimes the Lieutenant General of the Police himself did not know. It is clear from many of the published documents that these authorities often tried to obtain the release of a prisoner, or at least a liberalizing of his treatment, and were repeatedly frustrated in their attempts by an unexplained "No" from Versailles.

The more fashionable inmates of the Bastille enjoyed, for the most part, a rather active social life. They gave parties for each other and for outside visitors; some of these entertainments were as brilliant and lavish as any given in the more conventional salons of Paris. Mademoiselle de Launay, lady-in-waiting to the Duchesse de Maine, who spent the years 1718–20 in the Bastille for her part in a plot against the Regent, recalled that period as the happiest in her life.

This statement is more easily understood if one knows that the only time Mademoiselle de Launay knew love was during her imprisonment. She acquired two lovers: one, an officer of the Bastille, who acted like a perfect gentleman but with whom she was not in love; the other, a fellow inmate and fellow conspirator, with whom she fell passionately in love but who did not act quite like a gentleman. In one of the more bizarre episodes related in her memoirs, she tells how, one evening, the turnkey unwittingly locked her *amant du coeur* into her room, and how her jailer-lover, to whom she frantically signaled from her window, obligingly let her prisoner-lover out and never breathed a word.

For relaxation, those prisoners who were not restricted to their rooms could go bowling in the courtyard or take other exercise. In 1788 twelve Breton noblemen requested a billiard table and obtained it. Others raised dogs, birds, and many generations of cats (but not, contrary to legend, spiders). Many had musical instruments. The Duc de Richelieu and Mademoiselle de Launay, his neighbor, sang operatic duets from their windows and were joined by other inmates for ensembles and choruses. The prison library was well stocked. Under the regime of Lieutenant General of the Police Berryer, in the 1750's, such unusual concern was shown for the prisoners' morale that an order banned a religious poem from the library as being "too melancholy."

The prisoners' religious needs were not entirely ignored. The prison chapel contained several closetlike structures in which the inmates could attend Mass unseen by each other and by the priest. These closets were frequently used as mailboxes, and a lively clandestine correspondence took place among the prisoners.

Nearly everybody wrote. Pens, ink, and paper were liberally provided. One prisoner, it is true—Danry, the collector of linen and hosiery—chose instead to write to the authorities with his blood, on strips of linen or bread tablets, a habit which offended the sensibilities of the Lieutenant General of the Police. Yet whenever inquiry was made of the governor as to why the prisoner Danry was not supplied with writing materials, the reply was, invariably, that the materials had indeed been given the prisoner, but that he chose this unappetizing method of communication instead.

The nature of the prisoners' writings varied a great deal. In the Bastille Voltaire revised his *Oedipe* and wrote part of the *Henriade*; De Sade, amid his crimson hangings, wrote away at his novels; the writer La Beaumelle, who was addicted to hoaxing, wrote love letters, purportedly from a lady, to his fellow prisoner Allègre, a schoolteacher who wrote memoranda to the government on a variety of subjects including mathematics, engineering, and architecture; Allègre's roommate Danry, in turn, wrote memoranda on balancing the budget and on postal reform; and all, of course, wrote petitions. The prison authorities were no less literary; their reports to higher authorities testify that they had ample leisure to polish their literary style and adorn it with flowers of wit.

Men of letters, who were well represented in the Bastille, formed a special group in the sense that temporary imprisonment in that fortress represented an indispensable phase in their careers. "My career opened up before me," wrote the Abbé Morellet of his imprisonment. "Those six months in the Bastille were to be an excellent recommendation and an infallible road to success." When he was released, the Abbé exclaimed, "God bless those good tyrants!" Marmontel, whose reputation was at its peak when he was held in the Bastille, was treated as a guest of honor by the prison chiefs and left with equally benign feelings toward them. These experiences prevented neither Morellet nor Marmontel nor their friends among the *philosophes* from publicly inveighing against the cruel tyranny of their imprisonment; indeed, it was in their interest to contribute to the legend of the Bastille.

Not every prisoner, of course, was lionized by his jailers as Marmontel was, and life in the Bastille was by no means a bed of roses for lower-class persons caught in an infraction of the rules. There were punitive cells, some under the roofs and uncomfortably warm, some on the ground floor. The latter, *cachots*, were halfway underground, damp, and lit only by what daylight came in through a narrow loophole. Prisoners guilty of disciplinary infractions were often held there for months, in chains, and bedded on straw. They were not forgotten, however, and even to them the jailers extended whatever kindness they could under the regulations. Unfortunately, since many prisoners felt that they had been arrested without cause in the first place, they did not always appreciate the justice of being placed in disciplinary cells or always show gratitude for small favors. Thus the Major of the Bastille reported about Danry, who at the time was being held in a *cachot*, "Yesterday we had Danry taken out of his irons, and today he was given a cot, mattresses, a pillow, sheets, and a blanket, together with seeds for his birds, all this in accordance with your order of the first of the month. This prisoner, moreover, requested a different room, a new bed, a table, chairs, and a lamp or candle. I told him that he was pushing his pretensions beyond what was required of us."

Danry undoubtedly was not altogether sane, and many of the other long-term prisoners were plainly lunatics. Some became estranged from reality as a result of their long isolation, but for the most part their imprisonment merely brought into the open a psychotic predisposition which had landed them in the Bastille in the first place. In any event, they were better off than they would have been at Charenton, to which they were transferred only if they became violent. So accustomed were the jailers to the eccentricities of their wards that they did not recognize lunacy when they saw it. Thus the record of the prisoner Tavernier (a liquor-loving madman who was moved to Charenton in 1789) contains the following understatement: "His long imprisonment has given him an original character, so little in conformity with that of the people in the outside world that they would take him for a madman." Tavernier had spent thirty years in the Bastille at that time.

Of course, it was not always easy to tell when a prisoner was genuinely eccentric and when he was feigning. The case of the roommates Danry and Allègre was particularly puzzling, for both were genuinely eccentric and feigning at the same time. They also were the only prisoners who succeeded in preparing a startling surprise for their jailers.

For twenty-six months, beginning in December, 1753, Danry and Allègre, until then the most obstreperous of prisoners, perplexed the authorities by their peaceful behavior. As far as could be ascertained, their time was spent in studies: Allègre, who during his career as a schoolteacher had never had a pupil quite so captive as his roommate, was teaching Danry mathematics, mechanics, and engineering. But there were certain puzzling features in their conduct. Both spent their entire time, for two years, wearing only their dressing gowns; Danry, despite his hoard of shirts, was never seen to wear one; the room, moreover, was underheated, although the firewood supplied in ample quantities was always used up; and their bed and table linen was, for some mysterious reason, chronically ragged. Repeated searches of the room revealed nothing except meticulous tidiness.

On February 26, 1756, early risers who happened to be passing by the Bastille discovered an exhilarating sight. From the platform of one of the towers there floated, attached to a piece of artillery, a rope ladder 180 feet long, shining snow-white, with 188 wooden rungs, each carefully muffled with rags. From a wheelless pulley, attached to the same cannon, there hung a stout rope also gleaming white, 360 feet long. The wall, 4½ feet thick, that separated the moat from the outside world, had been pierced. A few crude tools were found nearby, as well as a wooden ladder with twenty rungs, consisting of several sections carefully fitted together by means of pegs and holes. Outside the wall lay a large leather portmanteau and two suits of soaked and grimy clothes.

Allègre and his pupil had indeed made excellent use of their linen and firewood. They had worked at making ropes and ladders for two years, and had concealed them under some floor boards whenever anyone entered the room. They had removed the bars blocking the flue of their fireplace; had climbed through the chimney to the roof; then hauled up the portmanteau, the rope ladder, the wooden ladder, and a number of tools; let down their paraphernalia; and finally climbed down the rope ladder. They had not forgotten to leave behind a polite note to their good tyrants: "We have caused no damage whatever to any of the furniture of His Lordship the Governor. We have used only strips of blanket that were no longer serviceable; the others are intact. If a few napkins are missing, they can be found beyond the water, in the large moat, where we took them to wipe our feet."

It is with regret that one must report the end of this adventure. Danry was discovered some weeks later in Amsterdam by a French police lieutenant disguised as an Armenian merchant; the Dutch government extradited him to France. Allègre, who was captured in Brussels, ended up in an insane asylum. Danry, after thirty-five years of imprisonment in various places, made a living, until his death in 1805, by selling his memoirs, which became increasingly fanciful in successive editions. He is remembered as Henri Masers de Latude, a name he fabricated sometime during his imprisonment. Much of the legend of the Bastille is the result of his fertile imagination.

"God bless these good tyrants!" Never was tyranny exercised by more gentle and considerate hands than in France just before the Revolution. Only two objections could be made to their debonair methods: first, that one was locked up in the Bastille without a trial, and second, that one could not tell how long one's stay there would be. But to reform this abuse it was not necessary to storm the fortress: a stroke of the pen would have sufficed, and in fact the system was about to be abolished when the Bastille was attacked. Four years after that bastion of despotic arbitrariness had been razed, the revolutionary government passed the Law of Suspects, by which any person, upon simple denunciation, could be arrested, tried (without benefit of counsel), and guillotined, all this in the space of a few hours, to safeguard the newly won freedom of the nation.

J. Christopher Herold won the National Book Award for Mistress to an Age, *his biography of Madame de Staël. More recently he wrote* The HORIZON Book of The Age of Napoleon.

BIBLIOTHEQUE NATIONALE

The Disappearance of Don Juan

What the moral indignation of three centuries could not achieve, our own age has done: the Don is dead, not because we are too puritanical for him, but because we are too licentious

By HENRY ANATOLE GRUNWALD

Madamina! Il catalogo è questo
Delle belle che amò il padron mio . . .
In Italia seicento e quaranta,
In Alemagna duecento e trent'una,
Cento in Francia, in Turchia novant'una,
Ma, ma in Ispagna, son già mille e tre!
V'han fra queste contadine,
Cameriere, cittadine;
V'han contesse, baronesse,
Marchesane, principesse,
E v'han donne d'ogni grado,
D'ogni forma, d'ogni età!

        . . .

Pentiti!
No! *   * —Don Giovanni

We think of our literature, no less than of our age, as loose and lascivious. Sex appears to be rampant. Writers treat it with a freedom and a wealth of detail which in other periods were permitted only to pornographers. We regard ourselves as a pretty wicked lot, and yet amid all this wickedness a strange fact—or, rather, a strange lack—stands out: Don Juan is nowhere in sight. The archlibertine has left the revels. His name remains in our language, but the character behind the name has disappeared. Since Shaw's *Man and Superman,* in 1903, no major work of fiction or drama has centered around the Don Juan figure. Seduction, adultery, fornication, rape, are readily found, but not Don Juanism with its characteristic dash of heroics and gay defiance. We can no more expect a true Don Juan in our literature than we expect to find a character with a cloak and sword at our next cocktail party, singing *"Là ci darem la mano"* to the pretty Vassar girl in the corner.

Among other things, of course, Don Juan is a myth. But as mythological figures go (compared, for instance, to the White Goddess, or Prometheus, or Ulysses, or Faustus, or Tristan), the Don is a newcomer. His existence and his meaning depend on a certain attitude toward love, and love is a relatively modern invention.

In antiquity the relations between men and women consisted mostly of frank sensuality or of domestic comfort. Love mixed with passion was considered a form of madness —and one afflicting women more often than men. Nor did the advent of Christianity, the religion of love, herald love in anything like its modern sense. For many centuries Christianity fought to subdue an unruly, violent, and still strongly pagan world to Christian laws in all matters, including sex. Carnal desire, even within marriage, was considered, at best, a necessary evil. Thus the concept of romantic love was completely alien both to what might be called the pagan underground and to the dominant Christian order. When romantic love made its startling appearance in the eleventh century, through the works and visions of the troubadours, it became a major revolutionary force—a revolution of belief, feeling, and behavior, not to mention literature, compared to which the Renaissance, as C. S. Lewis has observed, was a mere surface ripple.

In literature the revolution replaced the great epic themes of war, of faith, and of nature and made love between man and woman the center of the story-telling art. In life the revolution established love both beyond mere sexual enjoyment and beyond Christian-feudal ideas of marriage. In the elaborate patterns of courtly love the traditional role of woman was reversed; instead of dominating and using her, man treated her with abject humility and served her as if she were his feudal lord and he her vassal. He glorified her to a blasphemous degree, and courtly love, in effect, developed a rival religion to Christianity.

Whether or not it was, as has been suggested, a highly refined form of paganism rebelling against Christianity's moral order, courtly love glorified adultery. It held that love existed only outside the mundane, practical concerns of marriage. A famous ruling handed down in 1174 by a "court of love" under the patronage of the Countess of Champagne held that "love cannot extend its right over two married persons" because true love must be given freely, while in marriage it is given as a matter of duty and constraint.

It is not entirely clear to what extent this glorification of adultery was theoretical or how far it went in practice. There is no doubt that courtly love professed chastity—or at least moderation—as ranking high among its ideals. The self-punishment of frustrated love was held to be spiritually and even physically uplifting for a knight. When one troubadour sang, "I approve that my lady should long make me wait and that I should not have from her what she promised," he may have been expressing the insight that it is desire, not fulfillment, which is love's best part. Or he may have been driving at a more mystical meaning. In an

---

* "Little lady, this is the catalogue / Of the beauties my master has loved . . . / In Italy six hundred and forty, / In Germany two hundred and thirty-one, / A hundred in France, in Turkey ninety-one, / But in Spain there are already one thousand and three! / Amongst these there are peasant girls, / Chambermaids, townswomen; / There are countesses, baronesses, / Marchionesses, princesses, / And there are women of every degree, / Every shape, every age! . . . Repent! / No!"

Opposite: A nineteenth-century French costume design for the hero of Don Giovanni

ingenious analysis of the Tristan myth, Denis de Rouge-mont has pointed out that whenever the two lovers have an opportunity to settle down for a time to enjoy their passion, something happens to separate them—and the obstacles are often of their own making. This is so not only because the story must be kept going but because the ideal of courtly love demands it. That ideal, De Rougemont believes, was somehow linked to the Albigensian heresy, a movement of Manichean origin, which condemned both sexual intercourse and marriage as serving only to perpetuate a world intrinsically evil. Hence he sees in Tristan and Isolde not a desire for love's fulfillment but a desire for desire—kept alive by separation—and ultimately a desire for death.

Almost four centuries separate the heyday of courtly love and the first appearance of Don Juan—in Tirso de Molina's play *The Trickster of Seville and the Guest of Stone,* in 1630. In between lies the Renaissance, that titanic outburst of liberation as well as libertinage, of humanism as well as inhumanity, of man's glorification as well as woman's worship—the age of the passionate humanist, Petrarch, and the cynical amorist, Boccaccio. In a sense Don Juan is a Renaissance man, a character who might have walked out of the *Decameron.* But he assumes his true stature only when seen against the fading backdrop of courtly love. He is a kind of corruption of the troubadour, the exact opposite of Tristan. Courtly romances continued to hold the public imagination all through the turbulence of the Renaissance era; more or less at the same time that the De Molina play appeared, all Europe was entranced by *L'Astrée,* a long and preposterous chronicle of the handsome shepherd Céladon and his involvements with druid priestesses, princesses, wood nymphs, shepherdesses, and the God of Love in person. Not much later Mlle de Scudéry, in her novel *Clélie,* invented *La Carte du Tendre,* or "The Map of Tenderness," in which—much in the spirit of the medieval courts of love—the whole territory of love was laid out. There were, among innumerable other localities, the Villages of Great Heart and Generosity; the river Attraction; the towns of Honesty, Obedience, and Constancy; and the Lake of Indifference. It is as a sneering opposite of Céladon, an invader tearing up the *Carte du Tendre,* that the original Don Juan makes his entrance.

According to legend Don Juan was a Spanish nobleman, assassinated by Franciscans who, in the words of one chronicler, wanted "to put an end to his excesses and blasphe-

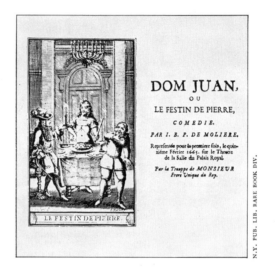

Molière's Dom Juan *first saw print under this title page, 17 years after its première in 1665.*

mies." At any rate, the outline of Tirso de Molina's drama is familiar enough, and simple enough. In the course of three acts Don Juan uses up four women: two of them highborn and two from the lower orders. His technique is fairly unimaginative and standardized. He wins the society girls by impersonating their true suitors, and the two proletarian girls—one a fisherman's, the other a peasant's daughter—simply by promising to marry them. He is capable of intoxicating flattery and lyrical speeches with all of them; but if anything, he is more poetic with the simple girls than with the ladies. Fiancés or honorable suitors are readily bamboozled and enmeshed in all sorts of wicked complications. Fathers, guardians, and other figures of authority are brushed aside with equal ease, until Doña Ana's father, whom Juan has killed, returns to life in the stony guise of the famous statue and drags the Don to hell, and damnation.

Several things stand out in a re-examination of this old play. One, obviously, is Don Juan's lack of any real affection for the seduced women. He plans his getaway before beginning his conquest: "Why, for her love I'm almost dying. / I'll have her now, then scamper flying."

Unlike Tristan, or any other typical courtly lover, he is interested only in physical satisfaction and sneers at any suggestion of moderation or delay, let alone chastity. He shares the troubadour's low opinion of marriage, but for wholly different reasons. Where courtly love held marriage in contempt in order to idealize passion and glorify woman—in order, one might almost say, to establish the sacrament of romance—Don Juan brutally rejects romance along with marriage. Above all, he totally reverses the courtly lover's worship of woman: "In Seville / I'm called the Trickster; and my greatest pleasure / Is to trick women, leaving them dishonored."

Don Juan is thus in double rebellion, not only against convention and the Christian order, but against woman herself. He fights not only churchly morality but romantic love. Far from serving the lady, he uses and abuses her, vengefully reverting to a pagan, a Greek—an almost Oriental—disregard for woman as a soul-bearing human being.

From this obvious characteristic, two opposite conclusions have often been drawn. The romantics believe that Don Juan, perhaps once disappointed in love, endlessly searches for the ideal woman whom he can never find. The psychological cynics, on the other hand, believe that he really hates women and that in his perennial conquests he is trying to punish them. Both views seem exaggerated. Not a line in De Molina's drama suggests that he is looking for his dream girl. Nor does his contemptuous treatment of women carry a suggestion of hatred: revulsion from the meek courtly tradition, yes, but nothing so personal as hatred. Women are probably not important enough to him for that.

And yet he seems forever ready to risk his neck for them —in countless duels, scrapes, and ambushes. The answer to this seeming paradox must be that what Don Juan is willing to die for is not merely women, or even pleasure as such, but the very act of risk, the very freedom of tossing his life away if he so chooses. To face death for a worthwhile ideal is to play the game; to risk death for transient joys is to defy the game, to be contemptuous of life itself, to sneer at the human condition. Don Juan sees in death a gesture of defiance against human limitations, against the *status quo* in the universe, and against God himself.

If this makes Don Juan sound like an existentialist, a case can be made for the notion that he was. Albert Camus saw Don Juan as a man who does not hope for another life: "He gambles that other life against heaven itself. . . . He has but one reply to divine wrath, and that is human honor." He is an ordinary seducer for all that— "seducing is his condition in life"—but he knows it. He does not "collect" women, but "exhausts their number and with them his chances for life. . . . Don Juan has chosen to be nothing." Again and again the first Don Juan play asserts that

N.Y. PUB. LIB. MUSIC DIV.

The 1801 edition of Mozart's Don Giovanni *(première, Prague, 1787) depicts its climax.*

"what you have done, you pay for." Don Juan is willing to pay the price even of hell-fire. That is an act of rebellion against God closer to Faust's and Prometheus's than to that of the mere libertine. It is an act, moreover, compared to which the ravished virginity of a few women—or even of *mille e tre*—is relatively unimportant.

There is a clear hint in the play as to where this rebellion springs from: in his attitude toward the supernatural, Don Juan anticipates the dawning Age of Reason. After the statue has called on him, he is frightened but calms his fears by telling himself: "But all these things, / Begot by fear on the imagination, / Are quite unreal. To fear the dead is baseness." There speaks the rationalist mind, which even at the last moment seeks to strike down the phantom—the supernatural—with a sword. To the end, pride—human pride asserted against God and the universe—is Don Juan's dominant quality. When the statue offers him a meal of "tarantulas and vipers," he declares, "I shall eat it / Were all the

snakes in hell upon one plate." The entire play contains exactly two lines of repentance, when Don Juan calls for a confessor; and this gesture is about as convincing as any moralistic ending tacked onto a Hollywood movie to appease the Legion of Decency.

To stress Don Juan's heroic insurrection against the supernatural is not to rob him, as Shaw did, of his sexuality and turn him into a mere metaphysical rebel. Both elements are interdependent and account for his fatal attractiveness. As a libertine without metaphysics, he would be a bore; as a metaphysician without his libertinage, he would (except for Shaw's wit) turn out merely a priggish liberal.

The intellectual distance between De Molina and Molière is great, but the core of the character has not changed in the latter's *Dom Juan, ou Le Festin de Pierre* (1665). The Molière play both simplifies and complicates the story: a few seductions have been removed; two vengeful brothers have been added; the comic servant, now called Sganarelle, has been built up; and a couple of typical Molière set pieces have been added—a duped creditor, two peasant girls wooed simultaneously. Not only has Don Juan become more amusing and unmistakably French—he has also become more of a hypocrite. He has actually married one of his women, Doña Elvira, and justifies his desertion of her with a dazzling show of Jesuitic reasoning. Above all he has become articulate; Molière's is the first Don Juan who really explains himself:

Would you have a man tie himself up to the first woman that captured his fancy, renounce the world for her, and never again look at anyone else? That *is* a fine idea, I must say, to make a virtue of faithfulness, to bury oneself for good and all in one single passion and remain blind ever after to all the other beauties that might catch one's eye! No! Let fools make a virtue of constancy! . . . Once one succeeds, what else remains?

This is the exquisitely cynical philosophy of the libertine, the philanderer's great charter, which went on to nourish the literature of gallantry in France and elsewhere. This particular speech, to be sure, omits the heroic, rebellious, heaven-defying side of the Don Juan character, but it is nevertheless very much in evidence elsewhere in the play. Molière's Don Juan, too, is a rationalist. He, too, rebels against the supernatural. After the statue first moves, he is momentarily frightened but recovers quickly: "Whatever it was, we will leave it at that. It is of no importance. We may have been deceived by a trick of light or overcome by some momentary giddiness which affected our vision." Later he adds: "There is certainly something there that I do not understand, but, whatever it is, it shall neither change my convictions nor shake my courage." And Molière's Don Juan is as unrepentant as the original. As he faces damnation at the statue's invitation, he once again announces his defiance: "Come what may, it shall never be said that I am the repenting sort."

In 1787, little more than one hundred and twenty years after Molière's play, appeared what remains undoubtedly the greatest Don Juan figure ever created in any of the arts, Mozart's *Don Giovanni*. In outline the libretto by Lorenzo da Ponte is not significantly different from earlier versions, although Da Ponte, a shrewd theatrical craftsman, added many stage tricks—masks, mistaken identities, abrupt and hilarious changes of mood. Effective though the libretto is, it is Mozart's music which superbly expresses the hero's nature, his extraordinary contradictions and ultimate tragedy. He is the character of whom the famous "catalogue aria" boasts so intoxicatingly (*"In Italia seicento e quaranta"*). He is also the character who can sing the ebullient, slightly coarse "champagne aria"— *"Finch' han dal vino"*—as well as the lovely, seductive *"Là ci darem,"* a sighing lyrical effusion. But above all he is the character who can prepare to receive the statue at dinner in the climactic scene, the scene that most perfectly epitomizes Don Giovanni's character. *"Io me voglio divertir,"* he announces with the arrogance of a crass hedonist ("I wish to amuse myself"). Yet in the music accompanying that line there is an unmistakably majestic strain, as there is during the farcical episodes involving food and the musicians. When the statue finally arrives, wreathed in unearthly music, Don Giovanni matches it in dignity, note for note. His order to his servant to open up—*"Apri!"*—shows no musical flicker of fear, nor does his reply to the statue's invitation: *"Ho fermo il core in petto: / Non ho timor, verrò!"* ("My heart is firm within my breast: / I am not afraid, I will come").

When his hand is already seized by the statue, his soul already in the clasp of hell, there is the great climactic clash: "Repent!" cries the statue, and *"No!"* replies the Don, unshaken and relentless, until the flames close in and a great scream of pain signals his damnation.

Mozart's is the last of the true Don Juans on stage or in literature. The eighteenth century provided a number of

striking autobiographical Don Juans, including Casanova, who was more jolly rascal than hero, and the Marquis de Sade, who represents Don Juan's rebellion carried to insanity. But the protagonist of Tirso de Molina's play had been gradually romanticized by audiences who insisted on a happy ending. The most notable example of this revised and redemptive version of the story is *Don Juan Tenorio*, by José Zorrilla y Moral, first produced in 1844 and still widely performed in the Spanish-speaking world on All Saints' Day.

Juan is a young nobleman who makes a bet with a friend to see which of them, in the space of a year, can do more harm and seduce more women. Despite such exuberance, Juan wants to marry Doña Inés; but when her father finds out about the bet, he forbids the match and places Inés in a convent. Amid innumerable police chases and hairbreadth escapes, Don Juan abducts Inés—she happens to be unconscious at the time—and in almost the next breath seduces another girl, betrothed to his friend and betting partner, after which he kills Inés's father. The father's statuesque revenge is considerably more elaborate than in the original—for one thing, there is also a statue of Inés, who in the meantime has died of grief. But the really basic difference is that in the end Don Juan repents: already on his way to hell, he lifts a hand to heaven, and forgiveness sets in at once. In a final tableau the spirits of Doña Inés and Don Juan sink together on a bed of flowers scattered by angels.

This preposterous beatification was preceded by another even more significant transformation which robbed Don Juan of both God and devil, sentimentalized him, and made him, like the troubadours, subservient to woman. The change occurred, as Leslie Fiedler has pointed out, in Samuel Richardson's novel *Clarissa, or The History of a Young Lady* (1747–48). In it Don Juan appears as Robert Lovelace, an aristocrat, a libertine, and a rationalist with contempt for religion, convention (including marriage), and women. But there are some major differences. Where the original Don Juan appears to believe in God but defies him, Lovelace seems not to believe at all; the metaphysical essence of his rebellion therefore is changed. And where Don Juan moves from woman to woman, hardly remembering their names, Lovelace becomes obsessed with one woman alone.

The plot, entirely told in the form of letters, is intricate beyond Borgia politics, Dickensian novel, or American soap opera. Lovelace is supposed to marry Clarissa's older sister

Though Byron's Don Juan *was sardonic, here its rapt hero gazes at Julia.*

FROM *Poetical Works of Byron*, LONDON 1860's

but falls in love with the younger girl instead. Her parents, however, wish to marry her off to an elderly moneybags. When Clarissa refuses, she is held a virtual prisoner until Lovelace carries her off.

Disowned by her harsh father, Clarissa is at Lovelace's mercy, but manages to escape. After innumerable complications she is recaptured and returned to Lovelace, only to be drugged and raped by him. She manages to escape again, is falsely imprisoned for debt, released, and goes into a physical decline. Throughout all this, Lovelace is beginning to suspect that if he cannot have her any other way, he will have to marry her. But she buys her own coffin and makes up her mind to die. Her relations forgive her, but too late. She is buried in the family vault, while a heartbroken Lovelace goes to the Continent where he eventually provokes a duel with Clarissa's cousin and is mortally wounded. Dying, he hopes to expiate his crimes and calls on Clarissa: "Divine Creature! Fair Sufferer! Look down, Blessed Spirit, look down!"

Lovelace is clearly a Don Juan figure, but a very great change from the prototype is contained in one fact: Lovelace is defeated by woman. Where the terrible hand of the supernatural, the breath of hell itself, could not move the original Don Juan to repent, a woman extorts repentance from Lovelace. In the eyes of the readers Clarissa was clearly the winner and the heroine: when, in the installment publication of the novel, she finally died, church bells rang throughout all England.

Delacroix painted the shipwreck that casts Byron's Don onto a Greek island and into a maiden's arms.

Part of the change in Don Juan is explained, of course, by the fact that Lovelace lives in a Protestant—and increasingly middle-class—society. Like the troubadours in the eleventh century, but for totally different reasons, the Protestant middle class in the eighteenth century re-established the superiority of the female. The Holy Virgin was discarded, but the virgin was regarded as almost holy. Despite a classic Christian belief that woman is the archtemptress, the source of sin, the Protestant middle class tended to see woman as pure and man as evil—a conviction still very much alive in the United States today. Also, it seems to have resented the cavalier attitude toward women, as it resented all aristocratic attitudes, countering leisure with thrift, nobility with diligence, combativeness with trade, paternalism with democracy, frivolity with sentimentality. In a sense, middle-class man needed woman to lean on because he felt insecure in the world. Where Latin-Catholic civilization used woman for procreation and delight, English-Prot-

estant civilization used her for procreation and uplift. In the Catholic tradition marriage is sanctioned not by love but by the law of God; adultery is a lesser sin than divorce —a comfortable situation for Don Juan. In the Protestant tradition marriage is indeed sanctioned by love as well as by law; divorce is not necessarily a sin at all, while adultery is—a highly inconvenient situation for Don Juan.

If in Richardson's treatment Don Juan succumbed to sentimentality, in Lord Byron's he escaped into humor. Appearing in 1819, more than half a century after Lovelace, Byron's Don Juan is once again an aristocrat and once again a rebel; in this immense and discursive work, in which digression seems to be the law of life and an aside may take a dozen stanzas, Byron castigates society, England, patriotism, power, money, women, poets, and almost anything that he was angry about. The work is a kind of limerick on an epic scale, ranging (as Mark Van Doren has put it) between the titanic and the cute.

In his satirical flights Byron's Don Juan is a figure to be reckoned with; but in his romantic escapades he is mostly a figure of fun. He is not a rebel against the supernatural, but only against human folly. The original Don Juan laughed, to be sure, but at the risk of death and damnation; Byron's Don Juan also laughs, but merely at the risk of offending respectability. Above all, Byron's hero is that modern oddity, a passive Don Juan—hence not a real Don Juan at all. Most of the time it is the women who pursue him, and it is he who allows himself to be taken. Among the types which the work satirizes are the era's Don Juans themselves, the lady-killers: "[Who] seem to say, 'Resist us if you can,' / Which makes a Dandy while it spoils a man."

Both Richardson's Lovelace, the repentant Don Juan who is ultimately defeated by woman, and Byron's passive Don Juan, who is seduced as much as seducer, jointly symbolize the fate of the Don Juan figure in much of the eighteenth and all of the nineteenth century; in other words, throughout the Age of the Novel. For the novel is essentially a female art form. It was not only the first art in history in which women distinguished themselves, but it was also addressed to a heavily female audience. The Seducer and the Persecuted Maiden continued their endless chase in countless stories, the more-or-less aristocratic villain relentlessly pursuing the pure bourgeois heroine; yet no matter what her fate, it is she who is the winner.

In the novel, as Bernard Shaw put it, Don Juan turned

into Doña Juana. The great rebels against society, against convention, even against the church, were all women. The three greatest heroines of the nineteenth-century novel, Becky Sharp, Emma Bovary, and Anna Karenina, who appeared within less than three decades of each other (1847–1875), were all fighters for a personal, emotional kind of independence, Furies avenging male inadequacy. Becky, in *Vanity Fair,* is an adventuress who uses up men the way Don Juan used up women, and survives them all. Emma Bovary may be a fool who comes to a tragic end, but that end can certainly not be blamed on male wickedness. Superficially Rodolphe looks like a Don Juan, but Emma is seduced by him only because she wishes to be. He and Léon, her other lover, are essentially the instruments of her obsessive quest for a different life. Similarly, Count Vronsky is not Anna Karenina's traducer: he may seem to be taking the initiative in the affair, but it is she who consents to it and pushes it to its doomed ending. He is more victim than she.

The world of the eighteenth- and the nineteenth-century novel, looking back as it does on the merrily licentious Restoration in England and on the heavily sensual Gallant Century in France, has its own libertine traditions. To judge from the novels, at least, men have love affairs constantly and discuss them freely. From the lavishly established semiofficial mistresses to the little flower girls and grisettes, adultery is a permanent, almost a respected institution. The point is not that the age lacks libertines but that the libertines lack the Don Juan spirit. There is an almost domestic tranquillity about many of these affairs, and always a certain lack of force on the part of the men as compared to great force on the part of their mistresses.

In short the image of man—even of the seducer—ultimately victimized by a female fate, applies not only to the stories of the Persecuted Maiden winning moral victories and the Misunderstood Wife bursting out of innumerable Doll Houses, it also applies to that third great category of the classic novel, the Glorified Courtesan. Triumphant or pathetic, genteel or vulgar, consumptive or peasant-strong, she gets the best of the men in the end—whether her name is Manon Lescaut, Carmen, Mme Marneffe, or Marguerite Gautier. The Lady of the Camellias may die pathetically, but how much more pathetic, and ridiculous, is her lover, Armand Duval, who when he learns that she will not see him again, swoons in the arms of his father. His is essen-

Goya based his Don and statue
on Tirso de Molina's early drama.

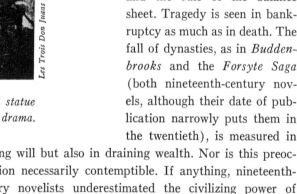

Les Trois Don Juans BY G. APOLLINAIRE, PARIS 1914

tially the melancholy passivity of Goethe's young Werther, perhaps the ultimate reversal of the Don Juan figure, the lover who has lost any impulse to force from a woman what she will not give and is reduced to an abject, tearful, almost feminine (in the old sense) surrender to his destiny.

It cannot be said that the novel lacked strong, memorable male figures. They appear abundantly in Dickens, Tolstoy—particularly in *War and Peace*—Dostoevsky, and elsewhere. Most of the time they are made memorable, however, not by their relations with women, but through their involvement with other forces—war, wealth, conscience, and God. One remembers the Karamazovs not for Dimitri's or Fyodor's wenching but for Alyosha's tortured spiritual struggles. Raskolnikov is as little driven by sexuality (though he is redeemed by a woman) as is David Copperfield or Jean Valjean. And though closer to Don Juan, the adventurer-heroes of Stendhal's *The Red and the Black* and *The Charterhouse of Parma,* and their somewhat debased descendant in Guy de Maupassant's *Bel-Ami,* are all far more remarkable for their ambition than for their womanizing.

There is everywhere in the eighteenth- and the nineteenth-century novel the clink of coin and the rule of the balance sheet. Tragedy is seen in bankruptcy as much as in death. The fall of dynasties, as in *Buddenbrooks* and the *Forsyte Saga* (both nineteenth-century novels, although their date of publication narrowly puts them in the twentieth), is measured in flagging will but also in draining wealth. Nor is this preoccupation necessarily contemptible. If anything, nineteenth-century novelists underestimated the civilizing power of money, a power—going far beyond either thrift or greed—that transformed the world as no revolutionary force before it. The fact remains that in the traditional novel love is made along with money; no embrace is ever free from the shadow of financial success or failure; and the dowry, the business lawsuit, and the unpaid debt are the background of seduction. And this atmosphere does not suit Don Juan.

A man need not be rich to be a Don Juan, but he must be financially independent—either because he has enough money not to worry about it, or simply because he is not interested in what money can get him. He must have the aristocrat's contempt for wealth. For Don Juan to give up a conquest because it might cost too much, or to make another because it might bring gain, is absurd.

When Shaw finally approached the Don Juan story at

the turn of the century, he in a sense ratified the changes that had taken place during the Age of the Novel. Looking at society about him, he reports that man is no longer the pursuer, if he had ever been; woman is now in full pursuit. "The sex is aggressive, powerful: when women are wronged they do not group themselves pathetically to sing '*Protegga il giusto cielo!*': they grasp formidable legal and social weapons, and retaliate." Thus turning Don Juan Tenorio into Jack Tanner, he also turns him from hunter into quarry; and changing Doña Ana de Ulloa into Miss Anne Whitefield, he also changes her into a relentless goddess of the chase, who stops at no deceit, at no trick—not even the ultimate trick of feminine weakness at the crucial moment—to track down her man. She is the Life Force in petticoats, fulfilling nature's overriding purpose of perpetuating the race. Tanner can rant against his fate, but he can no more escape than a beetle in the teeth of a lizard, or any living thing in the grip of evolution.

Shaw goes further than this. He not only illustrates the re-ascendancy of woman in Western civilization; he also reports the near-overthrow of God. Jack Tanner is not only unable to conquer women because they conquer him, he is also unable to carry out his rebellion against God because that rebellion has become commonplace. What, in the day of the original Don Juan, was a brave and lonely act of defiance has become, at the beginning of the twentieth century, the commonplace skepticism of the crowd. Shaw's Don Juan can no longer be a rebel against the supernatural. But, being Shaw's creature, he is a rebel nonetheless—a rebel with a positive program. Since the majority is skeptical, argues Shaw in effect, the rebel against the majority must be affirmative. Tanner is a socialist and an advocate of selective breeding. His cause is the dream of the Superman.

Tanner's alter ego, the Don Juan whom Shaw presents only in the dream interlude set in hell, is still another reversal of the traditional Don Juan figure. Unlike the Jack Tanner of the play itself, he has become immune to women. Unlike Jack Tanner, he is scarcely even concerned with such practical matters as socialism. He is dedicated to intellectual contemplation. He is neither libertine nor romantic, neither hedonist nor rebel against God. "I tell you that in the pursuit of my own pleasure, my own health, my own fortune, I have never known happiness. It was not love for Woman that delivered me into her hands: it was fatigue, exhaustion." In short, Shaw's Don Juan is a moralist and

In Zorrilla's 1844 version, Don Juan Tenorio, *the hero abducts Doña Inés.*

Les Trois Don Juans BY G. APOLLINAIRE, PARIS 1914

an ascetic, a sort of Nietzschean archangel—and more of a marble statue, except for his brilliant conversation, than The Statue itself.

Since Shaw, Don Juan has encountered what is his most trying time. The fact seems paradoxical, because perhaps in no other period of history has the preoccupation with sex been so intense and so widespread. The phenomenon is best illustrated by *Lady Chatterley's Lover,* written by a man who considered modern civilization insane and who dreamed of the natural life, of an unspoiled, unforced Eden. D. H. Lawrence was, among other things, a Rousseau of the four-letter word. But what makes his book especially remarkable are not those few Anglo-Saxon terms—poor, paltry, almost chaste compared to the vocabulary of a great many contemporary best sellers—but the overwrought lyricism of sexuality, which has done irreparable harm to a whole generation of writers who have learned from Lawrence not so much to call things by their right names (few will object to that) but to rhapsodize about sexual intercourse like overexcited and overeducated college girls.

It is, of course, not merely a matter of style. What Lawrence's language betrays, beyond the perfectly laudable desire to reproduce a human being's innermost reality, is an attempt to put sex through a mystical apotheosis. Sexual "fulfillment" becomes the only means of redeeming an otherwise empty life, of filling the spiritual void of modern existence. This whole attitude is entirely inimical to Don Juanism—as inimical as any other form of romanticism. The significant point is that the lover —exemplified in Lawrence's book by the celebrated game-keeper—is expected to be masterful yet sweet, strong yet soft. This is basically a feminine ideal, and perhaps an admirable one; but it is not Don Juan's.

The theme of the wicked seducer preying on the pure maiden has continued to thrive in popular fiction, from Theodore Dreiser's *Sister Carrie,* where the seducer is no longer an aristocrat but a mere businessman named Hurstwood, who himself becomes a victim of a harsh and greedy society; to *Bertha, the Sewing Machine Girl* and innumerable other melodramas in which Don Juan, twirling a villainous mustache and swinging a menacing cane, becomes a broad caricature. But while the seduction theme remained indestructible, the balance of power between male and female continued to shift. Where Clarissa was clearly the stronger in the end, forcing her seducer to repentance, where

Becky Sharp was a rapacious Doña Juana, where even Emma Bovary was anything but an innocent victim, all these heroines and their nineteenth-century sisters were tender souls compared to the female monsters that increasingly populated modern fiction.

Whether or not these women accurately reflected reality, their literary creators obviously thought they did: Faulkner, Nathanael West, Hemingway, Wylie, and O'Hara, among others, specialized in the literature of the bitch. Theirs were not merely forceful women seeking to ensnare a man; they went after men with an almost masculine savagery, with a hunger obviously not destined ever to be appeased.

When faced with such women, what does a man—even a would-be Don Juan—do? There are really only two possibilities. He can knock them down; and this impulse helps account for a large strain of violent sex fiction, from the Marquis de Sade to Mickey Spillane, in which Don Juan has exchanged sword for black-jack or gun and uses the weapon not on his rivals but on the woman herself. Or else he can take flight; and this accounts for another strain of fiction which is not concerned with sex at all, or at least not primarily. A great many American writers have returned to the older themes of nature, of man contending with the elements, of warfare and male loyalties. This literary escape really commenced with James Fenimore Cooper and Herman Melville—well before the female menace developed to its fullest in the Faulkner-West-O'Hara era. The western, rooted in Cooper but flourishing ever since, is an unmistakable escape from hag-ridden civilization. As for Melville, mere love or lust between men and women pales beside the monomaniac desire for revenge that animates *Moby Dick*. Ernest Hemingway has more to say about women; yet his romantic passages are usually his least convincing, and it can scarcely be an accident that the hero of *The Sun Also Rises* has been emasculated in the war. Hemingway was at his happiest as a writer when he spoke of the womanless world of guns and hunting, of companionship rather than love. The male loyalties and enmities in *For Whom the Bell Tolls* will always be more convincing than the preposterous sleeping-bag scene ("the earth moved").

But American writers escaped woman not only in the wilderness but also in society. In Henry James and Edith Wharton, men have appetites and desires, but ultimately we see the cut of their clothes rather than the texture of

JUAN GYENES—FROM *Don Juan y el teatro en España*, 1955

Sets for the 1949 production of Zorrilla's play were designed by Dali.

their flesh; and as often as not, the victories and defeats in these books occur not between man and woman or even man and man, but between family and family, tradition and tradition. John O'Hara, of course, fills his books with sex, regularly and almost dutifully, but the Don Juan spirit is excluded not only by the aggressiveness of the female but, more importantly, by the intense preoccupation with status. Ultimately O'Hara's men, to put it vulgarly, are more concerned with making the club or the team than the girl.

Despite these two streams of writing, in which the main preoccupation is not really sex, a mass of literature remains in which it is little or nothing else. Sometimes the emphasis is humorous: from Henry Miller to Peter de Vries, the seducer (somewhat like Byron's Don Juan) becomes a victim of circumstances, a burlesque version of the knight-errant. Such writers tend to see, as did James Joyce in *Ulysses*, the whole business of sex as a cosmic joke. But most of the time, sex is taken seriously, indeed solemnly. Sex is self-expression; self-expression is freedom; freedom is good; hence sex is good. Hence, libertines and philanderers in infinite variety abound in our fiction, in every setting and on every social level, at cocktail parties and on commuter trains, in offices and slums, among Bohemians and philistines. Yet they never seem to have—indeed, they cannot have—the heroic or even semi-heroic dimensions of a Don Juan. Today, we are enlightened about sex; we like our fictional characters to defy convention, to be "adult" about having affairs in a we-know-what-we're-doing spirit. We understand such motives as loneliness, boredom, or genuine attraction: and above all, we allow them their Lawrencean ecstasies. But the philanderer as such, the man who moves from woman to woman, we regard as somehow sick.

And here we have Don Juan's ultimate predicament in the twentieth century—psychology. In other ages he could defy heaven, earth, the female spirit of the Great Goddess come back to rule; he cannot defy what amounts to the new puritanism of the unconscious. He could pull the beard of the Commander of Calatrava; he cannot, or has not yet learned, to pull Sigmund Freud's beard. He thrives on being called a villain, a damned soul; he can even stand ridicule; but he cannot stand the earnest admonition that he is immature, neurotic, compulsive.

There is an ironic paradox at work here. To begin with, psychoanalysis, by putting the sex instinct at the very center of life, seemed to promise to be Don Juan's ally. But this really proved a trap. If all men and women, and even the baby in the cradle, are Don Juans, where is his special daring? If his impulses are the result of a vague, scarcely understood force called the unconscious, what becomes of his rebellion? The classic Don Juan sins because he wills to; the psychological Don Juan acts because he cannot help himself. The only conceivable tragedy involving this kind of Don Juan is the tragedy of any man in the grip of an obsession or addiction that he cannot control: he is no more tragic than the alcoholic.

Yet the cult of psychoanalysis robs Don Juan even of this form of tragedy because it teaches that the addiction *can* be controlled, that with the help of analysis it can be cured like any illness. Freud tells Don Juan not that he must transcend his nature and become a model husband or a monk; it merely tells him that he should understand his "problem" as some form of neurosis and that he should limit the riot of his libido to reasonable proportions. He condemns Don Juan neither to damnation nor to a painful life of self-denial or self-struggle, but only to mediocrity.

In a sense, in America today, Don Juan has gone underground. His figure persists—in a rather hazy, misunderstood, marked-down form—in a kind of sub-literature never noticed by respectable critics: the tough-guy paperbacks and comics, semi-pornographic magazines, certain TV serials and movies. The men in all of these have two characteristics in common: they "take no nonsense" from women, and they more or less openly, if with a leer, praise sexual pleasure. Don Juan would not recognize himself in them, but he would at least recognize his hedonist side. Significantly, this libertine half-world—unlike the middle-brow, middle-class world of the American novel—is relatively uncowed by Freud. Part of Don Juan's fate in modern times, including this semi-underground status, is at least a specifically American or Anglo-Saxon phenomenon. In the Latin world he was always better understood and still retains a greater degree of reality. And yet the forces that war against Don Juan are not confined to any one culture and touch even his traditional Latin home: the decline of aristocracy, the new status of women, the weakening both of convention and of religion that leaves a rebel so much less to rebel against, the fading of the supernatural, and the cult of psychology, which makes excess no longer a sin but merely a disease, all spell Don Juan's end.

In Shaw's Man and Superman, *Don Juan, here played by Maurice Evans, is victim.*

Don Juan's modern fate has been very aptly expressed in a minor but entertaining play entitled *The Death of Satan*, by the British playwright and poet Ronald Duncan, who has imagined what would happen if the legendary rake came back into the world today. Duncan's Don, possibly because of so many centuries in hell, has turned into more of a romantic than his classic model. For one thing, he spends his eternity of damnation pining for Doña Ana and writing her letters, in verse, that will never be delivered. Nevertheless, his return to earth is instructive: he rather recalls that other celebrated Don—Quixote—looking for knights to fight and for dragons to slay. Juan wants innocent maidens to seduce, jealous husbands to duel with, sins to commit—in effect, though Duncan doesn't say it that way, a God to defy. He finds none of these. When he sets out to make love to a married woman who is only too willing, the husband happens into the room and civilly offers Don Juan a drink.

When he finds Doña Ana, she has turned into a domineering modern career woman and a writer's fond, though scarcely passionate or faithful wife. Don Juan to her is now "obviously romantic and quite obviously immature." She is still woman enough to fall in love with him again—or something like love—and Don Juan is moved. But at the last moment he makes a discovery he cannot bear: the modern Ana does not believe in God. The cross she wears around her neck is a mere tourist's trinket. What the play is saying here is that Don Juan wanted nothing less than to be God's rival for Ana's love, in a sense to strike at Him through her. Since Ana no longer loves God, this is no longer possible, and before Don Juan flees back to hell in despair, he understands that—

If we don't love something greater than ourselves
We are incapable of loving one another. . . .
          Now I see that He Who was between us
Was the One Who drew us together.
Now there is nothing between us, we are forever apart. . . .

You leave me nothing to look up to,
Nothing to overcome. Flesh of my flesh.
A man doesn't love his own flesh.
And the last twist of the knife is:
When a profligate atheist like me
Finds that the only thing he loves was the soul which he denied.

Henry Anatole Grunwald, a senior editor of Time, *edited the anthology* Salinger: A Critical Portrait *(Harper & Row).*

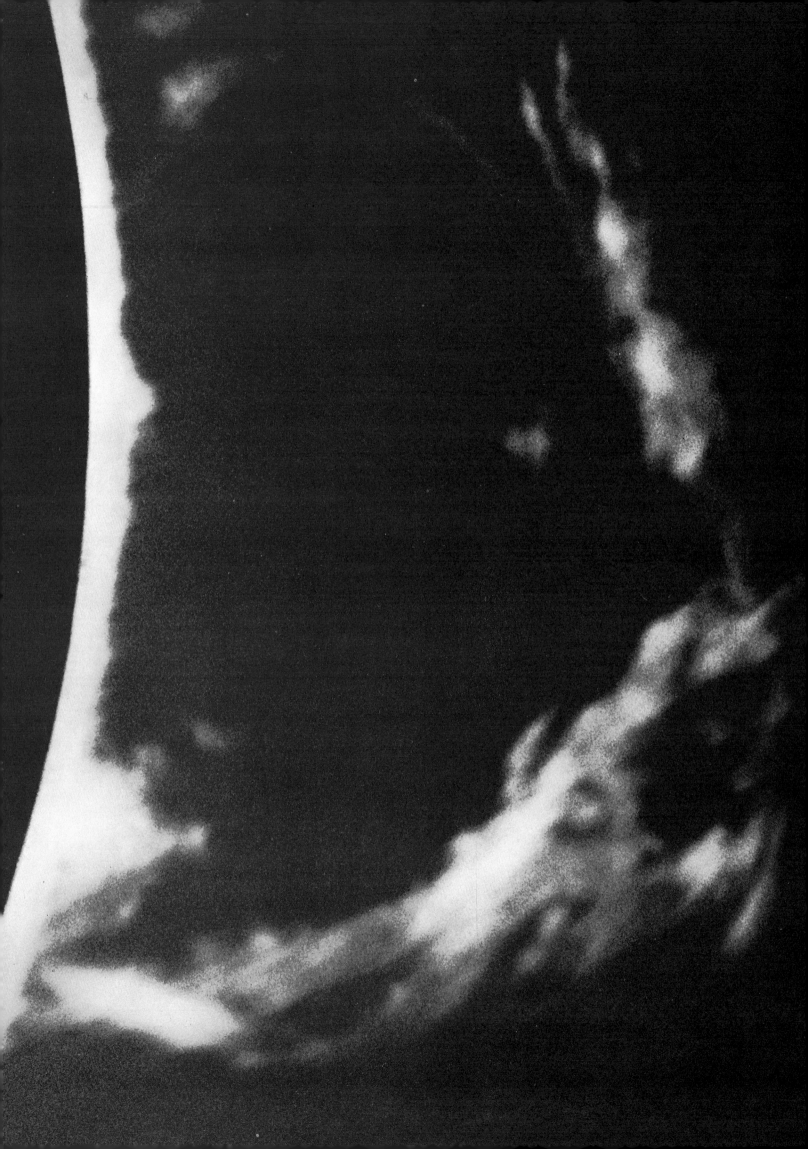

Is it old? Absolutely. At least 5,000,000,000 years. Relatively? As one week in the life of man. We are creatures of the dawn. It will grow colder, but we may move closer

By ARTHUR C. CLARKE

IN THE LIGHT OF THE SUN

Ra, the Egyptian sun-god

The only sun that can be "seen" is the scientific one, photographed in but a narrow fraction of its light and often (opposite) with its disc eclipsed, so that the hundreds-of-thousands-of-miles-high "prominences" are all that appear. For the most part, men have had to see the sun in symbols; a selection of them—from ancient to modern—follows on subsequent pages.

No man has ever seen the Sun, or ever will. What we call "sunlight" is only a narrow span of the entire solar spectrum—the immensely broad band of vibrations which the Sun, our nearest star, pours into space. All the colors visible to the eye, from warm red to deepest violet, lie within a single octave of this band—for the waves of violet light have twice the frequency, or "pitch" if we think in musical terms, of red. On either side of this narrow zone are ranged octave after octave of radiations to which we are totally blind.

The musical analogy is a useful one. Think of one octave on the piano—less than the span of the average hand. Imagine that you were deaf to all notes outside this range; how much, then, could you appreciate of a full orchestral score when everything from contra bassoon to piccolo is going full blast? Obviously you could get only the faintest idea of the composer's intentions. In the same way, by eye alone we can obtain only a grossly restricted conception of the true "color" of the world around us.

However, let us not exaggerate our visual handicap. Though visible light is merely a single octave of the sun's radiation, it does contain most of the power; the higher and lower frequencies are relatively feeble. It is, of course, no coincidence that our eyes are adapted to the most intense band of sunlight; if that band had been somewhere else

243

in the spectrum—as is the case with other stars—evolution would have given us eyes appropriately tuned.

Nevertheless, the sun's invisible rays are extremely important, and affect our lives in ways undreamed of until only a few years ago. Some of them, indeed, may control our destinies—and even, as we shall see in a moment, our very existence.

The visible spectrum is, quite arbitrarily, divided up into seven primary colors—the famous sequence red, orange, yellow, green, blue, indigo, violet, if we start from the longest waves and work down to the shortest. Seven main colors in the one octave; but the complete band of solar radia-

Thanks to special photographic films, we have all had glimpses of the world of infrared. It is an easily recognizable world, though tone values are strangely distorted. Sky and water are black, leaves and grass dazzlingly white, as if covered with snow. It is a world of clear, far horizons, for infrared rays slice through the normal haze of distance—hence their great value in aerial photography.

The farther we go down into the infrared, the stranger are the sights we encounter and the harder it becomes to relate them to the world of our normal senses. It is only very recently (partly under the spur of guided-missile development) that we have

strike at them even in complete darkness. Only in the last decade have our guided missiles learned the same trick.

Below the infrared, for several octaves, is a no man's land of radiation about which very little is known. It is hard to generate or to detect waves in this region, and until recently few scientists paid it much attention. But as we press on to longer and longer waves we come at last to more familiar territory; first we encounter the inch-long wave of radar, then the yard-long one of the short-wave bands, then the hundred-yard wave of the broadcast band.

The existence of all these radiations was quite unknown a century ago; today, of

Sumerian sun, c. 2700 B.C.

Old Hopi Indian sun-god

Sun wheel, Konarak, India

tions covers at least thirty octaves, or a total frequency range of ten thousand million to one. If we could see the whole of it, therefore, we might expect to discern more than two hundred colors as distinct from each other as orange is from yellow, or green is from blue.

Starting with the sun's visible rays, let us explore outward in each direction and see (though that word is hardly applicable) what we can discover. On the long-wave side we come first to the infrared rays, which can be perceived by our skin but not by our eyes. For infrared rays are heat radiation; go out of doors on a summer day, and you can tell where the sun is even though your eyes may be tightly clenched.

invented sensing devices that can operate in the far infrared. They see the world of heat; they can "look" at a man wearing a brilliantly colored shirt and smoking a cigarette—and see only the glowing tip. They can also look down on a landscape hidden in the darkness of night, and see all the sources of heat from factories, automobiles, taxiing aircraft. Hours after a jet has taken off, they can still read its signature on the warm runway.

Some animals have developed an infrared sense, to enable them to hunt at night. There is a snake which has two small pits near its nostrils, each holding a directional infrared detector. These allow it to "home" upon small, warm animals like mice, and to

course, they are among the most important tools of our civilization. It is a bare twenty years since we discovered that the Sun also produces them, on a scale we cannot hope to match with our puny transmitters.

The Sun's radio output differs profoundly from its visible light, and the difference is not merely one of greater length. Visible sunlight is practically constant in intensity; if there are any fluctuations, they are too slight to be detected. Not only has the Sun shone with unvarying brightness throughout the whole span of human history, but we would probably notice no difference if we could see it through the eyes of one of the great reptiles.

But if you saw only the "radio" Sun,

you would never guess that it was the same object. Most of the time it is very dim—much dimmer, in fact, than many other celestial bodies. To the eye able to see only by radio waves, there would be little difference between day and night; the rising of the Sun would be a minor and inconspicuous event.

From time to time, however, the radio Sun explodes into nova brightness. It may, within seconds, flare up to a hundred, a thousand, or even a million times its normal brilliance. These colossal outbursts of radio energy do not come from the Sun as a whole, but from small fixed areas of the solar disc, often associated with sunspots.

and radio telescopes dramatize the problem involved. If creatures with radio senses do exist anywhere in the universe, they must be far larger than whales, and can therefore only be inhabitants of gravity-free space.

Meanwhile, back on Earth, let us consider the other end of the spectrum—the rays shorter than visible light. As the blue deepens into indigo and then violet, the human eye soon fails to respond. But there is still "light" present in solar radiation—the ultraviolet. As in the case of the infrared, our skins can react to it, often painfully; for ultraviolet rays are the cause of sunburn.

ferent types of glass and assembled with great care into a single unit. The eye has only one lens, and it already has trouble coping with the two-to-one range of wave lengths in the visible spectrum. You can prove this by looking at a bright red object on a bright blue background. They won't both be in perfect focus; when you look at one, the other will appear to be slightly fuzzy.

Objects would be even fuzzier if we could see by ultraviolet as well as by visible light, so the eye deals with this insolvable problem by eliminating it. There is a filter in the front of the eye which blocks the ultraviolet, preventing it from reaching the

Roman mosaic floor from Egypt

Early American sunflower quilt

Buddhist sun medallion, India

This may be the reason why no animals seem ever to have developed radio senses. Most of the time such a sense would be useless, because the radio landscape would be completely dark—there would be no source of illumination.

In any event, "radio eyes" would pose some major biological problems. Because radio waves are millions of times longer than light waves, the corresponding sense organs would have to be millions of times larger than normal eyes, if they were to have the same definition. Even a radio eye which showed the world as fuzzily as a badly out-of-focus television picture would have to be hundreds of yards in diameter; the gigantic antennas of our radar systems

And here is a very strange and little-known fact. Though I have just stated that our eyes do not respond to ultraviolet, the actual situation is a good deal more complicated. (In nature, it usually is.) The sensitive screen at the back of the eye—the retina, which is the precise equivalent of the film in a camera—*does* react strongly to ultraviolet. If it were the only factor involved, we could see by the invisible ultraviolet rays.

Then why don't we? For a purely technical reason. Though the eye is an evolutionary marvel, it is a very poor piece of optics. To enable it to work properly over the whole range of colors, a good camera has to have four or more lenses, made of dif-

retina. The haze filter that photographers often employ when using color film does exactly the same job, and for a somewhat similar reason.

The eye's filter is the lens itself—and here at last is the punch line of this rather long-winded narrative. If you are ever unlucky enough to lose your natural lenses (say through a cataract operation), and have them replaced by artificial lenses of clear glass, you will be able to see quite well in the ultraviolet. Indeed, with a source of ultraviolet illumination, like the so-called "black light" lamps, you will be able to see perfectly in what is, to the normal person, complete darkness! I hereby donate this valuable information to the C.I.A., Ellery

L. TO R.: LUC JOUBERT—LOUVRE; N.Y. PUB. LIB. PICTURE COLL.; ROGER-VIOLLET;
The Sun in Art, GRAPHIS, ZURICH; N.Y. HISTORICAL ASSOCIATION; *The Art of India:
Temples and Sculpture* BY L. FREDERIC

Queen, or anyone else who is interested.

Normal sunlight, as you can discover during a day at the beach, contains plenty of ultraviolet. It all lies, however, in a narrow band—the single octave just above the visible spectrum in frequency. As we move beyond this to still higher frequencies, the scene suddenly dims and darkens. A being able to see only in the far ultraviolet would be in a very unfortunate position. To him it would always be night, whether or not the sun was above the horizon.

What has happened? Doesn't the Sun radiate in the far ultraviolet? Certainly it does—but this radiation is all blocked by

climbed through the opaque fog of the atmosphere. Beyond this, between twenty and thirty miles high, the ultraviolet sun would break through in its awful glory.

I use that word "awful" with deliberate intent. These rays can kill, and swiftly. They do not bother astronauts because they can be easily filtered out by special glass. But if they were to reach the surface of the earth—if they were not blocked by the upper atmosphere—most existing forms of life would be wiped out.

If you regard the existence of this invisible ultraviolet umbrella as in any way providential, you are confusing cause and effect. The screen was not put in the atmos-

short ultraviolet rays were blocked twenty miles up, did the present types of terrestrial life evolve. If there had been no ozone layer, they would doubtless have evolved into different forms. Perhaps we might still be here, but our skins would be very, very black.

Life on Mars must face this problem, for that planet seems to have no oxygen in its atmosphere, and therefore no ozone layer. The far ultraviolet rays must reach the Martian surface unhindered, and must profoundly affect all living matter there. It has been suggested that these rays are responsible for the color changes which astronomers have observed on the planet.

Aztec sun calendar, A.D.

Greek sun-god from Italy

Albrecht Dürer: woodcut, 1498

the atmosphere, miles above our head. In the far ultraviolet a few inches of ordinary air are as opaque as a sheet of metal.

Only with the development of rocket-borne instruments has it become possible to study this unknown region of the solar spectrum—a region, incidentally, which contains vital information about the Sun and the processes that power its nuclear furnace. If your vision were restricted to the far ultraviolet, and you started off from ground level on a bright, sunny day, this is what you would see.

At first, you would be in utter darkness—even though you were looking straight at the Sun. Then, about twenty miles up, you would notice a slow brightening, as you

phere to protect terrestrial life—it was put there by life itself, hundreds of millions of years before man appeared on Earth.

The Sun's raw ultraviolet rays, in all probability, *did* reach the surface of the primeval Earth; the earliest forms of life were adapted to it—perhaps even thrived upon it. In those days there was no oxygen in the atmosphere; oxygen is a by-product of plant life, and over geological aeons its amount slowly increased—until at last those oxygen-burning creatures called animals had a chance to thrive.

That filter in the sky is made of oxygen—or, rather, the grouping of three oxygen atoms known as ozone. Not until Earth's protective ozone layer was formed, and the

Whether or not this is true, we can predict that one of the occupational hazards of Martian explorers will be severe sunburn.

Just as ultraviolet lies beyond the violet, so beyond the ultraviolet lie still shorter rays. These are X rays, which are roughly a thousand times shorter than visible light. Like the ultraviolet, these even more dangerous rays are blocked by the atmosphere; few of them come to within a hundred miles of Earth, and they have been detected by rocket instruments only during the past few years. The solar X rays are quite feeble—only a millionth of the intensity of visible light—but their importance is much greater than this figure would indicate. We know now that blasts of X rays from the

Sun, impinging upon the upper atmosphere, can produce violent changes in radio communications, even to the extent of complete blackouts. Men have lost their lives because the Sun has disrupted radio; nations are equally vulnerable in this age of the ICBM.

You will recall that though the Sun shines with remarkable steadiness in the visible spectrum, it flares and sparkles furiously on the long (radio) waves. Exactly the same thing happens with its X-ray emission, even though these waves are a billion times shorter. Moreover, both the Sun's radio waves and its X rays appear to come from the same localized

boil at exactly the time when a good number of major space expeditions are planned —say around 1968. The astronauts may run into some heavy weather, for by then the Sun will be shooting out not only vast quantities of ultraviolet, X rays, and radio waves, but other radiations which cannot be so easily blocked.

We see, then, how complicated and how variable sunlight is—if we use that word in the widest sense to describe *all* the waves emitted by the Sun. Nevertheless, when we accept the evidence of our unaided eyes and describe the Sun as a yellow star, we have summed up the most important single fact about it—*at this moment in time.*

light is concentrated in the yellow band of the spectrum, falling slowly in intensity toward both the longer and shorter waves.

That yellow "hump" will shift as the Sun evolves, and the light of day will change accordingly. It is natural to assume that as the Sun grows older, and uses up its hydrogen fuel—which it is now doing at the spanking rate of half a billion tons a second—it will become steadily colder and redder.

But the evolution of a star is a highly complex matter, involving chains of interlocking nuclear reactions. According to one theory, the Sun is still growing hotter, and will continue to do so for several bil-

E. Cocker: calligraphic sun, 1657

Alexander Girard: sun, 1960

Saul Steinberg: cartoon detail

areas of the solar surface—disturbed regions in the neighborhood of sunspots, where clouds of incandescent gas larger than the Earth erupt into space at hundreds of miles a second.

For reasons not yet understood (there is not much about the Sun that we do *thoroughly* understand) solar activity rises and falls in an eleven-year cycle. The Sun was most active around 1957—which is why that date was chosen for the International Geophysical Year. Now it is heading for a minimum, and to take advantage of this, scientists made arrangements for a little IGY called the "Year of the Quiet Sun," 1964-1965. It is rather unfortunate that the Sun will be coming back to the

It appears probable, however, that sunlight will be the color we know for only a negligibly small part of the Sun's history.

For stars, like individuals, age and change. As we look out into space, we see around us stars at all stages of evolution. There are faint blood-red dwarfs so cool that their surface temperature is a mere 4,000 degrees Fahrenheit; there are searing ghosts blazing at 100,000 degrees and almost too hot to be seen, for the greater part of their radiation is in the invisible ultraviolet. Obviously, the "daylight" produced by any star depends upon its temperature; today (and for ages past, as for ages to come) our Sun is at about 10,000 degrees Fahrenheit, and this means that most of its

lion years. Probably life will be able to adapt itself to these changes—unless they occur catastrophically, as would be the case if the Sun exploded into a nova. In any event, whatever the vicissitudes of the next five or ten billion years, the Sun will finally settle down to the white-dwarf stage.

It will be a tiny thing, not much bigger than the Earth, and therefore too small to show a disc to the naked eye. At first it will be hotter than it is today, but because of its minute size it will radiate very little heat to its surviving planets. The daylight of that distant age will be as cold as moonlight, but much bluer, and the temperature of the Earth will have fallen to 300 degrees below zero. If you think of mercury lamps

L. TO R.: MUSEO NACIONAL DE ANTHROPOLOGIA, MEXICO CITY; LOUVRE—GIRAUDON;
N.Y. PUB. LIB. PRINT ROOM; VICTORIA AND ALBERT MUSEUM; LA FONDA DEL SOL,
RESTAURANT ASSOCIATES; SAUL STEINBERG

on a freezing winter night, you have a faint mental picture of high noon in the year 7,000,000,000.

Yet that does not mean life—even life as we know it today—will be impossible in the solar system; it will simply have to move in toward the shrunken sun. The construction of artificial planets would be child's play to the intelligences we can expect by that date; indeed, it will be child's play to *us* in a few hundred years time.

Around the year 10,000,000,000 the dwarf Sun will have cooled back to its present temperature, and hence to the yellow color that we know today. From a body that was sufficiently close to it—say only

preciated, results of modern astrophysical theories.

When the Sun shrinks to a dull red dwarf, it will not be dying. It will just be starting to live—*and everything that has gone before will be merely a fleeting prelude to its real history.*

For a red dwarf, because it is so small and so cool, loses energy at such an incredibly slow rate that it can stay in business for thousands of times longer than a normal-sized white or yellow star. We must no longer talk in billions but in trillions of years if we are to measure its life span. Such figures are, of course, inconceivable (for that matter, who can think of a thou-

—but our reaction to it is wholly irrelevant and misleading. For we are creatures of the dawn, with eyes and senses adapted to the hot light of today's primeval Sun. Though we should miss beyond measure the blues and greens and violets that are the fading afterglow of Creation, they are all doomed to pass with the brief billion-year infancy of the stars.

But the eyes that will look upon that all-but-eternal crimson twilight will respond to the colors we cannot see; aeons earlier, evolution will have moved their sensitivity away from the yellow, somewhere out beyond the visible red. The world of rainbow-hued heat they see will

Antonio Frasconi: woodcut, 1953

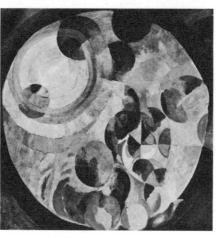

R. Delaunay: Sun and Moon, *1913*

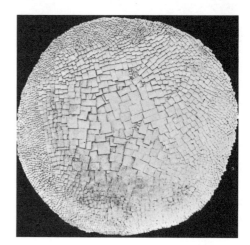

A. L. Toledo Piza: Mosaic #34, *1961*

a million miles away—it would look exactly like our present Sun, and would give just as much heat. There would be no way of telling, by eye alone, that it was actually a hundred times smaller—and a hundred times closer.

So matters may continue for another five billion years; but at last the inevitable will happen. Very slowly, the Sun will begin to cool, dropping from yellow down to red. Perhaps by the year 15,000,000,000 it will become a red dwarf, with a surface temperature of a mere 4,000 degrees. It will be nearing the end of the evolutionary track —but reports of its death will be greatly exaggerated. For now comes one of the most remarkable, and certainly least ap-

sand years?) but we can nevertheless put them into their right perspective if we relate the life of a star to the life of a man.

On this scale, the Sun is but a week old. Its flaming youth will continue for another month; then it will settle down to a sedate, adult existence which may last at least eighty years. Life has existed on this planet for two or three days of the week that has passed; the whole of human history lies within the last second—and there are eighty years to come.

In the wonderful closing pages of *The Time Machine* the young H. G. Wells described the world of the far future, with a blood-red sun hanging over a freezing sea. It is a somber picture that chills the blood

be as rich and colorful as ours—and as beautiful; for a melody is not lost when it is merely transposed an octave down into the bass.

So now we know that Shelley, who was right in so many things, was wrong when he wrote:

Life, like a dome of many-colored glass,
Stains the white radiance of Eternity.

For the radiance of eternity is not white: it is infrared.

British novelist and science writer, Arthur Clarke specializes in space and marine world subjects. His most recent books are Glide Path *and* Profiles of the Future.

L. TO R.: *A Book of Many Suns* BY A. FRASCONI; WALTER DRAYER—KUNSTHAUS, ZURICH; GALERIE LA HUNE, PARIS; OPPOSITE: THE METROPOLITAN MUSEUM OF ART, FLETCHER FUND, 1956

Richard Lippold: The Sun, *195*

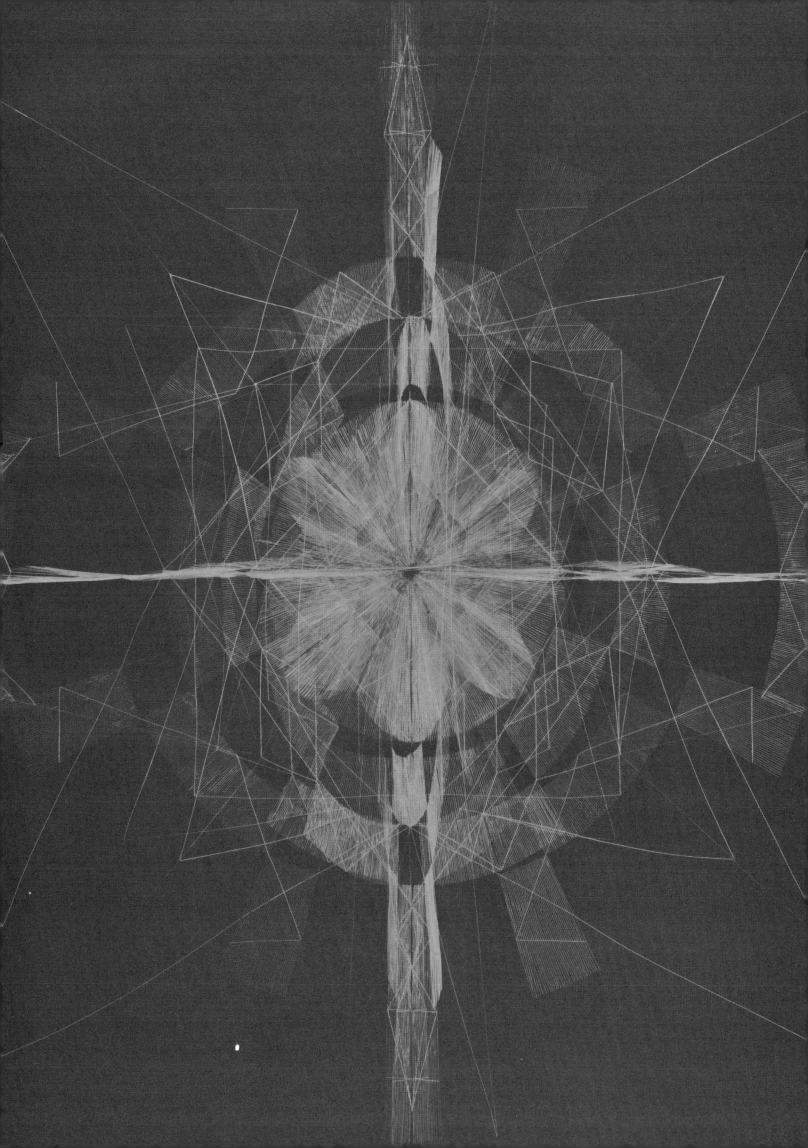

From Eden to the Nightmare

Dissatisfied with the world as it exists, men have always tried to imagine the world as it might become. Time, though, has darkened their utopian visions in more ways than one

By HENRY ANATOLE GRUNWALD

An early American Garden of Eden

Utopia has almost always been somewhere on the map of man's imagination. Every age, with some notable exceptions, has created a realm of Nowhere for its visions of the future. The frontiers of this realm are not precise. It should not be confused with Arcadia or the Golden Age, that space-time continuum (as we might put it) in which life was good and innocent; these dreams lie in the past. Nor is it the same as the land of Cockaigne or the Schlaraffenland of German legend, where roast fowl offer themselves up ready for the eating, where every prospect pleases and not even man is vile; those regions are merely playthings of fancy. Nor is Utopia the same as the Messianic Kingdom, where, in the words of the prophet Isaiah, "the wolf also shall dwell with the lamb, and the leopard shall lie down with the kid . . . and the lion shall eat straw like the ox." For that peaceable kingdom, though it may be located on this earth, can come about only through divine intervention.

Utopia is a city of man. Yet in their own way the utopians were prophets in the sense of predicting the future and also prophets in the sense of castigating the present; their very vision of things as they should be was a reproach to things as they are.

One of the extraordinary facts about our time is that its utopias are dark. They are no longer places of hope but of horror, no longer heaven on earth but hell on earth. How this happened is suggested by Nicolas Berdyaev, in a passage that Aldous Huxley used as his epigraph to *Brave New World:* "Utopias can be realized. Life is marching toward utopias. And perhaps a new century is beginning in which the intellectuals and the cultured classes will dream about means of evading utopia and of returning to non-utopian society, less 'perfect,' but freer."

In the past the triumphs of science led us to *hubris.* Today even greater scientific triumphs have led, on the whole, to fear. We can scarcely manage this world, we seem to feel; how are we to manage others? We have come to deride and deplore the Victorian era's unshakable optimism about man's destiny.

This involves a paradox, because in some respects we are still the heirs of Rousseau and of the Enlightenment, which held man to be essentially good and perfectible. This notion is reflected in our sociology and psychology, in our belief that good environment will make good people, that wrongdoing can be cured almost like a disease. And yet at the same time, with another part of our minds, we don't accept all this. We have seen too much blood and horror in this century, too much tampering with the "environment," too much "conditioning," too much "adjustment," ever again to feel easy about any attempt to achieve human perfection—and utopia is nothing if not a dream of conditioning, of environment wisely controlled.

Constructing a utopia used to be a fairly simple process. You substituted peace for war, altruism for selfishness, temperance for greed, love for hate. Today we do not turn the world upside down, we simply take it as it is and make it more so. The result is almost invariably nightmarish. In a recent address Huxley declared that "there are the near-in utopias, where people like

N. Y. PUB. LIB. RARE BOOK DIV.

ourselves have solved their social and psychological problems in ways which to us are unfamiliar. And there are the far-out utopias, inhabited by creatures unlike ourselves —creatures whose problems are either non-existent or so different from ours as to seem irrelevant." Past utopias, Huxley continued, were all intended to be positive, "but in every case an oversimplified view of human nature, combined with the lust for tidiness . . . has reversed the sign and transformed these ideal states into negative utopias which, in spite of their authors', underlying good will and sporadic good sense, are potentially as horribly inhuman as Orwell's *1984*." To see how this came about we must begin with Plato's *Republic*, the prototype utopia of them all.

What disturbs us about *The Republic* is quite simply the fact that Plato was more interested in order than in liberty. We feel that, when it comes to the people, the whole is greater than the part; individually they may be ignorant, but collectively they are wise. To Plato, of course, this notion would have been wicked nonsense. At best the people at large, like the false philosophers, might be capable of "opinion," which he considered an intermediate stage between knowledge and ignorance. The mob was merely "the great brute," and its rule could only be brutish. Not that in his view the common people are necessarily wicked or intractable. They are like children who must be led, and when necessary lied to, for their own good. "Our rulers," he says, "will have to administer a great quantity of falsehood and deceit for the benefit of the ruled."

As for the practical organization of the Republic, it is a city-state of strictly limited size; the optimum number of citizens Plato held to be 5,040, approximately the number of people who could be reached on a single occasion by a single orator before the time of public-address systems, radio, and television. The people are divided into Plato's famous metallic class structure, the rulers, or guardians, being symbolically composed of gold, the auxiliaries, or soldiers, of silver, and the workers of brass and iron. But there is a certain amount of mobility. "A golden parent will sometimes have a silver son, or a silver parent a golden son."

This mobility is aided by abolition of the family, at least among the ruling class. Theoretically all women are the wives of all men. At special festivals mating is arranged by lot, but only among partners judged likely to produce healthy offspring. Children are taken from their mothers at birth, and reared by the state. Thus there will be no private family feeling to detract from love and loyalty to the Republic. Nor is there any private property. This is particularly important for the guardians, for if they owned land and houses privately, they would become hateful masters rather than fatherly friends to the people.

The muses, like everyone else, are in the service of Plato's ideal state. Artists and writers are silenced or severely censored. Nevertheless, one finds in *The Republic*, as one is pushed on through the almost hypnotically reasonable interchanges, a serenity and clarity that are hard to resist. There is also a bucolic yearning that characterizes most utopias before the advent of technology, often remarkably naïve and detailed. The people will "produce corn, and wine, and clothes, and shoes, and build houses for themselves . . . they will work, in summer, commonly, stripped and barefoot, but in winter substantially clothed and shod. They will feed on barley-meal and flour of wheat, baking and kneading them, making noble cakes and loaves. . . ."

The underlying view of justice, of which the Republic is but a civic incarnation, is simply this: each in his own place and station, each performing his proper function, each minding his own business. Needless to say, with the exception of some lowlier matters that are not worth his while, the philosopher's business is to mind everybody's.

In various combinations, and with changing emphasis, most of these Spartan ingredients reappear in virtually all utopias after Plato. While we might conceivably tolerate the loss of property, privacy, family, and art, what truly makes Plato's Republic unacceptable to us, as democrats, is the notion of an infallible elite. What is unanswered in *The Republic* and in most other utopias is the immortal question: Who guards the guardians?

Plato and many other utopians can only present more or less impressive schemes for the guardians' education and training; they can only base their structures on the tautology that the wise man is wise. In few of the utopias is there a real check on the rulers; there cannot be, for everything depends on their goodness and wisdom. Plato was somewhat naïve about the nature of power, as are so many other utopians. He condemned tyranny, but did he fully understand what tempts men to become tyrants? Did he understand that a philosopher, once given power, might be so gripped by the passion for establishing the truth, his truth, that he would start working out his syllogisms in human lives? What troubles us, then, is not the notion that the philosopher should be king, but the serene assumption that a philosopher will never be a tyrant.

For nearly two thousand years after Plato, utopia almost never appeared on the map. Christianity looked to the City of God. Throughout the long Christian centuries until the Renaissance, mankind was taught not to yearn for heaven on earth; heaven itself seemed too close and too real. Only when the Christian vision of paradise began to lose its hold was it time once again to long for a secular paradise. It is surely no accident that Sir Thomas

The hero of Francis Godwin's Man in
the Moone *(1638) was unexpectedly taken
there, in just eleven days, by wild
swans he had trained to fly in harness.
The moon turned out to be utopia,
which—if still true—is the best reason
yet for trying to get there first.*

More's *Utopia* is, fictionally, a by-product of the intoxicating age of discoveries; for its narrator professes to have been a sailing companion of Amerigo Vespucci and to have found his happy island in the New World.

Following the lead of *The Republic*, More abolishes private property in Utopia. Since there is no property, there is no money. The citizens of Utopia just go to the nearest district storehouse and draw what they need. This material abundance More imagined as being created simply by the fact that everyone works—princes, rich men, would-be idlers. They toil but six hours a day, a condition that only a few of today's most ambitious trade unions have as yet achieved for their members. Besides, More established a kind of circular economic law: since there is enough for everybody, no one hoards; and since no one hoards, there is enough for everybody.

This seems a rather naïve way of doing away with greed, for it assumes that greed is caused only by the fear of want. In the matter of what he called "pomp and excess" More was equally simple. Precious metals are despised in his Utopia. Gold is used to make chamber pots and the chains of slaves. Pearls are playthings for children.

Unlike Plato, More was all for the family. It forms the basic social unit of Utopia, but it is subject to a good deal of regulation. Divorce is permitted for adultery, or insufferable perverseness, as well as by mutual consent for other causes, provided the government approves. While men and women are free to mate more or less as they please, care must be taken to prevent mistakes. The physical soundness of both parties must be ascertained and they must view each other naked before marriage.

Liberty was not the ideal in Utopia, any more than in the Republic. The ideal was stability. Like Plato, More considered the institution of slavery indispensable, if only to get the meaner jobs in life done. And, like most utopians after him, he had a touch of agoraphobia—particularly strange for a Renaissance man—in the sense that he yearned for the smallish, well-secluded corner of the world. In addition to this desire for seclusion, More set some other fashions for later utopians. Like most of them, he was preoccupied with sanitation. Like most of them, he called for as few laws as possible, and banished lawyers from the state. And like most of them, he had a passion for ceremonial and housekeeping details. But unlike many of his successors, More faced up to the matter of war and proposed that it should be waged by assassination of the enemy's leaders. Why kill so many in battle when a few well-chosen deaths might settle the issue?

More was far easier than Plato on the arts, music, and pleasure in general. He considered it to be man's natural goal in life, but he distinguished between higher and lower, worthier and un-

LHOMME
DANS
LA LVNE

worthier pleasures. While not spurning food, drink, or the feeling "which arises from satisfying the appetite which Nature has wisely given to lead us to the propagation of the species," he ranks as the highest pleasure of all cultivation of the mind. This is made abundantly clear even at mealtime, to which citizens are summoned by trumpet calls. All meals are taken in common in vast dining halls, on the doubtful theory that no one would want to go to the bother of preparing his own meal at home when it is so easily available in a kind of super soup kitchen. All meals are begun "with some lecture of morality that is read to them," and for educational purposes the young are placed next to the old, so that the old men may "take occasion to entertain those about them with some useful and pleasant enlargements." Whatever can be said for life in Utopia, one would scarcely want to dine there.

For a hundred years after More there was no sign of significant new utopias. Then, within a few years of each other in the 1620's, three visions of ideal commonwealths appeared, and together they reflected some major new forces that were stirring the age. All three were to some extent preoccupied with science, invention, and manufacture.

The best known of the three is Francis Bacon's fragmentary *New Atlantis*. It offers a suitably exotic and isolated location, wise rulers, and a well-regulated family life. But above all, New Atlantis is imbued with its era's almost vernal passion for science. Here it is no longer the philosopher who is king, but the scientist. It is the kind of realm that might have been dreamed, with due allowance for the intervening centuries, by the head of a large, modern, state university; or perhaps it is really the Rockefeller Foundation transported to Utopia. At the heart of New Atlantis is Salomon's House, a vast research institution whose aim is to find "the knowledge of causes and secret motion of things; and the enlarging of the bounds of human empire, to the effecting of all things possible." The Salomon Foundation, as one is tempted to think of it, has agents roaming the earth (traveling research fellows?) looking for new discoveries, and it tries to examine almost anything the seventeenth-century mind can imagine.

If New Atlantis was the first scientific utopia, Christianopolis anticipates the first industrial one. Johann Valentin Andreae, a German Protestant scholar, dreamed of an "abode situated below the sky, but at the same time above the dregs of this known world." Part Platonic, part Calvinist, Christianopolis is made distinctive by its industrial organization. The whole community is in fact a workshop. With that geographic neatness which marks most utopian writers, Andreae sees his city as a square divided into three parts: one to supply food, one for drill and exercise, and one, disarmingly, for looks. The industrial sector, which is lo-

*Until the mid-nineteenth century,
utopia was always positive; but then the
first negative ones began to appear,
such as the "Stahlstadt" of Jules Verne's*
The Begum's Fortune *(1879). It
was essentially a giant munitions factory
run like a concentration camp.*

cated outside the city walls, is divided into manufactures requiring the use of fire and those that can be carried on without it—heavy and light industry in modern terms. The economic planner has made his entrance into utopia.

The third and most far-out in this trio of early seventeenth-century utopias is *The City of the Sun* by Tommaso Campanella, an Italian Dominican monk who believed in astrology and spent considerable time in the prisons of the Inquisition, where in fact he wrote his fantasy. It is a fascinating mixture of Platonic communism, Christian radicalism, Aztec custom, astrological speculation, technological anticipation, and scientific instinct. Both spiritual and temporal matters are in the hands of the high priest, known as Metaphysicus, who rules jointly with three associates and is described as the most staggeringly well-educated ruler in the visible and perhaps invisible world. Below this top level there is a hierarchy of magistrates all of whom are also priests; the entire population confesses its sins to them, and it is their duty to pardon them forthwith, while in turn confessing their own sins to their superiors—and so on up in a continuous confessional ascent.

Yet amid this eccentricity there is a certain grasp of reality and of the future. Despite all its quirks, The City of the Sun is remarkably sound on education, scientific inquiry, and hygiene. Labor has become dignified, and the slave class of so many earlier utopias has been discarded. And there is a heady belief in "the wonderful invention of printing and arquebuses, and the discovery of the use of the magnet." Strange as were Campanella's visions, they mark, with those of Andreae, a turning point. With them, as Lewis Mumford has said, "we stand at the entrance to the utopia of means; that is to say, the place in which all that materially contributes to the good life has been perfected."

The remainder of the seventeenth century brought a veritable blizzard of utopian or semi-utopian works, including *The Man in the Moone,* by Bishop Francis Godwin, and *Oceana,* by James Harrington. The latter, an account of a strictly parliamentary paradise, was written in the days of Cromwell and is essentially a draft constitution, providing for land reform and a balanced legislative system allowing the rule of "King People." It was one of the very few utopias concerned with the preservation of private property and individual liberty.

Beyond this, and until the end of the eighteenth century, there is a considerable void in utopian literature. Instead of plans for perfect commonwealths, the Age of Reason yearned for the primitive. Its utopia was the forest primeval with encyclopedias dangling from the trees. Chateaubriand dreamed of the noble savage and Rousseau proclaimed man to have been pure before society corrupted him. This belief in nature and man's natural goodness

BIB. D'EDUCATION ET RECREATION, PARIS

was a strong radical force, since it seemed to justify razing the structures of society in order to start again from the ground up. Heightened to anarchic fervor, it fed the French Revolution. It also animated a group of oddly assorted idealists, by turns idyllic and radical, pacific and militant, democratic and tyrannical, who became known as the utopian Socialists. From the middle of the eighteenth century to the middle of the nineteenth, they drew up their schemes to tame the industrial revolution, until Karl Marx, sneering at their "unscientific" and vaporous dreams, began the movement that was to sweep them from the scene.

One of the first was Morelly (any other names, if he had them, are unknown), who is credited with originating the catch phrase, used with variations by most other socialists thereafter: "Each is to labor according to his ability and share according to his needs." Alarmingly liberal in some matters, Morelly felt that even incest should not be prohibited; authoritarian in other respects, he proposed that marriage should be compulsory, and that celibacy should be allowed only after the fortieth year.

More typical was Etienne Cabet, who in *Journey to Icaria* visualized, despite some romantic trimmings, a totally regimented community where the ideal of brotherhood is turned into the great relentless leveler. Since inequality of talent or intelligence is nature's fault, it is unjust to penalize the individual for it. Hence if some stand higher than others, they must be cut down to size; all dress alike, eat alike, learn alike, pray alike, and ultimately think alike. The environment is totally controlled: the city is laid out with mathematical precision, the sidewalks are covered against the rain, the streets are cleaned by special dust-collecting machines, and (Cabet shared the typical utopian's obsessive preoccupation with detail) the windows are designed to close noiselessly. People work for the state, love for the state, die for the state.

The most influential of the utopian Socialists was Charles Fourier, possibly because he approached utopia through psychology, though modern practitioners would scarcely recognize it as such. Human behavior, as he saw it, was a matter of the "passions" which, as we would put it today, had always been unduly repressed. They must be freed and harmonized with each other. In this he followed Rousseau and anticipated, however crudely, Freud. One cannot help wondering whether Freud's map of the psyche, with its division into id, ego, and superego, will a century hence seem as quaint as Fourier's map of the passions seems to us now. He counted twelve separate ones, from the "luxury" passions, corresponding to the five senses, to the "composite passion," or desire for union.

To harmonize all these passions, the proper environment is

needed, and Fourier prescribed it in minute detail as the "phalanx," an association of about fifteen hundred people on a small unit of land, self-supporting through agriculture and light industry. Fourier was obviously trying to escape bigness—the bigness of modern industry, the bigness of modern state. But he foresaw a world federation of phalanxes under a Great Chief whose residence was to be, of all places, in Constantinople.

Private property was permitted subject to certain co-operative rules. Everyone within reason was to be free to choose the kind of work he wanted, and to switch if he got bored. A very similar arrangement was to apply to choosing mates. In short, Fourier visualized a utopia of free love. He predicted that if mankind adopted his plan, it would face a glorious future of seventy thousand years, when lions would not only eat straw but draw men's carriages, when whales would pull vessels and sea water would be turned into lemonade.

In one way Fourier was the most unfortunate of utopian thinkers, for people made a major and fatal attempt to put his ideas into practice. The experiments were carried out particularly in the United States during the 1840's, when hundreds of utopian "associations" sprang up, many of them directly inspired or influenced by Fourier.

One of the most typical experiments was Brook Farm. It was set up near Boston by two noted Unitarian clerics, George Ripley and Ellery Channing, to show among other things that work need not mean industrial degradation but could go hand in hand with joy, dignity, and culture. In part the idea was that intellectuals would perform physical labor in order to free laborers for intellectual pursuits. To the regret of the founders, Ralph Waldo Emerson refused to join; he had tried physical labor and decided that it was not ordained "that a writer should dig." Charles Dana stated Brook Farm's purpose simply: "Our ulterior aim is nothing less than Heaven on Earth." He added that "the practical result we first aim at is wealth," an aim that constantly eluded them. The Brook Farmers adopted Fourier with reservations, particularly concerning his sexual theories, but their reputation suffered. After all the press could scarcely ignore the fact, regardless of what conditions actually were at Brook Farm, that in his ideal communities Fourier had provided for the entertainment of men by "Corps of Bacchae and Bayadères."

Nathaniel Hawthorne, who later wrote about it in *The Blithedale Romance,* joined Brook Farm as director of agriculture, mostly in hopes that the settlement would prosper and make him solvent. He described it caustically as "a polar Paradise," and was highly uneasy about his farm chores, especially milking. He complained about one particularly mean cow, "a transcendental

ROBERTS BROS., BOSTON 1890

heifer belonging to Miss Margaret Fuller. She is very fractious, I believe, and apt to kick over the milk pail."

Brook Farm dissolved amid a series of financial misfortunes and fires, sharing the fate of another famous community of the period, Oneida. It had been founded in Putney, Vermont, by a sometime clergyman named John Humphrey Noyes, who in 1848 moved it to Oneida, New York. From the time he attended a seminary at Andover, Noyes had been striving to reach a life of Perfection—but had fluctuated between evangelical triumphs and sordid scandals, partly because he often tried to convert prostitutes and was seldom as successful with them as they were with him. On one occasion, he asked two respectable young ladies to come to bed with him in order to test their virtue; they flunked. At Oneida he developed a system of "complex marriage" based on the notion that the foundation of Christianity is the ultimate selflessness of sharing mates. Economically, the community flourished when it was joined by Sewall Newhouse, a manufacturer who made and sold steel springs. Earlier, men and women had been forbidden to have children. When the commune started showing a profit, Noyes at last gave his followers permission to have offspring. But childbearing in an aging free-love community could only lead to confusion, jealousy, heartbreak, and eventually scandal.

All the "association" utopias were inevitably doomed, not only because of their eccentric doctrines, their amateurish administration, and their sometimes questionable devotees, but because essentially they were trying to flee, or hide, from the reality of the machine age. Similar escape attempts occurred in literature until much later. In 1890 William Morris in his *News from Nowhere* dreamed of a new London that had become a cluster of villages amid idyllic woodlands, the only remnants from the past being the Houses of Parliament, now used to store dung. In 1887 W. H. Hudson gazed into the distant future to find *A Crystal Age,* in which society resolved itself into great country estates, each a little world with its own history and traditions, presided over by a housemother who is part goddess, part queen bee, and part Mom. Although these communities were theoretically set in the future, they were really dreams of the past.

The other, the forward-marching utopias were changing with the contemporary world that produced them. More and more industrialized, they were becoming, in Lewis Mumford's phrase, merely "vast reticulations of steel and red tape."

One of the earliest of these Utopias of Steel was, appropriately enough, Stahlstadt (Steel City), and it made its appearance in an 1879 book called *The Begum's Fortune* by Jules Verne. Built in Oregon by a wicked German planner named Dr. Schultz, Stahlstadt is one vast munitions plant whose workers are attached to the factory as medieval serfs were attached to the land. Verne was deliberately creating a negative utopia, but he also put a positive one in the same story. The significant thing is that the "good" utopia is scarcely more attractive to us than the "bad" one. It is a kind of germless garden city with identical brick houses on identical plots, where wallpaper and carpeting are forbidden, to guard against bacteria, and for the same reason the city's hospitals are burned down each year.

Something similar happened a few years later in *Looking Backward* when Edward Bellamy constructed his own Steel City, or rather, Steel State. It was intended as a positive utopia, but it seems the opposite to us. The entire population works for the state in a vast labor army, and in good utopian tradition all receive credit in return for their work and thus may draw what they need from great storehouses. No money, of course; no banks; no want; no crime—for, argued Bellamy, most crime is caused by "inequality of possessions." If supreme trust in a wise elite is the first great utopian fallacy, here is the second: the notion that men need only be drafted, as it were, and issued with decent rations to make them perfect.

Yet, for all his simple-mindedness, Bellamy was a chillingly accurate prophet, even if he did not understand the meaning of his prophecy. He foretold a lot that has become reality, from Muzak and piped-in religion to the labor army. In this sense *Looking Backward* is one of the most significant of all utopias, because it makes us see the all-important point: we used to deride utopia because it was unreal; now we dread it because it *is* real.

The belief that everything was possible to science, to the machine, was the great source of Victorian optimism, but there were dissenters. One of them was Samuel Butler, who in *Erewhon* had created perhaps the first full-scale negative utopia. He brilliantly satirized his age, by exaggerating—but less than even he realized—what was possible. We are today not very far removed from the Erewhonian notion that disease is a crime while crime is only a disease. Above all, we are remarkably close to his fantasy of the machine. Well over half a century before machines learned to "think," Butler visualized what would happen if they ever did. The fact that they still lacked consciousness, he warned, meant little; after all, a mollusc also lacked consciousness, but there were other species ahead. And as machines grow more human, man becomes more machinelike. The solution in *Erewhon* called for man to destroy the machine. Years later the outcome in Karel Čapek's *R.U.R.* would be the opposite: the machines destroyed man.

HARPER 1899

The Machine Triumphant is a theme that was carried on, not too long after Butler, by H. G. Wells, and to him it suggested both hope and horror, both promise and threat. Accordingly, his visions are both positive and negative. In *A Modern Utopia* he set out deliberately to discover what could be done with the old utopian traditions in a new age, and he broke with most of them. He abandons the usual yearning for smallness and seclusion by making his a world-wide community with a common language. He allows and indeed encourages both property and money, with some limitations. Above all, Wells is concerned with freedom, which he feels all previous utopias ignored or slighted. He favors neither individualism nor socialism but a mixture of the two, with the state looming large in everyone's life, but hardly more so than we are already accustomed to.

Wells's Platonic guardians, called samurai, are a large, voluntary, ruling aristocracy subject to a rigid code of behavior. They are forbidden games, alcohol, tobacco, servants, and dramatic religion—the faith of Utopia being a kind of syncretism the basis of which is the absence of original sin. The samurai must avoid anything that accustoms the mind to applause, and once a year they must spend a week in the wilderness, without books, money, or other amenities, in order to meditate. Altogether, Huxley may have been a trifle harsh when he remarked that the Wellsian samurai "think, feel and behave like a cross between the Boy Scouts and the Society of Jesus."

Huxley obviously would have preferred the earlier, or non-Boy Scout, Wells. In the last decade of the nineteenth century Wells took several bone-chilling looks into the future that add up to a formidably negative utopia, in sharp contrast to the urbane and engaging commonwealth he put together later. In *The Time Machine* he forecast a distant scene inhabited not by a race of supermen but by a tribe of childlike, soft creatures, the Eloi, descendants of our ruling classes whose vigor declined when the need for effort vanished. Underground, in the bowels of the earth, live the Morlocks, descendants of our proletariat, who from ancient habit run the machines needed for the comfort of the privileged, but who feed on the flesh of the Eloi whom they serve. Yet another vision of the future is "A Story of the Days to Come," which anticipates Huxley's own anti-utopia by several decades. In this brave new Wellsian world, advertising is bawled everywhere from loudspeakers, deviates have their antisocial traits removed by hypnosis, dreams can be obtained to order, education is offered by telephone, food is rendered synthetic and eaten in automats, "face-molders" correct asymmetrical features, and in the end there is the Euthanasia Company always ready to be of service.

In *Men Like Gods,* written more than two decades later, Wells went to the opposite extreme and created a distinctly optimistic utopia, more or less based on evolution, which of course itself is one vast, biological utopia. In this positive mood Wells sees mankind as beginning to evolve toward a "nobler humanity, different in kind." While reading *Men Like Gods,* whose optimism revolted him thoroughly, Aldous Huxley decided to write a "derisive parody," a piece of "cynical anti-idealism" that eventually grew into *Brave New World.*

Huxley is to the negative or anti-utopia what Plato and More combined are to the positive. We are apt to be less familiar with the Republic's guardians and Utopia's jeweled toys than we are with Brave New World's Controllers, its hatched and identical humans, its sleep-conditioning, its feelies, its soma happy pills, and all the other paraphernalia of horror in the orgy-porgy of total organization. As Huxley himself has observed, mind control has become a reality in brain-washing, conditioning during sleep has been successfully attempted in experiments with sleep-teaching, Brave New World's mass pleasures that degrade and enslave the mind have their equivalent in our relentlessly distracting mass entertainment, and the soma pills of chemically induced happiness correspond to the millions upon millions of tranquilizers that our doctors prescribe every year.

Striking though these parallels are, it still takes a certain amount of straining to see *Brave New World* in our own. But it takes very little to see *1984.* George Orwell's masterpiece ranks, after *Brave New World,* as the greatest in the still somewhat specialized field of anti-utopias, and yet in a way it is not utopian at all. Big Brother and Doublethink are not, like the characters and devices of Huxley's work, cleverly extrapolated from the existing world; they *are* the existing world. They are what became of the Socialist utopia once it was subjected to Marx's "scientific" treatment. But how much ought we to blame on Marx, and how much was already present in those early revolutionary idylls and egalitarian schemes? The question must go even further back. For was not Big Brother born simultaneously with the Guardian, however noble of intent, ruling the Republic? And was not Doublethink invented with the principle that the people must be lied to for their own good?

The chief domain of Utopia today is science-fiction. The overwhelming majority of science-fiction utopias are negative, foreseeing a technologically supported totalitarianism. As is pointed out in Kingsley Amis's excellent *New Maps of Hell,* to which the following account is indebted, their villains are usually politicians

BALLANTINE BOOKS 1953

or businessmen, rarely scientists or artists. These utopias generally reflect and warn against our present world by the device of horror caricature. Advertising, for instance, is the starting point for *The Space Merchants* by Frederik Pohl and C. M. Kornbluth, a kind of Madison Avenue anti-utopia where commercials can be projected directly on the retina, where Congressmen represent not states or districts but business firms. The consumer-oriented society is the starting point of the short story "The Midas Plague" also by Pohl, who visualizes an anti-utopia of glut in which mankind is flooded with goods. True comfort, true riches, consist in *not* having to consume more than one's neighbor. In "Null-P" by William Tenn, *homo abnegus,* totally mediocre man, has taken over and is eventually domesticated by a race of intelligent Newfoundland retrievers who prize him for his stick-throwing ability. In Ray Bradbury's *Fahrenheit 451* the hero is a fireman whose duties are systematically to burn proscribed books according to a fixed schedule: "Monday burn Millay, Wednesday Whitman, Friday Faulkner."

In these anti-utopias, the true hero is always man and whether or not he physically loses, his spirit is not broken. Yet this rebellion is almost never for a detailed, positive program; it merely seeks to restore simple human values. What the rebels want to establish in all these totalitarian nightmares seems to be, as Kingsley Amis says, "a society just like our own, but with more decency and less television."

And that is basically where the matter of utopia rests today. Few, if any, serious writers attempt the form, and when they do, it is usually of the negative variety. That old negativist Aldous Huxley himself attempted a positive utopia in his novel *Island,* with generally disastrous results.

A maverick intellectual, Paul Goodman, in his recent *Utopian Essays and Practical Proposals* put forth several ideas, including the notion that first-rate writers and composers be commissioned to provide a better ceremonial for public school commencements; that the loneliness of old-age homes and orphanages might be reduced by having old ladies take care of the orphans; and that private cars should be banned in New York City. While all these may be ingenious and possibly even sensible schemes (particularly the last one), it is strange to call them utopian as Goodman does. It suggests that in our time utopia has finally come down to the level of a traffic problem. Perhaps what we really want is eighteenth-century democracy with health insurance and lots of room to park. Our true utopia, it seems, is in the past.

Henry Anatole Grunwald, who also contributed "The Disappearance of Don Juan," is foreign news editor of Time *magazine.*

Though holocausts, hatreds, and forgetfulness have obliterated vast treasures of past cultures, occasional good luck, later circumspection, and modern recovery have rescued a priceless part of our written legacy from oblivion

THE SURVIVAL OF RECORDS

By GILBERT HIGHET

The oldest surviving record comes down to us from the ancient city of Kish in Iraq, a pictograph inscribed on two sides of a limestone tablet dated c. 3500 B.C. Its images of a head, hand, foot, and threshing sledge probably record an agricultural transaction, preserved intact until its excavation in this century.

The other day I met a friend of mine, an author who is successful and ambitious. Asking him about his work, I found him profoundly depressed. In a few years, he said somberly, there won't be any books. They will all be destroyed, and there will be nobody left to read them anyway. It is difficult to argue with anyone who thinks he foresees the end of civilization; but I tried to console him. Mankind has endeavored to kill itself off before this, and its books have nearly all been destroyed. Yet as long as there was someone who wanted to read, books and records have been saved.

Nevertheless, it still strikes me with amazement when I open a book of speeches by Demosthenes and begin to hear the voice, the very syllables and cadences, of a man who died some twenty-three centuries ago. Surely it is almost miraculous that we can take up the *Aeneid* of Vergil, printed by machinery that would have astonished Vergil himself, on a material he had never seen, in a format he could scarcely have imagined, and after two millennia find that, undimmed by time and change, his poetry still sings, his mystical visions still transport us as they did his first readers, and the subtleties of his poetic architecture still hold secrets only half-discovered.

The miracle of the preservation of thought through marks on a smooth surface is commemorated every week by one of the most impressive little religious ceremonies in the world. Every Sabbath in every Jewish synagogue, a hand-written copy of the Torah, the first five books of the Bible, is taken out of its place. After a reading, the book is carried through the congregation before it is returned to the ark, and every pious Jew kisses it. It is always handwritten with a quill pen. It is always in the form of a parchment roll. Its text is always exactly the same as that of its predecessor, from which it was copied: the very letters are counted so that they may never vary by a jot, any more than the law of God Almighty can vary. By doing homage to the book in this way, the Jews express their devotion to the name of the Creator contained in the Torah; but they also, by implication, express reverence for one of man's greatest inventions—the written book.

The Jews, like the Moslems, have always carried their sacred writings with them: the book and the people have sustained each other. But among the Greek and Latin classics there are no such sacred books: the nations for whom they were written have disappeared; their very languages have assumed new shapes and sounds—remote, although not wholly different from the original tongues. How have the great books of the past survived through so many centuries?

First, we must sadly admit that many, very many, of them have been lost. In Greece and the Greek-speaking world, and later in the Roman world, there were many libraries and many hundreds of thousands of books. Literacy was more widespread in the second century of our era than it was in the eighteenth. The walls of Pompeii, covered with public announcements and private scribbles in three languages (Latin, Greek, and Oscan), show how natural and commonplace was the use of writing then. Nearly all townsfolk could read, freemen and slaves alike. Only on the farms and ranches were many people illiterate. In Egypt excavators now dig up large private book collections buried under the sand near villages where today few of the fellahin own a single book, or could read it if they did.

Although some authors of antiquity composed only a few works, to which they gave all their life's energy, there were many who produced an amazing number of them. The comedian Aristophanes left fifty-four plays. Aeschylus, first of the great tragic dramatists, wrote at least eighty. Livy's history of Rome ran into one hundred and forty-two volumes; and such polygraphs were not exceptional. But of many of the most famous authors we have only a few scanty though precious relics. It is as though we had the titles of all Shakespeare's plays, with some fragments quoted from most of them, but possessed complete only *Hamlet, Henry V, A Midsummer-Night's Dream,* and *As You Like It.* Of Aristophanes' half a hundred comedies, we have just eleven. Of Aeschylus's four score plays, only seven survive. We have a summary of virtually all of Livy's Roman history, so that we know what he covered in each volume, but only thirty-five of his one hundred and forty-two volumes remain. And while these great writers have survived in however meager a proportion, dozens of others have vanished almost without a trace. Aristophanes was only one of a large school of competing comic dramatists. From quotations and allusions, we know the names of about a hundred and seventy poets of the "Old Comedy" (the group to which Aristophanes belonged) with 1,483 titles of their plays. Except Aristophanes, not one survives. Where is his great rival, boozy old Cratinus? Where is the energetic Eupolis, whom Horace linked with the other two in a gay triad? Gone, except for a few jokes, some famous passages preserved in quotation, and many play titles. It is delightful to look through the titles and reflect how much fun the Athenians had in the fifth century before Christ; it is painful to remember how much of it has vanished.

But not all. It would scarcely be worth studying classical literature if it were a heap of insignificant debris. It is not. It is like a city which has been bombed and partially burned, so that whole sections are in ruins and some streets with their houses are irrecoverable; but at its heart many of the most important and beautiful public buildings stand unscathed, full of statues and pictures and memories, while others, although damaged, retain a noble tower or one magnificent wing. The two epics of Homer (or of the two Homers) are safe. All Vergil's poetry is intact. The works of Plato are complete and have even acquired some "Platonic" forgeries in the meantime. We have all that Horace ever published. We can read virtually all of Lucretius and Terence and Catullus in Latin, virtually all of Demosthenes

This antique double exposure is a page from one of the most famous of palimpsest ("rescraped") manuscripts. During the Dark Ages it was a common practice to scrape the writing from unread books and use the valuable parchment over again. But the ghost of the old text often lingered beneath the new, waiting to be discovered by the scholars of a later age (nowadays aided by chemicals and infrared photographs). In this case a fourth-century manuscript of Cicero's On the State *(double columns) was found to underlie a late seventh-century copy of a work by Saint Augustine. Until the Vatican librarian Angelo Mai recovered it from these pages in 1822, the Cicero was known only in fragmentary form.*

and Thucydides and Herodotus in Greek, and virtually all of a few other first-rate writers in either tongue. Furthermore, we have the complete works of a number of authors who, although not "classics" either in their own time or now, are amusing, shocking, informative, or creatively eccentric. We do not have too many of the classical books from Greece and Rome, but we have much of the best.

The great books of Greece and Rome were written down between 800 B.C. and A.D. 450. They were first printed and disseminated to many modern readers between A.D. 1450 and 1550. Once printed, they were likely to survive because they were so good or because there were now so many copies of them (duplication means preservation). But between the distant centuries when the classics were composed and the comparatively recent centuries when they were reproduced by the man with the machine, grave obstacles and recurrent perils often threatened to obliterate them.

First came the danger that haunts us all. Anyone born since 1900 has grown up with it always in his mind. It is the great destroyer, the waster, the terrible simplifier—war. It is always more violent than we expect. It is capricious. In the conflict of human wills, deliberation and choice and purposive action are often sacrificed to sheer destructive energy. When the Crusaders were sacking Constantinople in 1204, a drunken soldier was seen tearing up the sacred books of the Hagia Sophia.

King Matthias Corvinus of Hungary (1440–1490) had collected a magnificent library of manuscripts, some written for him by distinguished Italian calligraphers and some bought by his agents in Greece and Asia Minor (page 275). Part of it was captured by the Turks in 1541 during their advance into central Europe and some specimens were sent back to Istanbul. The others were left in storage, damaged by fire and carelessness, recaptured in 1688, and divided up among the conquerors. And yet a few manuscripts of the original library still remained together—at least until the end of the nineteenth century—in the Grand Seraglio at Istanbul, after the drums and tramplings of four centuries.

The most famous of all libraries in ancient times was the collection at Alexandria. In the Western world it was the first large public library; it was the cradle of literary scholarship and of responsible publishing; it was part of the earliest university. In one form or another it seems to have lived for seven hundred years, although many doubtful legends have grown up around it, and its final destruction is wrapped in silence almost total.

The library, along with the Home of the Muses (or Museum), was founded by Ptolemy I, Alexander the Great's marshal and his successor as king of Egypt. Its administrators strove to have the best, the most authoritative, copies of all important books, collated and catalogued with utmost care. After two hundred and fifty years it was burned during Julius Caesar's difficult struggle to displace the twelfth

Ptolemy and set up his own mistress Cleopatra as monarch. Mark Antony, who succeeded Caesar both as the real ruler of Egypt and as Cleopatra's lover, gave her as a replacement two hundred thousand books from the rival library of Pergamum in Asia Minor; these were stored in the sanctuary of Serapis, and this new library survived until the Empire went Christian. (Tertullian says that the original manuscript of the Hebrew Scriptures translated into Greek, the Septuagint, was one of its treasures.) Then the pagan sanctuaries were turned into churches, and Christians and pagans fought a cultural and religious war in the streets. In A.D. 414 the Christian historian Orosius wrote that the stacks of the great library "were emptied by our own men in our own time." If anything survived for the Caliph Omar to condemn as fuel to heat the public baths in A.D. 640 (according to a late legend), it was only a group of departmental libraries.

The imperial library of Constantinople, in an even more turbulent city, had still more drastic adventures. Its founder, the Emperor Constantine, intended it to contain both Christian and pagan works and caused fine copies of rare books to be made on durable vellum. Revolt, civil strife, and invasion struck the library again and again, but it was constantly restored by the Greek passion for culture. A rebellion and a fire in the fifth century A.D. destroyed it, with over a hundred thousand books, including one monstrous object, a copy of Homer's two epics written in gold letters on a snake's gut one hundred twenty feet long. Three of the most famous Greek statues perished in the same blaze. Rebuilt, refilled, reopened, the library was closed again for almost a century during the religious conflict over the worship of images and holy pictures. It was burned and looted, at least in part, by the Fourth Crusaders in 1203–1204. Restored once again, it was still in existence when Constantinople fell to the Turks in 1453. The Archbishop of Kiev, an eyewitness of the invasion, said that more than 120,000 books were destroyed. And yet many precious manuscripts survived in private collections. Lost in the outbuildings or substructures of some old mosque, some deserted church or forgotten barracks, there still may lie, in sealed jars or dust-covered chests, priceless relics of the classical past, more precious than the Hebrew manuscripts found not long ago in the Genizah, or storeroom, of a synagogue near Cairo. One of our foundations, which find it so difficult to spend all their money, could make its name world-famous by financing a really successful document hunt in the chief cities of the former Turkish Empire.

The invading barbarians from the North, after many attacks, at last split the Greco-Roman world into two parts, an eastern and a western realm. In the west, those who were the heirs of the Roman Empire spoke Latin and tried to teach it to their conquerors. In the east, the language was Greek. For some centuries the civilized Mediterranean world had been bilingual by practice and by sympathy; but after A.D. 500 or so, nobody in the west could speak or write

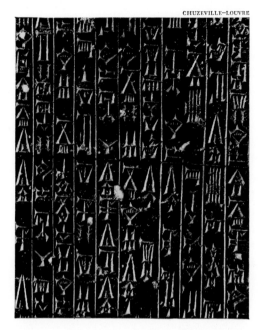

Many ancient kings have achieved immortality by committing their boasts and biographies to stone. Augustus's terse record of his achievements was carved, among other places, on a temple wall in what is now Ankara (above). The great Babylonian king Hammurabi (1728–1686 B.C.) insured the permanence of his famous law code by having it engraved on a diorite stele (left). A lesser monarch, Idri-mi of Alalakh (c. 1400 B.C.) is known to us only because he covered his own statue with his autobiography (right). The Persian Darius put an inscription on a gold plaque (below) in three languages: Old Persian, Babylonian, and Elamite.

Above are portions of three famous papyri discovered in inexhaustible Egypt. From the top, they are: Aristotle's Constitution of Athens, *copied in the 1st century and found in 1888; the speeches of Hyperides, found in 1847 and the first lost work of classical literature to be recovered in papyrus scrolls; and* The Tale of the Two Brothers, *the world's oldest fairy tale, written in Egyptian hieratic script in 1220 B.C. The Greek fragment at right, a label, bears the tantalizing words "Complete Pindar," but the book it accompanied was never found.*

Greek and nobody in the east could speak or write Latin. Now and then one still hears stories about Irish monks who alone were able to keep the knowledge of Greek alive in the west. Laudable, if true; but unfortunately false. An occasional scribe might copy out an occasional Greek word during the Dark Ages in the west, but the tradition of reading, understanding, and transmitting the Greek tongue—although it was the language in which the Gospels and the Acts and the Epistles were written—virtually died out (with the exception of a few lonely geniuses such as Grosseteste and Erigena) for a thousand years.

The second danger that confronted the Greek and Roman classics was not violent destruction but peaceful change. Nowadays it is almost impossible to purchase the piano works of Alexander Scriabin or to find scores of the music of Lully. Scriabin died in 1915; most of his music has been allowed to go out of print. Much of Lully still remains in manuscript, unpublished, unperformed, unknown. In the same way, those books which ceased to interest the Greek and Roman reading public ceased to be copied and studied, and were therefore not transmitted from one generation to another. After Vergil's *Aeneid* was issued, it was accepted at once as the great epic poem in the Latin language. It was learned at school, it was read for pleasure, it was admired and imitated. Naturally, it displaced all earlier epic poems, even the *Annals* of Vergil's greatest predecessor, Ennius. For a few generations, Ennius was respected, although little read. Then he was forgotten; his poem vanished. Nothing of it is left now, except fragments quoted by Roman scholars to illustrate oddities of archaic style—five hundred fifty lines in all, no fragment larger than a page. Only four poets of the early Roman Republic have survived entire, or almost entire: Lucretius, the philosophical missionary; Catullus, the brilliant lyricist; and the comic playwrights Plautus and Terence. All the others were neglected and eventually disappeared. No doubt some of them were trivial and others crude, but there were several masterful writers among them, such as the satirist Lucilius, and several lively works in minor genres, such as the Atellan farces, which we should dearly love to be able to read.

There was another habit of taste that tended to make books obsolete in the ancient world. This was sheer laziness. Partly to cater to lazy adult readers, and partly to create handy texts for use in schools, editors in later Greece and Rome reduced the complete works of many distinguished authors to small, neat anthologies, assimilable with little effort and easily portable. Thus, out of the eighty-odd plays by Aeschylus, the Seven Best were selected; out of more than a hundred by Sophocles, the Seven Best. These selections ousted the complete works, which fewer and fewer readers requested or even knew. So all the other plays of Aeschylus and Sophocles have vanished. With Euripides we are luckier because we also have part of one set of Complete Works.

If war is the supreme destroyer of books, it also, in another sense, creates them—as happened when the sack of Rome by Alaric and the Goths in A.D. 410 inspired Saint Augustine to write The City of God. *He conceived it as a reply to those who argued that the disaster, which in effect ended classical civilization, was a retribution for abolishing pagan worship. This French miniature was painted exactly a thousand years later, and shows Augustine offering his book to the pope even as the Goths are raging through the streets.*

Konstantin von Tischendorf

The page above is from what is probably one of the two oldest Bibles in the world, the fourth-century Codex Sinaiticus discovered by the German scholar Von Tischendorf on Mount Sinai in 1844 and brought by him to Russia fifteen years later. It is now in the British Museum, except for forty-three leaves in Leipzig and some fragments elsewhere. Its only rival for antiquity is the Codex Vaticanus of roughly the same date. Older than either, however, is the scrap of papyrus at left bearing part of verses 31–33 of the eighteenth chapter of the Gospel of Saint John. It was found in Egypt in 1920 by Bernard P. Grenfell and has since been dated to the first half of the second century A.D.—making it the earliest known fragment of any part of the New Testament.

Three thousand years after it was buried in the tomb of an Egyptian high priest, this papyrus Book of the Dead (a sort of guidebook to the next world) was unrolled in 1960 at the British Museum. It proved to be twenty-two feet long and, except for some wear at the beginning, in excellent condition.

But aside from these three, we have no Greek tragedies at all. Many of the lost books of Greece and Rome were not destroyed: they were allowed to slip into oblivion.

There were two further hazards that the classics had to survive before they could reach the age of printing. One was a change of format, the other was a change of script. The two changes sound unimportant, but they drastically altered our intellectual history.

Suppose that in 1970 all publishers decided to abandon publishing books in their present form and began to issue them only on microfilms; and suppose that we all accepted this, rearranging our homes around microfilm-readers and storage cabinets. If so, all the new books would be produced exclusively on microfilm. All important old books would be transferred to microfilm: the Bible, the encyclopedias, the scientific and technical manuals, the law books; and Shakespeare, Milton, Pope, Shelley, Keats . . . but who else?

At once the question becomes difficult. Should Butler's *Hudibras* be microfilmed? and Langland's *Piers Plowman*, which nobody reads except specialists? and Cowley's epic on King David, which nobody reads at all? A selective grid has been created. Through it must pass any book in the English language that is to reach the postmicrofilm future. The rest will be kept in storage for a while, will be forgotten, and in a few generations will fall into dust. (We have in our own lifetime seen a similar series of changes in recorded music, from the old phonograph cylinders to the flat 78 rpm discs, then to LP discs; and now tape threatens to make all discs obsolete.)

Suppose also that we were to introduce a new phonetic alphabet, say in 1970: all our important books would have to be transliterated into the new simplifaid speliŋ. Within a couple of generations only a few experts and antiquarians would be able to read the older script. All the books that remained untranscribed would be neglected, difficult, remote. Soon they would sink into decay and oblivion.

Now, these two changes actually took place during the centuries after the Greek and Latin classics were composed and while they were being transmitted to us: the format and material of books changed, and then the scripts in which they were written.

In the flourishing days of Greece and Rome nearly all books were written on long narrow strips of papyrus, in parallel columns arranged from left to right. When not being read, the strip was rolled up around a central rod and (although its material was thinner and its dimensions generally smaller) looked rather like the "scrolls of the law" kept in Jewish synagogues today. Although brittle, papyrus is quite a good material for books: if it does not get damp, it will remain firm and legible for a long time. The dithyramb of Timotheus can be easily read today although it was written on papyrus three hundred years before the birth of Christ. However, the specially treated leather called parchment (named for Pergamum in western Asia Minor, where it was perfected about 170 B.C.) is far more durable. Since it has a finer, smoother surface than papyrus, it will take smaller and clearer letters. And furthermore, a book with separate pages sewn together at one edge is far easier to use than a long continuous strip which must be laboriously unrolled in order to find and read a single column of writing.

Therefore the Greeks and Romans gradually stopped using papyrus and gave up the roll format. (Actually, "volume," which comes from the same root as "revolve," means a roll. The word for the flat book with pages is "codex.") This change-over was not at first encouraged by governmental

THE GREEKS
HAD A PICTURE
FOR IT

This stylish battle scene is proof that the lavish picture book is no recent invention, for it comes from what must have been an extremely handsome copy of the Iliad *produced—possibly in Constantinople—between the third and fifth centuries* A.D. *It is the earliest extant example of a Greek illustrated book, and in its original state it probably consisted of some 380 vellum leaves. Of these, only fifty-two separate fragments survive—and they only because a thirteenth-century collector who evidently preferred the pictures to the text cut some of them out and pasted paper over the backs. They came to rest in the Ambrosian library in Milan, where they were bound and catalogued merely as "a book of pictures." In 1819 Father Angelo Mai, the expert who discovered the Cicero palimpsest on page 259, peeled off the paper and recognized the text underneath as part of the* Iliad. *The inscriptions and captions had been added by later hands and were often inaccurate. This plate—which Mai numbered XXIX—shows the Greeks and Trojans in battle. At the left young Teukros is being congratulated on his successes by Agamemnon (wrongly identified as Diomedes), while overhead float the goddesses Athena, Hera, and Iris.*

266

ΠΡΟΛΟΦΥΓΑΤΟΔΑΚΡΥΧΕΟΝΤΑ
ΟΝΕΙΜΜΕΝΑΙΟΥΛΑΠΟΛΕΣΣΟΑΙ
ΕΣΕΛΑΣΙΟΤΑΤΟΝΠΕΤΕΗΝΩΝ
ΝΕΣΣΙΤΕΚΟΣΕΛΑΦΟΙΟΤΑΧΕΙΗΣ
ΠΕΡΙΚΑΛΛΕΪΚΑΒΒΑΛΕΝΘΡΟΝ
ΙΖΗΝΙΠΡΕΖΕΣΣΚΟΝΑΧΑΙΟΙ
ΤΑΓΕΚΑΙΟΣΗΛΑΥΟΣΝΠΟΡΝΙΣ
ΣΙΟΟΤΟΝΛΙΝΗΙΙΣΑΝΤΟΛΕΧΑΤΙΤ
ΡΑΛΑΝΙΑΣΩΝΙΠΙΣΑΛΑΣΘΩΛΙΡΕΡ

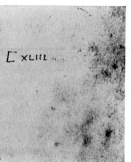

Since all books were copied by hand until the invention of printing, opportunities for error were limitless. At the left, in the middle of the sixth line down, is an example from the codex containing Tri-malchio's Dinner *by the Roman satirist* Petronius. *The copyist, who was probably a monk, has written* abbas secreuit, *"the abbot isolated him"; but the phrase in the original was no doubt* ab asse creuit, *which means "he started with a nickel."*

authority and took quite a long time. But the Roman law-yers liked the codex shape because it was so easy to consult. The Christians, too, who wished to read parallel passages in the four different gospel narratives and to compare the prophecies of the Old Testament with their fulfillments in the New, preferred the large book which could be opened out flat; and scribes, both pagan and Christian, found that a parchment page would take graceful script and elaborate decoration far more readily than papyrus. The eminent British papyrologist C. H. Roberts suggests that the change in format was connected with the first written versions of the life of Jesus. Saint Mark, author of the earliest gospel, wrote it in Rome in the handy format of a parchment note-book with pages. This he took to Alexandria, and there (al-though they continued to use the cheap local material, papy-rus), the early Christians grew accustomed to having their sacred writings in the form of a flat-paged book. By A.D. 400 the roll was obsolescent, whether in papyrus or in parchment. Any book that had not been recopied into the new format could survive only by exceptional good luck. And some Greek and Roman classics now lack their beginnings be-cause the outside of the papyrus roll, with the first few columns of writing on it, had perished before it could be transcribed. Others are only part of a once larger set. Aris-totle's *Poetics* was a two-volume work, one part dealing with tragedy and the other with comedy; but the second was lost before it reached the codex form and will now never be known—unless through a fortunate find.

All Greek and Roman books were, of course, written by hand. Great changes took place in Greek and Roman script between the fourth and the eighth centuries of the Christian era. In classical times the Greeks wrote most of their im-portant books in what we call capital letters, without much punctuation and often with no spaces between words. (The Romans, after hesitating for some time, followed them.) But, after many experiments both in the Greek world of eastern Europe, Asia Minor, and Egypt, and in the Roman west, a radical change to a script more like our own was carried

through: a script in which words are separated from one another and most of the letters are unemphatic, curved, and small (hence called "minuscule"), while only the emphatic letters beginning sentences, lines of verse, and proper names are capitals, or majuscules.

Then and thereafter all the books written like this, "ARMAVIRVMQVECANOTROIAEQVIPRIMVSABORIS," had to be copied in the new script, with its word divisions and em-phatic capitals: "*Arma uirumque cano, Troiae qui primus ab oris. . . .*" * But the work of transcription from one form of writing to another was laborious and difficult. A scribe who was accustomed to reading and writing "*Italiam fato profugus Lauinaque uenit*," sometimes made mistakes in reading and transcribing "ITALIAMFATOPROFVGVSLAVINAQVE-VENIT." Therefore when a scholar today sits down to edit a Greek or Roman book, one of his most important jobs is to reconstruct the various phases of copying and recopying through which it has been transmitted and to determine just what types of error were liable to be introduced at each transition. When a sentence in a Greek or Roman author looks doubtful or senseless, one of the first devices that scholars try is to write it out INTHEOLDVNDIVIDEDCAPITALS, and then see whether the misreading of one or two letters, or a failure to separate the words correctly, led to the error.

My favorite mistake of this kind is a matter of word sep-aration. At the vulgar millionaire's dinner party in Petro-nius's *Satyrica,* the guests are discussing a friend who has just died. "Ah, he had a good life," they say, "the abbot isolated him, and he died a millionaire." There were no abbots in the days of Petronius, and anyhow the second clause is meaningless. In majuscules the phrase reads ABBASSECREVIT. Divide the words differently and drop one superfluous letter, and you get *ab asse creuit,* "he started with a nickel" (see above).

These particular ordeals—the transference of books from one type of script to another and from one format to another —were mechanical hazards to the survival of literature. There was another, far more destructive, which depended on

---

* The Romans had no sound in their language corresponding to our *v.* They used small *u* and capital *V* for both the vowel-sound *oo* (as in *IVSTVS, iustus*) and the consonant *w* (*VIR, uir*).

The Italian writer Giovanni Boccaccio (*portrayed here by Andrea del Castagno*) *paid a celebrated visit to the monastery of Monte Cassino (below) in, most probably, the winter of 1370. According to one of his disciples, he wept in despair at the neglect of its once-great library and was given some books to take back to Florence with him (it has been suggested that he simply smuggled them out). Among them may well have been a great eleventh-century codex that turned up in Florence about that time. This invaluable book contained the only surviving copies of Books I-V of the* Histories *of Tacitus and Books XI-XVI of his* Annals; *Apuleius's* Metamorphoses, *better known as* The Golden Ass, *the only Latin novel that has come down to us complete; and two less important works by Apuleius.*

A. RUSCONI–*Montecassino*, 1929

DOMINVS IOHANNES BOCCACCIVS

269

the will of men. This was censorship. In pagan Greece we hear very little of censorship: although the emissaries of Antipater brought Demosthenes to his death, they made no effort to destroy his speeches. The emperors of Rome were more touchy. Even the clement Augustus felt himself compelled to exile the orator Cassius Severus and burn his books, which were full of personal attacks on the Roman aristocracy and the imperial court. Labienus's history of the civil war, which treated Julius Caesar as a traitor to the Republic, was destroyed; and, rather than survive his work, the historian killed himself.

The Christians, although considered an antisocial group by the authorities, were at first not known to possess any books worth destroying. But in the last of the pagan persecutions (A.D. 303) Diocletian ordered the Scriptures to be burned. That persecution, however, soon ended; and we know of no Christian books which were irrevocably lost in it.

A generation later the Christians came to power. Soon they were destroying the books of the pagans. Because of this policy, although we possess a good deal of Christian propaganda from the early centuries, no pagan counter-propaganda is preserved intact. The great Neo-Platonic philosopher Porphyry wrote a destructive analysis of the Chris-

tian doctrine and the Christian Scriptures in fifteen volumes. It was burned by imperial order, and only a few fragments, quoted by his Christian opponents, now remain.

In the Christian church there was always a sharp division between those who thought all pagan literature vicious and dangerous and would gladly have consigned it to annihilation, and those who believed that some of it was potentially good so that it could, under proper guidance, be used for teaching and study. Christians of the first type were responsible for much wholesale abolition of the Greek and Roman classics. Christians of the second type selected most of the books we now possess, copied them, taught them in schools, and so preserved them for the age of printing.

Of the many thousands of plays enjoyed by Greeks and Romans, all were allowed to rot away except eighty-one: forty-three tragedies (thirty-three Greek and ten Roman) and thirty-eight comedies (eleven Greek and twenty-seven Roman). One more complete Greek comedy and large fragments of others have been found in the last seventy years: these were not, however, transmitted through the ages by copying, but preserved as though in a time capsule. Drama was particularly repellent to the early Christians, for many reasons. They therefore banned plays. The professional

THE
LAURENTIAN
LIBRARY

Whether it was Boccaccio or someone else who saved the Tacitus-Apuleius codex from decay at Monte Cassino, the world has reason to be grateful. It found a home (beside an earlier codex, from Germany, containing the first six books of Tacitus's Annals*) in Florence's magnificent Laurentian library. Here the books were piled up on carved lecterns (left), with shelf lists at the ends, and secured by chains. Now there is only one to a desk and they are all protected by glass. At the right is a page from Apuleius's* Golden Ass—*a portion, in fact, of the charming story of Cupid and Psyche, which became famous in this version.*

theatre ceased to exist: for a thousand years men forgot the full power and meaning of drama, and the few plays that were permitted to survive were preserved mainly as models of fine Greek and Latin poetic and conversational style.

The pagan Greeks and Romans had also loved lyric poetry, which embodies or evokes song and the dance. Many of their lyric poems were loving glorifications of carnal experience: an invitation to drink ("the snow is deep outside and life is short") or rapturous desire for a beautiful body ("my eyes dazzle, a delicate flame runs through my limbs"). Others were hymns doing honor to pagan deities. Such poems were particularly hateful to devout Christians, so that the vast majority of them were allowed to perish. In Latin we have four books of songs by Horace and half a book by Catullus. In Greek almost all lyric poetry has vanished (or had vanished until the recent discoveries began): only Pindar survived, and only his Victory Odes. The rest disappeared, and even the Victory Odes came through the Dark Ages in one manuscript alone.

There was one curious way of survival for classical books, although it led through apparent destruction. For the sake of economy, scribes used to scrape or wash off the ink from pages on which a book had already been written and inscribe another book upon the cleaned surface. This could be done with papyrus, but it was both easier and more profitable with the tough surface of parchment. Usually it was a pagan book that was erased, and the Bible or a work of Christian divinity was written on the palimpsest, or cleaned-off, pages. But traces of the old writing would still remain legible underneath.

For instance: one of the best books by Cicero was his dialogue *On the State,* in which he discussed the rival claims of democracy, aristocracy, dictatorship (or monarchy), and a mixed constitution in which the powers should balance one another. He published it in 51 B.C. It was much admired and long read, but during the Dark Ages it vanished. Some medieval writers quote *On the State* as though they had actually handled a copy; but such citations are very shady evidence, for they might be secondhand or thirdhand. The great book hunters of the Renaissance were never able to discover a copy, although it was on their list of the Most Wanted Books.

However, in 1819, Angelo Mai, an expert in discovering old books beneath later books on a palimpsest surface, was appointed head of the Vatican library. There he discovered a commentary on the Psalms by Saint Augustine, which had been inscribed in the northern Italian monastery of Bobbio in the uncials of the late seventh century, over a manuscript of Cicero's *On the State* inscribed in the taller capitals of an earlier era (see page 259). Cicero's words could still be read and Father Mai published them in 1822. The book was incomplete, but at least a quarter of it was there. How many forgotten libraries still contain forgotten copies of forgotten works of doctrine, beneath which there sleep great classical masterpieces?

If you wish information to survive for many centuries, however, cut it on stone or bake it in clay; you can even paint it, if the surface is durable and protected from weather. Do not try casting it in metal, for someone will almost certainly melt it down.

The Emperor Augustus wrote his own autobiography, listing his chief honors, benefactions, and victories. It was deposited at the Home Hearth of Rome, with the Vestal Virgins, and a version in bronze was set upon his mausoleum in Rome. Both the original and the metal transcript have vanished. But a stone-carved copy was found in 1555 on the walls of a mosque in Ankara (see page 261); since then, two more copies, fragmentary but helpful, have turned up in southern Turkey. Only through these bits of stone do we know what one of the greatest rulers in history considered his greatest achievements.

Fifteen hundred years before him the king of a little state in what is now the Turkish frontier province of Hatay, after an adventurous and successful career, composed his own life story. His name was Idri-mi, and he was king of Alalakh in his time. He possessed less taste and less money than Augustus, so he had it carved upon his own statue—not even upon an epigraphic tablet, but over his actual face and his hard-earned regal robes (see page 261). Gazing out from eyes of black inlaid stone, his effigy sat enthroned in a temple for two centuries, speaking his adventures to those who could read. Then, in 1194 B.C., his kingdom was invaded by the northern barbarians called the Peoples of the Sea. His statue was wrenched from its throne and smashed into fragments. But after the invasion had passed over, a loyal courtier of the fallen monarchy crept back and salvaged the statue of the King, and buried it with respect. And there, underground, it was discovered by Leonard Woolley in 1939, and its long-silent boasts were read, and its eyes looked out again on a changed world with the same blank arrogance as before. His name and fame were forgotten; yet the stone that carried his message remained, with an immortality for which he could scarcely have hoped.

Two hundred years after Augustus, another public benefactor, on a smaller scale, went to a stonecutter with a document to be perpetuated. He was an elderly gentleman who lived in the small Greek-speaking city of Oenoanda in Lycia. Now it is a lonely heap of ruins in Turkey; then it was prosperous, civilized, but (the old gentleman thought) not quite happy enough. He was a devoted adherent of Epicurus. Epicureanism had taught him that the gods have no interest in this troublesome little earth; that terrifying phenomena such as illness and earthquakes and comets are all explicable, not through divine malevolence, but through nature; and that the duty of man on this planet is to cultivate his garden, keep quiet, and be happy. Old Diogenes, as he was called, had had a heart attack. He determined to use some of his remaining money and energy in showing his fellow citizens and their descendants the road to happiness. So he had a huge inscription cut and set up in the central square of his little city, explaining the chief tenets of the Epicurean doctrine. Now, all the voluminous works of Epicurus himself have perished; we have nothing from his own hand except three letters and some fragments and apophthegms. But the inscription set up by old Diogenes of Oenoanda, rediscovered by explorers and read by scholars in the nineteenth century, is one of the chief witnesses to an important philosophical creed that is not yet dead.

Laws and state announcements were often displayed on stone, for permanence and publicity. The earliest Greek legislation in existence is the code of Gortyn: it was incised on the curving stone wall of the odeum and still stands, perfectly legible, among the ruins of that city in central Crete. The names of Roman magistrates, some of them unrecorded in history books, appear on tablets of stone; so do the sums paid by the subject-allies of Athens to her imperial treasury; and so, too, the last effort of Roman bureaucratic government, the gigantic edict of Diocletian fixing the price of virtually every object of commerce throughout the Western world.

Records cut on stone or cast in metal were intended to survive as long as possible. Books passed from hand to hand and constantly recopied were deliberately kept alive. But there is a huge and steadily growing assemblage of documents that were, in the eyes of those who wrote them and used them, quite temporary. Many of them were actually thrown out as rubbish. Yet, by a combination of good luck and crazy chance, they have survived and become valuable. These are things written on ephemeral substances like papyrus and clay.

The records found in Mycenaean palaces (first in Crete) and deciphered by Michael Ventris in 1952, were apparently scratched on clay tablets that were not even fired: they became permanent only when the palaces were burned down.* Almost all of the papyri written in Greek or Roman lettering that we now have were found quite literally in rubbish dumps or in the ruins of abandoned houses. Since it scarcely ever rains in Egypt, they lay quite comfortably beneath the dry earth until modern searchers dug them up. The modern Egyptians thought it was about as stupid as digging in Western dumps for tin cans, but they co-operated, for a

* See "Homer's Age of Heroes" beginning on page 8.

wage, and even imitated the excavators when they found how valuable the rubbish was. In one day's work at Oxyrhynchus (one hundred twenty miles south of Cairo) Bernard P. Grenfell and A. S. Hunt got thirty-six basketfuls of papyrus rolls out of one mound alone. These had apparently been discarded as worthless.

Some papyri have been preserved because they were deliberately buried. One of the oldest Greek literary manuscripts, containing the only known copy of a dithyrambic poem by Timotheus, was rescued in this way. It is an absurdly bad poem (although interesting to literary connoisseurs); however, someone prized it, for it was discovered in a leather pouch, laid carefully in the coffin of a dead Greek soldier buried in Egypt. And a truly magnificent copy of Book II of Homer's *Iliad*, now in the Bodleian library, was set in a coffin as a pillow beneath the head of a young woman, whose fine skull bones, small regular teeth, and black hair make us believe she was a beauty: certainly she was beloved. Other papyri—mainly letters, accounts, and official documents, though including a few treasures of literature—were found glued together or squeezed tight with water, to make cheap mummy cases molded to the shape of the corpse. (Out of one of these cases came part of the lost tragedy *Antiope*, by Euripides.) Even stranger were the finds at Tebtunis, where Grenfell and Hunt came on a cemetery of sacred crocodiles. One dead sacred crocodile is very like another, and the job of excavating these saurian mummies soon palled. Eventually a workman lost his temper and smashed one of them to pieces. Then it appeared that the crocodiles, too, were incased in molded papyri, and some even had rolls stuffed into their mouths "and other cavities." From such absurd hiding places do we recover the records of the past.

We have as yet no idea of the treasures that are hidden in the dry sands of Egypt and the neighboring countries. The oldest Latin papyrus ever found and the oldest text of Cicero (part of his most famous set of speeches), written down not long after his death, is now in Leipzig: it was bought from Egyptian dealers in the Fayum in 1926— and where did *they* get it? In 1945 a Gnostic library of thirteen volumes was found in Upper Egypt, containing, among other things, a Gospel in Coptic, adapted from a Christian work written in Greek, which evidently preserved some beautiful traditional words of Jesus. And an Oxford expert once told me, with affliction in his eyes, that among a pile of papyrus fragments he was classifying he had found a label (see page 262) bearing, in Greek, the simple words:

COMPLETE

PINDAR

In vain I besought him to go back to the collection and look through it again. "No," he said gloomily, "it isn't there. It must have been on the site in Egypt. But perhaps the excavator missed it when he was digging, or it had already been found and lost again, or someone stole it and sold it in Alexandria. It may turn up in twenty years. It may turn up tomorrow. It may be lying at the back of a drawer forgotten."

Last, most absurd, and yet most natural of all the hazards through which the classics had to pass was the barrier of human stupidity. When barbarism comes to outweigh culture, through foreign invasion or social revolution or deliberately nurtured sloth and ignorance, works of art are often taken to be "useless" and destroyed. In waves of materialism and in revolutions, everything old is apt to be judged obsolete. It is a barrier to progress; or it is lumber; or it is reactionary; or it is inedible and unspendable—away with it! Only recently the commissioner of antiquities in modern Greece, Spyridon Marinatos, told a sad story of the Second World War. A farmer in the western Peloponnesus was digging a well. Twenty feet down he came upon a stone box. He smashed in its lid. Inside there was a big object "like a bundle," dark in color and crumbly in texture. He thought he saw letters written on it. He informed the police, who informed the local director of antiquities; but for some time they could not get out to the farm. It was 1944–1945, and Communist squads were trying to control the roads. When at last the director was able to reach the farm, the object was gone. The farmer had thrown it on the dunghill "because it was not a treasure: it looked like dung and it fell to pieces quite soon." Others, however, had seen "many letters" on it and said that, although fragile, it held together on the dunghill for some days. Clearly it was a book roll: papyrus, or more probably parchment; clearly it was precious to the man who buried it in a stone casket; certainly it would have been precious to us. But it was of no use to the farmer, and it is gone.

And so it has always been. Boccaccio, who was a great booklover and book finder, once visited the monastery of Monte Cassino (see page 269). He was particularly eager to see the library, with all its treasures of handwritten books. Very humbly he asked one of the monks for admission to it. "Walk up," said the monk, "it's open." It was. It had no door; grass was growing on the window sills; the shelves, the benches, and the books themselves were shrouded in thick dust. Some of them, he found, had lost pages or even whole quires, others had their margins cut off. Boccaccio wept. He cried tears of pity "that the work and study of so many illustrious geniuses should have fallen into the hands of scoundrels." As he left, he asked a monk how such valuable books could have been so odiously mutilated. "Well," said the monk, "some of the brothers wanted to earn a few pennies: so they took a page and scraped off the writing and made little psalters to sell to children; and from the page margins they made gospels and breviaries and sold them to women."

When a bibliophile sees good books neglected and on the road to destruction, his first impulse is to rescue them. Say not "steal." " 'Convey' the wise it call," as Pistol says in *The Merry Wives*. Some splendid books from Monte Cassino are now in Florence. If it was not Boccaccio who "conveyed" them there, it was an even more fanatical booklover, Niccolò Niccoli; or an agent of his and of the house of Medici. One of these manuscripts alone—bless the hand that saved it— is the only surviving book that contains Tacitus's account of the civil war after Nero's suicide and of the reigns of Claudius and Nero; it also has Apuleius's wonderful romance *The Metamorphoses*, sometimes called *The Golden Ass* (see page 271). This magnificent codex, written in the eleventh century, now rests peacefully in the Laurentian Library, above the cloister of the church of San Lorenzo. Near it is the only surviving manuscript of the first six books of another work by Tacitus, the *Annals*, found in Germany. Had these two manuscripts not been "conveyed," they might well have been cut up into amulets, and we should have lost one of the greatest historians who ever wrote of absolutism and the degeneracy of despotic power.

In 1844 a young Biblical scholar, Konstantin von Tischendorf, visited the remote monastery of Saint Catherine on Mount Sinai. There he found a great old book reduced almost to the same state as those which Boccaccio discovered in Cassino. It was a manuscript of the Bible, written in beautiful clear script between A.D. 330 and 400 and carefully corrected in or near that time. The book (see page 264) is now one of the chief treasures of the British Museum, which bought it from the Soviet Government in 1933 for a hundred thousand pounds. But when Tischendorf first saw it, nobody had paid any attention to it for seven hundred years. In the monastery, the latest intelligent markings on it, comments by readers, had been made in the twelfth century. Since then it had been brutally neglected. Fortunately, Tischendorf scented the value of this heap of waste. He copied out some of it and managed to get the monks to give him forty-three pages, which he took back to Europe and published. Fifteen years later he returned to the monastery, backed by funds from the Czar of Rusia. This time he obtained the remainder of the poor battered Bible, which he carried away and published. In exchange, the monks received nine thousand Russian rubles. They were disappointed. They said that Tischendorf had promised to get them a steamboat.

Stupidity; censorship; changes in format and changes in taste; war; and of course the inevitable accidents, especially flood and fire—such are the hazards to the frail life of books. How did the great classics, Greek and Roman and Hebrew and others, ever survive them?

Ultimately, they were kept alive by men who loved books and knew that books are an essential element in civilization. The biography of one single book would fill many chapters. The British Museum owns a copy of the Gospels in Latin and Northumbrian, together with some writings of the early Christian Fathers, that has outlived storm and fire, savagery and greed. A big book, over a foot high, with two hundred fifty-eight stout vellum pages, it was inscribed about A.D. 700 by Bishop Eadfrith in the monastery of Lindisfarne, now Holy Island, off the northern English coast. His successor, Bishop Æthelwald, bound it; and an anchorite living on the island made a jeweled case for it. In A.D. 875 the Danish pagans invaded England. The then bishop of Lindisfarne fled westward, carrying the sacred relics of Saint Cuthbert and this book. In a storm on the Irish Sea it was lost, but it was recovered at low tide as though by a miracle. For seven years it wandered; it survived more moves and invasions, and returned to its home at Lindisfarne, where it was catalogued (the simple boring work of librarians, which they think so unimportant and which is so valuable!). Next it survived the Reformation and the Protestant sack of monasteries, although it lost its jeweled case and its episcopal covers. Then, like many valuables during a revolution, it came into the possession of a government official (Robert Bowyer, Keeper of the Records in the Tower). From him it was acquired by someone who really knew what it meant: a genuine collector, Sir Robert Bruce Cotton. From him, because of a political dispute, it was confiscated by the Crown. It is now in the British Museum.

The most moving of all such stories, however, and most encouraging, would be the biography of an ancient book as a work of art and thought. First we should have to describe its author and the contemporary audience whom he meant to read or hear his work. Then, some time later, the Greek or Roman scholars who accepted it as a valuable achievement and edited it (as the work of Joyce and Eliot is being edited today); and then, as the Dark Ages set in, the far-sighted optimists (pagan like Symmachus or Christian like Cassiodorus) who preserved it from obliteration; and, after them, the monks who saved it once again by recopying it, to live on for many centuries; later we should meet the fine-scented book hounds like Petrarch and Boccaccio and Poggio and Aurispa who discovered it when it was forgotten and sometimes copied it out with their own hands; until finally, after more perils than a displaced person and more sufferings than a tormented prisoner, it emerged fifteen hundred or two thousand years or twenty-five hundred years after its birth, to be copied on a miraculous machine and multiplied through the work of scholars and publishers, and—incredibly—to reach an audience who loved it as dearly as those who were present at its distant birth. Even then the life of such a book is not over. It will be read by Shakespeare. It will inspire a picture by Rembrandt, a satirical parody by Pope, and a lyric by Keats. It will be edited by Housman, distorted by Picasso, translated into music by Ravel, and remain inexhaustibly vital, immortally versatile, today and tomorrow and into a long future, as long as there are a few men and women who can read, and understand, and appreciate true greatness.

Made in Italy for the fifteenth-century Hungarian king Matthias Corvinus, this copy of Ptolemy's Geography *(title page shown here) was carried off to Constantinople by the Turks in 1541, bought by the French government in 1778, and is now in Paris.*

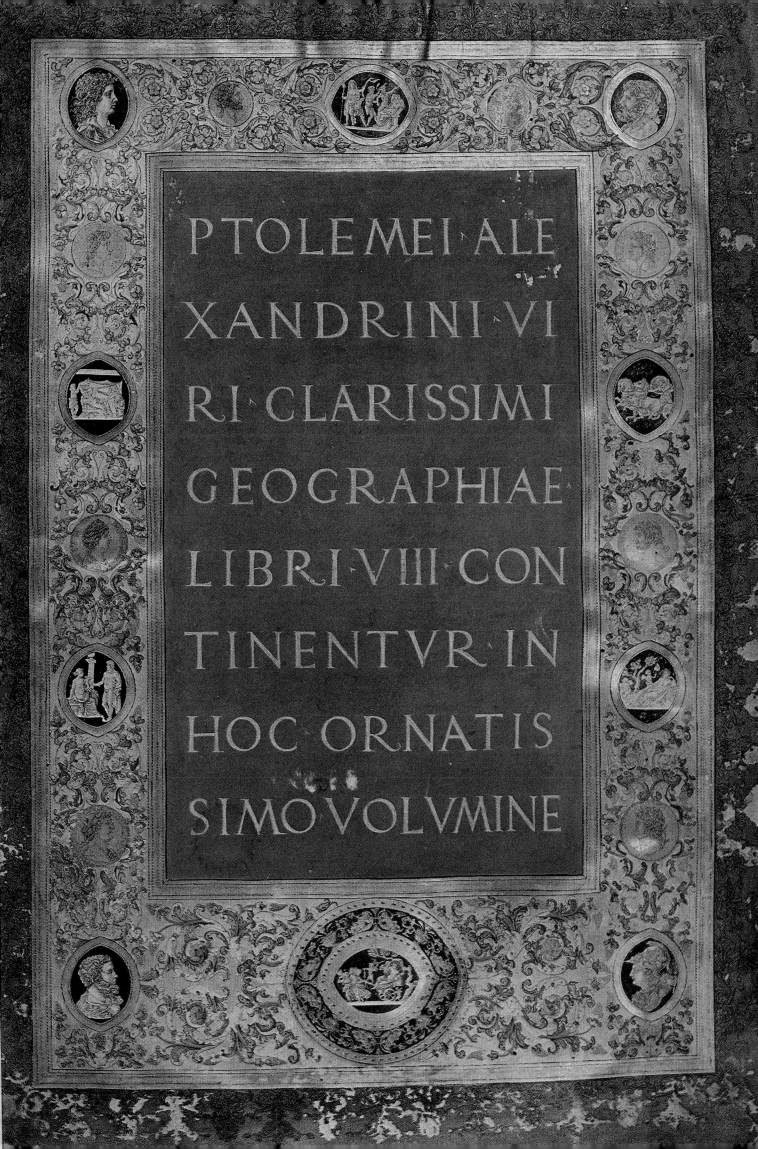

PTOLEMEI·ALE
XANDRINI·VI
RI·CLARISSIMI
GEOGRAPHIAE·
LIBRI·VIII·CON
TINENTVR·IN
HOC·ORNATIS
SIMO·VOLVMINE

I SHALL NOT LOOK UPON HIS LIKE AGAIN

Hamlet, Act 1, Scene 2

A few exceptions, assembled by Max Brandel

Sumerian head, limestone and
lapis lazuli, c. 2500 B.C.
Nelson Gallery, Kansas City

Arnold Stang

Roman sepulchral relief,
marble, first century B.C.
Metropolitan Museum of Art

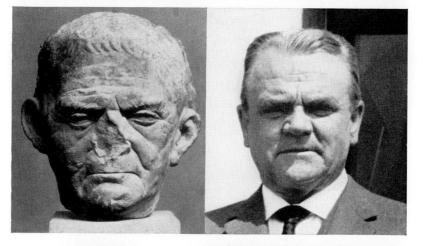

James Cagney

Egyptian magistrate
black schist, c. 300 B.C.
Cairo Museum

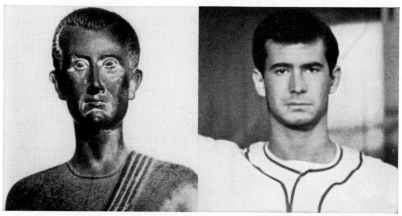

Tony Perkins

Roman head of Augustus,
marble, first century A.D.
Metropolitan Museum of Art

James Mason

Bette Davis

Roman head of Agrippina, marble, first century A.D. Louvre

Marlon Brando

Head of a young priest, Etruscan bronze, c. 200 B.C. British Museum

Jerry Colonna

Greek head from high-relief panel, after 570 B.C. Acropolis Museum, Athens

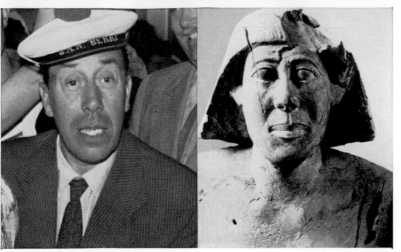

Fernandel

Egyptian functionary, wood, c. 2500 B.C. Louvre

By HERBERT J. MULLER

A symbol of our incomplete knowledge of the past, the giant statue of Emperor Constantine the Great in Rome survives only in fragments.

MISUSES OF THE PAST

HISTORY DISOBEYS THE LAWS THAT

MANY A HISTORIAN WRITES FOR IT

Writing in the middle of the last century, the historian Froude declared that "the one great Bible which cannot lie is the history of the human race." Americans have lately made this Bible a best seller too. "History is bunk," Henry Ford had said in the 1920's, the boom days when men believed that they had escaped from history, by progress, and that the past was something dead and done with. Today the past has become so popular that it got even me into the paperbacks—made me a kind of poor man's Toynbee. So I should add at once that this sudden interest in history is not really flattering to historians. The plainest reason for it is that men are no longer so proud of the history we have been making, no longer confident that it has been a progress, no longer sure where we are going or why. They are looking for the answers, which once upon a time they thought they knew. They are reading the great Bible anxiously, not reverently.

The trouble remains that this Bible can lie, or at least can yield meanings as radically different and often as dubious as those that Christians have found in their Scriptures. For the inalterable past—all that men have done that can never be undone and has made us what we are—is still not simply behind us, objectively *there* for all to see or read. It is within us. It is an image that changes with our image of ourselves, that differs as we differ. We are creatures of the past, and may suffer from its tyranny; but we are also its creators, and may suffer more from the tyranny of a mythical past. The history that most men know is in fact largely bunk. My present concern is with grossly simplified versions of the past that make the modern world more unintelligible, or more intolerable.

Eminent historians themselves have authorized such simplicities for understandable reasons. Henry Adams remarked that any historian who was not a pedestrian fact-finder naturally dreamed of discovering some grand law governing man's history comparable to Newton's law of gravitation; and by now we have a considerable choice in grand designs or dreams. In the last century Lord Acton, a deeply religious liberal, could still see in Liberty (which he habitually capitalized) the main theme of man's entire history, the key to "every nation, every epoch, every religion, every history." The growth of liberty was the measure of human progress—an idea the more inspiring to him because Progress (also capitalized by Acton) was as he saw it underwritten by Providence. Today Acton's faith is likely to seem naïve, even though he himself fully respected the power of conservative opposition. Other seekers of grand designs have generally had much less trouble finding or imposing their formulas—even when these have seemed uncongenial. In our own time, Oswald Spengler and Arnold Toynbee in particular have forced all history into neat patterns with a remorseless consistency that outrages most other historians but awes many readers.

Today the most obvious example of historical mythmaking is the nationalistic dogma that in all countries makes men arrogant and self-righteous. Americans can readily recall its dangers in prewar Germany, which had been taught by Treitschke and other historians to believe in its superior, manifest national destiny. But we Americans are less aware of possible conceit in our own national habit of proclaiming that we are the greatest nation on earth—a piece of news that the rest of the world may wish we would keep to ourselves now and then. Acton's faith was far removed from a popular image of American greatness, a fable of rugged individualists on the frontier, uncontaminated by foreign influences, giving birth to a 100-per-cent American spirit and going on to conquer a continent and to make the most spectacular progress of all time—progress still more wondrous because it was of an automatic kind that somehow emerged all by itself as everybody went about his private business, made money, and had fun. What made it automatic was economic freedom, the cornerstone of the American Way; and trouble began only when New Dealers started taking to un-American ideas. Herbert Hoover sounded the moral of the fable: "Our American system cannot be made to work part free and part regimented." In Washington such noises still pass for thought; so it seems necessary to observe that in America, as in all other democracies, business has been subject to increasing regulation over the last hundred years, during which time industrial progress has been most marked, and that when it was most thoroughly regimented, in World War II, it worked most spectacularly, doubling the national output within a few years.

Yet this was no simple success story either. It has raised more difficult issues that give thoughtful men deeper misgivings. Regimentation is indeed the order of the day—in business, labor, and entertainment as well as in government.

It has resulted naturally from an industrial revolution that nobody planned but that called out increasing organization and standardization throughout the whole society. It has not only antiquated the gospel of rugged individualism but has produced growing pressures against any real individuality, breeding such types as the "organization man" and the "other-directed" man. It leads many to fear that if we manage to escape catastrophe, we are inexorably bound for something like the brave new world of Aldous Huxley. Such fears point to the growing popularity of views that deny us any real control of our history and any reasonable choice in futures. Such views may make the simple faith of Herbert Hoover seem healthy by contrast. It is with these that I am chiefly concerned here.

In general, they reflect our fuller awareness of the deep, impersonal, unconscious processes in history, as in an industrial revolution that nobody planned. Up to a point such views may be quite sound. The danger point is marked by their common appeal to the "laws" of history—a signal for high, wide, and unhandsome generalization.

In the Communist world these are still iron laws that guarantee progress to a classless society and meanwhile justify violence and tyranny—iron methods of disposing of people who get in the way of this progress. In the democratic world, where few except visionary Marxists can any longer believe in an inevitable progress, the laws may be like those of Spengler, which instead make inevitable the death of our civilization, consistent with a supposedly invariable cycle of growth and decay in all civilizations. Meanwhile they proclaim a "coming Caesarism," or despotism. Or they may be religious laws like Toynbee's, which allow for a kind of spiraling progress as dying civilizations give birth to higher religions, bringing men closer to the One True God. But these also unfortunately require the periodic death of whole civilizations and indicate that we are most likely doomed, our sole hope lying in religion.

Typically they are more or less deterministic laws that drastically limit our choice in possible futures, if they give us any choice at all, and discourage rational effort to make history to suit ourselves. They reinforce the tendencies in fashionable literary and intellectual circles to despair of our godless civilization, condemn all its works, and scorn the idea of progress, especially in the name of Original Sin. Some men are taking an odd pleasure in insisting that man is first and last an incorrigible creature of original sin.

Now, we are indeed creatures of an inalterable past and cannot make any kind of history we have a mind to. Our choice is limited by irreversible tendencies. We might prefer to return to a simple agricultural society, for instance, or the survivors (if any) of a new world war might be forced to do so; but meanwhile there is no going back. It is inconceivable that men will deliberately call a halt to science and give up their machines, upon which now depend the lives of hundreds of millions. We are forced to work within the

Lord Acton saw liberty
as the key to history

Liberty was one of the great, inflaming ideas of the nineteenth century. It overturned governments, inspired poets, and gave themes to artists—even those who were not actively interested in politics, like the French painter Delacroix. He painted his Liberty Leading the People, above, to glorify the spirit of the French Revolution of 1830. Today we are inclined to be uneasy in the presence of personified abstractions, but to the great English scholar Lord Acton (1834-1902) this would have seemed an entirely natural expression of the guiding principle of history.

Acton is a currently stylish hero among those who require history to show an over-all meaning. In England, at least, his latter-day admirers are numerous enough to form a cult, and they are now proclaiming him one of the greatest historians of the past century.

Great he undoubtedly was—but he taught more history than he wrote. The few volumes that bear his name are merely collections of lectures and articles put together after his death. And his long-contemplated History of Liberty, for which he assembled some 25,000 notes, has been called the greatest book that was never written.

Less doctrinaire than Marx, Spengler, or Toynbee, he did not try to impose a system on history. But he did think that civilization had moved along a definite course in a single direction—upward. This was Progress. And the propulsive force had been Liberty. In his view it was the most profound of the causes that had transformed society; and because he was essentially optimistic and not afraid of moral judgments, he believed that—with a few setbacks—each succeeding transformation had been better than the one before.

281

conditions of industrialism, in a world that will continue to be revolutionary for as long as we can foresee. Yet I believe that within such limits the future is still open, its course up to us, and that history gives no reason to believe that we are inevitably doomed or damned. I suspect that many who are attacking the idea of progress, especially on religious grounds, are not fully aware of the implications of their attitude. For if man is as naturally depraved as some say, he is simply not fit for freedom and there can be no hope for a free society. And if we lose our hope of progress, we are pretty sure to lose our freedoms too—or more precisely, we will already have lost them.

I now propose, at any rate, to begin at the beginning, to give some consideration to history as a branch of knowledge and to the reasons why the great Bible is silent on the destiny of man.

Although few historians today would say what many did in the last century, namely that history is or ought to be a pure science, this idea is still in the air we breathe. Scholars often try to confine themselves to fact-finding, declaring that it is not their business to judge, and shy away in virginal fright from concepts of "value" as scientifically unchaste. As the ordinary man sees it, history gives us the facts and the facts speak for themselves; let's stick to the facts, he says. Actually, of course, the facts never speak for themselves. The historian always has to explain or interpret them. He cannot record the great Bible from nobody's point of view, any more than he can take a God's-eye view of it. And he cannot help judging, beginning with his selection of the pertinent and the most important facts.

Just how he decides this is not too clear. Historians used to concentrate on political and military events, or "drum and trumpet" history, paying little attention to the economic facts that have lately come to seem important. Thus everybody has heard of the Crusades, but few have heard of a possibly more important event of the same period and certainly a more beneficial one for mankind—the invention of spectacles in the thirteenth century by an obscure Italian, who thereby enabled many men to make better use of their eyes and heads. Saint Francis and Dante also seem important to us, though they had no apparent influence to speak of on either political or economic developments. So do Michelangelo, Shakespeare, Spinoza, Bach, and many others who made little if any difference in the main march of events. Importance, then, seems to have something to do with cultural values. In any case, for the sake of the very objectivity and impartiality that historians properly aspire to, we should remember that their works not only are to some extent personal interpretations, colored by their philosophical predispositions, but are more profoundly influenced by the climate of opinion in their age.

Here we might profit by heeding the old-fashioned Lord Acton, a Victorian who insisted on the necessity of strict moral judgment and deplored the common tendency of historians "to debase the moral currency" by explaining and condoning the crimes of the past as matters of local custom, products of "the times." If his own judgments may have been too simple and severe (as he himself confessed in his last days), they were always aboveboard and likely to be fair because he was not at all self-righteous, unlike some statesmen who mistake the rehearsal of earnest platitudes for an effort of thought. He was at least not deceiving himself as "scientific" historians are wont to do (the supposedly objective German historians of Acton's time were mostly serving the cause of nationalism). The many honest historians who try not to judge, and whose pages are strewn with judgments, might be more honest if they said in so many words that, like Lord Acton, they believe hypocrisy, fraud, treachery, torture, and murder are evil things. It is possible to excuse faults and errors without condoning the common crimes of history.

At any rate, the impossibility of a pure, unvarnished history becomes plainer when we look into the familiar idea of "cause." The historian always looks for causes and consequences, or connections between the facts; how does he make out these connections? They are not visible links or threads; they cannot be isolated, examined, measured, or tested. Presumably he makes them out by using something like intuition, insight, or common sense—which may be the limited sense of a particular age. And though his explanations may be plausible enough, the trouble remains that there is a whole web of possible connections, a complex of material and spiritual factors, so that different historians assign different causes—up to fifty, for example, for the fall of Rome. The trouble gets worse because many historians tend to speak of the "real" or the "ultimate" cause, as if some connections were stamped with a quality of superior realness. Thus we may now read that the real cause of the Civil War was not the issue of slavery but an economic conflict between North and South. The fact remains that a historian cannot operate on causes by any strictly scientific method, cannot verify his explanations, and above all cannot lay any claim to knowledge of an ultimate cause or *the* explanation.

We need not wonder when a study of the annual addresses of presidents of the American Historical Association, from 1884 to 1945, revealed that the various presidents disagreed about all their basic concepts. They agreed only on the idea that the subject of history is broad and rich. We need not scoff either—I, for one, also wish to keep history broad and rich. I would object to the now-popular "laws" of history if only because they invariably narrow and impoverish it. But here again the plain truth is that historians have been unable to agree on any comprehensive laws, and for a plain reason: they have no means whatever of verifying them.

None of these popular laws are scientific laws comparable

For Marx, history records
the class struggle

The Mexican muralist Diego Rivera painted this swarming pictorial roster of the villains and heroes of recent history, as defined by the disciples of Karl Marx. Among his villains: Wilson, Rockefeller, Clemenceau, the Czar.

His heroes: Lenin, Trotsky, Eugene V. Debs. Like Lord Acton—but how differently!— Marx saw history as a progression, with each stage in its forward march unfolding inexorably from the last. For him the motive

power was the struggle to control the means of production—a collision between classes that, in the Marxian view, was bound to engulf the world. And Marx had no doubt of the outcome: the victory of the proletariat.

283

to those in physics; they are not statements of invariable relations applying uniformly to all past events or making possible certain predictions of future events. All are man-made laws that man may break, as he cannot break the law of gravitation. Some, like Spengler's and Toynbee's, come down to pure conjecture, supported by a ruthlessly systematic disregard of inconvenient facts, which in the natural sciences would convict a man of dishonesty. Others may state statistical probabilities, as about pendulum swings or business cycles. Still others amount to rough generalizations, like proverbs. Thus Lord Acton's famous observation: "Power tends to corrupt, and absolute power corrupts absolutely."

This observation—so obviously true, but still only partially true—may do for a test. To begin with, it points to a fatal limitation of Marx's theory, namely his neglect of the eternal problem of political power. He, and Lenin after him, assumed that there would be no such problem once the revolution had been won—proletarian dictators were immune to corruption—so their theory made no provision for the brutal despotism of Stalin. This in turn points to the all too familiar but variable and incalculable "human" factors that invalidate any purely economic interpretation of history—the genius or the failings of rulers and generals; the devotion or the sluggishness of followers; the uses of knowledge and intelligence; the power of ideals; the power of sentiment, passion, or prejudice, racial, national, religious. Such factors should also warn us against the inveterate tendency to seek a single principle of explanation, in keeping with the philosophical tradition that the One is a more illustrious kind of reality than the Many.

We may now link Marx with the many respectable conservatives who also make economics the primary consideration, arguing that business comes first, sanctifying the law of supply and demand, and celebrating economic freedom as the most fundamental freedom. Marx and the conservatives both throw light on our own society, which has emphasized economic interests and the profit motive far more than almost all societies of the past. For the same reason both are poor guides to an understanding either of history or of human nature.

Yet Lord Acton's truism remains a half-truth and can be misleading. Power is as necessary as it is dangerous, necessary even for the maintenance of the liberty to which Lord Acton was so ardently devoted. There is no virtue in feeble or impotent government. While the fear of power has led to democracy—a political system designed to keep rulers responsible—it has also supported the fallacy that every gain in power by the government is necessarily at the expense of individual freedom. The power of government can be used to give people more effective freedom, for example through public education and unemployment relief. And if power tends to corrupt, it may also make a man more sober and responsible, as it did with many of the greater rulers in history, and as it often has in Anglo-American history. The uses and abuses of power depend upon culture as well as human nature.

More pertinent in our age of power, no doubt, is the truth of Lord Acton's observation. But the unprecedented power that men now command, the plainest threat to our civilization, brings up the plainest objection to the grand laws of Brooks Adams, Spengler, Toynbee, and the like. Those laws ultimately rest on arguments by analogy. They make some sense because of basic similarities in social need and response throughout history: broadly considered, history does repeat itself, most obviously in the familiar cycle of growth and decay, or rise and fall. Yet the great societies have all been dissimilar as well, the cycles never identical or neat; and in all history there is no real analogy to our present situation. Modern science and technology have produced an industrial society based on the machine. It is unique. So is large-scale democracy, with free education for all citizens. So is the extraordinary effort to create a United Nations, made possible by our technology and our knowledge of the entire world. By contrast with our civilization, the great Roman Empire was a provincial little hand-to-mouth affair. We may still learn something from its fate—we have the advantage of such knowledge, too—and we might share its fate, on a much grander catastrophic scale. Nevertheless there is no historical basis for Spengler's argument that we are *bound* to share it, or for Toynbee's argument that we can escape it only by praying to a God who failed to save the Roman Empire.

For the same reason history cannot tell us how to live with hydrogen bombs and sputniks, or how to build One World: men in the past never faced such problems. At this point history only gives us some warnings, tells us what to look out for. It may drive home the depressing platitudes about the corruptions of power and the besetting sins of self-righteousness; and doubtless this is the lesson men most need to learn. Yet even this is not simple. If human conflict always involves the ancient evils of selfishness and greed, it is usually intensified because both sides sincerely believe in the rightness of their cause and cannot understand the other side. The real tragedy of human existence, Hegel said, is the conflict not between right and wrong but between right and right. More precisely, I should say, the conflict is between men who, on both sides, are partly right and almost wholly self-righteous. Finally, Herbert Butterfield adds, we are face to face with the "absolute predicament and the irreducible dilemma"—the deadlocks that cannot be broken by sitting down around a table, any more than Catholicism and Protestantism have been able to reconcile their differences after centuries of discussion. We can only hope that men will somehow agree to live and let live, as Catholics and Protestants finally did after a century of atrocious religious wars; but the trouble is that when men are most fervent in their faiths, they are most likely to go to war.

Oswald Spengler

predicted the West's decline

Peter Blume's The Eternal City *looks as though it had been painted to a text from Oswald Spengler. It was not; it was simply one young American's reaction to Mussolini's Italy. But it epitomizes with stunning impact one of the final stages in the German historian's schedule of cultural decline and death: a time of ossified institutions, vulgar new Caesars, and manipulation of the mob.*

In the years of disillusion following World War I a great many people thought they had discovered a major prophet in Spengler, who seemed to echo and justify their own defeatism. They sought revelation in the pages of The Decline of the West, and found it in his melancholy prediction that Western civilization would be dead by A.D. 2200. The possibility is all too apparent — but few historians today would accept the deterministic theory of history by which Spengler arrived at his date. Cultures, he decided, live and die like any other organism: they all have roughly the same life span (1,000 years), and pass through an identical sequence of well-defined phases. He did not call these phases youth, maturity, and old age, but chose instead the seasons: spring, summer, autumn, winter.

There was nothing new in this notion; the idea is obvious and it had occurred to many historians before Spengler. What was new was the Teutonic thoroughness with which he worked it out. For him, the first three "seasons" are the growing, fruitful stages of a culture; winter is the moment when all is frozen into rigidity, when a culture becomes "complete" (his word). It is the end of the line.

The West, Spengler thought, was well into its winter months. He saw on every side the symptoms that he decided had marked the final stages of other cultures: the growth of monstrous cities, contention among empires, the rise of dictators, a political atmosphere of "Caesarism," and rule by "mobocracy" —all the things summarized with such virtuosity in Blume's painting.

Other cultures, when they died, have been reborn in the ones that succeeded them. But Oswald Spengler held out no such hope for the West: ours, he thought, would just dry up.

There remains a final paradox. The growth of an immense collective power, beyond the wildest dreams of men in the past, has made the individual liable to feel more impotent than ever before, and thus to conclude that man is now at the mercy of massive forces beyond his understanding and control. A more appalling thought is that this immense power is effectively at the disposal of a few individuals, in particular the leaders of America as well as Russia, who have secret information denied the rest of us. Upon decisions made by these very few depends the fate of our civilization. Any strictly deterministic theory of history founders on this fact; but so may the human race.

All this is to say that "history shows" a great deal more, and somewhat less, than men usually declare when they use this phrase. For those who do not pretend to know the one true interpretation of the great Bible it poses the problem of selection and emphasis. History is a record of all the great achievements of man, and of his repeated failures. It can make dismal reading, not only because all the civilizations before our own ended in failure, but because the causes of the failures are generally plainer than the causes of the creative achievements. Stupidity and folly are easier to understand than genius. The dark meanings of history are perhaps those that most need to be emphasized in the national forum, or in those business, political, and journalistic circles that boast of a purely material progress, glossed over with endorsements of moral and spiritual crusades that go about as deep as the testimonials used in advertising. (So most Americans applaud when their political leaders condemn the materialism of the Soviet.) For the more thoughtful, however, I judge that there is more need of countering the fashions in darkness, of risking sententiousness by dwelling on the creative achievements of man and in particular on the values of our own civilization. These might hearten us at a time when sanity and resolution seem as necessary as the religious faith that many say is our only hope of salvation. They are likely to be overlooked because they are a heritage we take for granted, the kind of thing that "goes without saying" and therefore without thinking.

Since we hear so much about the failure of science, of rationalism, of democracy, of our whole civilization, let us be really humble—even humbler than the specialists in humility. Christianity too is a failure by such standards—most clearly by its own standards. So have been the creeds by which all other societies lived and died in the past. But then we can add, in humility, that none of them completely failed in so far as they produced works that still live, ideals that men still cherish. In our immense and largely unconscious heritage we can point to all the lasting good that has come out of the historic failures. We can set realistic terms of historical judgment: partial successes, relative goods, mixed fruits. In these terms history does indeed show a progress, cultural and spiritual as well as material.

Today, to be sure, one must contemplate with some irony the verdict of Gibbon in *The Decline and Fall of the Roman Empire:* "We may therefore acquiesce in the pleasing conclusion that every age of the world has increased, and still increases, the real wealth, the happiness, the knowledge, and perhaps the virtue, of the human race." History certainly shows nothing so pleasing as a steady progress, with every age successively better than its predecessor. But just as certainly there has been an immense increase in knowledge; and all of us who read and write books must believe—in our hearts *do* believe—that knowledge does increase the real wealth of the human race and has some connection with its happiness, possibly even its virtue. It points to the wealth of values that man has realized and retained in spite of his repeated failures: skills and arts, ideas and ideals, including "higher" religions whose devotees may now condemn the faith in progress as sinful pride. In Western history it points to the political, intellectual, and religious freedoms that are no less cherished by most of these devotees, but were realized only in recent centuries. And a major inspiration to the effort to realize them, and extend them to ordinary men, was precisely the distinctive Western faith in progress stated by Gibbon. No such statement as his can be found, to my knowledge, in the whole literature of the world before his age.

The *will* to progress stimulated by this novel idea has been most apparent in America, a "land of opportunity" in which millions have worked to give their children better opportunities than they themselves enjoyed. Their hopeful spirit was not simply "human nature," for the peasant masses in all civilizations before our own accepted poverty as the law of life or the will of God. This suggests another reason why we cannot predict the future with certainty: prediction itself—that is, belief about the probable future—may make an incalculable difference in it. Marx's prediction that capitalism is inevitably doomed has helped to inspire a mighty effort to bring about that doom. It has also inspired efforts to reform capitalism and to control economic forces. Hence the free-for-all private enterprise system that Marx described, that Moscow still says is bound to wreck us and that conservatives say can alone save us, has long since ceased to exist. For such reasons the fate of a free society is bound up with the very hope of progress, or the despair of it.

"Realists" are now harping on a proverbial refrain: You can't change human nature. Those who insist that human nature is always the same always mean that man is naturally pretty bad, if not literally cursed by original sin; and given the long record of bloody failures, all history might appear to be on their side. Still, in a broad view of the evolution and the remarkable diversity of cultures that man has developed, one might be impressed more by the plasticity of his nature. Granted what any sensible man knows, that he is always frail and fallible and prone to unoriginal kinds of sin, the doctrine of original sin does not help much in understanding him, any more than it apparently has in getting

Arnold Toynbee
looks for a universal church

OXFORD UNIVERSITY PRESS

FROM *Ravenna Mosaics*, NEW YORK GRAPHIC SOCIETY

The brooding face above stares at us from the apse of the church of San Vitale in Ravenna. It is a mosaic portrait of Archbishop Ecclesius, who holds, like an exquisite toy, a model of the church itself. It was under his auspices that San Vitale was begun in A.D. 526, just as the Roman Empire was finally breaking up. But we need not know these details of history to recognize in this image a symbol of the all-pervading influence of a "higher religion" and a "universal church." These terms come from Arnold Toynbee, who uses them to describe the final

products of a disintegrating civilization. In A Study of History Toynbee brusquely rejects the blind determinism of Spengler, and says that "societies are not in any sense living organisms." But he does see a pattern in history, and it is even more elaborate than Spengler's. Civilization, for Toynbee, is the fruit of adversity, a successful response to a difficult challenge: harsh climate, poor soil. Success generates its own challenge, which—in a growing society—calls forth another successful response. But sooner or later a challenge comes along that is not met, and a

breakdown occurs. Here begins a rhythmic sequence of "rout and rally." The end is death, or always has been, but before the final rout the stricken society produces a "universal state." It also produces a "universal church." In the death throes of the Hellenic society, whose universal state was the Roman Empire, Christianity was born. And what of us? Toynbee's message is obscure. For the emergence of a new or revived universal church, which in his scheme has always preceded extinction, now seems to him the West's one hope of avoiding it.

287

him to behave himself. He behaved badly enough in the pious Middle Ages. As a product of our own cultural tradition, this cliché might warn us that the immutable human nature we hear about is likely to be the nature of Western man, or rather of some Western men. Many thinkers have assumed in man an inborn, ineradicable greed, a will to power, or an anarchic egotism that the great majority of men in other societies failed to exhibit. The least mutable types in history have been the long-suffering peasant masses, but they hardly look selfish and aggressive in their typically passive, fatalistic endurance; their "depravity" seems more a result of ignorance and inertia than of the old Adam in them. The nature of Americans has been rather different, for better and for worse. And the significant change that seems to be coming over our nature, in the growing conformism of "other-directed" types, also has little to do with the old Adam but much more with the growth of huge organizations and mass media.

Similarly with the worries over the "common man" or the "mass man." He represents problems that we cannot afford to minimize. He also represents a common failing of thinkers, who become victims of their abstractions and forget the infinite variety in type and talent among ordinary people. By definition mediocre, the common man is then made out to be mediocre in *every* respect, and so becomes a statistical monster like the "average man" with 2.5 children. At least he may be decent enough to call for some historical perspective. The so-called "new conservatives," for example, are finding their gods in the great conservatives of the past such as Burke—men who typically had little faith in ordinary human nature, and who may now seem wiser than they were because of the steady succession of failures. We forget that their class had its way throughout most of history. They held the power; they ran the great states and churches; they laid down the law; they set the social standards and goals. The privileged aristocracies and priesthoods that are usually given credit for the great cultural achievements must also bear most of the responsibility for the tragic failures. In their pride they invariably abused their privileges and repeatedly succumbed to the selfishness, greed, and stupidity they feared in the masses.

As we worry over the problems of a mass society and rightly deplore the quality of mass education and mass culture, we might keep in mind the fact that never before in all history have great nations made an effort like that of our own day in the West to educate their entire population and to enable all men to share freely in both their political and cultural life. It is hardly surprising if ordinary men abuse the first real chance they have had in history. Much more surprising, in a historical perspective, is the general acceptance of an idea that many oppose in practice but few would openly reject: the idea that every man ought to have a fair chance to fulfill himself. The peasant masses in the non-Western world, who still make up the majority of the world's population, are only beginning to get anything like such a chance.

Meanwhile, all our problems may seem worse because traditionalists are always disposed to simplify and falsify the past in the light of their characteristic ideal of stability and certainty. This is an ideal that man has never achieved and can never hope to achieve, short of the death he fears. Traditionalists overlook the basic conditions of man's creative achievements, which include the elementary principle of the inescapable costs of civilization, and more especially of freedom. These costs are implicit in the nature of the only animal that has the power of free, conscious choice, which means the perpetual possibility of foolish or even fatal choices. The costs rose with the rise of civilization, in which an increasing mastery of natural environment brought an increasing dependence on social environment, and in which new material and spiritual goods became new needs, new sources of deprivation and discontent. The costs became still higher as thought became freer, for it raised more questions than it answered, and finally settled nothing. Every major advance in freedom—social, political, intellectual—has meant new problems, including new threats to freedom.

In this view it also becomes important to discredit the popular idea of an automatic, inevitable kind of progress. Such progress as man has made has been only the sporadic realization of new possibilities. His bursts of creativity have always been destructive of cherished values and often fatal to the society that produced them. Nor is further progress guaranteed by any known law of nature, history, or God. It must forever remain uncertain, if man is in any sense free to make history. The painful signs of uncertainty—tension, instability, insecurity, disharmony, conflict—are the essential conditions of possibility, aspiration, idealism. We cannot fully appreciate our extraordinary adventure in freedom unless we realize that it has always been a precarious adventure, demanding the expense of resolute, arduous effort. The full worth of liberty is known only to those who know its full costs. To me, what "history shows" is that its price is indeed eternal vigilance, and that it is worth the effort.

Reversing Lord Acton, Herbert J. Muller writes history but does not teach it. He is Distinguished Service Professor at Indiana University. His most widely read book is The Uses of the Past, *but he has also written* Science and Criticism, The Spirit of Tragedy, *and most recently,* Freedom in the Western World.